Reclaiming Artistic Research

Expanded Second Edition

Lucy Cotter, ed.

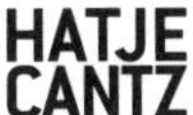

Contents

Artistic Research in a World on Fire

Lucy Cotter

Writing this, I am looking out on a garden that has hardly seen rain for three months. Its drought is witness to the encroachment of climate change, and the air outside is tainted by smoke from a distant wildfire. Yet today, the patter of my fingers on the keyboard is accompanied by the sound of rainfall, which is causing green grass to sprout out of the barren yellow. Slowly but surely, it takes over: here a few blades, there a flurry, until the overall sense of lack starts to recede into memory. It will not disappear entirely. Large plants that seemed hardy have not survived; small ones are

alive but struggling to thrive. It is a landscape that resonates with "post"-pandemic reality, where the human losses are permanent, where many are suffering from long COVID, and where the long evisceration of the lifeblood of the arts is still being felt. Arts programming has returned, yet it is not an easy transition. The arts landscape is still parched and struggling to reckon with its evident unsustainability, its precarious working conditions, the founding violence of many of its institutions, and its long histories and continued practices of exclusion.[1] In a world desperate for new ways of thinking, for alternate visions, and seeking radical social, cultural, and political transformation, artists are necessarily becoming more ambitious with their goals for artistic research.

In the United States, where I have been based since this book's first publication in 2019, artistic research does not have an established discourse related to debates about artists doing a PhD, as it does in Europe, the United Kingdom, Australia, New Zealand, and Canada, as well as in some locations in Asia, Africa, and Latin America.[2] "Artistic research" circulates as a free-floating term in the mainstream art world, little-noticed, it seems, except that more and more artists who engage with wider social, cultural, and political questions in their work describe their practices as research-driven.[3] There is an urgency to this work that is palpable and exceeds institutional demands or critical intellectual trends. Among other recent experiences, a two-year curatorial conversation with artist Christine Howard Sandoval, who attends to Indigenous-Hispanic legacies as she negotiates what is present and what is invisible in the physical landscape, brought home to me that much work being done by artists in the US – the first-hand archival research, the original thinking, the forming of connections through transdisciplinary inquiry, and the forging of relationships among and between people, and institutions – would not be done otherwise.[4] Indeed, artists worldwide are doing important cultural work that is not being done otherwise. In contexts where this inquiry is outside of governmental priorities, or even against national interests, this work exists and is being done with little support. In most countries worldwide, few sources of funding exist for the kind of long-term artistic projects that make especially significant contributions to wider social thinking and action. This is among the reasons why it matters now to look at artistic research and critically reflect on its wider value. What kind of infrastructural shifts need to take place to support artists to undertake significant artistic research on its own terms?

What are an artist's responsibilities (and possibilities) in a world that is on fire?[5] I hope that the publication of this expanded second edition of *Reclaiming Artistic Research* will further support artists, critics, curators, and art's many publics to articulate and embrace the singularity of what art does and has the potential to do in the world, at an individual and collective level. In this edition, I engage in four new dialogues with US-based artists Stephanie Dinkins, Cannupa Hanska Luger, Yo-Yo Lin, and Richard Mosse, whose practices navigate and exceed the studio-gallery system feedback loop in thoughtful and provocative ways, while attending to questions of human and nonhuman survival, self-care and collective care, new technologies, and the unlearning of ableist, gendered, sexist, and racist paradigms. Our discussions build on the twenty dialogues with artists (and curators) from the first edition to offer insight into what artistic research is in day-to-day practice. The dialogue form, which is based on oral knowledge, was chosen because it resonates with (embodied, material) artistic thinking in its ability to circle back over thoughts and peel into multilayered processes. Each of the contributing artists' and curators' practices in this book are singular, yet these dialogues are also in dialogue with each other, circling around overlapping areas like sound and spatiality, or engaging with questions such as the nature of history, or the reimagining of the body. The polyvocal echoing return of many qualities of artistic research points to some shared ways of knowing and unknowing in and through art practice.

HOW DOES ART KNOW?

The phrase "artistic research" establishes a connection between art and knowledge. It suggests that academics and scientists are not the only ones who can undertake original research and contribute new knowledge to the world. Initiated by artists, artistic research often comes into being through highly intuitive processes, and its unfolding through practice follows the inner logic of artistic processes, rather than academic protocol. It does not depend on an academic context or academic forms of research. This book is titled *Reclaiming Artistic Research* because there has been a tendency to view artistic research in academic terms, and thus overlook its singularity and potential. As I discuss in the introductory essay to the first edition (republished in this book), this misperception stems partly from the close association of the term with discourses surrounding the establishment of a PhD in Fine Art, in which programs often legitimate artists' knowledge production with academic criteria.[6] Yet, artistic research has many lives beyond the university context.

It is commonplace for artists today to engage with subjects outside of art, from environmental sciences and emerging technologies to disability studies and immigration flows. Yet, it remains underrecognized that these artists are not simply borrowing ideas or illustrating or creating aesthetic versions of existing academic subjects. Rather, many artists (including my interlocutors in this book) seek to create new questions and new forms of knowledge, using the kinds of embodied-material-conceptual thinking that goes hand in hand with art making. In doing so, they are often pointing to what has not yet been thought, what remains unknowable, or what has been overlooked or misperceived because thinking within the related field has been limited by the shapes and forms of standard academic research. (I use the term "non-knowledge" in the dialogues to refer to knowledge that exceeds formal categories of intellectual knowledge, often lying not only in unknown areas but extending into the unknowable.) Artistic making processes involve imagining, creating, and sometimes prototyping new forms, which can as easily take the shape of a social arrangement or a model for repurposing artificial intelligence as a traditional artwork. Similar types of thinking involving gathering, finding new constellations, imagining forward, and experimenting with possibilities exist as a continuum across these art practices. Even the most abstract work can involve artistic research processes.

Artistic mediums of all types lend themselves to ways of thinking beyond language, and even beyond consciousness. (I address these qualities more fully in my introduction to the first edition.) In its material fluidity and medium-specific processes of making visible, audible, spatially or materially palpable, contemporary art can bring about different multisensory modes of witnessing. The artists in this book were invited one by one, so that the medium-specific ways of knowing and unknowing unfolding through their practices could be built upon through each subsequent dialogue and considered from other facets. I have titled the dialogues to help orient the reader toward these underlying areas, and to make visible overlapping concerns among artistic bodies of work that may not immediately appear to be in dialogue with one another.

Instead of building on what is tangible, artistic research can pivot toward paying attention to human absences. It is attuned to gaps and strains in knowledge, rather than only what is evidently there. Through radical archival interventions and oral-material creations, artists can find ways to manifest and engage with the fragmentation and dispersal of human histories in ways that the formal discipline of history struggles (and often fails) to do. This matters in a world in which the traces of marginalized peoples, enslaved peoples, disappeared peoples, peoples who have been forced to migrate, and/or who have faced genocide and extinction seek to claim their own histories and trajectories. In our dialogue, artist Euridice Zaituna Kala described how, when she did archival research into the history of the eighteenth-century Portuguese slave ship *São José Paquete d'África*, she was faced not with ample material, but near silence on the 400 enslaved Mozambican people's experiences. Being an artist, she had other means of moving forward. "I am the archive," she realized, and continued this research by retracing the ship's journey with her own body and leaning into transgenerational embodied knowledge.

It is often through gathering fragmented, dispersed, invisible, unarchived cultural memory, and seeing the resemblances between forcibly separated materials and areas of thinking that a community or a culture can imagine forward. In grasping continuities across locations and temporalities, they can "move forward–both internally and externally."[7] The capacity for artistic research to bring together material, textual, and embodied sources of knowledge lends itself to these processes in ways that other (academic) forms of research seldom can. Artists bring the imaginative force and the associative, combinatory thinking of art making to bear on these materials, leading to potentially unforeseen outcomes.

In a new dialogue for this edition, Yo-Yo Lin points to art as a space for unlearning interlocking paradigms of ableist, racist, and anti-queer thinking. She leans into nuanced transcultural imaginaries around the body and incorporates experiences of chronic pain, chronic illness, and disability to create platforms for connectivity where new bodies of knowledge can be formed collectively. Like many artists in this book, Lin's work is multidisciplinary, cross-cultural, and intersectional. Art's long-held freedom to work in post-disciplinary ways enables artists to expand their research into the many facets of the subjects they address.

Several artists in this book self-position their practice in terms of the complex relationship between art and activism. Living in the United States, I have been strongly reminded of the ongoing need for artistic research into subject areas that are not wanted or are dangerous or undermining to governing bodies. Having witnessed first-hand the brutality of police violence, while living in Portland, Oregon through the 100-plus days of protest following George Floyd's murder in 2020, I deeply appreciate Forensic Architecture and Bellingcat's project, *Police Brutality at the Black Lives*

Matter Protests (2020–present). By geolocating and verifying over a thousand incidents of police violence, analyzing them according to multiple categories, and presenting the resulting data in an interactive cartographic platform, this artistic research is of widespread legal and sociopolitical importance. (Artist and audio investigator Lawrence Abu Hamdan discusses his work with Forensic Architecture in our dialogue.)

Artists can be keen researchers of scopic regimes, surveillance, and visibility because of their expanded visual registers and expert visual cognition.[8] Fluid thinking around media enables artists to use existing technology for different purposes than its inventors intended. In a new dialogue for this edition, Richard Mosse discusses multiyear projects like *INCOMING*, for which he repurposed military surveillance equipment to foreground the catastrophic conditions of migration into Europe. His latest film work, *Broken Spectre*, repurposes multispectral technologies used by multinational mining companies and redeploys scientific UV microscopy photography to create one of the most extensive and nuanced documents of the destruction of the Amazon rainforest in existence today. These artists' work is not made without risk, and in a world where the political climate is increasingly polarized and tightened, artists' relative freedom of speech and social visibility are crucially important assets.

The ethical and social repercussions of emerging technologies are constantly unfolding, and artists continue to address these questions in provocative and publicly accessible ways. The world is currently on the precipice of an artificial intelligence-led knowledge revolution that is mostly market oriented. It is no longer possible to talk about knowledge production without reflecting on these tech-led epistemic paradigm shifts, in which artificial intelligence's algorithms favor predictability and therefore the dominant and the known. In doing so, they herald in forms of "digital colonialism," "technological redlining," and the "default discrimination" brought about by artificial intelligence's logic of inclusion / exclusion.[9] Artistic research lends itself to counteracting the resulting absences and gaps in knowledge thanks to its tendency to move toward the invisible, the neglected, the unknown, and the unrecoverable. In another new dialogue in this edition, Stephanie Dinkins, one of the leading artists in the US, engaged with AI and emerging technologies, discusses what can be done and why it needs to be done by people from all walks of life, artists included. Moving beyond reactionary critique, Dinkins's interactive and immersive work offers models for reorienting emerging technologies toward social benefit, equity, and collective care.

As artist Cannupa Hanska Luger proposes in another new dialogue, technology is ultimately not mechanisms but ideas, and "[a] lot of Indigenous technology exists in our cosmology, in our homes, in symbols we create, in forms we express through dance and music" that "has not been allowed to navigate through material science and mechanisms."[10] In his ongoing *Future Technologies* project, Luger imagines past the exodus of the wealthy to other planets to consider adaptations necessary for the future survival of Earth. In resonance with Dinkins, who identifies the underrecognized knowledge and survival strategies handed down by enslaved peoples, Luger reminds us that this moment of impending environmental collapse is not the first time his people have faced extinction.

SELF-REFLEXIVE KNOWLEDGE

Artistic research may offer competing paradigms for knowledge in today's world, but it cannot neglect its own foundations. As Tom Holert summarizes: "The more contemporary art is accounted for and addressed as a platform, system, or institutional space of research, investigation, epistemological speculation, and decolonial struggles for the recognition of subaltern, Black, feminist, queer, Indigenous and other marginalized yet powerful modes of knowing and thinking, the more it is confronted with the task of understanding its own roles in the general intellect's current manifestations."[11] While many artists and arts workers have worked toward equity for decades, this moment of mainstream awareness of social justice issues offers ripe conditions for the art field at large to confront the problematic foundations and exclusionary norms of contemporary art's modes of existence and operation. The scope of artistic research, which exceeds the production of artworks, offers space to redefine artistic practice. It can be a means of challenging dominant definitions of contemporary art and, by extension, exploring alternatives to white cultural supremacy in arts institutions. In our dialogue, Cannupa Hanska Luger observes: "I work in an industry where art is considered an object, the thing that somebody makes. That couldn't be further from my personal definition of what art is. Art for me is the making. It is these processes that have been passed down from teacher to student, from ancestor to elder. It's a continuum. It's intergenerational."[12]

Contemporary art discourse's self-proclaimed autonomy and porous yet often inward-looking relationship to art has occluded the crucial question of how art relates to culture. Ariella Aïsha Azoulay points to the historic establishment of the art museum as a repository for colonially looted objects, leading to a necessity to present (art) objects as outside of living culture.[13] Some of the other legacies of colonial regimes of visibility and categorization of subjects and objects include the individual authorship inherent in the modern artist-function, which naturalizes the apparent cultural neutrality (and default whiteness) of artists in the West. Art has been rarified into something inactive and in need of preservation, and its decontextualization is reflected in the "professional" (distancing, socially detached) protocol for curators, art writers, and institutional workers.[14] What is the relationship between the self-perceptions of the art world as a field and how art operates (and co-determines perceived cultural value) in the world? These are questions artistic research discourse cannot skip over. The title of this essay is inspired by a Zoom-based performance by artist Pope.L, which exposed the performativity of the artist's position in society and the structuring force of the art world, which cannot assume to separate itself from a world at large that, in fact, "has always been on fire."[15]

Wider inclusivity in the art world matters as a means of reconnecting institutions with a more expansive sociocultural and political reality and as a way to counteract historically inbuilt measures of exclusion. This is not a simple matter of adding onto existing ways of thinking and working, but rather the bringing in of conflicting paradigms that should reorient institutions to question and relativize the narrowness of previous working paradigms. I felt this sense of reorientation when an artist in a workshop I attended asked, "Why does the art world always seek to 'include' the disabled in its activities, rather than asking what we are working on and thinking about and asking if they can join us?"[16] Julie Philips thinks far beyond the token acknowledgment of artists who are mothers when she observes that the life-altering and lifelong experience of maternity forges bodies of knowledge that are not otherwise available.[17] In her dialogue with Katayoun Arian in this book, Grada Kilomba offers a powerful reflection on the knowledge that is otherwise lost when people of color are not present as leaders and co-shapers of art institutions.[18]

It matters not only which artists or artworks are included in art discourse and institutions, but *how* they are included. Attending to artistic research as an entry point into all artists' practices offers an important counterweight to the identity-led framing of so-called diverse artists because it draws attention to competing cultural paradigms and alternate bodies of knowledge. Curator Karen Archey notes that institutional hyperfocus on an artist's biography is a way of cutting corners in the contextualization of these artists' work.[19] This covers up the inevitable lack of institutional knowledge and the paltry research undertaken within the tightly budgeted timeframes of the contemporary art institution. (The authors of *Post-Critical Museology* suggest that the contemporary museum can better let go of its claims to representativeness and return to serious research on art.)[20] Too often, "diverse" artists' work is represented in issue-led terms so that the institution can profit from the currency of hot topics, with discursive simplifications overshadowing the full complexity of an artist's inquiries. The artistic (material-spatial-embodied) sensibilities in their practice go under- or unaddressed, creating a false separation from other ("neutral") artists whose work is perceived as medium-led, abstract, philosophical, poetic, etc. (I have addressed this issue elsewhere in more detail.)[21] By undertaking in-depth dialogues that are three to four times longer than the standard artist interview, this book seeks to make space to articulate artistic practice in ways that keep these complex form-content-context relationships intact.

Many artists' work deliberately resists easy legibility as a counterweight to the tendency for the identity-driven neoliberal knowledge economy and click-bait-led public discourse to flow toward transparency and simplification. In response to the hypervisibility that accompanies identity-oriented framing of Black, feminist, queer, crip, and Indigenous practices, many artists embrace opacity, in Édouard Glissant's sense of a refusal of individuals or communities to be cornered into declaring an essential identity or essence in the face of the "transparency" demanded by dominant culture.[22] This doesn't make these artists' practices immune to opportunistic misframing, however. Artists today face difficult ethical decisions in this respect, as the sustainability of their practice or their livelihood is often dependent on contradictory opportunities. There is much to learn from artists who push back against this institutional and critical capture. One artist with whom I worked curatorially toward a site-specific performance requested to title the work with an untypable word-image, and to replace the usual press release with a crossword.[23] These gestures extended the critical ethos of the performance into all of the conditions of its production, exposing that standard formats are not neutral, and that curators and institutions have the agency to rethink and change them, should they so wish, or, as is often the case, "if they are willing to give something up."[24]

There is no such thing as a neutral container for art.[25] In considering how artistic research enters the world, art writing is an important interface to the public, as language is a source of security in the face of relatively opaque artwork. However, I increasingly think about the perfunctory role writing plays in the art world, which can limit the possibilities of creating a more nourishing and generative relationship between art and language (and the public). Several dialogues in this book manifest a move away from academic writing toward questions of how language itself can unfold new ways of thinking. (Sher Doruff writes from the position of inter-species; Manuela Infante writes in structures that follow plant thinking.) Several artists play with how text relates to objects, space, and territory (Falke Pisano sees where language ends and the object begins; Sky Hopinka uses song and calligrams to meld imaginaries and places). More and more artists, art writers, and curators are forging experimental writing practices that help to shift the status quo, and it seems that the publishing landscape is starting to make more space for the gray areas between the artistic and the literary, where artists' experimental material-spatial-embodied-led writing can thrive.[26] Having experimented widely with the "affordances" of different genres and writing styles that resonate with artistic practice in conversation with artists working at every level, I am excited to be working on a new book that will address writing as an artistic process and medium.[27]

EMBODIED MATERIAL KNOWLEDGE

Beyond the immediate concerns of the specific artistic practice at hand, what is at stake in the questions surrounding artistic research is a radical questioning of what defines and constitutes knowledge in the world–in university contexts, in the public discourse and the policies they inform, in our own minds and those of everyone we love, who has inherited and internalized these habitual ways of thinking through normal everyday life. This legacy includes the artist's sense of inferiority in the academic context, which relates to the inferior positioning of embodied, material, spatial, and lived knowledge relative to linguistic and numerical knowledge (with resulting narrow definitions of intelligence). The dominant consensus around what constitutes thought, or knowledge, art or culture is, of course, historically constructed. Its epistemological foundations lie in Enlightenment thinking from the seventeenth and eighteenth centuries (René Descartes, Francis Bacon, Immanuel Kant et al.). Europe's territorial imposition and power over peoples worldwide was partly justified by and made successful by the global indoctrination of defining and enforcing this white supremacist, Western form of thinking as the only real form of knowledge. This left on the scrap heap the forms of knowledge, worldviews, and ways of thinking intrinsic to over 80 percent of the world's population. The extent to which one feels included or seen within dominant definitions of knowledge, art, or culture complexly relates to this historical and continuous dynamic of internalized oppression and the embeddedness of this exclusionary logic in the norms of discourse and institutional logic. (As an extension of direct exclusion, imposter syndrome is a daily reality for many artists and art workers.) Among many other losses, the Enlightenment epistemic shift toward empiricism, rationalism, and scientific methodology meant that all human knowledge that lay beyond linguistic consciousness (over 90 percent of thinking) was (and still is) sidelined.[28]

With its fluidity of frameworks, and foregrounding of embodied, material, spatial, transgenerational, and temporally multidirectional knowledge, contemporary art offers possibilities to push against, question, and destabilize Western academia's epistemological monopoly, bringing in openness to other ways of thinking. Art "can provide in rare but important cases the very organizational structures, theoretical devices, and material contexts to sustain multilayered work on the dislocation and repurposing of knowledge itself."[29] This is why art's affront to (Western) academic knowledge is an important partner in efforts to decolonize knowledge in the university, and in our own minds. With its foregrounding of oral, material, and performative registers of knowledge, artistic research is starting to be recognized as a unique point of entry for Indigenous knowledge within academic contexts globally.[30] Art inherently aligns with and can support the work of activists and academics seeking to decolonize and to center Indigenous ways of knowing. The potential for artistic research to co-shape this wider negotiation of epistemological parameters is one reason why it matters now, more than ever, "to draw a line between conformist, depoliticizing ways of associating knowledge with art" and "the quest for different, oppositional modes of knowing" that many artists today choose to prioritize.[31]

I once attended a conference in which a young academic was struggling to articulate yoga as a form of embodied philosophy. It struck me that her argument would have been more successful had she invited her audience to do yoga together, precisely because most of yoga's knowledge is available in and through the body, bypassing conscious thinking and language. Because art's ways of working encompass inseparable body-mind and subject-object experiences, a comparable falling-out of knowledge happens when academics expect to be able to understand art's forms of knowledge through academic paradigms. In my "Reclaiming Artistic Research" essay (republished here), I reflect on what happens in the university context when artists undertake PhDs with expectations of having art's forms of knowledge recognized and embraced, only to find themselves in situations where academic requirements force them to prioritize already existing and nameable ideas and areas of interest over the opaque unfoldings of art practice.

The dominance of academic thought over artistic thinking is not only relevant in the university context, however. It is present whenever critics and curators attend to artistic research with the expectation that it will resemble or can be addressed using the paradigms of *academic* research. There will, in many instances, be overlaps with academic fields, and the long-standing theorization of those findings can contribute to deepening artistic inquiry, if this is done meaningfully. Too often art is framed using the most well-worn cultural theory, instead of looking further to find deeper resonances in the work of thousands of academics globally, thinking about overlapping questions. (This could be the entry point into collaborative co-thinking, instead of reinforcing knowledge hierarchies through critical juxtaposition of world-renowned thinkers with emerging or less established artists.) This is among many reasons why the PhD in Fine Art needs to be reoriented toward its stated ambitions of articulating practice-based knowledge.

While it is beyond the scope of this essay, I have elsewhere tried to articulate why practice-led thinking needs to be identified and nourished in curatorial discourse.[32] Practice-led curating unfolds in similar ways to artistic research processes and this kinship sets up the conditions to do more justice to artistic thinking. For those of us who started to curate as a way of attending to fellow artists' practices, curating is often led by material-conceptual and spatial-embodied thinking. This allows for a collage-like creation of thought-constellations and a material-spatial unfolding that cannot be expressed in critical jargon or academic terms. To curate in this way is in fact to say something that writing cannot capture. Today, when it is more and more difficult to fund exhibitions that are not designed to engage click-bait attention spans, I wish to emphasize that exhibitions have the potential to be experimental working sites. Their physical, spatial, and material presence can make space for ways of knowing that are embedded in the body, that make us see the performativity of knowledge; that make us witness the connection between voice and word, movement and body, space and subjectivity.

The exhibition's variety of modes of experiencing opens possibilities for anti-ableist forms of accessibility and its ability to draw attention to the performativity of knowledge opens possibilities for the decolonization of thought.[33] Exhibitions offer an unparalleled opportunity to attend to and foreground the value of the "extra-discursive significations of Indigenous art and culture-making."[34] Prem Krishnamurthy once wrote that exhibitions should be permanent, which is a powerful reminder that the knowledge (and potential paradigm shifts) exhibitions can produce should be taken more seriously.[35] Moving beyond simple notions of inclusion, and respecting the right for Indigenous "unbelonging" within given institutional structures, what might it look like for Indigenous values and principles to more fully inform and challenge the dominant frameworks of curatorial discourse? How can the rich multiplicity of Indigenous forms of knowledge "reformulate in unique and complex ways" the very concept and practice of curating?[36] How might the paradigms of artistic research support this process?

TEMPORAL SHIFTS, A MORE HOLISTIC APPROACH TO ART PRACTICE

When the first edition of this book was published, I was concerned that the absence of images might block artists from engaging with each other's practices, but something unexpected happened. Not being able to make quick aesthetic judgments, there was more space for artists to focus on what they have in common. This reminded me how often artists are set up to compete with one another, and how by being constantly asked what makes our individual practices singular, a sense of collectivity is undermined. As the pandemic brought to the fore, art is one of our survival mechanisms on an individual and collective level; it does not belong to a market or even to its makers, its temporalities are much longer. In our dialogue, Cannupa Hanska Luger suggests that art predates *Homo sapiens*, an expanded temporal framing that is reflected in some curatorial practices that work from Indigenous principles.[37] I want to close this essay with a reflection on why the notion of artistic research might alter temporalities within the process of day-to-day art making and help to shift public awareness and infrastructures toward a more sustainable art field in which artists can make their best contributions to the world.

The term "artistic research" implicitly encompasses more than the direct production of artworks and by doing so it crucially makes space for otherwise-unnamable activities that are intrinsic to the artistic process.[38] The precise nature of the activities included in artistic research is different for each artist, depending on their ways of working and interests. (These differences unfold across the twenty-four dialogues.) Importantly, however, the term "artistic research" grants permission to artists to take the necessary time and actions (or inactions) to nourish and inform their practice, to experiment and develop their work, and not only produce more work. This paradigm shift starts with artists' self-acknowledgment that this in-depth material-intellectual process (including times of sitting still and critically reflecting) is a necessity and not a luxury for their artistic practices. This acknowledgment needs to extend more fully into institutional recognition of artists' need to take time to invest in the unfolding of their process. If this clashes with the needs for quick institutional turnover, then those needs can in turn be questioned, which can only help to offset the stress levels of overstretched art workers everywhere.

The premise of artistic research, which foregrounds the material-intellectual processes involved in the making of art, challenges a tendency I observe in the US and other market-driven art locations, for even the very limited funding sources available to only be allocated for direct artistic output, and for awards and residencies to come with *a priori* demands of culminating exhibitions.[39] Not surprisingly, many artists hold back from long-term experimentation and in-depth research, being obliged to focus on continuous output to have any kind of sustainable practice.[40] In order to remain prolific in the face of inevitable time constraints, too many artists frequently skip over the necessary "restocking of the pond" of their creative process.[41] While inertia is part of any creative process, these conditions lead to long-term production of under-par work, and ultimately block the artist from reaching their full potential, creatively and professionally. Experimentation and open-ended research are, of course, the most difficult thing to finance anywhere and most contemporary art projects, even those privately funded, are being carried out by artists working at low pay.[42] However the agency of artists to determine the shape and form of their practices increases when these needs are widely understood.

The notion of artistic research as an *ongoing* process within practice shifts emphasis away from the production of "new" (art)work. It insists rather on multiyear time spans for artistic projects (that include but are not limited to artworks). In the dialogues, we witness how many years these processes take. This mental shift also redirects curatorial and critical attention from the latest work toward how an artist's practice unfolds from one project to the next, with an eye for continuity and growth, and the inevitable circling back and deepening of the process. (The practice moves at different speeds on different levels of its existence.) This perspective exposes what artists need to nourish within their practice to continue to grow and to thrive, and to not plateau mid-career. It shows what artists need to receive in terms of curatorial, institutional, academic, and public support in order to reach their full potential. Greater support of artistic research could enable artists to bring their work into every kind of social and public context that they could meaningfully contribute to.[43] Through this expanded view of artistic practice as a multi-sited entity that unfolds over many years, the world at large might better apprehend and appreciate the life-long contribution of artists, culturally, socially, and politically.

As an embodiment of this longevity of artistic research, I am picturing Simone Forti at the age of eighty, pushing her prone body across an ice-laden

Illinois shoreline as part of a late performance work.[44] The incessant stream of news on the transistor radio she carries is drowned out by the sheer physicality of her actions, and how they make palpable the connectedness of environmental and individual well-being—a quietly insistent message in a world on fire.

Endnotes

1 Data from 2022 gleaned from a survey of staff members from fifty-four art museums in the United States suggests that 60 percent of workers are thinking about leaving their jobs, and 68 percent are thinking of leaving the field altogether. Low pay and burnout are cited as the top reasons for this. This rate is higher among those who experience discrimination or harassment. Museums Moving Forward (2023), https://museumsmovingforward.com/data-studies/2023. The continuity between museums' colonial foundations and US museums' values in the present is examined by Laura Raikovich in *Culture Strike: Art Museums in an Age of Protest* (London: Verso, 2021).

2 James Elkins has mapped the existence of PhD in Fine Art programs globally. See https://www.jameselkins.com/yy/2-list-of-phd-programs-around-the-world, including some in the US (see note iii). See also J. Elkins, *Artists with PhDs: On the New Doctoral Degree in Studio Art* (Washington, DC: New Academia Publishing, 2009, expanded ed., 2014). See Danny Butt, *Artistic Research in the Future Academy* (Chicago: University of Chicago Press, 2017) for reflections and debates on the PhD in Fine Art's relationship to the university.

3 Sporadic independent institutions throughout the US center artistic research in their mission, including Rivers Institute for Contemporary Art and Thought, New Orleans, and the recently established Center for Art, Research and Alliances in New York City. James Elkins identifies seven arts practice-based PhDs in Fine Art in the US. Alongside electronic, digital, film, and performance arts PhDs, two of these are studio-based visual arts PhDs and one is a non-studio-based PhD in Fine Art. The wider contextual reasons for the PhD in Fine Art not proliferating throughout the US are considered by Elkins, *Artists with PhDs*.

4 Our dialogue led to an extensive solo exhibition *Christine Howard Sandoval: Timelines for the Future*. Documentation can be viewed at: https://www.oregoncontemporary.org/timelines-for-the-future.

5 I draw on Anna Jensen's formulation that art has responsibilities and possibilities. *Encyclopedia of In-Betweenness: An Exploration of a Collective Artistic Research Practice,* PhD diss. (Aalto University, 2023), p. 47

6 Silvia Henke, Dieter Mersch, Nicolaj van der Meulen, Thomas Strässle, and Jörg Wiesel's *Manifesto of Artistic Research* (Zurich: Diaphanes, 2020) pleas for art to stop being in competition with the academic, and to strike out and articulate its own research epistemologies, in relation to and drawing on a long history of aesthetics as a mode of thinking. This subtly argued philosophical reflection speaks back to the university in the dominant terms of Western philosophy. Centering Kant's philosophies on aesthetics, it overlooks the potential to challenge these frameworks for decolonial purposes.

7 Sky Hopinka, *Around the Edge of Encircling Lake* (Milwaukee, WI: Green Gallery, 2018), p. 75.

8 This heightened visual perception is discussed in, e.g., Stine Vogt and Svein Magnussen, "Expertise in Pictorial Perception: Eye-movement

Patterns and Visual Memory in Artists and Laymen," *Perception 36*, no. 1 (2007): 91–100.

9 Artist Morehshin Allahyari uses the term "digital colonialism" in an eponymous lecture performance from 2013 to refer to how the 3D-rendered digital archiving of cultural artefacts by museums often reinscribes property rights for perpetuity. Ruha Benjamin attributes the term "technological redlining" to Safiya Noble in *Race After Technology* (Cambridge, UK: Polity, 2019), p. 147. Benjamin addresses "default discrimination" in chapter 7, pp. 77–96.

10 Lucy Cotter, "Making as Future Survival: A Dialogue with Cannupa Hanska Luger," in *Reclaiming Artistic Research*, expanded 2nd ed. (Berlin: Hatje Cantz, 2024), pp. 42–63, p. 47.

11 Tom Holert, *Knowledge Beside Itself* (Berlin: Sternberg Press, 2020), p. 55

12 Cotter, "Making as Future Survival: A Dialogue with Cannupa Hanska Luger," p. 49.

13 Ariella Aïsha Azoulay's *Potential History: Unlearning Imperialism* (London: Verso, 2019) is a landmark critique of the relationship between looting and the curatorial gaze, and the artist-function, among other subjects, and seeks to radically rethink archives, museums, and photography. I had the pleasure of discussing Azoulay's writing, filmmaking, and curatorial work in *A Dialogue with Curator Lucy Cotter and Filmmaker Ariella Aïsha Azoulay*, YouTube video, 1:24:10 min., uploaded by Disjecta Contemporary Art Center, April 24, 2021, https://www.youtube.com/watch?v=p1u5qoxrMuA.

14 See Azoulay, *Potential History: Unlearning Imperialism*. Andre Lepecki reflects on how some artworks intrinsically refuse these protocols in "Decolonizing the Curatorial," *Theatre 47* (I) (2017), pp. 101–15, here p. 102.

15 Pope.L, *Notes on the Roll of the Artist When the World has Always Been on Fire??*, Vimeo video, 15 min. excerpt, uploaded by Berkeley Arts + Design, September 21, 2020, https://vimeo.com/462019660.

16 Dis/Rep: Liberating Words, six-week workshop by Curiosity Paradox engaging with art and access, 2022, https://thecuriosityparadox.com/disrep2022.

17 Julie Philips, *The Baby on the Fire Escape: Creativity, Motherhood and the Mind-Baby Problem* (New York: W. W. Norton, 2022).

18 Katayoun Arian, "Embodied Knowledge: A Dialogue with Grada Kilomba," in *Reclaiming Artistic Research*, expanded 2nd ed. (Berlin: Hatje Cantz, 2024), pp. 140–153.

19 Karen Archey, *After Institutions* (Berlin: Floating Opera Press, 2022).

20 Andrew Dewdney, David Dibosa, and Victoria Walsh, eds., *Post-Critical Museology: Theory and Practice in the Art Museum* (London: Routledge, 2013).

21 Lucy Cotter, "Mercurial States," Art and Education, 2019. This guest edition featuring five curated videos and related texts is now offline, but the essay can be accessed via my website: www.lucycotter.org.

22 See Édouard Glissant, *Poetics of Relation* (Ann Arbor: University of Michigan Press, 2010), pp. 189–94.

23 This "performance of keyon gaskin" and the related crossword is documented in *Turnstones: Season 10, 2020–21, Curator in Residence Lucy Cotter* (Portland, OR: Oregon Center for Contemporary Art, 2022).

24 I attribute this understanding to conversations with David Dibosa.

25 I discuss this in more depth in an interview with Marjoca de Greef, "Reorienting (Online) Spaces: An Interview with Lucy Cotter," In the Pause of a Gesture There May Be an Echo, 2020, https://inthepauseofagesturetheremightbeanecho.eu/index.php/en/?view=article&id=74&catid=22.

26 Some recent examples of artists' book publications include Steffani Jemison's *A Rock, A River, A Street* (New York: Primary Information, 2022); Na Mira, *The Book of Na* (New York: Wendy's Subway, 2022); Katie Holten, *The Language of Trees* (Portland: Tin House, 2023). Experimental texts are increasingly published in exhibition catalogs and academic books. For one recent commission, I had the bandwidth to create a series of text portraits of individual artistic practices in forms ranging from flash fiction and prose poetry to philosophical reflections; see *Fieldings: Propositions for 3rd Cycle Education in the Performing Arts* (Amsterdam: DAS Publishing, Amsterdam University of the Arts, 2021).

27 "Affordances" is a term used in design thinking. I borrow it from Caroline Levine who uses it to describe the possibilities of different literary genres in *Forms: Whole, Rhythm, Hierarchy, Network* (Princeton: Princeton University Press, 2017). In my book in progress, which has the working title *Writing as an Artistic Medium*, I trace how writing appears in and through everyday artistic practice (beyond text-based artworks) and look at the fluidity of writing and orality in contemporary artworks and performance, and related experimental artists' writings.

28 Doing justice to this epistemological legacy requires in-depth critical analysis of how the power dynamics and ideologies of Enlightenment and colonial thinking became embedded in the continuing dynamics of contemporary infrastructures. Those seeking accessible entry points into this vast area for art education purposes will find some in Louis Yako's "Decolonizing Knowledge: A Practical Guide," Counterpunch, April 9, 2021, https://www.counterpunch.org/2021/04/09/decolonizing-knowledge-production-a-practical-guide/, and Ijeoma Nnodim Opara's, "It's Time to Decolonize the Decolonization Movement," Speaking Medicine and Health blog, July 29, 2021, https://speakingofmedicine.plos.org/2021/07/29/its-time-to-decolonize-the-decolonization-movement/. The latter offers a sharp analysis of how to exceed the limits of acritical DEI-led thinking.

29 Tom Holert, *Knowledge Beside Itself*, p. 18.

30 See, for example, Estelle Barrett, Chapter 9, "New Frontiers of Research: Indigenous Knowledge Systems and Artistic Practice,"

in Margaret Kumar and Supriya Pattanayak, eds., *Positioning Research, Shifting Paradigms, Interdisciplinarity and Indigeneity* (London: SAGE, 2018), pp. 181–95; Danny Butt, "The Promise of Artistic Research in the Asia Pacific," *Manusya Journal of Humanities* 23, issue 3 (2020): 328–34; Mareli Stolp, "Artistic Research as African Epistemology," Arts Research Africa Conference Proceedings (2020), https://wiredspace.wits.ac.za/items/1256bcbe-8431-4871-b0aa-eb03f07d97c4.

31 Holert, ibid. *Knowledge Beside Itself*, p. 19.

32 See Lucy Cotter, "Unravelling: After Practice-based Curating," Bassam El Baroni, Bridget Crone, and Matthew Poole, eds., *Edinburgh Companion to Curatorial Futures* (Edinburgh: Edinburgh University Press, forthcoming 2024).

33 Amanda Cachia examines possibilities for curators to fold access into curatorial practice in *Curating Access: Disability Art Activism and Creative Accommodation* (London: Routledge, 2022). I have sought to use the exhibition self-reflexively as a decolonial epistemological space in two recent group exhibitions engaging with the exclusionary contours of art and curatorial value systems: *Unquiet Objects*, Oregon Center for Contemporary Art, 2021, https://www.oregoncontemporary.org/unquiet-objects, and *The Unknown Artist*, Center for Contemporary Art and Culture, Portland, 2020. Amelia Rina's review of the latter for *Art in America* can be found here: https://www.artnews.com/art-in-america/aia-reviews/unknown-artist-lucy-cotter-center-contemporary-art-culture-pacific-northwest-college-art-1202686594.

34 Stephen Gilchrist, *Belonging and Unbelonging: Indigenous Forms of Curation as Expressions of Sovereignty*, PhD diss. (University of Sydney, 2018), https://ses.library.usyd.edu.au/handle/2123/22301.

35 Prem Krishnamurthy offered this observation as part of *Endless Exhibition*, a curatorial-manifesto-as-artwork (2018–forever) at Kunsthal Ghent, Belgium.

36 In my formulation, I draw on Gilchrist, *Belonging and Unbelonging: Indigenous Forms of Curation as Expressions of Sovereignty*. See also Katya García Antón, ed., *Sovereign Words: Indigenous Art, Curation and Criticism* (Amsterdam: Valiz, 2019), and Bruno Brulon Soares, *The Anticolonial Museum: Reclaiming our Colonial Heritage* (London: Routledge, 2023).

37 Stephen Gilchrist reflects on how curating from Indigenous principles may include a shift in mental timelines toward tens of thousands of years in "Awakening Objects and Indigenizing the Museum: Stephen Gilchrist in Conversation with Henry F. Skerritt," *Contemporaneity: Historical Practice in Visual Culture* 5. no. 1, "Agency in Motion" (2016), pp. 108–21, p. 114.

38 For an extended reflection on the artistic process, see Kim Grant, *All About Process: The Theory and Discourse of Modern Artistic Labor* (University Park, PA: Penn State University Press, 2017).

39 In the United States, artists' public funding structures are typically state-based (and thus very limited almost everywhere outside of California and New York), and private patron-based or corporate funding is often based on the most conservatively drawn criteria.

40 Painting dominates the US art field, a medium that offers a more direct financial return than experimental, ephemeral formats that outnumber traditional artworks in other (publicly well-funded) art locations. In the US even the most established artists often work a full-time job, or several "side jobs."

41 I borrow this phrase from Julia Cameron's wise book *The Artist's Way* (New York: TarcherPerigee, 1992), a book of self-care and nourishment of creative practice.

42 I draw on Tom Holert's discussion of these conditions in *Knowledge Beside Itself*, p. 32.

43 Sher Doruff points out the need for more support for artists to engage in artistic research in contexts outside of the art world. "A New Format for an Artists' PhD: Conversation between Sher Doruff and Jeroen Boomgaard," in Yael Davids, *I'm Going to be Your Last Teacher-A Workbook* (Amsterdam: Roma, with Van Abbemuseum, Migros Museum für Gekenwartskunst, Gerrit Rietveld Academie, 2023), pp. 189–91.

44 Simone Forti, *A Free Consultation*, Vimeo video, 17:35 min., uploaded by The Box, LA, January 30, 2016, https://vimeo.com/154902507.

Making as Future Survival

A Dialogue with Cannupa Hanska Luger

Lucy Cotter The core focus of your current work is future survival and twenty-first-century Indigeneity. You work in so many ways – sculpturally, through performance and video, and with socially engaged and curatorial projects – but it seems to me to all revolve around making. Is that what drives you as an artist?

Cannupa Hanska Luger Yes, I'm more about materials and process than I am about concepts. My approach is, "The concept will show up. What am I working with here?"

LC Sometimes you've described yourself as a craftsperson and there's a sense that we can take things into our own hands and make a future – we can make in ways that bring the past into the present and the future.

There is so much political agency in what making can or could make happen in your practice.

CHL Yes, totally. I think it's funny that to be able to make something with your hands and create a thing somehow puts you in the position of being political. That makes sense because we've submitted our wealth, our collective knowledge of creation and making to the economic wheels that spin. We've removed all notions of manufacturing within society. Our economy is built on trading stuff, but we're not making any of the things for trade. You're just connecting one person to another to get a thing, sell a thing, and in that process you lose a lot of agency.

I like making stuff, whatever it is – making dinner, making dishes I would eat off. I like learning new skill sets. I'm a jack-of-all-trades, master of none, although I'm getting pretty close in clay. I've definitely put in my 10,000 hours in some random things, but there's constant knowledge to be gained. What I know is finite, what I don't know is infinite. I should look at the infinite, start from that place, and I think making, for me, is a way to take in information. It's a way to take in knowledge, take in recipes, and give meaning to definitions, materials, and other things.

Interacting with material, pushing it to its edge, allowing it to push me to my edge, there's a whole reciprocal experience that happens between me and things that are deemed inanimate, and I think their influence is proof of their animism. They're literally pushing and bending the way that I'm living my life. They're a participant in life being lived: How is that not the same? I think when you interact with materials, you begin to better understand that connectedness versus calling up Jeff Bezos and saying, “Send me a thing.”

LC One of your current major projects, *Future Ancestral Technologies*, delves into the relationship between making and knowledge in the past and the future. It is based around Indigenous futurism, and you also draw on speculative fiction and science fiction. Can we talk about the video work *We Live*, in which two figures can be seen walking across a landscape? We hear in the narrative voiceover that the colonizers have left, and those who have been left behind are the Indigenous people and those who have worked the land, and together they're going to create some kind of new cultures.

These people are wearing full regalia, with aesthetic aspects that invoke traditional Indigenous regalia, but they also incorporate futuristic, sports equipment-based elements. It seems like this storyline of imagining forward is a departure point for each of the various aspects of the *Future Ancestral Technologies* project. I'm interested to hear you speak about this coming together of past, present, and future, as well as the role of fiction.

CHL Yes, that's me just reading the room. “Okay, what's going on presently? If I'm going to imagine a future place, what's happening now?” Some of the wealthiest folks in the world are looking at space exploration. They're saying, “All right, we can go where there isn't going to be an Indigenous problem.” There's a notion of colonies, this notion of space exploration. I'm thinking, “I've seen it before. I promise you; you're going to call it the New World. You're not that creative. I've seen this happen.”

I'm also thinking, “How many things do I have to purchase to give you the capital to go?

You should totally go. I'm for it. It's going to be amazing. You should go and check out space. That'd be great."

LC And the rest of us should stay here. *(Laughs)*

CHL I'm totally staying, and they're not going to make enough seats for all of us anyway. I know how this operates, and they're going to take every resource they can from the perfect ship we live on right now to fulfill this dream of exodus. I'm saying, "You should go, take it, take what you need. I promise you we'll survive it." We'll survive after this toxic perpetuation of dominion and control has left the planet. I'm thinking, "You should totally go, we'll come up with something better."

I don't want to focus on it being an antithesis to those systems either, because I feel like the inevitable failure of those systems is nigh. We're seeing it crumbling right now, and there are some last-ditch efforts, like space exploration. It looks like, as Tesla and [Elon Musk's] thinkers are saying, a multi-planet species. I'm like, "Dude, the moment you spend six months out there, a year, four years, you're going to begin to resent the neglect of planet Earth." I'm like, "It's hard, space is hard, but you should totally do it." This pioneer intrepid spirit.

I'm thinking, "You know what you can actually do in space? You can lift yourself up by your own bootstraps." In outer space, in zero G, is the only place in the universe where you can lift yourself up by your own bootstraps. That's the myth of America. I'm like, "Nobody's ever done that, we're all super-reliant on one another. We're interconnected, we're interdependent, but you should go to space."

Where I'm interested in starting that conversation is beyond the exodus. What happens to those who remain and how do we develop and reinforce technology? Presently, we focus on technology being mechanisms, and it's not. Technology is ideas. A lot of Indigenous technology exists in our cosmology, in our homes, in symbols we create, in forms we express through dance and music. But that technology has not been allowed to navigate through material science and mechanisms.

LC Can we talk about how you enable these ideas to be recognizable as technologies? The word "technology" comes from *techne*, which has to do with making, a link that is foregrounded in many areas of your practice. In your *We Survive You* and *Tipi* projects you repurpose the detritus of industrial culture and future-proof and reintegrate Indigenous elements. While imagining a nomadic post-industrial way of life, we see the tipi becoming something that echoes high-tech mountaineering trek equipment.

One of your recent film projects, *Continuum*, shows your family kitted out in gear that is made by you, partly from repurposed packing blankets. I love the fact that rather than being dystopic or utopian, there is this very practical sense that we're going to work with everything we have, which is a mixture of this detritus and the constancy of the natural world, and the knowledge that lies in both.

CHL Totally, but I'm more inclined to talk about our customary practices than our traditions. Tradition feels like an imposition of ideas that makes it stagnate, makes it stick to a certain moment in time. Customarily, we would adapt to new material immediately. That adaptation is how we survive to this present moment. As a human species, we're one of the most adaptable creatures on the planet. We're everywhere. Even in places that would be hostile to us, we find a way to explore those regions. The exploration is in the question, can we live here? What would we have to do to live here?

The thing that I like about the tipi as a methodology, or a technology is that it is embedded in the nomadic existence, and it doesn't have to be much more high-tech than it is already. The high-tech aspect of it is a shift in mental perspective. The home I live in, the studio that I'm working in, the plot of land that I own is a technology that I was forced to assimilate into; this notion that these are mine now. This isn't my stuff. I'm borrowing this. I'm only here for so long. I think the tipi reinforces this notion of transience and movement, and, really, freedom in the core sense of the word, where I have more choices.

The more stuff I have, the fewer choices, so a tipi opens that up. Look at this entire generation of people interested in blowing off their parental modalities and saying, "I'm going to live in a van for a while and travel around. I'm going to see things and enjoy my life." That's not new, that's really old. It's probably truer to our nature than the systems that we're forced to navigate, which are ultimately traps to make us still, to settle us.

LC Some of your other works foreground these long-term migratory routes among peoples. I'm thinking especially of socially engaged projects like *Something to Hold Onto*, which sets out to make the statistics of the loss of life on the US-Mexican border tangible. There is an implicit insistence on the naturalness of that migratory route. I see it as a repair line across what has been forcibly separated.

CHL Yes, it's because this fluid migration, this movement of people and ideas and technologies and culture is absolutely natural and inevitable. When you throw something in the path of that movement, there will be a collision. The lives lost represented in *Something to Hold Onto* are the collateral damage of that barrier. To me, it's heartbreaking because we have no idea where we could be because of what we lost. It's called *Something to Hold Onto* because the impact of their lives on our lives has been stifled immediately. The last thing that we get to hold onto is their loss of life.

That project was a collective effort. I asked people to squeeze clay beads and embed their handprints into pieces of clay to represent data. I work in an industry where art is considered an object, the thing that somebody makes. That couldn't be further from my personal definition of what art is. Art for me is the making. It is these processes that have been passed down from teacher to student, from ancestor to elder. It's a continuum. It's intergenerational. These socially engineered projects are a way for me to share art by my own definition. Where I'm saying, "Help me make it." I simplify it so that it's completely accessible.

There's a lot of backend engineering that goes into how to simplify an overall thing. Working with data is a really great way to do that because data oftentimes is something very hard for us to wrap our heads around. Even when we get numbers, a large number is still only one number. Whether it's a trillion or seven, it's still one number, but seeing it at scale, you have a different relationship to it mentally. That's the driving force to these collective things, to look at numbers at scale.

LC The first collective project of yours that I saw was the *Mirror Shield* project where you invited people to make a wooden shield that could be used in protests against the Dakota Access Pipeline at Standing Rock. You made instructional videos of how to make these shields and put them on social media. In a related talk that I watched, you said this might be the first time that some people make something, certainly as an adult. For me, that project also seemed to include prototyping what an artist could be or what an artist could do.

That sharing of knowledge was one aspect of it. The other aspect embraced what physical material presence can do in the world. At the Standing Rock Reservation protest, having a visual material element in common created a more united front. This included a choreographed component where you had people collectively perform with the shields in space. There was a political weight and presence to that performance which manifested the agency of art as a cultural mover and shaper.

CHL Yes. It's interesting; that whole piece was built out of necessity. I didn't ever think of it as art. I just thought, "We need shields." That's the base, and I was trying to solve a problem, "I'm one person, what can I do?" The shield was built out of that question, what can one person do? There were GoFundMe things and on social media, there was a lot of interaction and participation through liking and sharing. I thought, "All right, that's a river that is wide and shallow. How do you make it a little bit deeper?" So, I created a prompt for people to make something, "You don't need to send money or supplies. For less than sixty dollars, you can make six of these shields. I'll show you exactly how."

When we talk about materials, it's also the economies and these systems that I navigate. "How can I build this in the parking lot of a big box store?" Something that I know is everywhere across America. What's the lowest common denominator between all these folks? I took that responsibility on myself as a person who makes things. I thought to myself, "Okay. If I can figure out how to make it here, I can put the instructional video out, and then people who may not have financial or other resources, or the health capacity to go to North Dakota to stand on the front line can participate in that and satiate a demand to do more." How to have meaning in their solidarity and transform an ally into an accomplice? If you're embedded and you're participating and you're making resources for us, you're in it now. You're in it from your home in a way that you wouldn't be by sending water bottles or whatever.

LC Can we talk a bit more about systems of distribution and circulation and their economies in *Mirror Shields* and other projects? The shields were subsequently sent on to various other protests, supporting different causes in different locations, which is significant in terms of circulation. I'm also thinking about *Every One*, a further project in which you asked grieving families to make round ceramic beads that collectively came together to form an image of an Indigenous woman. These 4,000 beads each represented a woman, girl, queer, or trans individual reportedly disappeared or murdered in the US and Canada over the past thirty to forty years, and every time it was exhibited, the fees went to a foundation supporting their families. Subsequently, with *Something to Hold Onto*, you didn't fire the

7,000 beads representing loss of life on the border but instead put them back in the earth and revisited that site to see how they were reintegrating with the soil. Each of these strategies seems to be a pushback against an extraction-based economy. Are you thinking about circulation with every project? Are you always creating or looking for a different system?

CHL Not necessarily. The socially engineered projects get really complex, so I end up learning every time I do one and apply that knowledge to the next thing. So, for the first one, the *Mirror Shield* project, I was using an address on Standing Rock to send the shields to, but it exhausted the PO Box once this thing took off. So many shields came in that were being redistributed and used for different things other than just as a shield. That was the first socially engineered project, and it made me understand something, "Oh, the Internet and social media, we can put more empathy in through creating projects like this." The next one was *Every One*. With that piece, we ended up firing all the beads because of the complexity of dyeing each one, stringing it, and traveling it.

I steward that collective work to this day. It's in Des Moines right now, and I have learned that stewarding it reopens trauma for me personally. Watching people with white cotton gloves carefully install this piece over and over re-triggers this notion, "You care more for the symbol than you did for the people that they represent. That's harsh." For the next work, *Something to Hold Onto*, I decided not to fire it, and to allow the pieces to go back to the earth into the location where the vast majority of those lives were lost, and the bodies were found. To allow the clay and these symbols of life to disintegrate and connect back into the landscape.

There's not a whole lot of economic return on that and on a lot of these social projects. It gets complex around the question of how to redistribute wealth and in what direction to do it. As the *Mirror Shield* project gets exhibited all over the place, there is an emphasis on the redistribution of the shields if people make them themselves, and the financial return on the project is redistributed into a variety of different channels and passages for all of that. These sorts of projects are complex. My general practice also produces objects, and I'm a little bit less inclined to worry about what these sculptural forms are as a commodity moving through markets. I'm saying, "I'm going to do something good with the money, I promise," but I'm less worried about it consciously than I am with the socially engineered projects.

LC That makes a lot of sense. It seems to me that in your general practice you're also constantly pushing your boundaries and operating at the edge of your comfort levels in terms of creating and engaging with new ways of working. A recent project I want to mention is the *Sweet Land Opera*, which took place in LA, just outside of Chinatown. I know that you came on board that project to create the costumes–you have an incredible practice of reimagining regalia and making garments. Yet, you ended up as a co-director of that opera, collaborating with artists like composer Du Yun, and librettists Aja Couchois Duncan and Douglas Kearney. It was interesting to watch the video documentation and follow that learning curve. I know that you have a background in hip-hop and slam poetry. It felt to me like the context of opera was a whole new genre, but at the same time maybe you leaned into that possibility of reconnecting differently with sound and the word and landscape. I see you reinventing those genres somehow.

CHL Yes. Well, co-directing this thing with Yuval Sharon, one of the first questions I was asking was, "What does opera mean? Translate it into English, literally translate the word." He said, "Well, it means to work." I thought, "I know how to work." Then it was more comfortable. I started to realize that it was about the presentation of art through many different dimensions. You've got the written word on the page, written music that then is transformed sonically, set and costume, and stage design which is painting and sculpture. All these things are moving from being one-dimensional to two-dimensional to three-dimensional, to a fourth-dimensional time installation. So, I'm thinking to myself, "Oh, this is durational installation work. It's not that far outside of the scope of what I am capable of."

I had a really great partner and instructor to pick up the slack, who was aware of the language of opera, so my ignorance became a resource. My intrigue and lack of knowledge around it sparked ways to reconsider doing things that, because folks had been trained so much, they'd never thought about operating in this other way. Some of my ideas were bad ideas and you learn that, and you have somebody who says, "Oh, we tried that years ago, it's a bad idea. It doesn't work in this instance."

I think the core of understanding all those different creative ways of intersection and plurality within the scope of opera is so incredibly close to something that is really familiar to me and to most human beings, and why opera exists in the first place, because it's ceremony. It is the gathering and the collection of people to express an idea through diverse materials and techniques, and it's a baby in that world. We hold it up in this place, but it's young. Opera is a young version of ceremony, and ceremony is the ancient version. I'm thinking, "See it for what it is."

LC Let's go back to talk a little bit more about *Future Ancestral Technologies* because several of the works involve exactly that, a reimagining and recreating of ceremony. I find it interesting that the making of regalia is a very important departure point for this and a lot of your work. You started moving your body to animate these sculptural garments and headpieces and that led to filming the movement. It's easy now to view you as a video artist because you have a lot of video work that is visually powerful. But it has grown from a recording of performative gestures that are rooted in a certain environment. I'm thinking again about the opera because it was so site-specific; it was an immersive environment and there was a sense of reinhabiting place. I'm thinking also about a video from your *Muscle, Bone & Sinew* project, in which two people perform in regalia that is inspired by the buffalo horn. They reinhabit a leftover industrial steel circle and we watch them move until their shadows eventually form a totemic figure. I'd love to hear you say more about that work.

CHL Yes, that's *Shadow Holding Shape to Experience the Energy of the Sun*. Well, a lot of that work is built on collaboration and cooperation with folks who are savvier than I am with the material. My introduction to film is a response to the question, where's the audience? Who's the audience? Working in museums limits your audience, but if you make a film and you put it out on social media, it's easier to ship and give away. There are object forms that are a part of the work, but the video itself is also something special.

A lot of the regalia hinders your capacity to see, and so you have to navigate the landscape on a feel basis more than the visual senses that we navigate with normally. That makes the landscape a collaborator as well. The land begins to choreograph those movements because you have to feel your way across it as you're moving through the space. By and large, in my performances, the primary audience is the land. By documenting those experiences, we can share them as video work, as a film for content desire, for where the audience is. I think art's primary function is about communication.

It feels good for me as an artist to wear this regalia and perform in it on the land, but I'm also asking other people to wear them and obscure their vision and navigate shapes to put themselves on the land. I try to direct that process from the sidelines, or they're skilled and I say, "Do your thing and wear this, and we'll see what comes out the other side of it." It's constantly changing and growing, but I'm beginning to build a vocabulary of film-based visual language by doing it.

LC I'd love to talk about *Continuum*, your recent and most ambitious work on that filmic level, partly thanks to your residency at EMPAC, an experimental media and performing arts center in New York. In terms of the visual vocabulary, I was struck by the many scenes of plant and insect life that bring forward the interdependencies you mentioned earlier. In this work particularly, the medium of film lends you a language to animate those things in a different way than in a sculpture or a socially engaged project.

CHL Yes. That film is the first time we had a legit resource and equipment to create something, which created a huge shift in me thinking about what a video can be, and how it can be presented. I'm used to looking at things on my phone ten inches away from my face or sitting down and watching a screen. EMPAC's space is incredible and that possibility of immersion and storytelling outside of the single-channel narrative was really interesting.

Up until that point, all of the *Future Ancestral Technology* work was tapping into the development of myth. In the creation of *Continuum*, what I wanted to resolve was the question of who believes in these myths? Who follows and perpetuates them? I was thinking, "This is what it looks like to be the people that hold and carry these stories in that place." I was like, "Let's not make a superhero movie. Let's just make it really slow. Let's make it normal," normalizing general tasks.

LC Often the relationship between the past and the present and the future is talked about in theoretical terms, or with reference to major political issues, but by inviting your family to be the protagonists in *Continuum*, you bring forward something that I experience myself very strongly: that raising children is a form of creating the future; that parenting is a political act and an experiment. What does it mean to you as an artist to think through how you invite your children into the world or invite them to believe what the world is, may be, or might become? I feel that parenting is the active working out of ideas that in my research often remained as theory; it's practice, it's manifesting and unfolding every day.

CHL That's how it is in the studio too. I create these ideas and it's all theory. Then even when we're working with science fiction, it's the presentation of practice. With a speculative formation, you have to assume that they're practicing it in some place that's not presently now. I think the thing that I'm trying to navigate and push forward with this future ancestral technology exploration is that we have a really limited sense of time that it is cause and effect. It's sequential, it's linear in this way, and I'm asking, "But is it? Is it really?"

How I was raised is that you are accountable to generations into the past and generations into the future; we call it seven generations. Time doesn't move in a linear sense in a forward trajectory and motion, but rather expands spherically from the present. You can end up doing something in the far future that references something in the far past, or some far past experience shifts the way the far future does things. The arrows in this line are going in both directions. Mathematics and physics and other theoretical thinking is okay to consider, but then let's add some more theories and reconsider what time is and how we relate to time.

Recognizing that a child is the future and that you're developing and setting in place a way for them to navigate truly, wholly, and accountably into the future, you also have to recognize and share these different notions of time. Otherwise, you end up becoming too selfish, you become monstrous. The annihilation of self in the absorption of continuum, of collective experience, of me being accountable to you, you being accountable to the land, to the animals. Once we start to build a better understanding of the way that we talk about time, history, and experience, there will be profound shifts. Things wouldn't be stagnated in this linear trajectory into the future. This is Indigenous knowledge; this is ancestral technology.

LC In *Continuum* it was palpable that children have greater intelligence than adults at certain moments. That it's not just that as a parent you are facilitating a child's unfolding, but that this process is also moving back toward you all the time. That you are being recreated through your children as they self-create and know more than you.

CHL Totally. What me and my family acted out on the landscape in upstate New York when we were shaping the film is not what we ended up putting out there. In the performance of it, we were grinding pigments, but it wasn't until we were sitting at the editor's table that we understood what we were illustrating. What shifted was that we recognized that the perspective of this three-channel film experience should be from that of our children and not of me or my wife as the leads sharing knowledge with them. It's about the children experiencing this present moment. I think that that's a really important thing for us all to learn presently as our world is radically shifting. There is incredible knowledge to be gained in us stepping off our high horse and considering ourselves in a position of power due to age. I don't know how to communicate like my kids communicate. They learn to communicate in a different way because there are external sources of information that flow in and out; it's really interesting.

LC Thinking about this spherical rather than linear unfolding of time and knowledge makes me think about your *A Way Home* project, which honors ancient clay practices. The wider project involves searching for knowledge through research, through testing of what it means to get back in touch with clay, what it means to make. It's neither recreating the past nor trying to preserve it. It's rather an understanding that this is all reinvention and that through your work you will be both re-finding and creating something. So, there's a dialogue across time in different directions.

There's one video showing an aerial view of a sedimented rocky landscape. A child's voice is narrating that sedimentation through time, but in a way that is always shifting, and making us part of that process. It rallies against the idea of preserving the environment or culture and foregrounds that it is firstly about letting nature go back to itself, and secondly, about maintaining culture and allowing it to be fluid. I'm thinking, too, of how your recent digital avatar works, *Bison and Seven Works* not only mourn the relative disappearance of the bison but also include imagining the bison being present again in great numbers. I really appreciate that there's never an elegiac,"That's the end of it," but rather, "We're in the process of these things which appear and disappear, and we have agency in that, so what are we going to do?"

CHL Yes. As I've worked more with museums and institutions, I've seen over and over in academia and in schools this emphasis on preservation of culture as the model for all of these spaces that I navigate. People from our community come and see these preserved versions of culture, and I'm like dude, you kill it.

Why have the jam when you can have the fresh fruit? I promise you it's better. It might not be as sweet, you can add all those preservatives and sugars to it, but you're transforming it from what it is to something you want it to be. What it is, is in a process of becoming, it's constantly in flux.

LC I want to think about your own positioning of your work as culture, which isn't always foregrounded within contemporary art. In several Indigenous artists' practices that I've engaged with, giving back to one's culture is a massive part of the practice; the community is always adjacent. Can we talk about that interdependence between artistic practices and wider cultural practices, perhaps also as an alternative to the economies that you've mentioned, which are very much capitalist economies? There is also evident generosity within your practice toward fellow Indigenous producers with projects like STTLMNT, where you created a digital platform to help make other creative producers' practices sustainable.

CHL Well, and this is oversimplified … and this oversimplification is where you develop stereotypes and limited understanding. But I'm in Indian country, I see, know, and operate within a living, thriving culture maintained under the most desperate of attempts to annihilate it, and so I'm asking myself, "What are you going to do? What could you possibly do?" Well, I can share space. All these institutional and academic and economic systems reinforce notions of scarcity. I'm saying, "Dude, we live on a planet of great abundance and we're greedy because of this notion of scarcity. You've put the cart before the horse."

I want to be in awe of us because I think we're brilliant as a species, as a creature. I know what we've done with ill intent. What happens if we do it another way? I still believe that's possible. I'm an optimist in that sense, but I also think that there is an inevitability in our own self-preservation. To recognize that self doesn't end at my skin, that the influence and the relationships are probably a much stronger bond than the hydrogen and carbon molecules that are keeping my meat inside. That self is bigger than that. If selfishness and self-determination and preservation is the model that you want to navigate from, well then let's expand the idea of self. Otherwise, you can just blend into and assimilate to Indigenous notions of community and being. We're not proselytizing this. I just want to share options.

LC Your optimism is a beautiful note to end this conversation on. I feel like there's a scarcity of optimism in these times.

CHL I question that. I think that because there are eight billion of us, clearly optimism is thriving, you know what I'm saying? If optimism was a rare commodity, there wouldn't be eight billion of us, I promise you.

LC That's nice to think about. Sometimes it seems that the further you go in the art world, the more the optimists are weeded out. On the other hand, you have to be pretty idealistic to stay working in this economy. *(laughs)*

CHL You're still participating, I don't believe you're that cynical! Give up then? No? Okay, well then endure. Let's figure it out. Art still exists. Art was here for a long time. Art predates us as a species.

LC That's crazy to think about.

CHL It is crazy. I'm playing with something older than my entire species, and I'm participating in it, and I'm creating within that vein. Once we start talking about a continuum, it's older than human beings, than *Homo sapiens*. That's incredible. That also tells me we value it in our core, in some place between our brain and our heart. I think it's been perverted within the last couple of centuries, but that's insignificant on that sort of timeline. That's a blip.

LC I watched a video interview with Breeze, one of the two artists who did the mural for *Something to Hold Onto*, and he made a direct correlation between the work of his ancestors in terms of early stone-carved petroglyphs and his current wall-based murals. I found his sense of continuity quite beautiful.

CHL Totally. I think one of the oldest things is supposed to be a tool, right? Those hand axes that they found are pristine. They weren't ever used. They were the original form. Somebody happened to say, "We should make more like this." Then they did and they used them, but this is a part of the historical record, and this is before *Homo sapiens*. There's an object that remains that's been like a perfect form of future things to this point. Knowledge and making. Understanding and making. I'm like, that is art.

Sounding Out the Law

A Dialogue with Lawrence Abu Hamdan

Lucy Cotter You describe yourself as an artist and audio investigator. In parallel with exhibiting your installations, sound and media works all over the world, your artist's audio investigations have been used as evidence at the UK Asylum and Immigration Tribunal and as advocacy for organizations such as Amnesty International and Defence for Children International. Did you start this path with a particular education or how did you start to think about sound in legal or political terms?

Lawrence Abu Hamdan The best education I got was from DIY music; people who were organizing gigs in Leeds during my teenage years, and seeing how they managed to build an infrastructure that could avoid the mainstream music industry but still exist beyond subcultural groups and cliques. So it was really about learning what music could be and how it could be tied into political organization. These were forms of experimentation that were both aesthetic and political and I was interested in where they met, a kind of folding of the aesthetic and political into one another. At the same time, this was facilitating ways of making music I had not heard before until that point.

LC Did you do any formal training as a visual artist or in sound or music?

LAH Yes, I then did the Sonic Arts course at Middlesex, and later an MA and a PhD with Eyal Weizman, who leads Forensic Architecture at the Department of Visual Culture of Goldsmiths. I was one of the first researchers on that project, so I helped shape it from the beginning and it also shaped and informed my approach. I've been working in parallel with and in collaboration with Weizman ever since, and my PhD is also with him.

LC Your PhD research was entitled *Forensic Listening*, which in a way is the underlying interest of most of your artistic works. It focused particularly on the role of the voice in law.

LAH Yes, I was fascinated by that and trying to understand how something like the law could conceive of sound and develop its hearings. Sound is very prevalent in testimony because many crimes happen in the dark and often parts of the event spill through the walls or into open windows. So the majority of witnesses to any event are usually ear witnesses. Yet it's easier to include an event visually as a form of evidence than it is sonically. I found it interesting that ear witness testimony has been prevalent in all the major high profile cases of recent years, like Trayvon Martin, Amanda Knox, and Oscar Pistorius. These highly sensational trials all hinged on sound. So it's not something niche, but it has not been dealt with, despite its prevalence. I wanted to return to the idea of how ear witnesses describe sound, and see how you could develop a way to produce ear witness interviews that were medium-specific and not only a bad form of eye-witnessing. So I started researching how you could unlock witness testimonies, memories, in ways that don't speak to the limits of sound but understand sound as something that bleeds between the senses, acknowledging that the way it is encoded often uses visual metaphors and touch; things that are understood through cinema.

LC You've recently opened up that world of touch and visuality of sound in *Earwitness Inventory* (2018), a work in which you present ninety-five custom-designed and sourced objects that relate to different ear witness cases around the world. Can you talk about what led you to create it, why you would present it in this way, and who may use it?

LAH The idea for *Earwitness Inventory* was conceived in 2013. I had at that point already been working a lot with what it meant to be an ear witness. I was fascinated by the ways in which sound was contested in legal forums because truth was being produced through sound. I found that interesting because sound is very hard to speak about and it's always collaborating with either space or memory, with people's subjective experience and description in language.

I had started to become interested in CIA Black Sites and was in discussion with an organization called Reprieve about ear witness testimony in response to the US prison and torture programme. You had people being hooded, blindfolded, and taken to countries where they had no idea where they were, and tortured. These "black sites" were all around the world: Thailand, Jordan, etc., and also in the European Union, but in 2013 their location was still unknown. At that time, I was on a residency in Sweden and went to a radio theater. There I saw a door with which you could create hundreds of different door sounds, hundreds of shoes, architecture that makes things sound as if things are more distant, and stairs with different surfaces. What I saw there was essentially a space to produce sonic illusion, but I saw it as a mnemonic device and something that could produce truth claims in an investigation. I started setting up a project but in 2014 the US Senate report released the location of the "black sites," so that project was shelved until I investigated the Saydnaya prison in Syria.

LC How did the Saydnaya project get started?

LAH I was invited by Forensic Architecture, with whom Amnesty had worked on a different project. Amnesty hadn't heard of the possibility of a sound investigator but they thought it could be interesting because, in this case, it wasn't about locating the prison but understanding what was happening inside. The prisoners there were blindfolded when they entered and never really left their cell the whole time they were there. So their experience of the place was mostly through the sounds that leaked through their cell walls.

LC One aspect of the Saydnaya project was that you reworked a type of technology that's normally used in architecture to render some kind of sense of the prison's inner buildings.

LAH Yes, that's one thing, but the most exciting thing was working on a level where we developed a language between ourselves. Amnesty had thought that they were hiring an audio expert. But actually, the job was much more specific to the role of the artist because it was really about producing language where there is none. I have the romantic idea that art begins where language ends or at least tries to reconstitute a language that we do not yet speak. And that's exactly what was the case in this project.

Sound is very difficult to speak about in a precise way unless you're technically minded. It just borrows from all kinds of language that have to do with visual sense – it's sharp; it's bright – all strange ways of describing it. Often these descriptions don't get you closer to the information you need. For me, it was very much about developing a language between us. So we were mouthing sounds, producing sound effects, playing sound effects from film. We were trying to understand both the technical things that could emerge, such as how many locks were heard opening and closing, from which you could estimate how many prisoners were inside, to things that pertain to more hallucinatory modes of experiencing sensory deprivation.

We tried to understand what constituted torture to them through the way they sensed things and the way that sounds were exaggerated and distorted. We were trying to make a case for the fact that some of the most lucid ways of understanding that place actually happened at moments of technical or factual inaccuracies. Distortions in memory were somehow more lucid than accurate descriptions because they contained within them the violence that was done to the senses. The withdrawal of the possibility to know is itself a kind of violation that was done to them. So the trace of that not knowing, that negative evidence, was also something to argue for. Maybe we are getting a bit off topic here …

LC No, I don't think we are, because not knowing is something that I'm also trying to bring to the fore in this book. Not knowing is an interesting area to embrace, not least given that academic modes of thought find it challenging to articulate.

LAH Yes, but it's *not knowing* in a postmodern sense. It's about making specific, almost positivist claims around negative understandings about things that are not present: silences, distortions, the inability to testify being itself a form of knowledge. I'm not talking about not knowing in a poststructuralist kind of way. I'm saying that there's something epistemic about the failure to speak to testify, to adequately remember in the ways that the law demands.

LC Your way of working is holding open space for epistemic failure as knowledge.

LAH Exactly. So ear-witness testimony is a really interesting place to do that from because you can have one punch described with a thousand different metaphors. Someone says it's an egg, someone says it's a watermelon; someone says it's a meat grinder. It's very strange things that are brought up. And you can't help but think about the role cinema has played in the construction of sonic imagination. Reading testimonies, it struck me that very often ear witnesses say that a sound didn't sound like itself, "It didn't sound like a punch, but a cinder block hitting the ground," etc. They always negate the event and replace it with an imaginary sound effect of their own devising.

LC You mentioned earlier that their original sonic inventory is very often film-based. So what the ear witnesses mean in fact is that it didn't sound like a punch in a film. So their subjectively experienced punch turns out to have a completely different sound from their received knowledge from media.

LAH Yes, but the description still demands a sound effect. So if it sounds like an egg cracking, it's clear that the event is inseparable from an egg in the person's mind, both visually and sonically. I became fascinated by those forms, by the way in which people encode events to memory and co-evolve cinema into it.

LC It's also interesting that it's not a metaphor. The choice of sound analogy is so random that it points to it being a subjective truth claim. Because if you were concocting such a claim, you would never say it sounded like an egg breaking. It points to the individuality of experience.

LAH Yes, and it also has very little to do with an egg breaking somehow. It sits somewhere in a very strange place between visual and acoustic perception.

LC Is it almost synesthesia at that point?

LAH I don't know, because it also includes memory. It's a recalling at the same time. It certainly bleeds between the senses and that's why in

Earwitness Inventory I wanted to show the objects in their mundaneness. These things look very familiar and are in the context of a display in an exhibition, which looks like bad conceptual art. Through those conditions, they start to transform into something that sits in your mind's eye as a sound, not in the space.

LC So when you see an object – like an egg – that you imagine it creating a sound effect?

LAH Yes, but there's also a text in the space that narrates the objects. It moves alphabetically through the list. Every object I've collected forms part of a witness description or could have been used in an investigation to recover sounds. Some of the objects, like the customized metal door, could be used as an investigative tool, whereas others act only as mnemonic triggers. So it's quite a strange place. You have these sound effects, a laboratory that sits somewhere between cinematic theatrics and forensic re-enactment. That's what I was going for with the feeling of these objects. As I said before, I want to activate the sonic imagination of the visitor, rather than their ears. That has very little to do with the sound they make and more to do with the sound you can make them make.

LC Is that because the imagined sound can be stronger or different than the sound that is heard?

LAH Yes, or it can be surprising and that's what you have in Foley sound effects when things are used for something other than their original purpose. Like videotape being used to sound like a forest floor. What Foley shares very closely with torture is precisely the fact that things are not used for what they are supposed to be used for. One of the main strategies of torture is to de-civilize objects so, for example, a table is used for torture or a chair is used for torture. The idea is that the world unravels; that everything is a weapon. That emerged through trying to understand what torture meant to people and the way it became articulated in these contexts where objects took on this strange role. Where they are neither the thing nor the sound nor the memory but they sort of exist between those things.

LC You mentioned that sight is more accessible than sound; that the visual also provided some accessibility to that sonic imagination.

LAH It can be. All strategies are on the table with regard to my own works. If I feel that something needs to be seen rather than heard, that makes sense. So, for example, in *Conflicted Phenomes* (2012), I worked with convicted asylum seekers from Somalia who had been rejected from the Netherlands based on the fact that they pronounced certain words in a way that suggested they were from the North of Somalia and not from the South. The project was trying to show that speech is the last place you should look for a faithful account of where people are from, for several reasons, and even more so for people who live itinerant lives. In that work, recording their voices and playing it back would reproduce the forms of violence that have been done to them. If they had stayed silent in those interviews, they would also have been deported. So it was about producing very visual and almost silent maps that would work to give them back the right to silence that they had lost. Not having the choice not to speak is, in a way, a weaponization of free speech.

So in that case you can understand why the visual takes precedence. And why it's political for the visual to take precedence even though it's about something phonic, about acoustic substance.

LC It seems like the expectation of an origins-based sound within the accent is already a complete misunderstanding of the conditions of an itinerant life or the conditions of war.

LAH Yes, or the conditions of the voice itself. Right now, I'm speaking to you differently than I might speak to other people. The very act of speaking is to lie. You create yourself every time. You're in dialogue. So what does it mean to sit in front of someone and have to give an account that is faithful to your origins? That's a very Western, Christian, Protestant way of understanding.
The work on Saydnaya is similar in that it didn't exist only as sound, even though the prisoners' main experience was of sound and of hunger. All of these things need to find more adequate ways of being represented. The ways the prisoners experienced architecture wasn't really visualized. They saw their memories in their mind and it's increasingly irrelevant for me to approach sound as sound. It's about trying to activate sound as an imagination that involves images as much as sound.

LC The investigative process also involves the analysis of images of sound, as much as sound itself.

LAH Yes, if I think of a case like *Rubber Coated Steel* (2016), which revolved around the sound of gunshots, I couldn't hear the difference in those sounds until I saw them because it's much easier to pick apart colors than a frequency spectrum.

At least I don't have really good ears. In that case, it was a constant process of picking apart a sound by looking at the crowd reaction and the frequency spectrum. It involved just as much looking as listening and I think that's the case with a lot of forensic cases of sound.

LC Clearly you use technology to make sound visible within your work. Like a lot of artists, you also work with these media long enough that you are able to make them more fluid. For example, in *Saydnaya (ray traces)* (2018) you used "ray tracing," a tool used in architectural design to map potential acoustic leaks in a building for the very different purpose of mapping an unseen prison space three-dimensionally within the gallery. I'm also thinking of *Walled Unwalled* (2018), the single-channel video installation and performance that work in parallel with and speak to the emerging technology of "muons," invisible cosmic particles that are being harvested for their ability to penetrate matter. In some ways that work tries to exceed what is even technologically available to you.

LAH Yes, you've said it basically, and that's been the whole philosophy of Forensic Architecture from the beginning; that designers, artists, and musicians have a very intense relationship to the tools with which they create. They not only produce artifacts but also through doing that, they gain a kind of expertise and insight. Through the intensity of looking at things like color, form, or frequency for other purposes, you might be just as able to use that technology to say something or to analyze the world through it. Again, we are people who are trying not only to use technology but also trying to articulate images or sounds and find their meaning. If you spend long enough doing that, you are in a position to do those things, to give them language, which otherwise may be in a kind of linguistic poverty or have not been adequately addressed in a context like the law, where it really matters.

Oftentimes we leave investigative work to people who are not as interested in images and sounds, or their relation to those things is not as developed as part of a continually observed practice. So it's really about finding ways in which aesthetic practice can function as investigative. So it is about technology, but a lot of the technology I use is not even that specialist and that's the point. It's stuff that anyone can pick up and use and turn back and if you're a musician or a DJ or whatever, you've already accessed this material. You've already looked at sound; maybe done a tempo analysis or any of those things that teach you how to listen to the world and analyze it. It's not only about mobilizing specific technologies, although you have to follow what's out there, but also about you developing language and developing ways of imagination and thought around sound. So, for example, arguing in the Saydnaya case that a whisper is actually evidence, whereas normally under legal conditions they would never accept such a thing.

LC Can we talk about your choice of presenting material within and outside of an artistic context? Maybe we can take the *Rubber Coated Steel* works and their link to a criminal investigation as an example, because your research was brought forward as evidence and had a concrete effect on the case, but it later also became the departure point for a gallery installation and film. With regard to artistic research, I'm interested in the registers of knowledge that artists open up and these new languages being used outside of an artistic context, and at the same time how an artwork can exist in a form that does not exist elsewhere. There are not too many examples of artists who have this double status within their practice, so I'd like to know more about your decision to do that.

LAH Let me just clarify that the work that I've done and the artworks that I have shown are distinct. I don't exhibit my artworks in legal contexts, although there has been one exception. I've also worked on several cases with Forensic Architecture, but I have developed very few of them into artworks. I only work with the ones that, for me, can speak to a more generalized experience or the ones through which you could get a deeper understanding than the case itself demands.

LC I was wondering if you could perhaps reflect on the decision to invest energy in both directions precisely because one situation doesn't transpose into another context. In *Rubber Coated Steel*, for example, you undertook specific research in response to a case about two unarmed Palestinian youths shot by Israeli soldiers, who were said to have been shot using rubber bullets, and you helped to solve that case by proving that live ammunition was used. But you chose to also make an artwork, a film, and an installation related to the case. Can you elaborate on that choice to create a work and present it in an artistic context?

LAH Taking the *Rubber Coated Steel* case, I was immediately asked to do something that, for me, was politically compromising, which was to argue that the Israeli soldiers were not firing rubber bullets but live ammunition. It was assumed that if they were firing rubber bullets it was OK. That's where my problem comes in, because rubber bullets, especially in the Israel-Palestine context, are constantly being shot in people's faces at close range. They do horrible things and in that particular apartheid, it's turning out that maiming is more effective for them than killing. They actually want to humiliate families, creating conditions where people are dependent, rather than increasing the death toll.

LC They want to create lasting visual reminders …

LAH They want to also destroy the idea of the martyr in Palestinian resistance. So the idea of saying that rubber bullets are OK in this context was really a problem for me. I did it anyway because that's what the situation "demanded." In the context of human rights advocacy that's where we're at, the lesser evil. But then something interesting happened because I started to understand that you could use this as the biggest way to argue against rubber bullets, because what they were actually doing is a kind of alibi. They were using the rubber bullets argument as a way to work the international legal system to continue to kill. You can understand the sound of live ammunition sounding as if it is rubber, meaning it's a kind of serial killing sound. It's a new kind of sound that speaks to another kind of violence that includes human rights within it.

The more I worked on that case, the more things happened that made me think about the role of human rights. For example, the families of one of the two teenagers buried the boy immediately. The thinking of human rights was that they were religiously conservative because they did that, because in Islam you should bury on the same day as the death. But it was actually a form of silencing because they wanted to put the body in a mass grave of colonial violence, rather than put it in a morgue for the very people who do those things to pretend as if they care, to pretend that they had done an investigation. Their decision was actually about understanding what happened to their child, not as something individualizing but as part of a collective violence. It was a very powerful statement. But where it gets stronger is that the other boy's father, despite the humiliation, submitted his child's body to be investigated by the people who had just killed him. This meant being accused of collaborating etc., so the fact that he did that, I find equally brave. So there's a strange phenomenon, where the body was being used both as speech and as silence. In the human rights context, there is no way to speak about that. Because it's about urgency, it's about producing knowledge but in a very specific framework where only specific kinds of things mean things. So, for me, the space of the artwork allowed me to understand that apartheid, or to express and reflect on it in ways that I felt had not necessarily been seen before or represented. So it was a moment for me to make a work, a film, containing not only the case but through that story you could understand and unfold all of the complexities of those particular ways of colonial violence and what it means to resist them or to be suppressed by them.

LC So you were articulating and deconstructing the terms of the discourse, with regard to both legal and human rights discourse.

LAH Yes, and to do that I had to write a trial myself because there was never a trial that did any justice to those kids. Even the trial that I wrote doesn't just come out as justice, but it includes the discourse itself, as you say. It offers a way in which you could understand the technologies of listening to people in a trial and what that means and its politics. So, in order to adequately tell the tale, I had to fictionalize a trial, which for me adequately contained those complexities. So that's what the artwork allowed me to do.

LC So, here we come to the need to move into fiction to make an expanded truth claim.

LAH Exactly. And not like my predecessors, who had more of the post-structural way of understanding things where it was about undoing truth. It's not about putting people in a context where they're constantly asking, "Is this true or real?" Actually, it's kind of negating that question as even being meaningful.

LC Yes, in a way they are not even relevant questions. This also reflects the conditions of the world we live in, in which technology infiltrates to an extent that the location of the real is a very questionable thing. You talked about the cinematic imagination and how that affects the sonic imagination. But if we move into the virtual and through digitalization, the virtual imagination also adds layers to that which are beyond the cinematic.

LAH Yes, and I think artists are some of the first to realize that, because I think there was always another mode of truth that was never about accurate representation but, let's say, in the romantic sense that I am attached to, that a painting can be a more adequate image of someone than even being with them. So it's also more specifically about mobilizing the mode of truth production that I think art does, which is different than the truth production that the law or science do. I think I try to articulate art as a methodology of truth production, just like the law and science. But it has its own way of making truths and that's what's at stake often in making artworks and using the discourse.

LC Within the *Walls Unwalled* piece, there are interlinked narratives of forensic evidence. I think one of the ways that contemporary artists produce truths is precisely by collecting various narratives or pieces of information that should not go together, and through the spaces between those things something emerges that otherwise could not be seen. Whereas when you talk about the legal framework, there is also a push to stay within one narrative because it's not rational to work like that.

LAH Exactly, and I think the law always tries to isolate its pieces of evidence. It's either a fingerprint that we can draw a thing around or the emission of powder from a gun, and these things become fragments. There are many cases where an accent is separated from the context of its biography or a gunshot is separated from the space or the communities in which it resounds. This often means that, in its will to separate, you lose the meaning in those leakages. This idea of collecting or in making collectives that you mention is something I'm increasingly interested in. By that I mean, for example, that Pistorius, a mother in South Africa, a prisoner in Syria, and a guy who is growing weed in Oregon all start to produce this strange collective of people who are able to speak from their perspectives but also create a coherent collection of narratives. It's the same with *Earwitness Inventory*. Those are things from all over the world but they join up. I find that a productive way of working, to produce collectives.

LC In your writings on *The Hummingbird Clock* (2016), you also mention the idea of artists making records. You say you turn these tools to the people. In that work, you literally offer the public the means to geotag their experiences the way that governments do, using surveillance. But there's also the creation of records by artists. I can see that by moving toward these collectives, you're actually forming records that are meant to exist as records. Maybe that's without knowing what their future use is also.

LAH Yes, exactly, that's a good observation.

LC Let me ask you one more thing about imagination. You have talked about sound and its relationship to imagination, but I'm also thinking about how that works in the *Walls Unwalled* piece, the idea of these muons descending into the earth's atmosphere and the idea of penetration by something that we cannot see. Like the war on terrorism, it invokes fear of what can't be seen. So this technology and the idea of the penetration of walls seem to be a war in the imagination. You also talk about torture like that, that it's a war that takes place in the imagination somehow.

LAH Yes, definitely. Certainly in torture, it's more about the anticipation than the actual thing.

LC We normally talk about imagination in a way that's so free and creative.

LAH Yes, but it can also be ideological.

Healing as Becoming

A Dialogue with Yo-Yo Lin

Lucy Cotter You have an interdisciplinary practice, working with video, animation, sound, performance, dance workshops, and publication. A lot of your recent work has engaged with embodied knowledge and has specifically sought to move away from the medicalized body to make space for chronic illness and disability as part of a whole experience of the embodied self. I'd love to start by talking about your multisensory performance work *The Walls of My Room Are Curved* (2019), which you describe as "a movement-generated sonic performance of the body living with a connective tissue disorder." It feels like such a turning point in terms of centralizing your own body and embodied knowledge within your practice.

Yo-Yo Lin (林友友) Yes, *The Walls of My Room Are Curved* was a very big leap for me because I wasn't trained as a dancer or a performer, and I was very much working with time-based media and video and animation at the time. All of my work has an element of sound, and I also work together with different kinds of electronic artists, including my friend and collaborator Despina (Mica Matchen), who was my roommate at the time. I came home one day and I thought, "What would happen if we sampled my internal body sounds and turned them into music?" They were just like, "Yes, of course. You can totally do that." At first, we were just experimenting and suddenly we said, "Wait, we can really make music with this, and we can actually make a performance like this."

We experimented with a bunch of different ways of putting microphones on my body and ended up creating a process with contact microphones. We kept playing with different tools until we found the right ones that I could still move around with. It just grew from there. I think the embodied nature of that piece was coming from a place of questioning: How do I activate my body in order to create these sounds from which we can create music? The performance uses several microphones attached to my moving body, capturing the live sounds of creaking and crackling bones and joints as they shift, transfer, extend, and rotate. While I move, Despina samples, processes, and synthesizes the sounds of my body into a musical score in real time.

LC The process of experimentation that led to *The Walls of My Room Are Curved* incorporated sound and free dance movement, but you also looked to other body-based practices.

YL Yes, slowly, as I began moving, I realized that the movement languages that I was gravitating toward were moving with a more internal eye, a more inward-looking sense of space, and so I started working with different dancers and exploring tai chi and other somatic-based practices to access different kinds of movement vocabulary and a structured and improvised performance emerged from that.

Every time I move, different sounds are produced and every time, with different sounds, we create a different soundscape and I move in my response to that soundscape. It was a very in-the-moment kind of piece. I think, initially, the impetus was also reading about the work of Milford Graves, who was a jazz drummer, scientist, and artist.

LC I just saw a retrospective of his incredible multidisciplinary practice at the ICA in Los Angeles this summer. His practice incorporates everything from botany and herbal medicine to cardiac research and sculpture.

YL Yes, I had read about his practice, and a lot of what his work was about was channeling different parts of the human body into material for sonic-based art. I really wanted to think through the material of my illness and how we explore that in a way that doesn't come from a place of looking at what's wrong. Not coming from a place of deficit, but just actually really looking at it as its own kind of aesthetic and its own kind of knowledge and starting point for art.

LC In many ways, your later performance *Channels* builds on this unfolding aesthetic and its resonance with embodied knowledge. It visually resembles *The Walls of My Room Are Curved* in the sense that there is a translucent screened-off space within the larger performance space in which you're dancing as a solo figure inside. There are also sequences of projections onto these fabric screens and ongoing sound-based elements, but it moves through a series of chapters, each one unfolding a different experience. You speak to the audience, and danilo machado describes the sound in the performance live through speech-to-text software.

YL Yes, *Channels* was an extended production version of *The Walls of My Room Are Curved*. It was commissioned by The Shed, which is a massive creative arts venue in New York. I really wanted to expand on the idea of creating music from my body, but also think through a more expanded performance – an act one, act two, act three kind of performance.

The first movement, "Channel 1," investigates the internal pathways within the body, exploring the energetic channels of *qi* moving through the body as conceptualized by Chinese medicine, and the cyclical nature of the body living with chronic illness. "Channel 2" explores external pathways of the body through movement and sound, and the final movement, "Channel 3," invokes ways of being together across distance.

The generative feedback loop of dance creating music and music creating dance blurs the lines between body and musical instrument, organic and synthetic, human and device. During the work, I also ask a series of questions, like "Can pain be a portal? What are the electrical currents that we signal to one another, reminding us that even in continued isolation, we are not alone?"

LC I was struck by the sense of closeness between your body and the technologies you use, which is something I don't feel with my own body. Your very fluid relationship with technology makes you able to perform with it in ways that are very intimate and haunting.

YL The piece itself was very much rooted in this liminal space of body and technology and how they continually speak to each other. How they're always in relation to each other when it comes to my body. At the most simple level, it really is just like, "I rely on technology to stay alive because of my disability, I require lots of technological machines to enable that."

But beyond that, this piece explores the complex relationship chronically ill or disabled folks have with technology. There are a lot of different ways you can move through working with technology and being in relation with it. Technology can be a violent tool, a tool to control others, but with self-agency it can also be used for amplifying oneself, transcending boundaries, and fostering community.

So much of what technology has offered me has been a feeling of, "We can connect from anywhere in the world. We can have these networks that didn't exist before." This piece also exists as an homage to the movements of the disabled community, whose connections are made, and togetherness found, without leaving the walls of one's own room.

LC It struck me that the work is being made from the interior of the body outward, rather than trying to connect from some external point. There is a resonating chamber of self, a dark space, and within that space there are experiences. I had the feeling as a viewer, that I was invited to come into that resonating space. The performance also makes it possible to come to that space communally. We move through different interior realms as we are watching.

YL I think so much of what I was trying to create was a feeling of deep isolation when it comes to being disabled, and so much of what I ended up doing came from the confines of my room, especially during the pandemic. Yes, I don't know. I think there is a lot about being within hospital space, behind a curtain, and there are a lot of recurring spatial experiences that involve being isolated or being behind something – being hidden or not being very straightforwardly seen.

I think that also has a lot to do with it since a lot of my disability experiences have been coming from a very interior space because so much of my illness is not visible. Yes, there's also an element of just inviting people in to experience this, and also knowing that the performance space is not a place that can always be permeated, for safety reasons. There's a need for opaqueness, I guess as well.

LC Is that opaqueness also a form of self-protection within the performance space?

YL Yes. I think there is an element of that too, where the walls are both confining me but also protecting me at the same time, and then, like in the final act, it becomes more like a portal to be in connection with my collaborator, Pelenakeke Brown.

Through the work of graphics artist Torin Blankensmith, Pelenakeke slowly emerges as a projection silhouette, and we dance together through describing our movements using audio description, using description as a way to move together with and through the glitch stream. Pelenakeke also made live drawings on projection screens through an online interface by Avneesh Sarwate. She illuminated the room with her drawings, depicting her home in Aotearoa, New Zealand, and dancing with me through her digital pen strokes, which played with presence and expanded ideas of what dance performance can be.

LC You are responding live to each other, and perhaps this relates to the emotional and social spaces you're invoking, but there is such a strong sense of both presence and absence. You and Pelenakeke seem to connect in the space between them.

YL Totally. That is also literally how we've been connecting over the past few years. She was based in New York when we met, and then the pandemic happened, and she had to go back to New Zealand.

A big element of that part of the performance was bringing her into the space, but also knowing that her presence isn't always going to be guaranteed. It isn't always going to be smooth. It was pretty glitchy, it wasn't a very clear experience, and we were working with live Wi-Fi feeds, so a lot could have gone wrong. Part of the performance for me was like, "Well, if she gets disconnected, then that is the performance."

LC This interdependence and fragility is referred to within the performance narrative. The phrase "Are you still there?" is a repeating refrain that becomes metaphoric and existential. There is also a constant undoing of presence through the ever-changing and always-moving lines that heightens awareness of the experience being fleeting. It's almost ethereal.

YL Yes. Imagery-wise, Pelenakeke and I play a lot with computer shaders and fragmenting her image, and at the end, she becomes a field of stars, and it's quite beautiful.

LC It seems as if her body dissipates into space, as if she has transcended physical limits or broken into another time-space reality. That feeling of transcendence is present in several other moments in the performance, especially when your body is completely immersed in blue light. There is a feeling of channeling energy or other modes of being.

YL I appreciate that thought deeply. I can't fully speak for Keke, but I feel that we tend to approach technology with a sense of ritual embodiment, that our ancestors inform how we interface with these tools. There is always a sense of creating worlds and wonderment through our collaborations together. Though in many ways I feel Act 3 with Pelenakeke was less of a transcendence *from* and more of a radical re-imagining *toward* what is and what could be. What does it truly feel like, look like, sound like to channel one another, to reach for one another across distance?

LC The possibility of extending the limits of the organic physical body is also suggested by the delicate cyborgian attire you are wearing, which you commissioned from the couturier Weijing Xiao. You have talked elsewhere about wishing to reclaim the cyborg figure as a crip figure.

YL Yes, and I want to mention Alison Kafer's brilliant piece on cripping the cyborg in *Feminist, Queer, Crip*. It has been fascinating to reclaim the cyborg as a disabled, crip figure. As someone who was often called a cyborg, it was liberating for me to re-imagine that and reclaim what this figure truly was. In the performance, the cyborg's "final" form was a shimmery, genderless insect-like creature connected to tubes and wires, harnessing both organic and synthetic forms. Weijing Xiao was brilliant in embracing such hybridity, combining materials for my body in a garment that seduced and perplexed audience members at the same time. My favorite material for the garment was Japanese stainless-steel organza, a silk fabric woven from metal threads. It was mind-blowing to touch it and see it in movement, and it encapsulated the soft yet resilient engineering we wanted to create with the crip cyborg figure. The garment was also designed with openings for wires to attach to my skin. We worked closely incorporating that into the design, knowing that the nature of the performance was this delicate and at times fragile connection of wires connected to my skin being pulled back and forth between Despina and me, while also designing the garment to be robust enough for ample movement and sweat.

LC You have been connecting widely with other people whose embodied experiences include illness or disability. In 2020 your *Resilience Journal* was published, which started as a personal tool for yourself to keep track of the nuances of living with a chronic condition, but through workshopping became a collective tool for self-knowledge, resilience, and advocacy. As well as asking questions about lived bodily experience that move away from hard medical data, you created a means to visualize the changing experience through gradations of color that can be filled in on a wheel-like diagram.

YL Yes, I was thinking through how to create language for my illness and document it, archive it in a way that was coming from my own terms, in my own way. I was interested in finding language for it that didn't come from a medicalized space and that charted the fuzzy embodied experiences that are typically overlooked in my life and often shelved away because they were deemed not useful. I began to realize that the journal served more than just a personal tool for me to keep track of the nuances of living with a chronic condition – it became a collective access point for acknowledgment and self-acceptance, giving people a tool to put into words, images, and ritual their complex living experience on their own terms.

It's interesting because I grew up always having this disability, and I was coming into my late twenties when I made this project. I feel like at that age there was a very big reckoning of me asking myself what happened when I was a child and what happened when I was becoming an adult, and what are the ways in which I have learned some destructive ableist ways of thinking about my own body?

LC The *Resilience Journal* asks its users to chart their social experiences as they relate to bodily experience, including social pressures, logistical challenges, and efforts to get care. You mentioned in a previous talk that you're often gaslit about your illness or your disability, that someone else tells you, "No, you'll be fine," or underestimates your needs and makes you feel small. I think about how in Milford Graves's practice, too, there's a political aspect to the work, which is saying "No" to the knowledge I've been given through the system, and "Yes" to what it would look like if I started to create the knowledge myself.

YL The journaling was a way to unlearn that and to really recognize that in my daily life and to see how my body was in relation to the structures around it. I think that was really necessary for me.

I grew up in a very, yes, pretty ableist environment, always pinpointing this experience as something that was a personal issue but, in fact, it was something so much more than that.

The *Resilience Journal* came from a lot of discussion with numerous friends who were also chronically ill and disabled. It came from talking through the fact that it's not just a personal experience, that it's also very much a shared experience, and it's an experience that is threaded into the social structures we live in. We can continue to deny that, or we can actually recognize that for what it is and move forward with the knowledge that we're not alone and that we are all combating a system that was not designed for our bodies.

LC In a text on your website reflecting on the *Resilience Journal*, you refer to the disability scholar Colin Cameron's notion of "the disabling gaze." As you suggest, this gaze is very much related to a colonial mindset, a white supremacist ableist vision of the body that is either the desired body or an othered body that will be rejected. This highlights a continuum across ableism and white supremacism. The process you're describing is an intersectional process, a simultaneous decolonization and "de-ableizing" of your mind, and an invitation to others to do the same.

YL Oh, yes, absolutely. I think they're intertwined. There is a lot of unlearning involved, and there is the need for refusal, continued refusal, of these overbearing perspectives. I don't really know another way for me personally because I wasn't raised in an environment that was very politically or socially active. It was quite insular, so I think this was really an invitation to myself to be like, "Okay, how do I exist within these structures?

Can I give this framework out into the world and allow it to also be something that other people can access for their own self-knowledge?"

LC You situate yourself and your practice in relation to a wider movement of people looking to change the language and thinking around disability, which is also a generational shift away from disability rights toward access and equity. I linked through via your website to a text by artist and activist Patty Berne on disability justice in which they reflect on how the shift to talking about disability justice has mostly been a change of vocabulary, but not a real changing of the process or end goal. As I see it, *Resilience Journal* is about imagining new processes, co-creating the process, and rewriting the script individually and collectively.

You have also actively sought to create different processes around relating dance and illness or disability with the movement workshop series Rotations you co-established with Pelenakeke Brown, which is building a transnational community, and looking to co-create new processes of dance, of understanding the body, and being together, and gathering new knowledge as you're doing it.

YL Yes, totally. Rotations is very much bringing into practice with others what we've been talking about when it comes to creating spaces for us and by us and knowing that there are very limited avenues for disabled dancers to learn from each other and to learn together, and also to learn in general. I think that was the core desire for us.

I was in New York for a while doing all these different dance classes and realizing that there are very few classes that allow people who did not have the quintessential athletic dancer body to thrive in. We were all very frustrated, me and my other disabled dancer friends. During the pandemic, everything shut down and we were very much just desiring a space where we could continue to move and continue to grow and learn from each other.

We thought it would be a good idea to do a collectively facilitated workshop series where in every workshop there was a different leader, who led us through their practice, essentially. What were they exploring in their movement practice, what kinds of warm-ups and exercises do they do? It was just learning by being together and learning by practicing together.

LC Both in the *Resilience Journal* introduction and in the Rotations open call you state: "If you have a relationship to illness or disability, this is for you." In doing so, you acknowledge that "disability" is not in everybody's personal vocabulary, or they haven't culturally been brought up to see themselves in these terms, but that this way of looking might bring a particular kind of agency.

YL For me, so much of disability discourse in the United States and a lot of the disability community building is very white-centric and also rights-based, and so much of what I was encountering within the disability arts realm was very much not that. We were really wanting to offer nuance and to offer space to be able to say, "Hey, if you have a relationship with disability, then you're welcome in this space. You don't have to necessarily identify or be clear about where you are in that identity to be a part of this because so much of disability is very fluid."

People go in and out of disability and this is a space to invite people in. It's not a space to delineate who is what and who is not. I think, for me at least, coming from a family with a non-American, Taiwanese immigrant background, I have the sense that a lot of the language around disability hasn't been exactly welcoming or historically useful for people who aren't white.

LC Is this why you and Pelenakeke specifically state that you are queer artists with an immigrant background doing this work, as well as being artists with a relationship to chronic illness or disability?

YL Yes. I think there is a lot there to unpack about what happens when I say that I'm chronically ill or I'm crip or whatever. I think there's a lot of different language that's still emerging, but the most important thing is to just be like, "Yes, and … ?" There is this identity and there's more, and this is all something we can witness and be in relationship with together.

LC Beyond Rotations, you and Pelenakeke experimented with finding other visual and performative languages through your Zoom-based *Glitchual* performance, which happened during the pandemic. I'm conscious that virtual space has long been a space of gathering for people who are chronically ill or have differently abled bodies to come together and create and perform. Although the pandemic shifted the world at large in the direction of doing that, it feels like that space in the arts has already quite quickly waned, undermining those possibilities for access. I'd love to hear you talk about what technology meant to you on that creative level in community with Pelenakeke and others, which speaks to the importance of maintaining that space.

YL Creatively, technology has always been a part of the work. I sometimes wonder if what I do is considered technology-based or is it just using tools that look technological, and somehow fooling everyone that I know everything about tech. *(laughter)* I think that's also, maybe, just the constant imposter syndrome feeling.

Glitchual was making use of the medium of live streaming performance into a kind of video-based performance in and of itself. For that piece, we actually had a big gathering of people on Zoom for a remote access party. Kevin Gotkin, who is an amazing disabilities activist and artist, had been doing a remote access party series all through the pandemic. We would have these Zooms with hundreds of people, and everyone would be dancing, and Kevin would be DJing or we would invite someone else to DJ. It was always an amazing time, so we started thinking through, what if this was a real club and there would be shows? *Glitchual* was a performance within that space of the nightlife party. I love that piece because it came together so organically.

LC How did you go about making the work together?

YL My collaborator, Pelenakeke, was in New Zealand, I was in New York, and Kevin was DJing in New York. We had been thinking, what if we created a piece that was all about the computer glitch and the rituals that we have within the computer space? Kevin has a dissertation on glitch as a disability aesthetic. He wrote and recorded a kind of lecture performance on the glitch and mixed it with his DJ set, and I started creating all of these different visuals for my home space and recording things with my camera phone. So did Keke, and during the performance we collage them together live.

We both do dance-based work, so the collaging was its own choreography within the screen. I think, for me, as someone who also doesn't always do live body-based performance, it's really interesting to think through how movement can exist outside of the body and within the gestures and within the movement that we have within screens.

LC I am curious about something you said on a video profile for *Now This*, which is that interdisciplinarity is for you a crip space. I wonder if this is connected to that act of gathering.

YL Oh yes, absolutely. It really is, because I think so much of what is so fluid about the disabled experience has been just like working with what you have in the moment. A lot of that changes for me all the time. I think the interdisciplinary nature of everything has been a necessity, a very necessary choice.

LC Looking through each of your works, from the earlier sonic-movement performance works we discussed until now, there's also the question of how to make everything present. How to not close it down, but to make these different languages and bodies of knowledge present in relationship to each other.

YL Yes, totally. Well, yes, so much of the work is about presence. I'm so glad you mention that. I don't know, I always feel as if I'm just gathering things in my life and putting them together. I think collaging is always a part of the practice.

LC This collage aesthetic comes to the fore in your recent video work, *Re:collections*, which you describe as "an experimental memoir." In it, you explore the relationship between the interior journey of your body and the experience of being Taiwanese-American.

The video recounts how your parents always brought you back to Taiwan for medical care and the trauma of those experiences. Weaving in and out of the past and present, it also moves into nuances of overlapping transgenerational experiences of illness, dislocation, and loss.

YL Yes, and in *Re:collections* I was for the first time very much thinking through language and thinking about the language I use to speak about these experiences that often aren't spoken about. So much of my understanding of the body is different when I'm in Taiwan than when I'm in the States. I started realizing more and more that going to see Chinese medicine doctors in Taiwan is often like a complete reconceptualization of what the body is.

Suddenly, I had different body parts than I thought because the way that we treat the body here in Taiwan is different than the body that we have in the US. The idea that the body can be so different in a different place and context, even though it is the same body, was very strange to me. *Re:collections* was a way of recognizing that seeming gap that existed between those two bodies and reconciling it somehow, seeing how I could put them together in one place.

I think a large part of *Re:collections* is just moving through grief, through a lot of hard-to-deal-with memories and emotions that arise when coming back to the place where I did so much medical treatment. It's also about knowing how embedded that experience is within my family, and in Taiwan, where I grew up in many senses of the word–the intensity of going through medical experiences as a child and as a young adult.

Having had some distance from it for twenty years, I think this was the first time I was able to put language to that. In many ways, I think it's like a memoir film. It's a way of understanding my existence since that date. Also, just knowing that it was such a quick project. I made the film in two weeks.

LC Wow, and it's such a layered work.

YL It was very much a process of, let me cut together something that feels right, and let that be the piece without having to massage it too much, because, yes, for me, it was important to understand and encapsulate that moment of coming to terms with all of these ghosts of the past and also the remnants of medical trauma and the trauma of losing language and coming back to language. It's a pretty emotional piece for me. It's also the first film that explicitly deals with my Taiwanese heritage.

LC Part of that heritage is transgenerational knowledge around the body and an experience of navigating across different forms of embodied knowledge. The video explores how your life story interweaves between different sites of knowledge including Buddhism, traditional Chinese medicine, and mainstream Western medicine. The video is broken into chapters revolving around heat, cold, warmth, etc., so the narrative structure already invokes a Chinese medicine orientation toward the body.

YL I think a lot of that film has been an exploration of the sense that this is me so far. I think the ancestral knowledge and all of that is something that I'm continuing to explore and continuing to try to build language for. Learning about the body in Chinese medicine has also been something I've been continuing to do research on.

LC Right now, you are in Taipei for several months and your website bio says that you are "reconnecting with land, body, and ancestors." Can you say something about what you are learning or unlearning through that process? What are you thinking about in your current practice, and do you have even a vague sense of what that reconnection might mean for your future practice?

YL I am in Taipei for now, tending to my health and reconnecting to my family and motherland. I'm reconciling with a lot at the moment, figuring out how to maintain an artistic practice that is rooted in prioritizing my health and well-being while also reimagining my community to be one that is global and not so New York-centric. I'm learning more about Chinese medicine, and the way Chinese medicine is integrated into the Western medical system in Taiwan and the US, and how quality of care is enacted in the healthcare system in Taipei. It's a different world here, and I'm dreaming of ways the US healthcare system can change for the better. I'm unlearning "urgency"–I'm realizing that is a term that is often used by nonprofit art organizations and I don't have a need for that type of rhetoric in my artistic practice. I'm constantly reminding myself that my body is unique and moves at its own pace because so much tells me otherwise. I'm setting myself up for longevity. I'm centering soft unfoldings, quiet awakenings, gentle blooms.

History as a Question

A Dialogue with Natasha Ginwala

Lucy Cotter Artists have always researched. In that sense, the demarcation of artistic research articulates something in existence, rather than being something new as such. Yet when I am working with emerging artists and art students, I feel that there is a distinct generational shift concerning how artists use and regard research within their practice. Do you see some kind of shift in the young artists' practices that has to do with artistic research?

Natasha Ginwala Yes, I do believe in this generational voice, which is one that is aware of the way that research can become a working surface. I see a more conscious approach toward dealing with historical material in particular. I think this has a lot to do with how pedagogy has changed. There are far more interdisciplinary thinkers and teachers entering art schools and courses, who provide an environment for this generational voice to appear. What is being read now in critical theory has also so much to do with a kind of art and science collision, with social scientists updating their ideas and using visual vocabulary to mobilize their ideas. There is a whole range of events taking place in the intellectual sphere, which are very conscious of critical theory and very close to it; that proximity has increased radically in the past ten to fifteen years. This shift is visible in the work of the artists who are now gaining some form of recognition. Of course, the making of art continues to involve material research – what kind of paper you are going to use, which frame, etc. – which is of equal importance to going to an ethnological museum and going through archives. I wouldn't separate those activities; I would call them all research.

I was just talking to someone at a conference, who was suspicious of artists using archives; he commented that there is a lot of nostalgia. Yes, some artists are superficial in their approach to archives, but what I am talking about is not a simplistic take on research. It is not just picking and choosing from an archive and making some kind of collage. The generation I work with is constantly deconstructing knowledge. It is in their makeup to use archives the way one would conceive a drawing. This is how they conceive their ideas, through other subject fields. It is not separate.

LC Yes, that's an important distinction. It's less about making an artwork and then researching something within the work, it's more often now about moving within other subject fields and the work partly emerging from that encounter. I am interested in how *Landings*, your curatorial collaboration with Vivian Ziherl, makes space for that shift and works with it.[1] I remember being struck by your openness to show art in a state of fragmentation or flux in *Sensing Grounds: Mangroves, Unauthentic Belonging and Extra-territoriality* (2013) at Witte de With Center for Contemporary Art in Rotterdam, for example, which was one of the first presentations of this multi-part project. This, again, I feel was a generational shift. Young artists do not use a "research aesthetic" in the explicit way that previous generations have done, but they may include more source material in their work or show something in a more raw state, which may shift again into another state in a subsequent artwork.

NG I think that's a very important point. If you are an independent curatorial project like *Landings*, your infrastructure is not a site but mental connections and relationships with others. It's much more committed to the questions artists come along with. It is committed to the question of how to find a form for an artistic project, which is an ongoing process. How are artists able to find forms that are not going to blow the display budget but focus on the microscopic reading of what they are primarily interested in? There is a live-ness in bringing in this vocabulary, in using film, in bringing together performance and source material. All of the *Landings* displays are focused on making that live quality happen so that it's not a kind of academic research that needs to be in a PhD format. It's not about turning the artist into a PhD researcher. But the fact is that the *Landings* projects have constantly brought academics together with artists and this has brought about conversations

1 From 2013–15, Ginwala and Ziherl led the multi-part curatorial project *Landings* presented at Witte de With Center for Contemporary Art, David Roberts Art Foundation, Neue Gesellschaft für Bildende Kunst (as part of the Tagore, Pedagogy and Contemporary Visual Cultures Network), Stedelijk Museum Amsterdam, and other partner organizations.

that have in turn become source material for their next work, or for new kinds of collaborations.

LC I have been trying to identify for myself what the nature of the shift is from the discursive turn in art to the kind of talks that *Landings* makes happen through events like the *Confrontation and Confession* symposium (2014). One of the things I am left thinking about is the phenomenon of the talk itself *as* research. There is a centralization of the question in a very open way. Through this live quality, it becomes research in progress in the presence of a public that is encouraged to participate. It is less of a spectacular model, it has a more collaborative drive. I also find it interesting that you refer to *Landings* as "a visual culture artistic project" and an "archival research" that incorporates these things. You centralize research and a broader cultural approach – "art and." Can you say something about that choice of framing?

NG We found ourselves needing this kind of condition to bring in our own histories, more social and political histories, dealing with having a certain colonial backdrop, having had a certain kind of relationship to territory, having had a form of visual aesthetics that considers the city and the village. Vivian and I felt that there was so much content coming from our own backgrounds that suddenly felt urgent. We started seeing that artists are also breaking these research boundaries. But *Landings*, as you say, is bringing visual culture and archival research; it has a cloud of subjects that it deals with. It isn't going to pick and choose. We are dealing with the colonial model, with land, with earth, we are dealing with earth history from the geological to the ethnological, all things which bring about this approach in any kind of event format. There is a sort of horizon from which the talks come, which has to make an arc somehow. This all has to do with our commitment to certain subjects. It is dictated by what, for us, is part of curatorial research. You need to have a frame, a horizon of conversations, with which you make new records as you go along but you don't lose sight of this frame.

I would position *Landings* more in terms of the question of what it means to come from the South, for both of us to come with all of our curatorial research and transform that Southern position. There have been conversations like *The Anthropocene Project*, a two-year project at the House for World Cultures, which go toward addressing that, as well as the idea that there is a geological age, which will now be called the age of man, the age of humans, which is so much more the age of the white man in the way in which it is being formatted. Vivian and I were conscious that within science there are certain changes going to be urgently discussed. *Landings* is also partly in response to that, to go back to the politics of what made the human impact on the earth, of this density and directionality. What happens when you have another hemispherical position from which to address these very issues? What happens when you do that in the domain of art? That was partly the beginning of *Landings*.

LC It's interesting to hear that you and Vivian took your own biographies as an entry point because you have an organic selection of critical territory, which doesn't leave you. You are originally from India and Vivian is from Australia, so it's also a question of negotiating across those positions. It's South, but the South is a big place!

NG Exactly, the South is no longer necessarily located in the South, so it's a bit of a paradox.

LC In your solo curatorial practice, you often engage with history. Can we talk perhaps about *Double Lives*, the exhibition you curated at the Ethnological Museum in Dahlem as part of the artistic team of the Berlin Biennale in 2014? Rather than showing artworks, you presented glimpses into the research worlds of nineteenth-century individuals like Emma Hart Willard, the women's rights activist and radical pedagogue, and Emin Pasha, an Ottoman-German physician and naturalist. Can we discuss the role of biography there and its relationship to research, and in particular the frontier between reality and fiction it sets up?

NG Yes, *Double Lives* basically foregrounded biography, but it didn't foreground the individual. I think this is an important distinction to make because historical research can go in different directions when it deals with certain subjects. If you take a human subject as the protagonist, then you can deal with them as *the* individual, using the terms of a Western enlightenment ideology, or you can deal with their biographies in a way that crosses the lines of reality and fiction, which is what happened in the exhibition. I was interested in using the real to destabilize certain kinds of constructs of that person. I find it much more useful not to conceive abstract stories because that is not fiction in the real sense, but to *look* at a photograph from the 1800s and actually *feel* that there is fiction being crafted in the grammar of this image. That's something very different. That is why the exhibition was also not simply engaging the biography and the archive as fixed entities, but also the history of image making.

LC Can we discuss the role of the stereoscopic, which in the exhibition was one of the most prominent expressions of this interest in the history of image making?

NG I started to think of the stereoscope and stereoscopic images as a form of thought apparatus to really approach what *Double Lives* was meant to stand for. Because the more I decided to go into the gray areas, points of the journeys that these individuals undertook, I felt there was a multi-located self that adopted differential purposes and "presences" on these world-charting endeavors. I started to conceive ways to present that, but I was not sure what mode I was looking from to address this asynchronous mode in which they lived. How to address the asynchronicities in the way they proceeded. These asynchronicities could include turning from being a linguist to an anthropologist and then suffering depression. I prefer to say asynchronicities rather than "the amateur"–what it means to live your life in that way, rather than saying, "I am just an amateur and will stay that way in all manner of actions."

So I felt that the invention of the stereoscope, a device that moved in parallel with the daguerreotype and therefore became a system of making mechanical images, needed to be treated in an epistemic way. How do you treat that device? You can look at it as an unwieldy object and then say, so what? I wanted to treat it as an apparatus and then look at how the whole field of visuality shifted drastically when you had this device to look through. If you view an entire life from the same period through this device, then these civilizations make sense. Because those characters and their actions were moving together in this project of world-making and making sense of this world, I think it somehow spoke to very different kinds of audiences. It wasn't just a case of, "Alright, now I'm in this room where they are presenting some kind of self-conceived archive." It was a form of storytelling, a form of intersecting the image with narrative; it worked on levels that I think those factors really added to.

LC Art is obviously not a purely visual thing but when it comes to research methodologies, both the sophistication of artists' visual engagement, as well as their material engagement, give something which should not be taken for granted. In a way, by following visuality in this technology of seeing, you also engaged with all of the material from a position of being aware of the act of looking as you looked. Not just as an intellectual construct, as critical revisionism or another theoretical position but actually as a mode of seeing – I would even say an artistic mode of seeing – image, text, and material. By weaving along those lines, you make very different selections in terms of what is interesting than someone who is choosing from a non-visual or non-material mode. It is different from someone who approaches the image looking for "content," rather than seeing the actual image or the drawing as a carrier that works inseparably from its aesthetic means and not only as a conveyor of information. I felt that, by taking a position that I see as being close to an artistic way of working, you gave a sense of new epistemological possibilities. I would like to consider this in terms of the potential for how the methodological approaches of artistic research could operate in other fields.

NG Maybe your book will help me to position myself. I am not dogmatic about these divisions between artist and curator, yet at the same time, I am quite clear about my previous training which involved journalism, political science, and only later art history from a broader visual culture perspective, as it included studies in film and theater as well. I just feel that these forms of exhibition making, and *Landings* as a project, are somehow trying to renegotiate what curating can pursue as a more complex exercise in knowledge production and cultural processes. Art students and sometimes art historians come to me and say that this is some kind of artistic act, which is something that I prefer to refuse unless it is turned into an engaging conversation. If someone says my work can have the sensibility of an artist, then I understand, but I do make a distinction. The immanent condition a lot of us are working from is the question of what curating can be. We respect the professionalism and the divisions at play.

LC Can we talk more about the historical? I recall that on reading an article you and Vivian published in *e-flux*, "The Negative Floats: Questions of Earth Inheritance," I was struck by its historicism; its gesture of forefronting the historical, which doesn't happen so often within the contemporary art field.[2] You did that at the Ethnological Museum but it's different to see this level of historicism in a contemporary art journal like *e-flux*. There is a fairly rigorous division between contemporary art curators and art historians, even if they curate. I feel like you are opening up an interesting position, which is very much engaged with and driven by questions coming from the historic, yet as a contemporary art curator. You are not afraid of bringing very rigorous academic historical research into the field of art discourse and into the field of contemporary art curating. Maybe this is partly in response to the somewhat faddish approach to curating

2 Natasha Ginwala and Vivian Ziherl, "The Negative Floats: Questions of Earth Inheritance," *e-flux Journal #58*, October 2014.

following the curatorial turn of the early 2000s? Of course, someone could critique your approach as just another fashion, something cutting edge that will pass quickly, but I see it as something sustainable because it is not afraid to take that weight with it, even though you are searching for a kind of lightness of touch in your curatorial approach.

NG I was thinking about this question too when I read the other texts in the same edition of *e-flux* and shortly afterwards when we were in the House of World Cultures for *The Anthropocene Project: A Report*, the conclusion of the two-year project I mentioned. We were sitting with scientists, archaeologists, artists, and anthropologists for three days and the kind of discussions that were taking place raised the question for me of what this methodology of dealing with the historical can mean as an ongoing language. Because even in the structures of what we do and how we present talks and writing, in the conclusion or in the grain of what is being addressed through all of our references, there is always a will to address something, like here, for example, using the history of the earth in terms of the fossil and the mountain as a way to address the extractive industry. How do you address this very important activity? Mining is as old as when Pliny wrote about it, but it is rapidly changing the ground on which we live to an extent that is accelerationist; not in the sense derived from the flows of cognitive capital but in a visceral sense, for the corpus of the earth itself.

We have also chosen not to confront certain philosophical developments in the sphere of new materialism, coding the object's agency without a political premise. Such strategies in thinking can easily become fetishized by the art world without real value to the larger cultural community *per se*. In terms of research or aligning ourselves with certain kinds of new philosophy, we feel safer and more excited to go back to a form such as the fossil in the mountain and the surrounding discourse of natural philosophy linked with present-day debates in geology. Instead of becoming a follower of certain newer philosophical approaches, I have chosen to make an alliance with ancient ideas of Western polymaths, as well as non-Western understandings of time, earth, and cosmos. These provide us with a more digressive passage of "origins" to decode the climate of Modernism. The question for us as curators is, how can we bring those into the present, into the urgencies of the present? When arriving at the exercise of writing or curating, artists' practices become starting points for these broader inquiries or, at other times, they form a visual or aural culmination of a certain thought procedure.

LC A lot of the historic material you've engaged with comes from the nineteenth century in particular. From what you are saying, it sounds like there's also a search for the repositioning of the artist after or through modernity.

NG Exactly. This particular point of revisiting the nineteenth century is something that a lot of artists and thinkers are adopting at this point. The nineteenth century is being excavated as the long nineteenth century, somehow; this enduring mode of life and knowing the world and knowing the self, through empirical findings, through the phases of industrial development. I think we still haven't resolved the question of how to deal with the modern, also in relation to the question of the failure of the nation-state. It has to go back to the nineteenth century because, at that point, knowledge was still attached to empire and nation-state as an unsteady dynamic; it wasn't yet a resolved condition. It was only in the mid-twentieth century that several non-Western nations became liberated, which is why the nineteenth century is a space from which we are still learning.

LC Thinking about the seven nineteenth-century individuals whose personal research worlds you engaged with in the *Double Lives* show, isn't this also a question of the possibility of the non-specialized individual? The rigor of specialization was only emerging then and somehow we are dealing with the non-institutionalized individual because of it being an entrepreneurial age where the kind of individuals you engage with do self-driven research projects from a secure but very much self-funded individual basis, with very diverse outcomes. This is a very different imperative than the notion of applied research or doing research from an institutional base in the twentieth century.

NG Yes, that is exactly why I didn't shift my focus from the nineteenth century in the exhibition. Those practices of knowledge and the application of knowledge were possible in a way that we are not in the circumstances to do, or that we are re-adapting to. That's why I'm so fascinated by it. Of course, I was on the one hand just positioning this as a general condition of the nineteenth century, where there has been industrialization in its first phase, where territories have been discovered but the potential of that discovery is not yet known. It was through these individuals that the potential of those territorial discoveries became visible. That visibility is addressed very richly as we can see now in all of the material that I present in the exhibition. So yes, it's linked to the general condition of the time and how, in some bizarre way, we are now coming back to that mode of life.

LC You mentioned earlier that you weren't looking for the big curatorial moment, but that you are trying to make these small statements that are mostly about questions and that stay questions. I again see it as a kind of artistic strategy to allow knowledge to remain in an emerging state of what I would call non-knowledge; it isn't allowed to get to the point where it crystallizes and becomes a statement. Some of the individuals you looked at in *Double Lives*, for example, had not traveled but were engaging with subjects as if they had traveled, so we get into imaginary geographies and so on. Of course, we have already seen a critical turn in discourse that comes through revisionism and postcolonial discourse but what I find interesting, and maybe this is the lightness also, is the taking of this path of knowledge that never sits comfortably in terms of fact or fiction. There isn't space for dogmatism; there isn't space for knowing. This age we are in is clearly not an age of confidence, so we have to stay close to that kind of fragmentation and that modesty about not knowing. I feel that the work you are doing is very critical but not in the old-fashioned sense; it's something else, it's more exploratory. It's not outlining what is wrong or right; it's saying that this is where things are at, it's all unstable, but I'm trying to negotiate something. Maybe this says something about the current generation too. It doesn't have the luxury of declaring critique, not out of fear but as an open acknowledgment of a lack of knowledge.

NG I feel that there is currently a reluctance to be declarative within the arts as well as scientific communities, which may or may not be a generational voice. That reluctance comes from a sense of consciousness of what is common. It's becoming clear that if you declare something in a finished sense, you remove it from a common purpose, from being something that can be looked at in common. I really think that it is a rather neo-liberal position to declare an authentic closed space of operations and to thereby claim a certain ground or term as authentically yours, as something that is finished and held beyond sociality. I really appreciate it when, on the one hand, I meet peers and on the other hand, very established scientists or ethnographers who have established the same thesis through their experience, which is that they are not going to declare. It is too painful to declare; it is redundant. That's not the way in which they want to formulate their knowledge.

LC I started out having an artistic practice and at a certain point I turned to other modes of working; for example, I did a PhD in cultural analysis. One of the reasons I started to engage with the academic world is that I felt that within artistic practice it was difficult to declare your contribution to a wider area, even to declare your sources. Despite the existence of collectives, there was always an emphasis on authorship in a different way than within academic thought, where, for example, ethnographers are very conscious of being part of ongoing research, of a discussion that maybe runs for a couple of hundred years. I see a different modesty of position possible now for the curator or the artist who steps back, but by doing so joins into this greater whole. It's one of the things that excites me about artists being more open to direct dialogue with experts from other fields, this sense of aligning practices to have this common ground. To take on the riches of somebody else's practice and be able to work with that, away from the authorial stance of "I am influenced by" or "That was my source." What is happening now is not declaring itself self-consciously as interdisciplinary or transdisciplinary; it's a more spontaneous case of "Hey we're interested in this and so are a lot of other people from other fields, so we naturally intersect at this point." This for me is a more "natural" inception of how artistic research invites this greater dialogue. It's not that I want to identify this as *the* big thing that's happening. It's more that there are small shifts, shifts in the individual practices of academics, shifts in artists' heads, and in artists' ways of working. I think artists are moving toward a different way of operating.

NG Yes, I think that at every level of institution-making, there is a shift of awareness in terms of what we claim as our reference points or our example; this collective reference point is not Conceptual Art in America anymore. The whole trajectory of institutional programming and teaching needs to be included in the understanding of what is taking place, in terms of research approaches constantly being updated and expanding horizontally. It is as though there's a new sociality being built into these processes, a sociality that is mobilized through a shared perspective, through friendship, through thinking collaboratively. With a lot of projects, like *Double Lives* or *Museum of Rhythm* or *Landings*, it's so much about this sociality, what it means not to be content with this very stable level of art historical strata. It's a model of immersive, asymmetrical thinking, of conjoining artistic practices with documentary evidence that is located in the history of science, anthropology, and allied fields. It's not artists alone in their studios and curators alone in their offices, but being with authors and writers and anthropologists in a more horizontal way. This non-knowledge you mention is inherent to this approach; what you're looking at now and where you're looking is being shaped together. The spaces of work are also shifting as cultural discourse and curating-as-research practices become more process oriented and stage themselves in diverse settings, with changing temporalities in their publicness.

LC I have noticed you tweeting interesting material and I think that the use of social media is an important part of that horizontal movement.

NG Yes, that's why I refer to sociality; there is no division in that sense. What you share is also this reading of what is relevant as news. That's why, for me, it's also about this journalistic mode of reading in an asymmetrical way. How do you read the same material that is circulating in mainstream media? How do you co-opt it and read against it? The way you share it and the networks you share it in also change what the news is. So I think all of those things are moving together in some way.

Fact as Fiction

A Dialogue with Rabih Mroué

Lucy Cotter Your artistic practice engages with existing political situations, as well as fictitious events and personae and concepts from different fields of practice outside of art. I'm curious as to the role of research in making your work and how you come to bring such an eclectic mix of ideas from different fields into play with each other.

Rabih Mroué Research is very important to me in the production of my work, as is the case for most artists. I don't have a particular research methodology or a method for how to start a new work. I may start from an image of a form in my mind without any context, and this leads me to find what I want to talk about. Sometimes a work comes from an idea or a sentence. I also read extensively and seek out videos or other works that deal with the topic that I'm engaging with. While I am in this process, I'm not afraid to depart from my original train of thought completely. If I am working on a new piece about probability and someone recommends a book to me, I will look it up. However, if I find a sentence on the second page that intrigues me, I will stop reading to engage more fully with the meaning of that sentence. This may in turn take me to another book, where I come across a further idea of interest and go in another direction with my thoughts. I am quite open to letting go of my initial idea and following an entirely new train of thought that opens up in the process of working.

Sometimes I try to combine these divergent sources. I'm interested in how to put together different kinds of material where there is no apparent connection between them. I aim to construct some kind of narrative or question or the work itself by bringing them together, even when it doesn't appear possible. In *Probable Title: Zero Probability II* (2013), for example, I brought together dental records, architectural plans of BO18 nightclub, and a mathematical graph that my father made in asking the question of how to find the identity of a missing person in a mass grave.

LC Do you think this possibility of following up on multiple lines of inquiry that don't appear to have any relation to each other is something specific to art practice?

RM Many thinkers address this idea of putting things together and trying to find a connection between them. Walter Benjamin's idea of how the past comes in flashes comes to mind, for example. How is it possible to put those flashes together and to think about history in a non-linear way? It may be pretentious to aim to shake the official history, or even to talk about the official history and to try to enter into it with another narrative. The result will clearly be nothing like the official history, which is so established and holds so much weight. We should not be so optimistic and say art can change things. I don't think so. But it does bring ideas and questions for people.

LC I want to think a bit more about how art does this. I remember an interview you once did with Maria Hlavajova, in which you said at a certain point, "I take *not knowing* as the departure point for all my work."[1] I wonder if art partly raises questions and ideas through its insistence on *not* knowing. What does it mean for you to take this as a starting point?

RM Art is where I can put my doubts and uncertainties; it's where I can raise questions. My process of doubting doesn't have a clear destination as such. Being honest with the process of having questions inevitably means not having answers. I try to continuously challenge myself, to question what I am doing and what form it should take. The key question, for me, is how one can start from something that one doesn't know about. When I make a work, it should bring me some knowledge, explore something new, enter into the unknown. I take myself as a departure point because I cannot put myself in the place of an audience and assume to know what the unknown is or what something new might be for the audience or spectator. I try not to take up any kind of position of statement-making or invite the audience to follow or take up my advice.

LC How do you see this in relation to coming from the position of trying to make knowledge based on having

1 Cosmin Costinas, Maria Hlavajova, and Jill Winder, eds. *Rabih Mroué: A BAK Critical Reader Series in Artists' Practice* (Utrecht: BAK basis voor actuele kunst, 2012).

a particular proposition or already knowing something? I am thinking here about how, in academic discourses, one often works with an existing body of knowledge, even if one is trying to undermine it or extend it. How do you see the relationship between those approaches?

RM Art is a kind of reflection, which extends to philosophy and to various intellectual fields. I read theory and philosophy and am influenced a lot by the ideas and propositions I come across. But when I make a work, I try to play with these ideas, even if I am not on the same level as the philosopher in question. I try to push myself into uncomfortable territory and propose ideas that may look playful, banal, or naive but potentially shake up the whole field. To offer an example, if you ask a very simple question, like whether every kind of art is political in some sense, this raises questions like how much politics we should put in art and still be able to say that this is an artwork. This rather naive question forces us to ask a series of fundamental questions, such as: What is the difference between politics and political? How do we do theater? What is theater? etc. By asking such simple questions, we enter into a realm of complex matters that push us to rethink our norms, our stereotypes, and beliefs but the questions themselves remain rather difficult to answer.

I can also think about this in terms of the definition of a line. As is known from geometry, any line is made up of an infinite number of points that are placed next to each other. This means that between every two points, there is a cut. So, for me, what makes these points look like a line is our movement. I came to this idea while I was thinking about the duality of stillness and movement in dance and how one can create choreography for a still dance with continuous movement at the same time by using this idea of the line that is made of points and cuts.

LC When you and Hito Steyerl did your collaborative performance *Probable Title: Zero Probability II* (2013) at the Stedelijk Museum in Amsterdam, you engaged with the question of whether it was possible to calculate a space where it is possible to be one hundred percent alive and one hundred percent dead. What do you imagine it would be like to repeat this performance at the mathematics department of a university? I'm wondering about this because the emerging field of artistic research makes it increasingly possible for artists to work directly in the university context. What do you think mathematicians would make of your use of mathematical theories of probability in this work?

RM I imagine that the scientific aspects of our research would be of little interest to mathematicians, given our rather basic level of engagement with mathematical problems as such. However, coming from another field of inquiry and posing particular questions to mathematics can intrigue something in mathematicians' minds. They may potentially develop an idea in response, or this engagement may trigger new lines of thinking. Let me take the example of my own father, who is a mathematician. In the performance at the Stedelijk, I talked about giving him the case of going from A to B, passing through a checkpoint, and covering all the possible outcomes that exist, which included death, safe arrival, etc. I asked him to calculate the probability of getting from point A to point B, but he failed to do so. Despite using the correct method, his final sum did not add up to the desired hundred percent. This forced him to consider why, but he couldn't find a logical explanation for this shortfall. This led to my proposition that perhaps we have to find the answer in our daily lives and not in mathematics. I don't know what he has done with this within his own work, but he was interested in this as an approach.

LC Can you say more about this in terms of the agency of not knowing? I am interested in what it means for an artist to claim that space, using the relative authority of their artistic position and making something happen that might not happen otherwise.

RM Well, mathematics is a predominantly abstract field of thinking. When mathematicians propose an equation or offer a case to be solved, it is always based on the ideal circumstances for calculation; it's a world that does not exist because you have to be fair with everything. However, there are, as Hito and I mention in the performance, the kind of impossible events referred to in the theory of probability that happen constantly in life.

The performance gave us a chance to revisit this relationship between how, in mathematics, we should exclude these impossible events to come out with an equation for understanding the world and at the same time acknowledge that there is something parallel to that, namely our daily life. We cannot apply these equations to our daily lives, so there are two conflicting needs confronting each other. What we have done in this performance is not so much to criticize mathematics for its inability to calculate the existence of missing people during the civil war in Lebanon but rather to find a new logic for how to think. We force ourselves to think about a different logic coming from another direction and try to open up a relationship between two modes of thinking. How can we put them together? How can we talk about impossible events in a mathematical way or in a scientific way?

LC Can we think a bit more about the kind of political space that opens up through artistic research? You've come from a theater background and from an interesting line of family members who were politically and intellectually engaged. One of your works, *Grandfather, Father and Son* (2010), presents some of the different thinking spaces that have been forged across the generations in your family at key historical moments in Lebanon, for example. Another performance, *Riding on a Cloud* (2014), is based on your brother's experiences in the aftermath of the Lebanese Civil War. Working within artistic discourse seems to open up possibilities for engaging with the autobiographical as well as with the philosophical in approaching political subjects. What do you see as being possible within and through this space?

RM Let me first distinguish between the artist's life on a daily basis and the artwork that an artist is making. One isn't an artist all the time in the sense of making art all the time. The relationship between activists and activism or between art and artists is an ongoing question for me, for example. An artist can, of course, also be an activist, yet when this artist produces work, the role of activism becomes problematic. For me, art raises questions, creates doubts and new ideas and these are necessarily unfinished ideas. They are still in progress, still in process. Crucially, they require the other–whoever that other might be–to to share, debate, and develop these ideas. In this sense, any activist role for the artwork breaks with the basic concept of art itself and becomes rather a kind of tool to serve a particular purpose. For me, art always means betraying one's self, going against one's own beliefs. It is the place where one can ask "what if?" This is a theater tool *par excellence*, which classical theorists like Stanislavsky proposed for actors to always ask. This magic "if" puts you in a different situation because you ask yourself "What if I am …?"

LC You make an important differentiation between the person and the artist and notably between the politically-engaged artist and the activist. They interact at moments but they're not necessarily the same and can be mutually exclusive. However, I'm still interested in the possibility that within artistic research you can bring in the autobiographical or you can bring in the position of the self. It's something that's very difficult to do within academic discourse, for example. It happens to a certain extent through feminist and post-feminist academic writing and the notion of positioning oneself at the departure point of an argument, but I'm wondering what you think the autobiographical can do. What does it do to the possibility of creating knowledge or creating doubts? How does the possibility of bringing in the self change the content or the outcomes of the subject areas that you're dealing with?

RM Just to clarify, this is not a rule of thumb that I follow, just a strategy for addressing questions to myself. It opens things up and avoids directly provoking others. At the same time, it's not a confessional thing. The autobiographic is good material to play with or to use as an example of some ideas. Sometimes I invent a biography or an autobiography to insert myself in a situation, based on this notion of "what if?" This hypothetical question can lead me to insert myself in a case or situation and invent a kind of autobiography. My intention here is not to cheat or fool the audience. I always try to reveal my tools or mechanisms so that it's not hidden, a Brechtian approach. The work is not about whether it's truth or fiction but beyond this. It's about what this material brings as a question.

LC You started out in the world of theater. Making the transition to working in the field of visual art seems to have made other things possible through engaging with the specificity of certain media, like video. Can you say something about the possibilities specific to particular media available to an artist and what they mean for representation? In the work with Hito at the Stedelijk Museum that we mentioned, there seemed to be a political layer underlying the comments that concerned the medium of video specifically. I'm curious to hear more about what you were trying to make happen through that; through the use of that medium in relation to the subject areas that you covered in the performance.

RM Yes, I always have to insist that I come from the history of theater, not from the history of art and visual art. I find it beneficial to work in other media where I feel insecure and cannot even pretend to be in control of the tools and the skills as I can in theater, or I think I can. This forces me to push the work further, to think deeper, to carry out more research, etc. However, it's always a question of representation at the end, how one represents something on stage. I refer to theater because it is so clearly about how to represent. The issue is not to run away from representation but to go beyond it. I'm interested in words, in the written word, in reading, and going much further with, for example, the idea of the absence of the speaker and the role of words in representation.

To be honest, it started with a very simple question: How can an actor stand on stage and represent the war through his body? How can we represent war in art? It's a simple question, but it's difficult to find a convincing answer. It is, however, not impossible to find an answer and this led me to start to work with the representation of the absent body. I found different ways to deal with the absence of the actor, using words, through language, images, media, videos, etc. I found that the more I created representations of representation, the more distance I could create for people to think and to feel comfortable with the material. In other words, to give them time before they come to any conclusions about what they are watching.

LC It seemed to me that by dealing with representation through the medium of video in that lecture-performance with Hito, you were able to say more about the subject of missing people and open up a playful relationship between the seen and the unseen within the political. You address what gets lost within the cuts in video edits and you eventually disappear into that space yourselves at the close of the performance. I'm wondering about the wider repercussions of this; what art can do for the non-represented or the non-representable through media like video. You work with this in different ways, of course, with works like *The Pixelated Revolution* (2012), where you're using video in a whole other way.

RM In fact, the work that I did with Hito at the Stedelijk Museum was not the first time that I proposed this particular form. I've also done this with my partner Lina Saneh in *33 Rpm and a Few Seconds*, which is a proposition for doing a theater piece without actors on stage. As for the performance with Hito, we usually presented this performance as a straightforward presentation by being physically on stage. Hito was presented as Hito and I was there as Rabih, with no characters to play and no hidden layers in our theatrical representation. But the work in Amsterdam went much further with representation in that both of us were not on stage. We were represented by projected video images of ourselves, so there was another layer to think about, to shake the representation.

Whatever we use as a means of representation–actors, characters, ourselves, as performers on stage, or as images, videos, etc., what is important is to keep the discourse and the ideas open to interpretation. We try to keep open space for critique, for others to have an input and push the ideas further, which is essential for me when I make my work. When I first started to show *The Pixelated Revolution*, I often had impromptu talks with the audience after the performance. Members of the audience pushed the ideas further or triggered something in my mind that pushed my ideas further. I think this phenomenon of discussion is very important, even if it is not between the artist and the audience. It can also be between two individuals from the audience or a group from the audience. It can be between others and not include the artist herself or himself.

LC You seem to be interested in the artist taking a non-hierarchical position in creating a discourse, but we could also think about the public position you inhabit as a well-established artist. What did it mean, for example, in *The Pixelated Revolution* to take videos of these men as they were being shot in Homs in Syria and to bring it into a certain space, where you have attention from an international public and the media? Can we look at the position of the artist and what you do or what you can make happen through that, as opposed to thinking of the artist as having a non-hierarchical relationship with an audience?

RM Well, to start with the issue of the international and local, I had never thought about where I was going to present this work. I felt that I had to make this work, and I was making it while in Beirut. I started the process of making the work by writing an article for a Lebanese cultural quarterly called *Kalamon*. Maybe we can talk later about this issue of what it means to take a work outside the context of its production. In any case, in *The Pixelated Revolution*, I don't take up a neutral position. I'm clearly on the side of the protesters against the regime, and the videos that you see in the work show the suffering they are going through. I don't stop there, however, but aim for a more intellectual aspect of the work. The work is about the image and the use of the Internet in revolutions. It's something beyond what's happening now in Syria.

The reflection I've done in this work bothered some Syrian and Lebanese people, because they could not understand how I could be so cold-hearted as to pose intellectual questions as people were being killed a mere few kilometers away. For me, this is the role of art. It is not to mobilize people. Revolutionaries insist that we have to be in solidarity to fight the authority and that this means postponing our questions and doubts because we operate in a state of emergency. When I make art, there is no such urgency. If I have a question, even if it's against the revolution I'm in support of, I should ask it. Otherwise, I am not making art. When people come to see an artwork, they give the artist a kind of authority over them for a certain period of time. Artists have to act responsibly in taking up this role and not misuse it. People generously grant this authority to artists by sitting silently in a performance for one hour or quietly viewing an exhibition, even if the work is bad. The issue is how to use this authority.

LC You mentioned that *The Pixelated Revolution* started with an article you published in a Lebanese quarterly. I'm interested in what it meant to work with words as opposed to working with the media that you used when you showed *The Pixelated Revolution* as an exhibition and as a performance. What happened in the gap between these different media? What did they make happen differently? I'm thinking about this in relation to artistic research and the possibilities that open up with the different media within art discourse, as opposed to a written-only discourse. It seems to me that through the medium of writing, you're forced to choose particular possibilities and present them in a more or less linear way. And through the medium of video, you can maybe introduce three ideas simultaneously or hold them open, perhaps hold open contradictions in a different way.

RM Can you be more specific?

LC I'm thinking of how you used video or flipbooks or blown-up images taken from mobile phone screens within *The Pixelated Revolution* exhibition when it was shown at Documenta, for example. I'm interested in the knowledge that opened up that you almost can't put your finger on, but that comes through material possibilities that stem from the use of particular media. I'm wondering what was possible through text when *The Pixelated Revolution* was an article, and what happened in terms of translation across the media of performance, video, and installation for you in terms of content.

RM There are some differences between the performance of *The Pixelated Revolution* and the exhibition that was shown at Documenta. The performance was far more similar to the text than the exhibition. In fact, the exhibition was not a translation of the article but an addition to it. The flipbooks were not referred to in the article, for example, although I did address the idea of seeing a video frame-by-frame in order to understand it. However, in the article I never had the idea to make the video flip in order to create difficulties for people to see the video and to raise this question of what we are looking at. If we watch this video, are we really seeing what is happening in Syria or not? It's related to other series of questions that are not in the article as such.

LC Do you think the flipbooks are not in the article because they can't be? I mean, are they not in the article because their content is not linear enough or it cannot be adequately held in words?

RM Perhaps, but of course an article doesn't necessarily have to be linear. Some writers can write in a non-linear way in articles as well as novels. One issue that I faced was the question of how to show a video in an article. I knew I had to describe it in detail, as if you are watching it while you read the description. Of course, enabling you to "watch" a video through words allows you to imagine it differently or translate it in your mind somehow. Maybe when you see the video physically you will even be disappointed, so there is always a surprise element. I tried to keep that quality when I did the performance. I showed the video to the audience without talking, without saying anything, and when the video was finished, I replayed it and started to describe what they had seen in detail by creating pauses in the video and using the description from the article.

This did something in addition to the article that I could not make happen in a text. It had the quality of something that had just been seen, but that one is not able to describe in any detail. So I took this experience and started to describe it in detail, which left the audience questioning their own spectatorship. Had they seen these things or not? It left them unsure and wanting to see the video again. So there was an uncanny situation, an unsatisfying situation, which I found interesting. It planted doubts in the audience and by doing so, created an immediate distance from emotions. This was a particularly confronting piece of footage to watch and I have often been criticized for showing such videos. They are inherently violent, despite the fact that they don't show any blood or corpses. If you take the sound out of them, then you don't understand anything. It is just a shaky movement and then the camera goes down.

LC In the Stedelijk performance, I had the feeling there were almost parallel tracks on the level of content. At moments when you or Hito appeared to be talking about mathematics or philosophy or representation, I was actually dealing with violence and death. I could feel myself being manipulated as a viewer, but not necessarily in a negative way. There was a certain manipulation of my brain to hold open more space for that violence or death than I would normally be able to hold open in a sustained way through this other parallel discourse dealing with mathematics and representation. It's as if there was a puppet show going on, but the real story was somewhere else. As an audience member, you are watching the puppet show but I had the feeling, watching the performance, that I didn't have time to process the level of violence I was dealing with in the performance. This seemed to be a way of making me take in more violence and let it go deeper so that the repercussions would be after the performance.

RM I find this an interesting interpretation. I don't have comments, just that I like what you said.

LC Living in the Netherlands, I don't find so much openness in people around me to try to imagine or want to understand war and what it does with people, or to engage with physical-psychological violence in general. There is so little space for the possibility of thinking about what violence is, what it really is, and not just making it belong to the other. I felt that one of the things that was going on within the performance was a widening of that space within the minds of people with no direct experience, an attempt to somehow stretch the space. I don't know if that was your intention or not, but maybe this also brings us back to the question of context. You wanted to get back to the notion of taking very local work outside to an international audience.

RM Yes, in short, I don't care where I am going to present – in this context or that one. When I make a work and go out with this work, I present it in the same way as I made it in my own city. I'm not afraid that if the work addresses a situation in Beirut, the audience outside Beirut will not understand. Even without knowing the history of Beirut, the audience can understand a lot and sometimes see different elements in the work than a Beiruti audience. This becomes evident in audience discussions after performances. I think it's important to keep all of the complexities in place because simplification always leads to false realities. It may put things in black and white and separate them into the good and the bad, which is dangerous. This is what the media always tries to do.

LC So you try to bring the audience to realize their own not knowing? To keep the known and the unknown together to get a sense that the picture cannot be complete?

RM Definitely, yes, although I can't tell if I am successful or not in doing so.

Embodied Knowledge

A Dialogue with Grada Kilomba

Katayoun Arian You are an interdisciplinary artist and writer with an oeuvre consisting of different registers of knowledge, such as publications, staged readings, performances, installations, and theoretical texts. You also have an academic background, with degrees in psychoanalysis and a PhD in philosophy, and have taught for over fourteen years. In fact, your classes on decolonizing knowledge at Humboldt University have become a huge source of inspiration for Black and POC students in the decolonization movement in Germany. In the past years, you have chosen to leave academia and to work more in the art context. I am interested to know when you decided to transition to a more art-based practice and why and how you made that move.

Grada Kilomba Well, firstly let me say that it makes a lot of sense to be having this conversation today at Witte de With Center for Contemporary Art because of the current discussion about the colonial name of this institution. Each space I perform in has a new meaning and when I performed *Illusions* this evening, it felt like the performance was speaking to the physical building itself and that was very inspiring for me. I think this says something about my reason for leaving academia – well, I didn't leave academia as such. I was always a hybrid person, transgressing fields and disciplines and still always out of place somehow. It's not that I finished one discipline and started a new one. After starting out by studying clinical psychology and psychoanalysis, I worked a lot with war survivors in Lisbon during the time of war in Angola and Mozambique. I was very interested in documenting their histories and narratives, so I started writing a lot. Psychoanalysis is very powerful because it works with the unconscious, with metaphors and symbols, so it could give me a lot of symbolic and metaphoric material with which to work on stories that were silent. From there, I sought to bring these stories into performance. I was interested in knowledge; which knowledge we produce and how we produce it. How can I bring this knowledge into performance and make it vivid? How can we make it felt in the body and in the emotions? I wanted to bring in all of these different levels of knowledge production, which are usually not there.

KA Do you mean that these different levels of knowledge production are lacking in academia?

GK In academia, there's a long old colonial tradition of creating an object that you observe from a distance. You describe, classify, and speak about it. You are supposed to be a disembodied theorist and artist. That's why, when we enter these spaces, we only have heads without bodies, as you have noticed; usually white men with a neck and a head, which is so symbolic of what knowledge is, something that stays here *(gestures to her head)*. It's not related to the body, the heart, or the belly. You are supposed to create others, an object that you should never be in relation with. So you work knowing that most of the disciplines function with this dynamic, which is strongly connected with colonial and patriarchal discourse. When we come to speak and to produce knowledge, you have to transgress those disciplines and those methodologies. You cannot work with those disciplines that have placed you as the other, that have described you, that have spoken about you. We come with subjectivity, emotionality, physicality, memory, spirituality, and so on.

KA You are now doing performances in which you stage readings yourself to accompany your video works, which in turn include performers you have choreographed. How did you make the transition to creating this kind of work, and how different is it to be working in an artistic field?

GK I became very interested in bringing part of political and theoretical texts into performance. That was a period in which I worked a lot in the theater and brought things to the stage. I usually work with the same ensemble of actors. They are five people, actors of color, Afro-Germans who usually work in the National Theatre, as well as dancers. I formed this small group that I have worked with on all my different projects. I left academia and went more into the arts because

I felt very incomplete. I wanted to work in a field that is open enough to be experimental. In academia, we can't be very experimental. In theater, it's also not so possible. It's very traditional, extremely conservative, and extremely racist, like contemporary art. The difference, however, is that in contemporary art there is space to raise questions, whereas in other fields you are supposed to give answers. I find it much more fascinating to produce works where, after seeing the work, people leave with new questions. So in art, you produce knowledge by producing questions instead of giving answers. I find that more transformative somehow. It has been a long path. After working on stage and staging a lot of things, I got more interested in visualizing the stories and visualizing text. That's, for instance, what *The Desire Project* (2015–2016) is. It's a visual work divided into three videos: *While I Speak*, *While I Write*, and *While I Walk*. Its main visual element is the word.

KA You work in so many different formats, including publications, staged readings, lecture performances, video installations, and theoretical texts. How did you come to these different formats?

GK I'm interested in telling stories and particularly interested in experimenting. I think we have a lot of experimental work to do because we have to transgress these borders and these disciplines. So we're a generation of artists who are searching for a language. Looking back at my work, I see that each project has a different format and a different language, and I like that. I am not especially interested in being a filmmaker or a performer or a writer or whatever. My interest lies in telling stories and working with the different disciplines to create a format that fits me or fits that story somehow.

KA I also notice that, next to text and visuals, you make use of music in your work. In *Illusions* you tell the myth of Narcissus and Echo, recasting it as a colonial scenario. A recurrent element in the video was the song "I Put a Spell on You," which in the end we understand to mean that white supremacy has put a spell on us. What is the role of music there? Why did you choose this particular kind of music to work with?

GK I chose the music because I loved it. I love the work of Screamin' Jay Hawkins and Nina Simone and was searching for all of the variations of "I Put a Spell on You" to use them in different moments. It seemed very apt to that moment because we are all put under the spell of white supremacy. *All* of us. She plays with that quite well: "I put a spell on you and you are mine. It doesn't matter what *you* want, I put a spell on you." I like to use these contradictions because the film, as you know, is a silent film. I chose not to have any sound besides the music and the beats, which are, of course, also music. With *Illusions*, I wanted to recreate a kind of storytelling. Over the past few years, I became very interested in the African tradition of storytelling, with the oral tradition as a way of producing knowledge, in counterpart to the usual forms of knowledge production that we have in Western structures. The oral tradition always involves storytelling, the body that tells the story, and music. It involves a whole setting, a *mise en scene*, which is very closely linked to the past and the future.

It's fascinating to create knowledge through storytelling. I wanted to tell a story we all know, but perhaps don't know why we know it and to bring a new meaning or reading through staging it. What is in that story, that myth of Narcissus and Echo? What is that love story and what could it represent? It has so many different layers. The layer of colonialism is one of them. This fascination with itself, the reproduction of its own image, this consensus of loyalty that Echo has to Narcissus, even though she is not loved by him. She remains loyal, and she does not want to know. I find those different layers of gender, sexuality, and race fascinating to transport into a postcolonial society. I thought to tell this story and to come as a voice, as a storyteller, like a contemporary Creole storyteller who tells the story so that everybody can hear it, but this time we hear the story we know in a different way.

KA How did you conceive of the translation of those words into images? How did you get to these images and to the overlapping of words and images that we experience in the work?

GK The projection of the video is a little bit like the visualization of the words of the storyteller; it's like a dream. Music is also very important. For example, in the *Desire* project, which is a video installation in three acts, I decided to subvert in a different way, to do a video installation without any image besides the words themselves so that the message becomes prominent. So that the audience has to read what I want to tell; it's about coming to voice. Instead of having a voiceover, I worked with Moses Leo again, and he did the drumming you hear in the videos. We did a lot of research, which led to us composing that. It took several weeks for Moses to compose that music and once it was ready, I wrote a text according to his music. I re-edited the films countless times until the words fit physically, like a breathing body, with the music. It's as if the music is the voice and the words are the body. I wanted to work with that for a very political reason. I think music has this element of political resistance, especially for the African diaspora, but for many other diasporas as well. Because we have been entering so many spaces through music.

KA Some of the most important questions in your work are: Who can speak? What can we speak about? What happens when we speak? I wonder how you consider the use of music to be related to these questions.

GK We have, in fact, been denied entrance to many different spaces, but music is something metaphysical. You can deny entry to someone, but once that person is outside playing their music, they enter the space anyway because you cannot filter music. You have to hear it. There is a long historical tradition of Black people occupying spaces through music–actually, also as musicians. Not as artists, as writers, or as academics; this series of labels that we are not allowed to enter, as such. But as musicians, we can enter, as such. Music itself has the power of entering and occupying spaces. If you go to certain spaces, like hotels, you can hear the music of Black people constantly, although you do not see any Black people inside, besides the ones washing the dishes. I wanted to play with that power of occupying space and also that tradition. I wanted to use music as a form of narrative that is also part of this African tradition of storytelling. You narrate something through the music. People understand, even if they don't know what story I'm telling; they can understand what is being said somehow. I find that fascinating. In this project, I wanted to play with the silence and the storytelling, and with the other one, I wanted to tell a story and narrate it through music. To play with and experiment with all of these subversive practices. To subvert more common artistic practices somehow.

KA The mythological characters are presented as metaphors for a colonial past and as a politics of representation that only reflects their self-image. But at the same time, you are speaking about racism through Greek mythology, through the dominant narratives that we have been fed. I find this subversion very interesting. Can you elaborate on how you relate to subverting existing and dominant frames of knowledge and history-telling?

GK I think that with any project, we are always doing the same thing but we go around in circles, and the question becomes more and more refined. It's about my own questions; wanting to understand who I am, knowing that as a Black woman, there are a lot of things that I do not know. Things from my history that were hidden, that were not published, not documented. Names of many people that I would like to know that I do not know. Books I would have liked to have in my library as a child, as a teenager, as a student, but couldn't. There is so much fragmentation in my everyday life that I urge to complete.

From project to project, you have a question that you are concerned with, and then you put all these pieces together and start turning the pieces to make the puzzle. You start putting them together and you complete this puzzle, and the question is, for you, answered. It's a very spiritual process of completing things, of putting things in place, of naming them, of giving a proper burial to these ghosts, so that they're not ghosts anymore. Even in installation, we put things in their place, knowing that a big part of our history did not have a dignified burial or ritual, was not properly named or documented. I think it's a part of that process.

With *Illusions* I very much had the question of how to work with this. Franz Fanon once wrote, "All this whiteness that burns me." That sentence has always stayed with me. I was asking myself how to create a project that can bring exactly this to life. How can I make it visible? Without us realizing it, we have created this normativity and normality that is not normal at all. How can we dismantle that? I thought, "It is Narcissus and the Echoes." The day of the premiere of *Illusions* at the Bienal Internacional de São Paulo was the day of the US elections. I was there with my curator Gabi Ngcobo and we were reading that fifty-three percent of Donald Trump's votes came from white women. They are Echoes. We were talking about the power of that, about the force of transporting this myth into today's politics.

KA It's wonderful to learn more about all of the different layers of your work as an artist, as they are so very rich and distinctive. I also wanted to talk about your curatorial practice. You've just finished curating a two-year series of talks called "Kosmos[2]," which took place at the Maxim Gorki Theater in Berlin from 2015 until 2017.

GK I wouldn't call myself a curator. I was lucky enough to be invited by Shermin Langhoff, the director of the Maxim Gorki Theater, which is one of the most important and fascinating theaters in Germany, I would say in Europe. Making a revolution in art, winning prizes every year, partly because it is very political. She is the first woman of color, a Turkish-German woman, directing a national theater and she has had the courage to really transform the space. The Maxim Gorki Theater was originally called the Singakademie, two centuries ago. As was common back then, Alexander Humboldt, the great scientist, went on several journeys to South America, especially to Cuba, to study, classify, name, and document the cosmos. This knowledge production was financed by Spanish royalty. They would pay people to travel, to study, and create knowledge because they had a huge interest in having a new topography, new maps, and detailed information on the places they wanted to exploit further, deeper, and harder. Even today, it's a factor in who receives scholarships, fellowships, or commissions to create knowledge with certain political interests. Anyway, Humboldt did his research and came back, and I think he was treated like a kind of pop star. He gave a series of incredible lectures that were called "Kosmos" at the Singakademie, which is today the Maxim Gorki Theater.

KA What questions were you and Shermin concerned with? What were the themes that you wanted to work with, and why?

GK We faced the question of what to do with a historic space that has this colonial legacy. How can we occupy or rename it? How can we interrupt spaces, appropriate spaces and transform spaces? Shermin called me up in the summer of 2015. As you know, that summer many people were crossing Europe from the Middle East, in particular from Syria, and arriving in Berlin, in Germany. It was physical, it was not just something you read in the news. We had to do something. What should we do? We were doing many things and then this idea came of doing a new "Kosmos" at Kosmos Square. Shermin and I put something together, I loved working on that. My concept was to do a series of artists' talks that lasted for two years. The intention was to occupy the space, to remember the history of that space, and transform it by changing the configurations of power and knowledge. We can only create new knowledge, new concepts of knowledge, if we change those configurations of power. That means that people who do not usually have entry to those spaces can enter. We change those configurations of power: Who can sit here with a microphone? Who can be here? Who can deliver knowledge, questions, and concepts? Who can create new formats that were not there before because these people were not here? When I entered this space – Witte de With Center for Contemporary Art, Rotterdam – I met many people working here but I did not see any Black people. You are the first woman of color I've met who works here.

KA I am not working here. *(laughs)*

GK Exactly. We do not work here. How can we build a curriculum, an agenda, if we are not here? If we are not defining what should be here? If we are not bringing questions that are not, cannot, be posed here? How can we bring methodologies if we are not here? How can we bring new paradigms if we are not here? We can only bring new questions if we are here to ask these questions. Questions that might not be relevant for most of the people who have the privilege of always being here. We can only bring new methodologies, new formats of working, if we are here and say, "I don't want to work with that format. I'm going to revert that; I am going to use something else, I have another idea." We can only bring new paradigms, new perspectives to approach those questions, if we are here. What I'm talking about is epistemology, *episteme logos*, the acquisition of knowledge. How do we acquire, how do we produce knowledge? It's through questions, methodologies, and paradigms. And this is only possible when we change the configurations of power. That means people who are usually outside of these spaces have to be inside to produce knowledge that has never been produced before. This is how we decolonize. I thought, this is exactly what I want to do. I want to bring artists who have just arrived or have been here for a while and have, or have had, the status of refugees. But they come to talk about their work–their methodologies, questions, techniques that they use–and not about being refugees.

KA How did the audience respond?

GK Well, there was no Q&A because people should listen, and that was very challenging for the audience because they were curious and familiar with asking questions. The concept I created was that people were going to come to listen to them. They were not going to tell about which boat they took or how many hours it took; they were going to talk about their work. It was fascinating because suddenly you inverted the gaze. It was challenging but inspiring to realize that some of the people were here because they made a certain film and went to prison because of that film, because of their music, because of their choreography. They were artists from a whole range of disciplines. It was fascinating that many of them were there precisely because of the art they produced and the knowledge they produced. It was challenging for the audience but also inspiring to listen to them without the voyeurism of wanting to hear private stories. When we give an interview, everyone wants to know where we come from, when we arrived, where we like to be. And I always interrupt, "I want to talk about my work." You cannot talk about your work because it's so focused on voyeurism. It was a beautiful experience; the lectures were always packed, throughout the two years. That just shows us all that the audience is much more avant-garde, it's more futuristic than the institutions themselves. When the institutions dare to change their curriculum, there's a huge audience more than ready to come. That's always been my experience. It is the institutions themselves that are fixated on this very old curriculum and agenda that actually does not speak to most of the audience. Sometimes, as we know in contemporary art, it is very detached from reality and from political reality. Many times you pass by works, but physically you don't even stop because it is detached from your reality.

This text is an edited transcript of a live dialogue that followed a performance of *Illusions* by Grada Kilomba, curated by Katayoun Arian as part of First Things First's program "Decolonial Options: The Futurity of Decolonial Practice." It took place as part of *Cinema Olanda: Platform* at Witte de With Center for Contemporary Art, Rotterdam (2017), curated by Lucy Cotter and artist Wendelien van Oldenborgh (with in-house curator Natasha Hoare and director Defne Ayas) as an extension of the Dutch representation at the 57th Venice Biennale. First Things First consists of Katayoun Arian (researcher, curator, writer), Louise Autar (activist, organizer), and Max de Ploeg (activist, political/cultural programmer). Postscript: Witte de With Center for Contemporary Art changed its name to Kunstinstituut Melly in 2020.

Language as Film

A Dialogue with Sky Hopinka

Lucy Cotter Working mainly with film and video, your deconstruction of language through cinema is, in your own words, a way for you to be free from the dogma of traditional storytelling. Your recent film *Dislocation Blues* (2018) engages with a camp set up as a protest against the construction of an oil pipeline at Standing Rock in North Dakota. Rather than providing a backstory, the film enters that highly politicized context through a very intimate encounter; namely through a Skype conversation in which a person talks about how they experienced their gender identifications in the context of the camp. Can you share some thoughts on your decision to open up that film in that way?

Sky Hopinka Entering that space was about trying to locate myself as an Indigenous person but also as a filmmaker, thinking about the priority of how I want to experience this moment. Am I here for a project or just to support the movement? I was asking myself constant questions, not only in negotiating what I shot but also in considering how I participated. I wasn't going as an unbiased reporter or a documentarian. I was going as a Native person. That ethical position was important for me to define. What were the things I was dealing with when I was there? How was I approaching representation? What did it mean to listen to audio in the background in shots where I didn't mean to record it? The conversations I picked up were very vivid to me and still are. It took me a long time to edit this piece. I didn't start looking at the footage until three months after I shot it because it was difficult.

The conversation with Cleo [Keahna] was the thing that tied everything together. It helped me make sense of the footage and why it was difficult to look at the footage. That became a part of the film itself. Having someone else, someone who had a totally different experience of camp than I did, both asking ourselves "How do we talk about this?" was important. Trying to navigate these different de-colonial spaces, these different reservation spaces. As the conversation between Cleo and I turned to the question of processing the experience, it became clear to me that that's what this work was actually about. It's a step in thinking about things, like asking how to think about my own nostalgia. Audiences with their own experience of Standing Rock, who have seen the film, have asked this question too. It was also about trying to find others who are going through the same process. It's an important part of the healing process. So how can the film function in that trajectory?

LC Cleo talks about the sense of solidarity, how it felt to see banners saying things like "Palestine stands with Standing Rock." The tension between that passionate and shared spirit of resistance and the sense of distance created by the mediation of the event is really striking. There are a lot of references to how Standing Rock appears on social media and how gaps open up between what appear to be very personal accounts and actual personal experiences. The desire for solidarity, for a coherent political narrative, brings a sense of loyalty and with it a practice of not critiquing. We can sense that double bind and how it makes a "true" account impossible. The underlying focus of your film seems to be about enabling those gaps to be legible and undoing narratives as such.

SH Yes, I think so.

LC This undoing of coherent narrative or legibility seems to be present in your approach to the cinematic image as well. In many of your films, there's a visual transition from realism into abstraction, even into pure color at some points. What does that visual sliding scale, from realism to abstraction, make possible for you as a filmmaker?

SH There's a freedom to it. Looking at things on a timeline, looking at landscapes that I shot, being able to play with them, being able to explore what the possibilities are, what's hidden in the camera's sensor. These are the things I think about when I'm editing or correcting color. When I turn up the contrast there are more details in certain areas or vice versa. So I'm asking myself how I can use the information the sensor has captured to recreate something, either that I remember or that I want to see in these spaces that I was formally in.

There's a remove between shooting the footage, where I may adjust the aperture, adjust the shutter speed, use a filter, remove the lens from the body, or anything I can do in-camera, and editing that footage, where it becomes more of a recreation of memory and space. I try to oscillate between different modes. I deliberately don't manipulate too much or use too many visual abstractions in *Dislocation Blues*, for example. I didn't feel it was appropriate for that film and I also wanted to challenge myself by making it in a different mode than many of my previous films.

LC Can we talk about some of those previous films, where abstraction and color play a more pronounced role? I'm thinking, for example, of *Anti Objects* or *Space Without Path* or *Boundary* (2017) and *I'll Remember You as You Were, Not as What You'll Become* (2016).

SH I entered *I'll Remember You as You Were, Not as What You'll Become* thinking a lot about color field paintings and Helen Frankenthaler's in particular. I was thinking a lot about her paintings and those images and what these things are around color or representations or challenges with the semiotics that we associate with those different approaches.

LC One of the entry points for your artistic practice was your being critical of ethnographical documentary filmmaking practices and the representation of Native people in cinema. Does that continue to inform some of your formal choices, like the semi-abstract rendering of the powwow in the film's opening scene? The viewer is watching a powwow but in a visually fluid form, like a kind of oil stain in which people emerge and disappear into translucent colors.

SH Yes, this confluence of different reasons allowed me to think more about the uncomfortable feeling I had while shooting the scene. I had helped to set up this powwow and I had been invited to attend and document it. I felt protectiveness toward these people, and there were a number of people

I've known for years. I was asking myself how I could make this *not* about the powwow. I initially had a more realistic rendering of the powwow in the opening scene but I was quite uncomfortable with it. A powwow is a giant thing with these people, the sounds, the dance, and so on. I was asking myself how I could focus attention on these dancers, their movements, and the colors of their outfits, which are very vibrant. How could I have this moment read, not as a spectacle but as a procession of movements of color and light? I felt that within the conceit of this film, which is about reincarnation, spirituality, and the afterlife, I could do that. It offered me a chance to sustain that conversation, that topic of the film.

LC I've noticed that a lot of people writing about your work use words like "hallucinatory." I would think about your artistic strategies more in terms of breaking away from rational time or space, which perhaps also relates to possibilities like the afterlife or reincarnation. I get the sense that when your imagery becomes more abstract or more manipulated, you're trying to open up a space between coordinated space and time, as such; it acts as a kind of placeholder for that possibility. Does that make some sense to you? Do you read it in those terms?

SH Yes, I do, definitely. I wouldn't describe my films as hallucinogenic or psychedelic, although I understand why people go there or use those words to describe the movements and everything else. The problem I have with those words is that they imply some sort of loss of control in the viewer or the person experiencing it. It suggests that they are without their faculties or agency, in a sense. For me, those different techniques are more about communication. They are ways of creating languages that are not verbal but visual.

There's a logic in how they are constructed that's very deliberate. It's about how to communicate in a way that I can't communicate with my own voice or through the things that I write. So the question is how this language can speak to you in a way that is visual, but not auditory or text-based.

LC Before you got into filmmaking, you were studying and working with Indigenous languages. Are those things still closely related, for you? I'm not sure if you still work directly with language practices in parallel with your filmmaking.

SH Not in recent years, although I'm still actively involved with language revitalization as a speaker and as an educator. I started learning and teaching Chinuk within four or five months of first picking up a camera and making a film, so they are very closely related. How I view teaching, how I view languages, and how I view sound work are tied together.

LC In *Wawa* (2014), which is quite an early work, you directly represent the process of language transfer of Chinuk Wawa but in more recent works, there's a humanization of language processes. We witness the intimacy of language transfer in *Anti-Objects* or *Space Without Path or Boundary*, for example, where we listen in on a conversation between Henry Zenk and Wilson Bobb from the 1980s, presumably in preparation for Zenk's later dictionary of the Chinuk Wawa language. It appears to me that your film is not so much about the acquisition of that language as it is about the loss of language; how gaining a language is about learning the existence of gaps between languages and how to inhabit them.

SH Yes, as you said, it's about those gaps.

LC In a way, poetry is also about opening up spaces that can't be articulated in everyday modes of language. Some of your earliest video work, like *Tangles* (2012), departed from Native poetry. Poetic language returns in several later works. Do you see a relationship between the manipulation of language in poetry and the abstraction we have talked about in relation to cinematic image making? Is there a parallel in the use of language to enter into realms that are not everyday experiences?

SH *Tangles* was my second video and the first time I used a DSLR camera. I studied English literature in college, so it was my entry into the moving image realm, while I was trying to make my first films. Having the poetic voice be a part of the process of trying to understand how I fit into the world of film has been important to me. I've become more comfortable in incorporating my writing into works and trying to have literal poetic prose in the films. It has been nice to complement that with how I've constructed these videos.

LC There's a very interesting relationship between culture, consciousness, and language throughout your films. By using IPA, the International Phonetic Alphabet, to transcribe English and by employing different scripts and fonts, you seem to use language as a kind of material that's slightly divorced from its everyday functionality.

SH I think a lot about how text is a source of information to understand different parts of our lives. My engagement with IPA began with my language revitalization work. It's used by tribes and linguists to create a writing system for languages that don't have one. What does it mean to create ethnography for a language that has never had a writing system? How do you represent sounds through text? I try to be very intentional with the font and typeface. I think about those things constantly, and not only in how I view certain visual techniques as language but also in how I view language itself as being representative, whether it's something in need of revitalization or one that is spoken every day.

LC I came across an interview in which you used the term "ethnopoetic" in relation to your own work, which implies that things can't be explained in a standard form of documentation.

SH I've used that term less in recent years because it still has "ethno" at the beginning; it's still tied to that. How can I *not* think about my work within the framing of ethnography? I'm interested in the poetic but it's a very broad term. I think a lot about words, about the power of words, as well as just finding a word that describes what you are thinking about or feeling. That's what I love about language, that there is always some way to describe your feeling. I'm fascinated by how language shifts, how new words are created.

LC Your new film *Fainting Spells* (2018) almost becomes a visual narration of a poem. Like *Dislocation Blues*, it opens with a laptop screen in a dark room, this time showing a flowering plant. Then it moves through semi-abstract imagery of a side-tilted landscape, which becomes a dystopian image of burning woodlands. Throughout those image sequences, there is a horizontal line of handwriting unfolding across the screen. It appears to be an interior monologue but on the other hand, it also seems to be a kind of myth. There's something happening in that video that feels a bit like a search for how to place some kind of a mythic realm in very real contemporary circumstances. It evokes an association between the political and the mythical.

SH Yes, absolutely. My interest in this area began with questions like whether new tribes can be created in the US. What does it mean for tribes to continue to grow and form? That brings us to the level of thought where we could ask the question of whether we can make myths. What does it mean to relate to documents, written down in the 1900s, which have removed the relationship, not only to their contents but also to the creation of them as an act and a part of a culture?

I think there's something romantic about the *Xąwįska*, the Indian Pipe plant, and its relationship to myth. The plant is beautiful and really delicate and there's something eerie about that. Looking through Ho-Chunk myths that have been written down and finding out there was nothing about this plant made me wonder how this knowledge was passed down and what has been lost. What is the utility of myth or mythmaking? If someone made a story and it came to them, what else was going on in their life and what were they feeling? Was this a way to teach about mores, but also a form of catharsis? I wanted to make up a story about a plant and to do something cathartic. By making it a bit opaque, I'm not trying to enter the canon of Ho-Chunk mythology. It's more of a proposition in thinking about how we relate to these stories and to our own need to be part of these stories as active participants in these tribes or communities.

LC In the film's opening song, a child asks an adult to tell them the story of *Xąwįska*. It was only later that I noticed in the synopsis that this is a story about the Indian Pipe Plant used by Ho-Chunk to revive people who've fainted. But as a viewer with very limited knowledge of the heritage you're working with, it's impossible to establish even a vague boundary between the received myth and the fictional space created by you as an author. I'm wondering how that informs the reception of the work. Do you want to give the feeling that an existing myth is being revisited somehow or is it more about evoking the possibility of a contemporary myth?

SH I would say the latter. I've thought a lot about context and how much information I'm giving or withholding. I don't see it as being withheld; I'm not keeping information. I just don't feel I need to talk about it. One rarely watches a film, especially a short film, without access to a synopsis so I do try to include some relevant information there. The synopsis is an opportunity to set up the film in a certain way so that I don't have to do that in the film. But it's not important whether it appears as something established or authored.

LC At the same time, the film's landscape imagery relates to circumstances that have a distinctly political aspect. There is no sense of departing from current political conditions. I'm wondering if *Fainting Spells* is perhaps a further step in thinking about some of the questions that came up in *Dislocation Blues* to do with where to place desire and the possibility of fabrication as a making process, of self as well as of community. Does *Fainting Spells* step into other, slightly more abstract but perhaps also more bold territory to open that possibility?

SH The formal similarities between the two films are deliberate. I was also imagining what it would be like to move from *Dislocation Blues* to *Fainting Spells*. Even that process of viewing creates a certain nostalgia for what you've just seen; it evokes the memory of what you have just seen.

Both films operate in the same field of desire, as you said. It's a desire to process and a desire to heal. Both of those things are important in how to relate to the work. Also, that sentiment is provided without a vocal soundtrack or voices. There's a certain lyricism at play in the images in themselves, in what's going on.

LC Can we talk about the role of song? It doesn't only appear in *Fainting Spells*, but in earlier works like *Jáaji Approx.* (2015), in which you record conversations with your father and play recordings of his singing. There's a haunting presence of song, and often it's Indigenous song, returning through different works. The fact that it's sung from the body in a very unmediated fashion makes it have a different presence than music. You often cut from bodily song to silence or very subtle sound, so there is also a high contrast.

SH I'm often motivated by songs that I find or record. Those are things that I constantly return to, outside of the films. All the songs in *Jáaji Approx.* are songs I've listened to hundreds of times. In some ways, I made the video as a way of incorporating those songs, to share those stories. I didn't intend to make a music video; it's more that music is often how I experience the world. I like to play it, record it, to find a song that describes how it feels at that moment. To have these different spaces, to have music evoke a feeling I'm feeling is another way to communicate through a non-verbal language, a musical language. The sound edits and sound design are very important. What do they say about sound in film? That you don't notice it when it's good, but you do notice when it's bad.

LC In most of your videos, the aural reality runs in parallel to, but at a distance from, the visual reality. In a way, it forms an audio collage that's juxtaposed with a visual collage and they move in and out of being in sync.

SH I don't often shoot sync sound. Even when I do, I like using the audio on my camera body. Whether things are in sync or out of sync, there is always a play between the relative veracity of what you are experiencing or seeing. If things are out of sync, the film stutters for a minute. Like there's a shot in *Dislocation Blues* where Cleo is talking and I make the cut, not in the video but in the soundtrack, so his voice goes out of sync. I try to be very attentive to these small things, especially in the pacing of the film and the relationship between the sound and space. I like the sound of silence, especially as a way to give weight to an image but also to pause and unburden an audience from what they have just seen or heard that may have been intense or had a lot going on. I think a lot about the rhythm of the piece, and it may be balanced or unbalanced with text and sound.

LC The silence often moves the viewer toward the non-veracity of the representation. You can register the silence, but it also confronts you with the film being a form of representation. When we discussed *Fainting Spells*, you said that you don't deliberately hold things back but that you often don't feel the need to say certain things. Can we talk about the power of making this choice not to be transparent? I didn't experience it as a willful holding back, but rather as being attentive to the productive force of opacity.

SH I do think about that a lot. I think about who my audience is, who my intended audience is, and how I can focus the nature of a video toward my audience. Because my intended audience already knows these things, it's not about withholding but not needing to talk about it. But even still, when I'm editing and thinking about those things, it's often in some ways like I am my own representative for my own experience. It's not as if I'm making these experiences for myself, but I am. So what kind of shorthand can I make for myself? Can I think of myself as my own representative of my tribe? I don't think that's accurate, but it makes sense to me and if I feel good about it and if it doesn't feel disrespectful then I know that I'm doing OK. So, what are these boundaries and how do I think about them? One example is the calligram of the Bird Effigy Mound containing a text by Paul Radin in *I'll Remember You as You Were, Not as What You'll Become* (2016). A lot of Ho-Chunk people know who Paul Radin is and know not to trust his books. If you're Ho-Chunk, and you know what the effigy mound is, you know how to read those calligrams. I don't feel the burden to explain what those things are, because it's not about the explanation of them but about what the film is trying to do.

LC It seems to me that part of the feeling of intimacy in your films comes from the sense that you are not explaining things. By not being didactic, they bring the viewer quite deep inside a situation, and plunge them into it. At the same time, they also make space for the viewer to be confronted with their own lack of knowledge.

SH Yes, there's no small talk and there's no education. It's not a classroom.

LC Are there other forms of research or thinking that you do or draw on that are important to your artistic practice?

SH I try not to limit myself to what I'm exposed to, to give me a spark or a moment of curiosity or an idea. I like to be open to whatever crosses my path, whether it's in my field, my profession, my art practice, or outside of it. I don't watch as many films as I should. In fact, I only watch films that are really inspirational to me once. I don't want to study those films; I want to have the effects that they made me feel transfer onto something else. Or even techniques like the scrolling text, which I very deliberately borrowed or was inspired to make by James Bennings's film *American Dreams: Lost and Found*. That's a very important film for me.

I've done three book trailers for the poet Adrian C. Lewis at various stages of my career: in 2012, 2013, and 2018. I often use those trailers as spaces for what I want to try out for the short films that I've been working on. The recent one I did for Adrian's book *Electric Snakes* is something I've wanted to do for a long time, using a green screen and keying out images or tracking shots. That was a way to try things out for the feature film I am working on at the moment. When I did *Fainting Spells*, it was also a way to carve out some space to begin thinking about things in a form that didn't have to be a feature right away.

LC What is your feature film about? Does it have a title yet?

SH It's about the relationship and effects of myth. It's called *Małtini*, which means "toward the ocean," and it also means "toward the shore." It's a directional word that means moving toward the shore, whether you're at sea or on the land. I think it's a beautiful way of looking at the world and the boundary it describes that's representative of the relationship between life and death that I am working through.

LC You say that myth is an area that is really opening up in your work. There's a moment in *Dislocation Blues* where Cleo talks about the camp and says, "We were all having the same dream; all our pieces fit together." Do you think myth is a shared concern at the moment with other artists and filmmakers?

SH I don't know. I think that Indigenous artists are working through what it means to be Native in the world right now. We are asking a lot of the same questions in different ways. There's a lot of discussion about "What am I doing and how can I support my community and myself?," exploring these different possibilities and I think that's a larger conversation. I hope that other people are thinking about myth and I'd like to talk to them in this way. I don't know if it's reflective of the society we live in or the progress that Native speakers, scholars, and artists have made.

Making as Translation

A Dialogue with Christian Nyampeta

Lucy Cotter You often describe your practice as working in art, design, and theory "in search of a new narrative of how to live together." This includes seeking out new or unfamiliar ways of collaboration, like your so-called *scriptoria*, a form that has reappeared over the past few years and will take place again at the Contour Biennale 2019 with the poetic title *A Flower Garden of All Kinds of Loveliness without Sorrow*. How did you come to this form and how does it manifest itself in practice?

Christian Nyampeta A *scriptorium* is inscribed in theology; it was a designated environment in the monastery in which monks wrote or made transcriptions. So it's a place where "scripts" were produced. You can also see it as a place where rules are codified. *Scriptoria* were perhaps the only spaces of writing whose output would have a wide circulation. I thought the word was still very evocative, particularly within the context of some kind of cinematic images that might first be written in one way or another. I saw it as a practice of thinking, as spaces of making visible, or spaces of play.

Also, I partly came to this as a pragmatic solution when I was doing a residency at the Camden Arts Centre in 2017. At the time, I wanted to translate texts from French to English. The estimates we received from translators were way beyond our budget. So I had the idea of undertaking the translation as a work in itself, to allow the translation to form the basis from which an artwork would be made. However, I had been thinking about translation for a long time before that. Those thoughts even prompted me to start a PhD in visual cultures at Goldsmiths to try and translate – very immodestly – Roland Barthes's lectures "Comment vivre ensemble: simulations romanesques de quelques espaces quotidiens: notes de cours et de séminaires au Collège de France" (How to Live Together: Novelistic Simulations of Some Everyday Spaces) (1976–1977) at the Collège de France. So, translating and thinking about these writings has gone on for about six years and that coalesced more or less as a cooperative.

LC Cooperation and collaboration are very central components throughout your practice. You typically go through a process with many people, but there's also an afterlife of the work that takes several forms including, but not limited to, artworks. In the *scriptorium* at the Camden Arts Centre, the translations had an afterlife in the form of the film that you made for your solo exhibition there, which was titled *Words after the World*. What about other afterlives? Is there an ambition for the *scriptorium* to create translations that will go into the world in other ways? Is that something you foster or want? Or do you place more emphasis on experiencing this process together, and does that necessarily result in an artwork?

CN The ambition is always much bigger than the outcomes. An artwork is usually one of those outcomes, but it's more of a stage within these possible directions. To take the example of the *scriptorium*, its most important activities have not been made public yet. The translations are not yet published, for example, even though they circulate in a more intimate community of practices. In this way, French-speaking colleagues in Rwanda are able to read texts by colleagues in New York who only publish in English. We go through the effort of producing quick translations, which are circulated for the benefit of our own discussion. I hope they will mount up into a more sustained form of publication but for now, my interest is not to produce something final. I prefer to think along the lines of a journal, which would allow ongoing revisions of the same text. But all of this comes with financial limitations. Besides, it's not always possible or desirable to accommodate these processes within short-term projects, like at Camden Arts Centre. In fact, we are still working on the *Words after the World* film, which is taking a long time. The exhibition cycle and the demands of the work are sometimes incompatible. To sum up, although this process can become an artwork, I also see it as a journal, an entity that can gather new iterations as it goes.

LC Your description foregrounds the fact that a journal is also a place of convening. There seems to be a distinct parallel between, not only the *scriptorium* but also ways of working from earlier projects like *How to Live Together*, in which you more explicitly combined art, design, and theory in interventions at Casco in Utrecht and The Showroom in London, or in workshops you have collaborated on, like *People Who Think Together Dance Together* at the Centre d'art Waza in Lubumbashi. To put it differently, convening seems to be a central means of artistic production, which the journal replicates, including the fluidity of that situation, because there is no sense of having a fixed outcome.

CN Yes, that's a very good way of putting it. In this sense, an artwork bears my name. I'm fine with that and honored by it. It's good to be responsible and to account for the aesthetic choices and the ethical imperative involved. At the same time, it's only one of many possible outcomes for working in this way. The object of working in this way, such as making a film, is not only for my own enjoyment; it's really a form for thinking together. It's something that can bring together spaces, histories, and most importantly, memories.

LC Your collaborators on the upcoming *scriptorium* are all Rwandan-born or of Rwandan descent, so there's a shared focus on Rwandan culture and the deep imprint of the Rwandan genocide. In *Sometimes It Was Beautiful* (2018), the film you made in Sweden, there's a focus on thoughts around a particular period of Congo's history. Are you interested in looking in more depth at certain contexts and then moving across contexts to open up this larger conversation? Obviously, there's an overlapping relationship between the history of Rwanda and the Congo, but in several works you refer to "thinking about Africa." So there's an ambition to consider a larger picture of Africa as a continent, as well as its relationship to European colonial history. How do you negotiate cultural specificity?

CN Theory can help, such as the idea that thinking is necessarily thinking the world but you have to learn somewhere. For the activities I will be convening at Contour 9 with artists of "Rwandan" descent, I'm studying how we artists negotiate the demands of history. My focus is on history and how our actions informed by history may produce more hospitable models for futures. The emphasis is not on culture. The recent history of Rwanda is a global history, from which the entire world should learn. If we go back to the question of translation and language, I can think of at least two models: Ngũgĩ wa Thiong'o, for whom the language of all languages is translation. He is renowned for having written in his own language. Alongside that, Souleymane Bachir Diagne, who's here in New York, suggests that French, English, and Portuguese are equally African; there isn't a way to separate thinking Africa from thinking the world. I suppose that's why, at the end of the day, the defining aspect of my projects is dialogue, more so than collaboration.

Over the last five years, I have worked on *How to Live Together*. And yet I realize that I'm not part of any collective; that I'm not part of any communitarian living arrangement beyond a few very extensive collaborations. I am, however, part of a long-term research network that works together as collectives in order to share resources, funding, hosting, etc. But there is still a stark contrast between the stated claim of how to live together and my lived reality. Maybe that's because of the Rwandan history I have lived through, which makes me fear being defined by belonging to one single cultural community. I feel like I have a "mission" to move beyond the need to only be understood through one single marker of belonging. I ask myself how to honor the need for an elective “isolation,” without being excluded from partaking in a community or society. This is where dialogue can help. I feel that translation is one of the strategies that demand a dialogic exercise. But also, I consider translation as an inconclusive negotiation. I’m not a “native” French or English speaker, and my Kinyarwanda is truly appalling. I have learned every word I use somewhere, maybe at a young age. So in a way, I am always translating to make meaning. I guess cultural specificity is sometimes good and sometimes limiting. It’s a problem when it’s denied but it’s also a problem when it is enforced. I navigate across it, as you were saying, with the films or the works.

LC There is also the aspect of convening in physical space. A further claim and departure point for *How to Live Together* is that you incorporate art, design and theory. In projects like *Words after the World*, the physical construction of spaces seemed especially important. In the exhibition, many of the works manifested multi-functionality, such as a table and chairs that could be used but that also functioned sculpturally as an artwork. Moving away from words, there’s something about the languages of aesthetics and materiality in creating a space to convene that seems quite particular in your practice, relative to other artists working in this way. I’m curious to hear what you imagine that quality makes happen or what your ideas are behind this foregrounding of form within your exhibition installations. Don’t you also have a background in design?

CN Thanks, that’s a beautiful question. I studied industrial design at Central Saint Martin’s in London. I am trained to think in terms of space. During my studies, I was interested in the theories behind industrial design and its connections to global production and relevance for formerly colonized countries. I was naively surprised to learn that political systems like socialism, communism, capitalism, etc., are defined by who controls the means of production. I wanted to study the means that allow us to "make a living," ranging from making a tent all the way to making cities. I was mostly interested in these processes, and only then in the aesthetic qualities of their outcomes. But I hit a limit. Industrial design is linked to most other processes of contemporary production, but the objective of those courses is to train students in producing a chair or a phone, following the demands of the industry. I was disillusioned with the course and its future practice. I was somehow more comfortable working as an artist.

But material thinking is still a necessity. Think about how hard it is to work only standing up or lying down! I like to think about this kind of choreography. Also, I'm attracted to the possibility of a "simulation," as Barthes suggests: how to live together through novelistic simulations of some living spaces. I think about the spaces of convening as simulations that might emulate actual living spaces. In other words, they are models. I don't think these models are complete; they are passing spaces, which can teach us about our actual everyday spaces.

LC You mentioned that these models act as an impetus for a particular choreography in space. In your earlier work, the relationship between the body and structures often concerned the immediate environment of daily living. Recently there seems to be more emphasis on the choreography of the body in relation to an object that is more overtly a part of a larger system of fabrication, which in turn relates to political structures. Your practice forms a movement across all of those things. I was conscious of how in your recent film *Sometimes It Was Beautiful* (2019), for example, passages of the film engaging with colonial experience in the Congo are interspersed with scenes of two dancing figures, which bring us back to the presence of the body in space as a point that we must always return to.

CN At the beginning of my practice, I was exploring "self-making" and "self-fashioning," which are terms that have a long philosophical heritage. They are still relevant in queer studies. I approached "self-making" in a literal sense: making "our own" spaces, which includes thinking about architecture. I felt that we can't only leave matters to those who are supposedly in charge. It made sense for me to think about how we sit, how we walk, how we think, how we move, how we dance. I felt compelled to translate these insights into structures that host each of our presences within these spaces of display.

These "hosting structures" are a system of production that creates models. They generate a system of how to assemble, how to disassemble, how to pack, how to ship away, etc. Hosting structures are also a metaphor for interdependence. They're made through modes of assemblies or slotting mechanisms that form an entity only when they are together. Apart, they seem like an abstraction.

I am still fascinated by these material forms, but I think I have moved on. At the time of my design studies, I was interested in inverting the primary design attribute of "mass production" into "production by the masses." I was wondering what it would mean if we, "the masses," were able to exercise "self-making" so that our homes could become sites of material production. I would make bread, which I would then exchange with a friend who made shoes, etc. A lot of my work at the time was focused on this supposedly economic question, in reference to the histories from which it grew, including asceticism and marginal communities. At the moment, I think a shift has occurred in my work, where this material thinking is more oriented toward forms of knowledge. I'm not sure how else to describe this. As an example, we can again take this idea that a group of us can produce a philosophical text and translate it, although none of us is a "proper" philosopher. This "forming of knowledge" is still a domestic economy, in which the private realm is a site of production, but its orientation is toward a much wider horizon.

LC If we consider the *scriptorium* as a model for producing knowledge collectively, do you relate it to creating other economies for the production of knowledge? It's a slightly different form, but it seems to work in parallel with the idea of self-fashioned material production, which is collective and moving in the opposite direction to industrial production. There is a distinct parallel between those economies.

CN Yes. Previously, my "self-fashioning" revolved around self-learning. Activities like workshops demanded exterior expertise. At the workshop, we had different forms of unknowing that came together, driven by divergent ulterior motives. For instance, in 2014 at The Showroom for the exhibition *How to Live Together: Prototypes*, I wanted to organize a party in the spirit of *People Who Think Together Dance Together*. We then embarked on a study of how to make vessels to drink from, and in doing so, we learned that the soil around The Showroom gallery has amazing clay deposits. We ended up learning about geology, medicinal herbs, etc. A year later, the party took place. But right now, I feel that this "self-learning" has become "self-pedagogy." Its scope is much larger; it demands further planning and collaborative efforts that are a bit more complex. It needs to speak to different forms of history as well. In the example of the previous activities at The Showroom, we produced about ten workshops over one year. Now I'm more interested in what remains after that, and how this knowledge can be kept and preserved.

LC Is this perhaps a question of how the work would re-enter other, larger, systems of knowledge?

CN Yes, in the end, it is and maybe it also speaks to the question of cultural specificity that you raised earlier. It's not always the case, but often in this mode of workshops, people separate afterwards and it can feel as though there's little at stake. Once the workshops are finished, the outcomes are given to those who participated and it ends there. Now, I'm interested in how institutional collaboration might continue afterwards. That's the difference in the shift from a material orientation to a "systemic" one.

LC You've mentioned that dialogue has become foregrounded in your recent practice, both literally and metaphorically. It would be nice to hear you reflect on the texture of that dialogue, which emerges in an artistic context. Perhaps that allows for certain freedoms, certain possibilities; forms not only of interdisciplinary inquiry but also cross-material manifestations. Can you comment on attributes that are specific to those dialogues emerging out of the artistic context?

CN Yes, I have to think of the three films I have made, which all share this dialogic aspect and in which each of the conversants inhabits totally different worlds. Some of the protagonists are alive, while others have passed away. *Life after Life* is based on *Guelwaar* (1993), a film by Ousmane Sembene in which a man is buried in the wrong grave. As a sequel, *Life after Life* begins when its protagonist wakes up in the wrong heaven and must find how to get by in this unforeseen condition. In its form and content, the film is made of conversations between different times, but also between incompatible realities. An idiom is created in which it becomes possible to ask a historical figure banal and everyday questions so that a relationship is established. The questions are not only for the sake of questioning but also for mutual learning, despite antagonisms or differences. In *Words after the World* dialogue comes about through facing the exhaustion of possibilities. The film follows a writer trying to tell a story at a time when certain undisclosed words are prohibited. The writer has to invent synonyms or borrow them from elsewhere. The writer then channels herself into a mausoleum-like space, where historical philosophers lie in repose. It's unclear if the writer finds meaning in their words. But still, a dialogue is established.

In my last film, *Sometimes It Was Beautiful*, actors and actresses play the role of historical figures, even though the actors don't look like their supposed personae. So the dialogue here partly takes place through speculative portrait making, in order to give a face to agents of history and to address their actions. It's a way of reducing absence through abstraction. In this film, the monumentality of the Swedish filmmaker Sven Nykvist is undermined by showing him at a vulnerable time, as a young boy left alone by the absence of his parents, who were Protestant missionaries in Congo. But the subject of *Sometimes It Was Beautiful* is a fictitious meeting between unlikely friends, who gather to watch *I fetischmannens spår* (In the Footsteps of the Witch Doctor), the first of the six films that Nykvist made in or about Congo between 1948 and 1952. What these unlikely friends have in common is that they have visited Stockholm's Museum of Ethnography in the past, where an archive of Nykvist's parents is kept that documents their life in Congo as Swedish missionaries, alongside the artifacts they brought back to Sweden. These strange friends include politician Yasser Arafat, postcolonial theorist Leela Gandhi, human rights activist Rigoberta Menchú, politician Robert Mugabe, playwright Wole Soyinka, and Crown Princess Victoria of Sweden. Several other colleagues of Nykvist also attend his screening from both sides of the grave: film director Andrei Tarkovsky shows up, and somehow activist and politician Winnie Mandela also has something on her mind, while the fourteenth Dalai Lama is rumored to be nearby. When I was making this film, I wondered what would happen if younger artists convoked me into a situation like the one I was bringing Nykvist into, fifty years from now. What if, from the "hereafter," I am brought back here and asked probing questions about my current failures and blind spots?

LC When Sven is asked critical questions about his representation of this colonial context by contemporary individuals, he always returns to the notion of film as a composition of shadow and light. At the end of the day, these are the terms by which he insists on judging, not only the aesthetic quality of his films, but also their ethics. There's an interesting moment in that dialogue, which revolves around untangling the complex relationship between formal discourse and art's return to, or ongoing engagement with, formal discourse and the distance from humanity that it often implies. Is that scene also a self-reflection on the contradictions and incompatibilities within artistic practice as such?

CN Yes, in the end, such a dialogue really is an artistic question: how to intervene in history and its moments of crisis? *Sometimes It Was Beautiful* is really a film about itself. There are parallels between what the protagonists address and the film itself. For me, before I'm able to comment on anything else, I have to comment on myself first. In that way, the film is an intervention *within* itself. But it's also a contribution to history. The claim to distance from history, which we sometimes invoke, is not always convincing. Sometimes it's necessary to claim distance from social struggles, for example in cultural situations where art can exist only when it claims distance from politics. But this distance can also be an excuse not to engage with the demands of our moment.

LC It appears to me that the opening sequence of *Sometimes It Was Beautiful*, which starts with a story about a protagonist who is "roller-skating through the mountains of history," is written in such a way that it sounds like the result of a cut-up technique using found words. I don't know if I'm projecting from the narrative of *Words after the World*, but you seem to be still working with a certain imaginary around the self-fashioning of words. What are you trying to open up in those two films in this respect?

CN Thanks for this fascinating question. In *Words after the World* what's at stake is the question of how to surmount the interdiction of speech. Is it enough that we can't speak anymore? Should we contend with such interdiction? What conditions can we put in place in order to navigate around these prohibitions? On the one hand, the film is addressing a lived reality. Historically, philosophers in Rwanda and the Great Lakes region could only become philosophers by first studying Christian theology. It's as though they never used their own words. I feel like they were faced with a crisis of discourse. Their efforts were monumental and I don't think I will ever equal that in my lifetime. Yet, for me, their work has shortcomings; the philosophers don't seem to have surmounted their crisis of discourse. Maybe it's unfair of me to say this, and others might disagree with me, but I feel that this contentment resulted in politically untenable situations.

I may "accuse" those historical philosophers of not having dealt with that crisis. But in my conversations with contemporary philosophers, I have also learned that some of them consider contemporary artists to be failing because they are supposedly not learning from history. "Our" elders were apparently more inspired – in fact precisely those that I am accusing of shortcomings. In other words, there's an understanding that we don't share time. As if those who are living now live in the past, and we are living in a present that is more related to what is to come. The particular problem faced by any of us then is to learn how to share time, how to align our temporal expectations and understandings. It's not so much about space. I feel that ultimately the dialogue is about how to learn to share time–history, the present, and the future–in a spiral manner.

LC In *Sometimes It Was Beautiful* the film cuts from the discussion of Nykvist's films to contemporary scenes of paper manufacturing processes. Through this anachronistic juxtaposition, we sense some kind of relationship between those production histories and economies that you elaborated on earlier in relation to industrial design. The imagery silently pulls those stories together. But what about the processes involved in making the film itself? I sensed, for example, that there was some kind of cut-up or found language process in the writing of the opening monologue. It felt like it engaged with that process of deconstruction and its histories, going back to Dada and re-emerging in the 1950s and 1960s. I don't know if that rings true for you.

CN Maybe it does, and if so, that might have to do with what can be called "desedimentation," a term I came across in *Toward an African Future: Of the Limit of World*, a book by Nahum D. Chandler, which is about how W. E. B. Du Bois understands history. Chandler doesn't discuss desedimentation in depth but, for me, that's one way of understanding translation; it's a convocation. But unlike unearthing, which suggests returning to the material conditions of internment, in *Sometimes It Was Beautiful* this "unearthing" is really pulverizing, making dust. The film unearths a substance that is no longer what it was when it was interred.

LC It's a reminder that you can't just dig up the past?

CN I'm not so sure that it's always possible, or that it's always desirable. In the case of the film, it was not possible. This brings me back to the narrator of *Sometimes It Was Beautiful*, which is a divinity that was once shared among the peoples of what are now the border regions of Congo, Rwanda, and Uganda. This divinity is mostly described as the wind, or as an "old woman." It's not a goddess. "She" is an intervener, someone able to perforate time and to see the past, but also able to see ahead to what the consequences of our current actions could be. This entity is able to stitch time, which is expressed in words, and these words enable worlds to be stitched together, and to convoke this unlikely group to gather and watch films from 1948 and comment upon them today.

Art as Non-Knowledge

A Dialogue with Sarat Maharaj

Lucy Cotter When we first met, I was very struck by your engagement with the notion of non-knowledge, which at the time you defined as a kind of knowledge that was beyond the radar of conscious thought and could hold open contradictions and incorporate intuition. I'd like to revisit that notion and think about what it means in itself and in relation to the potential of artistic research.

Sarat Maharaj Yes, the idea of non-knowledge has intrigued me in one way or another over many years, not being entirely happy to treat the processes of thinking through art entirely in academic terms. Learning from the academic but not being reduced to the academic, and then on the other hand, to ask the question, "What sorts of processes of thought open out without practice?" I have been trying to probe this fog, or foggy region, between history, theory, and practice. This fog was taken as a figure of thought from Marcel Duchamp's *The Large Glass* in which many transformations, many translations, many transfigurations, take place, from one kind of knowledge – scientific processes, chemical processes, biological processes – translating into religious, theological processes and sexual processes, from the virgin into the bride. I'm not too bothered whether it sounds spiritualistic or if it sounds materialist. Those distinctions do not entirely trouble me.

LC In the ten or more years since our first meeting, I have come across various definitions of non-knowledge, among them Georges Bataille's references to non-knowledge as something that is on the other side of knowledge. He proposes that if you really get into any kind of knowledge, you come to reach its limit and arrive on the other side of that knowledge into a kind of non-knowledge. This is as opposed to non-knowledge being in any way antagonistic to the production of knowledge. I wonder if artistic engagement with non-knowledge can circumvent that route through knowledge as such to get to that point of non-knowledge. It might start with non-knowledge or come from a place where you could enter non-knowledge, let's say, without taking the route through knowledge.

With regard to the spiritual, Bataille also refers to Henri Bergson saying that maybe the mystical is one of the few areas of thinking where you can also suspend consciousness or the rational, and that might open up other possibilities. I notice that when I theorize non-knowledge from my own perspective, I end up in a kind of a zone that is about some kind of otherness, almost an existential otherness. As someone who grew up Catholic, I find it interesting that this place, this thinking space, is a place of being, but also a place of mystery. I wonder if some of the problems surrounding the possibility of a discourse working across the academic and artistic are about the existence of this space that could contain some kind of a level of otherness that hasn't been named or pinned down.

SM Yes, you've put it so clearly. I think that all those references are very important, and I think they give one pause for thought and make one really think of a sort of cultural studies map or philosophical studies map of recent times, which has had a very strong kind of gain to being materialist, and is deeply suspicious of claims that cannot be somehow validated or examined or questioned from a materialist or experiential and empirical basis. I have, generally, in thinking this, found that one could continue that tradition. To me, it's also a very binary tradition, and it has its limits. At some point, some further "t" word has to be introduced apart from translation, transformation, and transfiguration. In thinking about these issues, the issue of transcendence also has to be taken on board, which is one that sticks in the gullet of our recent history.

Bataille's grappling with the notion of the sacred and trying to understand the economies of the sacred, I find deeply interesting. But ultimately, Bataille, being the brilliant thinker that he is or was, understands that the tradition of philosophizing in the West is to build a system. And for me, straightaway, this would grate against the notion of non-knowledge, that one could ever have a system of non-knowledge. For me, non-knowledge would be, as Bataille calls his system, an incomplete system, just because he senses that the notion of a system is deeply contradictory.

LC And there is a necessity for the unfinished.

SM For the unfinished, for the incompleteness. Therefore for me, it is the work in "pregross," the Joycean term, not progress, but *pregross*, that you never reach the gross form, the full bulk; you can never flesh out the full thing. It will always remain in this pregross form and that might be also, as a pun on the term, the very grossness of the project. That it's about size, it spills over, it's sprawling and so on, so the work in pregross is about the incompleteness, the definitively unfinished. If we shift back to Duchamp, which are terms I've used to say why this should not be seen as a project in system-building philosophy, we must retain that notion of the do-it-yourself engineered patchwork that an artist's practice involves.

LC A kind of bricolage.

SM Indeed, and then we move from Bataille, backward to an engagement with Bergson's thinking, the sharp notion of intellect versus creative intuition, which is so central to the mapping of knowledge that he gives us.

LC Bergson's writings on intuition are the closest I can find to being able to think through some aspects of artistic thinking, and also the potential for what that means in terms of the production of knowledge or something other than knowledge as we know it. But, on the other hand, Bergson was interested in creating a *method* of intuition, and I would like to also disassociate from the creation of a methodology. I would prefer to rescue some of his ideas around intuition, to look at how it functions, and what makes it possible.

SM Absolutely, but if we move beyond Bataille, then I think of the newer systems of non-knowledge that emerged in France. Lowell's thinking is a huge system built around the notion of non-knowledge, whereas my views to some extent draw a little bit from the struggle over the sacred and refer, rather, to the great Christian mystic, Meister Eckhart, who for me transcends continents, transcends cultures; he is the most eschatological of speculative thinkers. I think this has remained something to tussle with, this strand of the spiritual-sacred-ecstatic experience, which comes from nowhere and is going nowhere.

It is this nowhereness of non-knowledge that for me is the creative moment that you cannot reduce to a program or a protocol and therefore takes away that systemic quality that philosophical thought gives to it. At the beginning of an art project, we don't know where the work's inspirations, nudges, or hints, come from; we just don't know. We might say, "Well, it was when I heard this composition that I went down this road of making it." But we don't know how this slow gathering of elements takes place and this configuration emerges that we begin to work at and call art, and we don't know where it's going. This is why we have to retain the indeterminacy of this non-knowledge space.

LC In a lot of recent discussions around artistic research, there has been a sense that it's a discipline that has been almost forced into birth, through the Bologna Accord and so on. But when we return to a notion like non-knowledge in relation to artistic research, you can sense that it's a search for a more organic relationship, for something that is already inherent and which exists, but is now being hammered into methodologies, into temporal structures. In an earlier conversation, we talked about your thoughts about Paleolithic caves in relation to economics, and I am interested in how, through one person's interest, and also through the creative interests that arise partly from their personal biography and the routes they've taken in their life, that you can have this kind of an organic coming together of things which would no longer be allowed to sit next to each other. There is a freedom within the artistic, maybe because this personal element will always weave things in unexpected ways and point in directions that have nothing to do with the existence of disciplines; it is freed from making those divisions.

SM Absolutely. This is why I have somewhat gravitated toward thinking that the practitioner – I wouldn't even want to use the word artist at this stage – gets involved in a practice that's created. The practitioner is a person I would like to describe as "clueless," and this state of "cluelessness" is my most recent way of describing the terrain of non-knowledge. I've tried to find more colloquial ways of describing this thing, so cluelessness in everyday, idiomatic language means you haven't a clue about this thing, where you're stumbling around, you're blundering, you're flat-footed.

I rather like the idea of the practitioner being flat-footed because then they're dabbling in all sorts of academic disciplines without having the rigor or mastery over those disciplines, but they're quite happy to take a bit of physics, a bit of chemistry, a bit of anthropology and use that to jumpstart their artwork. Some people might describe it as a moment of ignorance, but I would tone it down and say flat-footedness, cluelessness. This brings down the slightly daunting term non-knowledge, which I have in the past tried to unpack through John Cage's reference to certain aspects of Indian, Hindu Buddhist thought, where he uses the phrase "*Neti, neti, neti*," which is attributed to Buddha. In his philosophical debates, he always refused to either found or negate the notion that there was an ultimate reality. This is why there is a kind of skepticism that's peculiar to this phase of ancient Indian thought, which tries not to simply say that something exists or doesn't exist because this binary opposition leaves one trapped in the same problematic way.

This also exists in Pyrrhonistic skepticism in the ancient Greek world, but it largely disappears from Western thinking until it surfaces in philosophy of science with Karl Popper's skepticism, his hypothesis that we can never know what knowledge is. We can only say that we have failed to attain it and in failing, we get a glimpse of what it might possibly be; an approximate to the state that we call knowledge. Knowledge production isn't about verifying something only, bringing all the evidence to back it up. It is only when you are able to disprove a hypothesis and show that it doesn't work that we have a glimpse of knowledge. So it's about an approximation and the importance of failure, then, in the heart of scientific production of knowledge that is crucial to our understanding of that whole scenario of knowledge production.

LC Considering failure also brings up the question of success and the relationship between art and the art market. An Irish artist, Brian Maguire, once suggested to me that the existence of the PhD in Fine Art might protect ways of working that could not survive in the market. There isn't a lot of space at the moment, even within artistic discourse, for long periods of not knowing, for failure, for very open-ended experimentation. There is a tendency toward branding an artist, expecting particular discourses, wanting references, wanting a press release, almost before the work is finished. Instead of polarizing the academic and the artistic, I want to acknowledge that there is a really creative space within both. I think they're both suffering from the difficulty of keeping that open space intact, which in the past has been called "research." Whether we're talking about artistic research or academic research, it's a space for thinking or creative development that can embrace the quality of not knowing as something valuable rather than tracking a route.

SM I think that's a very, very perceptive point. It's also important that the question of non-knowledge is not just posed outside of institutions. It must first begin by questioning the state of knowledge production within the institutions. And one of the biggest institutionalizing forces we face today is the rise of the creative industries. We have technology that makes people actively involved in making something, which leads to claims around these technologies, that everybody can be a creator. Everything is being, as it were, rethought in terms of creativity and the fact that you yourself are the agent who is the doer in this, so you are an artist essentially and you are an entrepreneur at that too. Our workday has changed. You're not a worker anymore who then finds leisure, but you can be sitting in Starbucks with your laptop and you're a creator. You're both working and playing and relaxing and inventing and that goes on for twenty-four hours, regardless of the old division of the day.

So it is against this background of the creative industries in which the logic of many of our funding organizations for art–who do good work in many instances–see the production of artwork entirely in terms of this new entrepreneurial creativity. It has to do with making sure that you can parcel out and partition, in a new division of labor, what has to be produced. And in this instance, everything gets programmed, organized, so that the delivery is spot on and on time. Against that then is the cultivation of the space of non-knowledge, which comes from nowhere and is going nowhere, which is clueless. These non-values, or looked down-upon values, again become important to defend because they rub up against the grain of the general trend in which creativity is being captured and made captive to notions of entrepreneurialism. So I think that's how I would want to see the institutional setup.

LC I think another aspect of that is keeping space for the political because it's something else to be protected. What about the production of knowledge that nobody wants or wants to think about?

SM Yes, and also the production of knowledge that deals with domains that we would rather sweep out of vision and consider as absolutely rubbish or non-knowledge in a sense, what in the past was described as "excremental knowledge." And in this instance excremental comes back into the scene of vision and puts in new claims, but it is also a new validation of the epistemological map, a new validation of art practice as a form of search-inquiry-research-thinking-examination, possibilities of it being a scrutinizing instrument or tool of its own making that stands in its own right, that doesn't have to look over its shoulder, to be offered a crutch from the academic disciplines or anything else. So it is an attempt to really validate from within, from the nature of its own vagaries, from the nature of its own nowhereness. I'm using the word "nowhere" from Samuel Beckett here, but with other resonances and connotations added on.

LC Maybe this is why we arrive at these questions now, because we're dealing with multiplicities and complexities that cannot be broached, not to mention encompassed, within the kind of epistemological order that we've come from, the clean temporal lines. Maybe the artistic allows us to move into a space for what cannot be named.

SM Yes. Let's think out of the art practice itself and out of people like Cage, Beckett, Joyce and Duchamp, exciting practitioners who were grappling to open up a new space in which you understand creativity and its thrust in new ways. And above all, it was to introduce a new linguistic order, a new emotional order, a new somatic order, a new sonic order, if that's the right word. Maybe "disorder," if we are Joycean about this. A new kind of set of spaces opened up and these multiple or countless dimensions that Duchamp speaks of are not just three dimensions, but four dimensions and beyond four dimensions. He speaks of the possibility of there being multiple dimensions in which our existence comes to flourish and define itself.

LC This complexity has always existed but through the global, we're especially forced to deal with that complexity in the present.

SM Exactly. On the global level, we are dealing with so many times, so many cultures, telescoping together in ways. We're all "monolingual translators" in Richard Hamilton's sense, so one is not talking about translation as simply the mastery of many languages, but one is pressed upon in everyday experience to be in an act of translation. Again, the second point that you mentioned was that maybe all these questions of non-knowledge come up in a time of complexity when we have to think about cultural forces in terms of a model of chaos and complexity, rather than in nineteenth-century thermodynamic notions.

LC Precisely, because even the monolingual is now forced into that position.

SM We are forced, indeed, to model it in different ways, to try to understand it, and develop new figures, new metaphors, and new maps. Also, the world of physics tells us – for example, the brilliant physicist Lisa Randall and her scientific mate Raman Sundrum have been working together on the notion of there being an infinite multiplicity of dimensions in which we exist. Or Peter Higgs's great discovery for which he has been awarded the Nobel Prize comes to shed light on some things. It makes even more difficult how we sink in a large understanding of the universe with this quantum level of understanding.

There's no theory yet to bridge these two understandings of the universe we have, and also physicists apparently only understand four percent of the universe that is visible to us, so the invisible has become very important. Randall's and Sundrum's work is around this notion of the invisible dimension, the countless dimensions in which we exist. We seem to have fragments of understanding that we piece together, but bits of the jigsaw are missing and we cannot find ways of piecing them together.

LC I often see science as a more natural partner to artistic research than the humanities, precisely because it's forced to deal with acknowledging its own lack of knowledge and take this departure point to try and figure out the other ninety-six percent. It has findings that it doesn't want. Quantum physics has discovered things that nobody wants to deal with, like the phenomenon of pieces of matter, forcibly separated by geographical distances, apparently "communicating" with their counterparts.

SM That's exactly my point, yes, because it is, in fact, questions which are asked today–and I don't want to say too much about this, but just so that we can see that we're not just a bunch of crackpots *(laughter)*–these questions are being asked elsewhere with other rigor and other systematic thinking going on, like the question of whether consciousness itself is a product of a brain, as is being asked today.

LC In fact, Jung asked this question much earlier in very specific ways in *The Structure and Dynamics of the Psyche*. Where is the psyche? Where is the brain? What is the relationship between the two? He looked back at a history of philosophers from the pre-medieval period and found more openness to levels of complexity that tie up with some of the issues that we're dealing with now. And when I read Jung's discussion of those philosophers, I feel they're quite close to the position of the artist.

SM Yes, and hence Joyce's great fascination and involvement with Jung. There's a wonderful and dreadful pun in Joyce where he said, "They were yung and easily freudened."[1] *(both laugh)* So maybe it's the youth of Jung that we have in this kind of post-Freudian space perhaps, to reaffirm Jung, not as somewhat discredited because non-scientific, but someone who is thinking creatively and bringing together a new map through which we might understand.

LC Yes, through his intellectual journey, he was forced to encounter that other side of knowledge and enter the space beyond the known. If you read *Memories, Dreams, Reflections*, in which Jung addresses the more personal experiences informing what was going on in his other writings, then you can follow this profound and difficult confrontation with the unknown. Maybe what is comparable within the artistic realm is the courage to deal with that lack of tangible coordinates to hold on to. There is a kind of swimming through the darkness to find something, and that's a very confrontational space to work in. I think one of the reasons why the artistic has often operated on that delicate borderline of existential and psychic health is because it's not afraid to go into those places. And that's not something you can put on the agenda of the academic or the institution lightly.

SM Indeed. One very blunt sort of distinction I make is that in the academic context, you are in a state of tutelage to some notion of a ready-made body of knowledge for a long time. Until you've mastered that, you cannot find or speak within the discourse. Part of the flat-footed, cluelessness of the art practice is that there is, certainly in contemporary art, no sense of tutelage to a master. The old Zen Buddhist notion was, "If you see the master,

1 Joyce makes this observation in *Finnegans Wake*: "Be who? farther potential? and so wider but we grisly old Sykos who have done our unsmiling bit on alices when they were yung and easily freudened in the penumbra of the procuring room and what oracular compression we have had to apply to them." (New York: Viking Press, 1958), p. 202.

kill him." Now this wasn't as violent as actually killing your Zen master but getting rid of authority, feeling that there is an authority that you have to bend your knee to, each time the project has to be thought from scratch, and fresh with understanding given by the masters, but not with the reverential relationship that you're in with this position of tutelage.

LC Yes, one of the interesting things here is the question of discipline. There is a sense, looking at the artistic from the academic perspective, that one steps into a space of anything-goes; that there's a kind of sloppy openness in art but I think it's much closer to that kind of discipline. The constant self-confrontation requires discipline and also a discourse because art has its own internal orders. There is a sense that other people have been on this journey before and that it's important. It's inevitably a different journey and the outcome will be different, but people have been on this journey. As we enter non-knowledge, we also brush up against knowledge. We go in and out of those spaces.

SM That's a nice way of putting it and this is the indeterminacy I talk of, that we cannot therefore draw clear borders and boundaries around this notion of non-knowledge. I would not want to systematize it too much because I feel each time it is an exploration. The long periods of tutelage, learning the terrain, the territory, which is the academic world's task, is a tremendously disciplined rigor of its own when done well. There, too, there can be sloppiness, as we know. There can be the mannerisms of academic rigorous thinking, but not really the rigor that comes with exhaustive thinking. Ultimately for a long time, you can remain in what we could call the domain of exposition. You go there to do an exposition of Nietzsche's thinking, to take it apart, to understand how it works. It's a kind of secondary, a part of the *commentaria*; you are commenting on this text. Now, in the world of non-knowledge, the urge is for you to be in a creative activity. Something has to be not put through the paces of exposition but possibly through exploration so, for me, these are the distinctions between the fields.

LC In debates surrounding the establishment of the PhD in Fine Art, I have observed at times almost a feeling of envy from the academic perspective toward the position of the artist. Because when we talk about what it means to be on the other side of knowledge, the academic gets there through a slow route of accumulation. When somebody has reached a certain level of thinking, they can allow themselves the authority and the personal freedom to maybe break into that space, whereas the artistic often takes it as a departure point. It's already bestowed on the very young artist who hasn't earned it as such. Of course, they may incorporate given knowledge and go through some of those other routes by choice, but through *bricolage* they will only bring it in as they need it. But from an academic perspective, the fact that you do not have to earn to be in that position, the fact that it's a departure point almost seems...

SM Scandalous.

LC Scandalous. Yes!

SM Which is again part of the liberty, part of the flat-footedness, part of the cluelessness, part of the permissiveness of this space that we're talking about. An academic would make a very, very, very long journey through philosophy, only in the end to say that the answers exist in a painting by Paul Klee. So what is that about? At the end of all of Gilles Deleuze's work, he'd say, "Yes, but it is in the reading of D.H. Lawrence, in the understanding of Virginia Woolf's *Mrs. Dalloway* that we come close to the intensity of life that philosophy looks for." So why are the philosophers gesturing in the end to an artwork where the intensity of life lies? Whereas the artist, of course, is starting there! Ultimately it is that immersion in the musical, the sonic surge that counts. But all along we're doing musicology, we're unpacking what Beethoven did and so on, how Mozart did it, how John Cage did it, how Philip Glass did it … but ultimately, people like Glass take us right into the intensity of those moments.

LC Yes, this is also what Bergson talks about in terms of "false problems." The reason we can't find answers is that our questions are based on false problems in the first place. I have that sense also with discussions around art's relationship to artistic research. For me, this is art being able to claim or reclaim a space which it has always inhabited. I can almost hear a sigh of relief from artists of the past saying, "Now finally you can take art on board in relation to the formalist, the political, the philosophical, the intercultural, the spiritual, the in-between spaces, without contradiction." There have, of course, been major revisionist projects in art history to shift the frame of how we receive art, but it's not the same thing because it's reconstructing brick by brick. Artistic research enables a widening of the frame to allow the very organic relationships between artistic discourse and other discourses to simply emerge. They've always been there. The cutting out of a disciplinary frame, a linear temporality, a particular canon, that drive toward the product has always been tied up with the rather antagonistic presence of the art market. Artists themselves have always intuitively felt the freedom to be non-linear, to weave, to be aesthetic and political, to work across disciplines and art historical temporalities. Unfortunately, this openness is what the streamlining of art education seems to be closing down.

SM Yes, indeed. That's why I think some of us would like to defend these spaces or evoke them and nurture them, and elaborate them, and open them up in different ways. Maybe outside the formal status systems altogether, maybe the events of the biennale, forward on the edges, with new people coming in from the countryside in some of these events. The governments have one official agenda in mind, but what happens with artists around them? Something totally different. I'd like to imagine that somewhere deep in the Alps there are art schools that people have forgotten about with only three students and that these would be left out of Bologna, the culture industries, not plugged into the gallery systems or anything. But people are there doing something. Maybe in these kinds of spaces, the chinks exist where …

LC I don't think we even have to find those colleges deep in the Alps, because every individual artist has that going on in themselves. The thing is that artists have learned not to share it. I think artistic research maybe makes a little bit of space where some of that pre-thinking, that notebook phase, that rather internal, undefined space that cannot be well-articulated in art discourse, can be allowed to exist in some way. Maybe it can make more space for what doesn't seem acceptable to contemporary art discourse.

SM I mean the school in the Alps as a resistance to the systematization and the over-academicization and institutionalization of art studies. I mean some places might be left out and therefore offer spaces for community; communities and friendships and affiliations. That they are places where we can gather and create an ambience of friendship, through which things blossom, as happens elsewhere. But my other view is that each individual practitioner carries an academy in themselves, and this academy is something that you take out, unpack, and invite people to, wherever you are, and then the academy folds up. It's a portable academy of sorts; it's carried in you. So that too should ultimately be borne in mind.

LC The first time I tried to publicly unpack this area between art and knowledge was in a spontaneous once-off talk for art students. I gave this talk before I was visibly engaged with any discourse around artistic research. They were young art students, I knew the academy very well, and I felt free to speak from my personal experience as an artist and as someone who had just stepped into academia. At some moment during the talk, I mentioned spirituality and I remember one student coming up to me afterwards and thanking me for that. I was struck by her vulnerability and the sense of being silenced. Afterwards, I thought a lot about the fact that there are artists today who enter the art world because they have a personal relationship with art that connects to some kind of interior and even spiritual space. When they enter into a system where there isn't much openness to consider those things, they are confronted with whether they can or want to translate their creative practice into something which can stand on two legs and apply for funding and be considered as legitimate in relation to existing discourse.

I think there's a certain level of impoverishment in that unspoken transition. On the one hand, it can mark an initiation into the intellectual life of art, which I think is extremely important and very enriching but on the other hand, there's almost a banishment of interiority. I see artists who are close to this inner process being some of the least successful, the ones who drop out. They cannot risk making this space tangible; it's too vulnerable. Very often this process is complicated by questions of cultural integration and assimilation in a very rational, atheist environment.

SM Absolutely, and if you travel in the wider world, and you look at ordinary people's creativity and the things which they've created, you realize to what extent we've whittled down what we mean by creativity to this very, very narrow definition of artistic creativity and the contemporary art world. If we were to follow that, we'd simply disregard and dismiss the greater part of the world's creativity. And it takes forms that are so tied up with people's understanding of what we call the sacred or the spiritual. Our last thirty to forty years of cultural studies discourse have been so Marxist and materialist. This has been a great enlightenment in some ways compared to what existed before, but it also needs to be questioned. We need to move on and we need to see now, as it becomes clearer, that there are many blind spots in that materialism too, packing out the notion of genius, of authorship, of creativity. Suddenly, the world of technology, IT, and science are talking about creativity. And biology.

LC And art isn't talking about it. Art is embarrassed to talk about creativity …

SM Art is truly embarrassed and it's coming through the back door and has hit us in a way in which we cannot understand, but we were being so enlightened and materialist. If you're using the mystique and mystifications of creativity and authorship and genius and talent, then we even begin to speak about the work of art during this time. We begin to see that labor brought industrial production closer and closer to art and aesthetic production.

LC But this is another reason why knowledge production came back knocking on the door because if the arts no longer claim their uniqueness and their position in relation to creativity, they have to claim something. So if it's not a utilitarian social use, such as happened in Britain in the 1990s, then where is there to go? And knowledge – of course, you have the knowledge worker and so on – but knowledge is a space that may encompass the intellectual inheritance of the artistic, to re-enter and claim some kind of a position that distinguishes itself from industry.

SM Indeed. It has to, because by the very processes in which art thinks, it cannot program creativity in the way this is done in post-industrial production. It might call itself knowledge production and I call that "production" still in my writing because I'm generally opposed to the notion of it being seen only as transmission and transfer, as though you have ready-made knowledge and art can only be a site of transfer of that. But art is a point where knowledge is made from scratch in its own terms; from its own model something emerges which we value and which forces us to think about our experience, forces us to think about knowledge also in embodied terms, in digital terms, in algorithmic terms, whichever the case might be.

Artists see something lying there; they drag it in, and stitch something else onto it in this collage way of thinking. I think that because these processes are so intrinsic to art processes, they will crop up and question how creativity is understood in the creative industries, whether it is in the cultural creative industries or the hardcore material production industries, or in the immaterial, digital, algorithmic industries of IT. In all of these domains the question of creativities is posed but art, because of the very distinctive way in which it emerges, will pose questions to them.

LC Yet there is still the pressure of entrepreneurialism you addressed earlier.

SM Yes. Obviously, in an age where we have to survive through these institutions, defined by those notions of research and creativity, we have to play the game. By "we," I mean artists. Artists have to play the game of it along the way in getting their funding, in getting their works sold, or whatever the case might be, but that's a different issue ... But one has to be careful also that this other–what should I say?–non-university or non-academic validation of art research which takes place in the art system, in the art world, is of a kind in which all the discourses–philosophical, intellectual, conceptual–are not being used also to prop up or give an intellectual face to artworks, in order to market them; that they will become part of the promotional atmosphere of the work. Contemporary art is now, to a great extent, being promoted on the grounds of its intellectual credentials. We want to buy this work because we are told the artist is such a deep thinker and he's thinking about the world, he or she is saying this about politics, has this to offer on ethics. These have all become offerings as part of the promotion. So I think that is unexamined largely in the art system, in the gallery system, in the collector system, in the biennale system, in the big sales of art, that more and more the artist is managed and promoted and pumped up to be this intellectual, researching, thinking figure.

LC Yes, and what doesn't happen in that scenario is that the artist meets other thinkers who challenge and infiltrate their work, as well as those thinkers being confronted with artistic thinking. This is simply a case of sovereign, legitimated thought propping up the artwork, as you said, whereas the other way round, there's a possibility for new thought and the deepening or furthering of the artwork.

SM Yes, the artist is under more critical scrutiny too, and also the role of the curator here is questionable. The curator, who's not often a deeply scholarly person, is often very quick to pontificate about the scientific credentials of the work, the philosophical credentials of the work, and string it together and package it that way as part of The Big. That's the big danger of not making these terrains quite clear and not arguing them out; that curators, well-meaning as they might be, might sense something in art but they don't have time. They're dealing with a mega-show. They've not looked at these things in any detail, so they string it together and it all becomes part of the packaging.

LC Do you think the existence of the PhD in Fine Art creates the possibility and the demand for the artist to go deeper into existing discourses, and both claim their position of not knowing in a valid way, while also taking knowledge on board in a way that they haven't previously?

SM Exactly. They're questioning who knows, utilizing this possibility of unpacking and scrutinizing, questioning why I'm making these claims for creativity in my work, which might, in fact, lead to nothing – to a dead end. Many artists might find that, frankly, they've got nothing to say and in a way, like Wittgenstein, might call a halt to it all. The genuine ones will take the process right to the very end, I suppose. Many, like the great artists of our time, would stop creating, but others might just then find that this is a very, very valid activity of having this kind of scrutiny, examination, debate, going deeper – you as a tutor saying, "I'm sorry. If you are claiming that idea to illuminate this particular patch of your practice, then I don't think you really have understood that properly. Don't you think the rub-up between them is either a contradiction and that you should make something of that contradiction, or try to understand this body of thinking you're using more carefully?" Because one of the points about non-knowledge is that we are dealing with a world in which we do not follow a given map. We construct a map and we're paying some sort of acknowledgment to people who have made this journey before us.

LC This is the discipline and the rigor. It is there, it's just non-linear.

SM It's not linear, yes. So I think there are many questions and we can't take those outside the PhD in Fine Art, as it were, as having a better answer than those in the PhD, I suspect. And I think in this we share the same sort of aspirations, that the PhD space makes a framework available within which we can put under scrutiny;
a four-year process in which many things will be examined with a kind of intensity and continuity that doesn't happen elsewhere, because it

happens in a haphazard way or gets claimed very quickly by the curators and then becomes part of curatorial jargon.

LC It's also that the speed of the art world doesn't allow for reflection. It's production, production, production.

SM Exactly. And circulation and sales. As much as a curator might say–and I'm speaking as someone who has been in curating–"Let's slow it down, let's examine this, let's set up a seminar, let the work itself be the seminar." All sorts of strategies to delay the process. It's caught up in a circulatory system where the intellectual focus has been drawn in, very much, as I say, this promotional discourse and dialogue and ultimately, whether we like it or not, it's all for sales promotion.

If we just look at how someone like Thomas Hirschhorn begins in Documenta 11, and how deeply persuasive and convincing his own research is, that had nothing to do with the PhD but as a genuine artist in research in the city, with the unemployed, with the migrants, through his reading of Bataille and then moving on to the Davos project. Now, he's doing with Benjamin Buchloh and Hal Foster a kind of legitimization of the artist as knowledge producer. Hirschhorn's work didn't have to be re-academicized and passed through the most conservative art history departments of Harvard, Princeton, and Cambridge, which are only interested in validating the artist in some scheme of things, ultimately having to do with the American art market.

The fact that Hirschhorn worked with as rough-and-tumble, interesting, obscure, difficult-to-understand and digest a philosopher as his co-partner, Marcus Steinweg. It was precisely that opacity that was important in understanding the experience of Hirschhorn's projects. That he took Deleuze and just ripped up the pages, that we had to walk knee-deep through Deleuze texts in order to understand the drag of textual life, the drag of textual and intellectual thinking. This embodied way, as we understood it. The fact that Steinweg doesn't add very much clarity to it; he just adds to this further opacity in which we have to, as it were, walk through honey or some viscous material. You have to struggle to make almost bodily sense of these installations. That gets lost as soon as the art historian's voice is put over it, clarifies, and says, "But surely you have made a little bit of a mistake with Bataille there. And now we've got it right. This is the quote. That's the footnote."

LC This is the discontents of what artistic research could be … and *is* sometimes.

SM Yes. Exactly. So there is a lot to question across the whole thing. I don't think any one side has the answer, except I do see this potential, which we both have acknowledged, that is a space in which a certain scrutiny that is not possible elsewhere and a pace that is not possible elsewhere anymore, it seems, can exist.

Performance as Philosophy

A Dialogue with Manuela Infante

Lucy Cotter You have often described your practice as a playwright, theater director, writer, and musician as a "lab for embodied philosophy." Can you elaborate on why you see your work in those terms?

Manuela Infante Since I was very young, I've read philosophy more than fiction. I thought about studying philosophy at the university, but another part of me was into music and there was a level of abstraction in music and a level of mystery that I couldn't find in academic thinking. I later found that theater could be a place where I could do philosophy without having to respond to the academic structure or environment, and where I could allow the unknown to be given space and time. I wanted to try out ideas. It was like, "OK, you philosophers are saying the world is like this and that, and here we have a little machine that makes worlds, so why don't we try it out?" I just went to an architecture exhibition in Chicago where they simulated skyscrapers. They put tiny models of skyscrapers into wind tunnels to know if they're going to be able to sustain wind pressure. I feel that theater is a bit like that. You can create a little model of a world that uses the same actual forces: time, space, human beings, things. It's the real thing, it's not even a replica of it. You can actually try out philosophical ideas and see what happens. I don't think what's happening is a representation, I think it's an experimental world.

LC You also incorporate real historical figures and political situations into those experiments. Your earliest plays, like *Prat* (2002) and *Juana* (2004), underlined the fictional invention involved in writing history, and your current work engages with philosophy through performance in ways that have been described as "genre-bending."

MI Yes, on the one hand, I am interested in being able to think through reality, representation, humanity, history, colonialism, etc., but by giving a large amount of space to what we will never know about those things. If we put that in the center, I think we can produce knowledge. That's not the right way to say it, but I think we can think through the world, having the impossibility of knowing at the center of that thinking. For me, the academic world wasn't a place to do that.

LC A few years ago, you started to digest some thinking from the nonhuman turn in philosophy and also object-oriented philosophy. Artists Peter Fischli and David Weiss's video *Der Lauf Der Dinge* (The Way Things Go) (1987) was also an important departure point for your research into non-human performance. You started to develop the idea that you wanted to create a post-human theater. Can you say something about that transition in your work?

MI I have always approached my practice from the perspective of a post-structuralist theoretical education. I have done an MA in cultural analysis, so I was all about constructivism, gender as a construction, reality as a construction, etc. One of my early plays, *Christo* (2008), for example, is all about how Christ is layers of representation on top of representation and there's no original. The idea of the post-human was a 360-degree shift. The political idea of decentering humans turned my practice around. This movement counters any over-attachment to the radical constructivists of the last sixty years. I'm interested in what that means in terms of where we stand. Maybe posthumanism is the only thing I can do because "human" is a concept that has always excluded me, as a woman, as a lesbian, as a South American. Human has always been something that I am not, so posthumanism allows me to find a new center, which is not the white straight heterosexual thinker. Aside from that, it's also such a great way to break with the norms of theater! The Western theatrical tradition is anthropocentric; it's discourse oriented. It has a structure that has to do with a character, a human that finds an opposing force and deals with it.

When I came across Bruno Latour's actor-network theory, I found that he was speaking about actors and actions in ways that would totally disrupt theater as a discipline. In *Reassembling the Social* (2008) he asks, "When we are acting, what else is acting?" That's when he comes up with the idea of the "actant" to include other forms of agents. I'm fascinated by that politically, but also by how this thinking could transform theater as a thing. I'm a very big fan of formal exploration, so exploring the limits of what theater can do is fascinating in its own right. I do a lot of work that is devoted just to that. In the 1970s, the European avant-garde was able to explore formally what painting was, what theater was, etc., and now we're sort of "not allowed" to do that anymore because art has become so instrumental to institutions and politics. I think theater has become very utilitarian in that sense.

LC Your "post-human turn" started with your play *Realismo* (Realism) (2016), which is ironically titled because it undermined just about every possible aspect of realistic theater. The underlying narrative is a story about five generations in a family but the only continuity is the household objects that are always present, turning the humans into props. But the possibility of non-human theater seems to come much more fully into being in your latest play *Estado Vegetal* (Vegetative State) (2018–19), which moves into plant thinking, and the plant as "other." It's a play in which one woman takes on seven different roles, but you could say that plants are the main protagonists. How did you move from thinking about objects through performance to thinking about plants?

MI *Estado Vegetal* came from two different directions. First, there was an image that I had in my mind for a very long time. This idea used to be called *A Conference to Plants*, and it was just an image of a person speaking to plants. Like a plant audience in conference with a human. I had that image long before I ran into any of this thinking. I have a piece called *Rey Planta* (The Plant King) (2006), which is about a character that is still because he's in a vegetative state. So the main protagonist, the king, is sitting in a chair, and he can't move. You see him not moving and you hear his voice. That show was about separating the voice from the body, how that works in the theater, and what it would be like to watch a show in which someone is not moving. But the plant thing was also there.

On another level, every element that I feel has failed in a work is what I want to develop next. Whatever I fuck up in one show turns into the center of the next show. What I felt had failed in *Realismo* was something very political, which is the idea of representing otherness or giving voice to another. I've always been very critical of documentary theater because of that; the privileged position of this artist that gives voice to others. Even though these people are put on stage, I still feel that there's an authorization to speak that has been given by the artist. Momentarily, I felt that I was doing the same thing with things. I was trying to put objects on stage to "speak for themselves," and at the same time, I was hating them because I wanted to do beautiful things in this material opera and it just didn't work the way I wanted it to, which is obvious because these things have their own agencies. I was hating everybody and everything until I found myself in this paradoxical moment of realizing, "OK, there's something here that *I'm* not doing right."

LC How did thinking about plants help you out of that scenario?

MI Well, it was at that very moment that I came across Michael Marder's plant thinking or plant philosophy and he helped me to understand that what I needed to do was not represent these othernesses but rather find the otherness in me, which meant finding that plantness in the discipline. Not finding what is human in plants, which is something I really dislike about some new materialist thinking when it's very vitalist. I feel that they're trying to imprint life onto everything. They seem to imply that if we are living and we have a consciousness, then what we can do to make the world non-hierarchical is to think that everything else has life and consciousness. So what Marder was saying is, "Don't look for humanness in plants in order to read plants, just do something that's more humble and try to look at plantness in you." This idea was important for me in developing how I was going to work methodologically with the non-human for this new show, *Estado Vegetal*.

LC In *Plant Thinking: A Philosophy of Vegetal Life* (2013) Marder talks about plant thinking as "non-cognitive, non-ideational, non-imagistic thinking," which I thought was a wonderful analogy for how art comes into existence. How did you start the process of developing your play?

MI I started by finding ways to imitate plantness with the body of the theater piece. It was a very simple idea. Later I went on to read Stefano Mancuso, the plant neurobiologist, and I started to isolate certain concepts around plant behavior, like modularity, ramification, polyphonic communication, photosynthesis, and phototropy. I was thinking about how to make performance and undermine theatrical norms in those terms.

LC Most of *Estado Vegetal* was not conceived or "written" in the traditional sense but evolved using improvisation as a research process into planthood, undertaken in close collaboration with the play's sole human actor and co-author Marcela Salinas. What kind of improvisation and research process did you go through together?

MI We did the whole thing using improvisation, but there were a lot of different kinds of improvisation. For example, I would practice branching in a narrative with Marcela. I always work with actors that are able to allow their consciousness to flow. I need them to be able to produce material and not to be second-guessing themselves. I always look for people that I know can follow their gut feeling and speak it, and not be afraid. A lot o the work starts with creating an environment to be able to make that happen. Then we start practicing these concepts – for example, with branching I said to Marcela, "Tell me a story, starting with any character you want and whenever you quote somebody else in the story, whenever another human subject comes into the story, you need to branch off into that person." We would practice this branching for hours and hours. Many of the characters came from those branching improvisations. They were all characters who were somehow related to plants in a lateral way, like the fireman who crashed his motorcycle into a tree, or the old woman who talks to her houseplants. Later I realized that they were all characters who are somehow considered less than human. There's a weird little girl, there's a guy who doesn't live in the city, there's a woman who's a mother. It wasn't conscious, but I think we chose characters who were all marginal humans in a way.

Many things happened through these really simple exercises. If Marcela said things that

I liked, I would write them down and I was seeing how this branching thing worked so that later I could write it. I developed the phototropic aspect with the play's designer, Rocío Hernández. We talked a lot about phototropy, about how plants are always moving toward the light, whereas in theater the light follows the actors. We made a rule that the light would move when the actress was still, and the actress would move when the light was still so that they never happened together. We did silent improvisations to try out this idea of light changes. We practiced it a lot and the best moments came out of that practice.

LC Clearly, improvisation was central to developing the play, but *Estado Vegetal* is also partially a written thing. You used text as a medium to create a branching, modular, and repetitive form of narrative, which was very striking in its own right. To arrive at that structure is to really use the medium of writing as a craft.

MI In my memory, I never wrote, but I know I did. Usually, I write down everything actors say in an improvisation that I like, and then I work it through in a more literary way. Or they will say something that will spark an idea and I will develop that. But later, the actors also help me develop that writing from the character's perspective, considering how they would speak those thoughts. Then there's the writing that I do on my own. There are scenes where I really just sit down and write as a writer would. In every show, there's a mixture of these three things.

LC When I picture the structure of *Estado Vegetal*, I see two things. On the one hand, the play has a branching structure but on the other hand, it has a circular structure, like a vine plant, a creeper. It creeps around all the time, while also branching out. I'm trying to imagine how you sat down to arrange the words to create that particular form.

MI I knew I didn't want to touch the issue. I had "dancing around" as an image. I had the branching as an image. On my wall at home, I had a map of the scenes and things that I had liked and I sort of slowly sculpted it at the same time that everything else was happening. I would go back and forth between the rehearsal space and my home, so the structuring happened at the same time as the material. The really small things were coming to life at the same moment. They sort of informed each other. I think that's also a not knowing. I get this question a lot, "How does this happen?" I don't really know how this happens.

LC Well, you've already answered that question, because the form *is* the content and the content and the form were developing simultaneously.

MI Absolutely, and the content will also tell me the form. It will whisper the form to me. There's a lot of hearing back what the thing is saying. It's not like film or television, where you imagine a structure and fill it with dialogue, and then turn it into a thing. That makes no sense to me, although I do that writing to make a living. I guess it's more like how a visual artist works with materials. It's also a path in time, a rhythm more than a text. That's why I love Laurie Anderson so much. I feel very close to her medium, which is rhythm. I am sure her stories are the last things that happen, just like for me. What the show tells is the last thing that takes form.

LC What about modularity? You mentioned it as one of the qualities of plant structures and I see it coming back in the structure of the play. I think it's an interesting idea in terms of how to build or construct something.

MI Modularity is basically the defense mechanism of plants. Since plants cannot run, like animals do when they're attacked, they have evolved a form of passive resistance. It revolves around being replicated into identical models a million times so that every module has all the repeated organs. I love that idea. I don't know if it's Marder or Mancuso who says this, but it's a non-unitary form of government, a non-centralized government. Every local unity has its own brain, for example. The ends of roots are all brains. Each end is one brain but they make decisions together. I thought about modularity in terms of how to challenge the structure of theater in two ways. The first was that I would practice having the same lines of text be said by every character. My original aim was to have the characters speak the exact same words as each other, but it became very monotonous and difficult. In the end, about fifty per cent of the text is repeated by every different character but said or organized in a different way, so that it seems like a different story. That was how we imitated modularity. Another aspect of modularity is the idea that every part of the plant is self-contained. I worked toward *Estado Vegetal* being a piece in which every scene could be done on its own; it's self-contained. It has a narrative structure of its own, so there isn't a sense of unity. There's no centralized government in the narrative structure, I hope. That's what I tried to do.

LC Did the modularity of plants also lead you to think about multiplicity?

MI Yes, the multiplicity idea comes from the same point, since plants are not individuals because they're dividable–they're dividuals. We speak of multitudes; we cannot consider a plant to be a single plant but rather a "them," which is very interesting in terms of new gender identities. I have thought a lot about post-identity as a form of acting but multiplicity is a very plant thing. So I was thinking, "How can I make Marcela multiple? How can I make her a 'them'?" That's when the looper pedal came in, which is a pedal that musicians use to record layers of music so that one musician can turn into a whole band. So I thought, "That's what I need, I need her to turn into a choir." The looper also became a tool to rethink playwriting. What does it mean to write in layers? Piling time onto each other instead of moving forward. I tried it out in one scene and it's something I really want to explore in my play about rocks. I am wondering how sedimentation can be a narrative structure ... but that's the next show.

LC Going back to post-identity, you mentioned in a recent lecture that you are interested in the work of Ursula Le Guin. In some of her early novels, she also dealt with the multiplicity of gender and sexual identities, with characters that could take on or have different aspects of their identity present at different moments in their lives. For me, this also related to some of the multiplicity of the plant structures that you've talked about. There aren't many lines explicitly addressing gender identity but there is a sense of gender multiplicity weaving in and out of *Estado Vegetal*. I'm wondering if there was a conscious relationship between how you are querying some of the structures of theater and some of her ideas. Especially because Le Guin has a speculative-fiction take on multiplicity, gender, and sexuality.

MI Yes, and I only realized that myself when the idea of multiplicity came in and I wanted Marcela to be multiple. This happened during a big feminist wave in Chile and I was with my students thinking about how post-identity can come into theater and what it does to theater. Not only in the sense of messing up the genders, but also in the sense that in classical theater one actor equals one character and that's very essentialist, in a way. I realized while working with the students that I had never done a show where one actor does one character. I've always had them coming in and out of different characters. In a way, I think that was me doing post-identity in theater before I even realized it. With Marcela and the multiplicity of plants, it became super evident. I was watching the play the other day and I realized that I had also forgotten the fact that she is playing men and women. To me that's not even something anymore, I don't even see it. But I like this idea and I'm going to take it further in my next work.

Going back to *Rey Planta*, maybe dividing the body from the voice somehow allows me to enter multiplicity. Plants are polyphonic; they communicate by means of chemicals so their voice is chemistry. Their smells are actually messages; they are the way that plants speak to each other. They are also polyphonic in the way that they send multiple messages in what we consider to be one smell. They're saying, "I'm hungry. There's sun on this side. We're drying up over here," all at the same time. When I started studying polyphony, I moved on to thinking about rocks, which is the subject of my next play, because of the birth of polyphony in music. Music used to be monophonic not that long ago. The idea of breaking music into harmony is a relatively new thing. That's why there's a little Bach piece in *Estado Vegetal* and why there are a lot of choirs in the show. So the chemical polyphony translates in the show as breaking into musical harmony. There's a moment where Marcela does a harmonic layering of a voice that turns into the way the plant speaks in the end, so it's not only layers of voices, but it's layers of voices that are in different tones, and that's relevant to how baroque exploded into polyphony as a way of composing music. So there's that and there's the idea of what would it mean to work multiplicity into acting. Multiplicity in very multiple ways.

LC In the play's synopsis, you quote Marder as saying that "recognizing a valid 'other' in plants is also beginning to recognize that vegetal other within us."

MI When Marder says we have to not think about what of us is in plants but what of plants is in us, he's referring to DNA. He's really referring to the plants as our ancestors. As humans we're always thinking about some thing, one thing, even in this conversation, no matter how branching it is. And academic writing is all about unity. Marder asks how a piece could branch out into every direction at the same time, never coming back to the center, just like a plant. To me, this is a serious idea about how to break unity. Really branching out at the same time, which is something I haven't accomplished yet, and resisting the desire to tie things up back to a core and to make them resonate. Allowing something to branch endlessly away from the center.

LC Can we talk about that difficulty and that sense of resistance? You have mentioned wanting to put not knowing at the center of your work, which is not an easy thing to do. In your performances, you have tried to think how to keep these unknowable elements present in the work and create space for them but if there's still a pull toward unity, how do you negotiate those two things in relationship to each other?

MI That was another problem with *Realismo*, precisely that. It tried to bring in or make sense of the unknowable in a unified structure. It tried to organize. *Estado Vegetal* is more subtle because it happens in a disorganized manner. The way the unknown comes in and out of the show is there to pull the show further away from unity, not move toward unity. In *Realismo* the way the unknown comes in and out of the show is a way to make the show unitarian and comprehensible. I do feel that I make music with words and concepts and images.

LC It seemed to me that the way Marcela Salinas used her voice and her breathing started to open up the fact that the voice already contains so much that almost feels non-human.

MI It's fascinating that you say that. I have a new project in Singapore called *Eloquence* (2019–), which is a sound inquiry into women and voice, thinking about the voice in non-human ways. If I say "My voice is not mine," you're probably going to think that my voice is a construction of cultural, gender norms, etc., but there's another way in which my voice is not mine. It really is not mine in the sense that it only happens in resonance in a space outside of me. It's an ecstatic event, in the sense that it's outside of me. This new project will work halfway between a concert and a play, music and theater, sound and meaning. It will continue my previous work with electronic live processing and layering of voices to produce soundscapes. I'm very interested in choirs and voices precisely because of the way they negotiate human and non-human and how they negotiate discourse and matter in relation to each other.

LC By discourse and matter, do you also mean the moment the breath turns into a sound that can be decipherable as a language? This brings to mind Jean-Luc Nancy's book *Listening* (2007), where he reflects on the sounds that precede the voice and the body as a resonating chamber for sound.

MI Yes, I do mean that distinction Nancy makes between meaning and sound, and I also mean that in relation to the formation of the voice. There's a process that produces, that informs that waveform, which I think is informed by discourse and matter in a very intermixed, impossible-to-figure-out way. Also in the way that it's formed, it helpfully mixes up discourse and matter and it messes up nature-culture as a distinction. That's what I really like when I'm investigating voice. I like voiceovers and GPS voices. There's a Japanese duo that I love called the Formant Brothers. They have invented instruments that actually sound like voices. So, for example, they made an accordion and a piano that is able to speak. It orders a pizza; it's a very funny performance. Then they come into the whole idea where they say, "OK, what we finally understood is that our instrument is an interface to something that is speaking, but what is speaking?" There is no human actually speaking there. I think that the same question, even applied to human speaking, is pertinent. What am I an interface of? As a voice. And I think I'm not only an interface of whatever cultural norms you want to describe, but I'm also an interface of many non-human factors and elements.

LC That's fascinating, and the humor in their work also makes me realize that we've perhaps been talking about your plays in ways that might make them sound too like a dry reflection on philosophical topics. All of your works that I've seen are also very funny. They don't hold back from doing things that look absurd and weird. Like the scenes in *Estado Vegetal* where the plants start to whisper and become a kind of crowd, or the moments in *Realismo* where people talk back to the furniture. Can we talk about what performance makes happen when it turns to the comedic, which is unlikely to turn up as philosophy?

MI All of my work is very silly, it's always been like that. I always choose people who enjoy working with absurdity and silliness. I think that it's not far from philosophy, actually. For me, part of this learning the non-unitary and non-human has to do with allowing the piece to go wherever it's enjoyable. I don't know how else to say it. A lot of the rehearsal work is fooling around with stuff and it's very beautiful. I often say that theater is like dancing around a fire, the fire being the issue that you're working with. You can't touch it. You can just fool around with it. Fooling around is a way of alluding to something. You're acknowledging the fact that you cannot really speak about that thing. For me, fooling around is a very serious method for a non-human theater and you can't do that in the academy. It's really acknowledging the fact that I cannot speak for these things, or to these things, or on behalf of these things. I can only fool around with these things.

LC I remember that hilarious scene in *Estado Vegetal* when Marcela rolls a fake-plant-covered ball across the stage, which was like a deliberately unconvincing image of the earth going back to a state of planthood. That kind of comedic absurdity remains imprinted on my mind. I laughed a lot during *Estado Vegetal*, which seemed to make room for things to shift inside, to let go of the sense of who you think you are, watching the show. Some kind of malleability of self comes in and that humor is doing a lot of work to put one in a place where one might be open enough to receive a new perspective.

MI I like what you're saying about humor making space. When I was very young and had just started with theater, I had this premise that I said the first thing I'm going to do with people is make them laugh and love these characters. Then I can do anything else I want to do. I don't think of it like that anymore but there's also an idea that laughter is a nervous reaction to a paradigm change.

LC Yes, Georges Bataille talks about that in his writings on non-knowledge. He says that laughter can signal the sudden invasion of the unknown.

MI Laughing is just the body being moved from one place to another. I use laughter as a very strong tool to know what to keep. I use other tools but when I'm in rehearsal and I'm laughing, I follow that path.

Seeing as Unknowing

A Dialogue with Richard Mosse

Lucy Cotter Over the past thirteen years, you have been working on what we might loosely call a trilogy of films and related photographs that explore alternatives to photojournalistic modes of reportage. Often, you do this by subverting photo or film technologies that are originally designed for military use and using them for other ends. *The Enclave* (2013) engages with conflict in the Democratic Republic of Congo. *Incoming* (2017) examines the humanitarian crisis of immigration into the European Union, and *Broken Spectre* (2022) engages with the devastation of the Amazon basin and its related ecosystems. How do you determine your subject matter and the specific media with which you will engage with them? Maybe we can start with *The Enclave*?

Richard Mosse I'm looking for aggravated media, media that have some agency in the story that

I'm telling and can help the viewer unpack the complexity of it in ways beyond the literal thing that's depicted in the composition. With *The Enclave*, I was interested in using the film stock that Kodak discontinued in 2009, which was developed by the US military during World War II to identify camouflaged targets.

I was interested in several situations, but it struck me that the situation in eastern Congo was tragically underreported. According to projections by the International Rescue Committee, 5.4 million people had died of war-related causes from 2008 to 2018. Yet, the genocide in Darfur, which was far smaller, was generating ten times the amount of column inches in international newspapers because it was a pithy sound bite that celebrities could talk about, with clear victims and villains, whereas Congo was anything but black-and-white; it was super kaleidoscopic with over fifty armed groups at that time.

LC This impossibility of having an overview of the conflict is translated into a physical experience of disorientation within the six-channel film installation which, as I remember it from the Irish Pavilion in Venice, were juxtaposed as hanging panels. Each channel is thirty-nine minutes long, and as a viewer, it's unsettling that there's no sense of an overview or clear narrative. Instead, you're constantly repositioning yourself in relation to these different soundscapes, mentalscapes, and visualscapes. You feel implicated by the material in a different way than by a documentary film you can distance yourself from.

RM Eastern Congo's armed groups are frequently nomadic, moving through the forest whenever it's an advantage to them. We wanted to try to represent the kaleidoscopic nature of news coming out of the forest around Goma, which was very hard to verify and full of hearsay. You'd hear something one night, and the next morning you'd hear the opposite. We were walking into the forest for days to meet these armed groups on muddy trails across no-man's-land into their territories, often meeting them in the middle of nowhere and walking with them for another couple of days to their encampment or their HQ.

This is something I went off and started on my own in early 2010. I had quite a lot of contact with some of those paramilitaries and their leaders. I must have reached perhaps a dozen armed groups, certainly more than eight. That level of access would be quite unusual for a journalist, actually.

LC There are several moments in the work where danger is really palpable, but scenes of conflict are also juxtaposed with scenes of local people, carrying on day-to-day life with resilience and joy. I was conscious that when you show moments that would be dramatized by photojournalism, like coming across the body of a dead soldier on the ground, the visual representation is deliberately pulled back. In fact, we encounter some of the most harrowing information through sound overlaid on footage that doesn't show violence. This seems central to your rejection of a photojournalistic mode of looking.

RM *The Enclave* is oscillating between styles and grinding the gearbox in a way that is intentionally disrupting and challenging received viewpoints of eastern Congo's conflict, trying to bring out the inherent problems with photojournalism, which has been the bee in my bonnet for a long time and was certainly my subject, particularly with the work in Congo, which was very much a critique of photojournalism and its limitations.

I was trying to push, amplify, and extend the language in my own idiosyncratic way, which, of course, upset a lot of photojournalists. I have always felt deeply ambivalent toward photography. I find photography inherently predatory and problematic. I think that self-loathing is generative for me as an artist.

LC The fact that the apparent reality we see is equally a constructed representation is foregrounded by your idiosyncratic use of infrared film. A lot of the visuals have an intense, almost bubblegum pink color so that viewers are immediately plunged into something that is both real and surreal. There's a lot of footage of a dense forested or bush landscape, but the greens are also rendered red through this infrared film.

It feels more like an internal image in your own mind as a viewer watching it. There's something about the fictive nature, the dreamlike aspect that plants it more deeply in your mind, even though you know it's constructed. There's a paradox there in terms of how it works on you as a viewer. Usually, if you see that level of abstraction from reality in an image, it's in your dreams, so it feels like an externalized dream sequence that you somehow take back into your own body.

RM Yes, for sure. That film's palette is "false color." That's what they call it scientifically, as it doesn't relate to what we see. We're primarily looking at a spectrum of light that's invisible to human eyes. Alongside anything else that you might bring to it, a film made in false color foregrounds and emphasizes the fact that it is constructed. That was at the foundation of the whole work. There was something transgressive about this willful violation of photojournalism's naturalism and its claims of truth and transparency.

LC There were times when I felt a pushback of my own expectations as a European viewer. One was the scene where a little girl is coming down a path and ahead of her there are corpses of dead soldiers. I had the expectation that the innocence of the child would be ruined by this traumatic sight, but you see the child's face and watch her facial expression change as she breaks into a smile and jumps up and down. To me, this felt like the undoing of certain tropes that relate to photojournalistic storytelling.

RM Anna, that little girl who is the star of *The Enclave*, and her family and community – who are Mai-Mai Yakutumba who were at large in Fizi in South Kivu – were very interesting. Some of their older members, ones who were in the rebel group, claim to remember Che Guevara from when Che crossed Lake Tanganyika in the 1960s and tried, and failed, to convert Congo. In that scene, I think Anna is excited by the camera, so she starts dancing. She doesn't care about these simulated battles.

LC As viewers, we can't tell that it's simulated.

RM There's a tension there and a lot of decontextualization at play. That's what we did in a bunch of situations, but we weren't just alluding to the conflict because the conflict caught up with us too. My collaborator Trevor Tweeten and I were almost killed in the Battle of Goma. We had artillery coming down on us for about fourteen hours, all evening and throughout that night of November 19, 2012. We started shooting scenes the next morning after the M23 had won the battle and taken the city. There were plenty of real dead bodies. That's the scene right at the start and end of the looping film, which we deliberately graded with a desaturated, low-contrast palette, depicting scenes of the chaos of battle and sobering scenes of relatives who had come to identify the corpses on the street.

LC At one of the most brutal moments where we can see these bodies strewn along a road, this *cinema verité* is extended to include your presence and that of your team. We can hear you and your collaborators speaking about changing the film reel and there's a disjunction between your voices, as English-speaking white men, and what and who we are looking at.

This is the reality of much of photojournalism, which you make us experience, but what about your position as an artist? I thought about your next film *Incoming*, which addresses the refugee crisis on the doorstep of Europe. I wondered whether this chosen context was also a result of a wish to reposition yourself.

RM No, it wasn't a reaction or a defensive position. That was the year, 2014, when we had an exponential increase, a huge wave of illegal immigration, as they call it, across seas to southern Europe, and a lot of people were dying. I think it was more than a million people landing by sea in 2014 alone. At that point, Sophie Darlington, who works at BBC Planet Earth, who met me at the London opening of *The Enclave*, introduced me to this thermographic camera. It was a very strange and sinister technology, and I was blown away by it, as a potential tool. It didn't take a whole lot of thought to realize that the European refugee crisis, as it's known, would be the ideal subject for that unicorn medium, because the technology itself was designed for purposes like long-range border enforcement, insurgent detection, tracking, and targeting. But few would have chosen to turn this sinister technology on the vulnerable figure of the refugee crossing international borders.

Many refugees are climate refugees, so there's a great overlap between the two films in terms of the resource extraction for rare earth minerals in eastern Congo that's at the heart of that conflict. To take that to *Incoming* felt like a very organic evolution. I also kept working in Congo. In 2015, I brought *The Enclave* back to Goma to show it to people there, which was a very interesting experience in its own right. That was a really big undertaking. I had to buy all the equipment and ship it from Berlin and install it with generators, voltage stabilizers, and security. We had to build the whole setup in a hotel ballroom. It had a substructure interior chamber with sound-absorbing fabric; we didn't compromise the work whatsoever.

LC *Incoming* is an extensive film. It's fifty-two minutes long and it's filmed across Europe, the Middle East, and parts of North Africa, tracking the movement of people with this thermographic camera. Can you talk about the kind of visual capabilities you were working with and what they enabled you to do?

RM The camera can image human body heat from eighteen miles, which is thirty kilometers, so the first concern was one of privacy. The refugees we were documenting are vulnerable people, who don't necessarily want to be identified because there's an EU law called the Dublin Regulation that tries to limit the movement of people north across Europe from southern countries like Greece and Italy. The camera we were using doesn't depict the individual in a recognizable way. It's medium wave infrared, so it shows the radiant body heat rather than the individual. So, it provides anonymity for the individuals being filmed.

I felt that this medium was more appropriate than the Canons or Nikons used by armies of photojournalists on the coast of Greek islands to document these individuals, whose images could be used by EU immigration officials to send them back to Greece or Italy. A lot of them were trying to get to Germany or Sweden, for example, and wealthier nations that had better support for asylum seekers.

LC In *The Castle* (2018), the publication accompanying *Incoming*, there's an essay by Judith Butler in which they say that the problem of the immigration crisis concerns the media because a life cannot be perceived as a life. They talk about the evaluative structures around that. While the heat camera anonymizes, it also foregrounds the shared physical vulnerabilities of being human. By making us look differently at these human lives, they can be seen again as individuals, as flesh and blood, no different than our own. *Incoming* challenges us as viewers to be accountable, but it also challenges photojournalism as a field, and it exposes government surveillance techniques to the general public.

RM The thermal camera is seeing the radiant body heat of the individual depicted; the respiration, the blood circulation, the sweat–all these bodily functions–as biological organisms, the traces of life. It foregrounds the fact of mortality faced by people crossing cold seas, some of whom drown. If they get there, and even on the way there, they have to live in tents exposed to the elements. I believe the International Organization for Migration calls the Sahara the "Second Sea" as a lot of people die crossing that, which is in the film too. We worked in northern Niger documenting trucks of refugees traveling across the Sahara to try to make it into Libya and Algeria. Usually, they stay there for several months to work or be detained and then they try to bribe their way onto illegal boats in an attempt to make it to Italy, Lampedusa, or Malta, or simply be rescued by a passing ship and taken to Europe, where they would claim asylum.

The camera comes loaded as a medium with this extraordinary materiality of indexically measuring heat. It's deeply aggravated. It's part of weapons systems; it's not designed for filmmakers like me and Trevor. It's designed for governments, militaries, and police forces, and it's not generally sold to civilians. That upset some people, but it was intentional, the idea of using a weapon to tell the story of mass migration of refugees and asylum seekers who were being failed by the EU.

LC I want to talk about a moment in *Incoming* that, honestly, I was digesting for days after seeing the film. This relates to the effect of the subtlety with which violence is portrayed within the work. In one scene, we see a child receiving some kind of CPR. Then the image falls away and we're only left with the sound, which is becoming frenetic, and then an abstract, minimalist sound. But that sound resonates with the medical equipment, and in that resonance, there's a beeping that stops. It's subtle, as a viewer you're asking yourself if this means death. The next scene shows people in full surgical gear attending to a body. You assume that there is a need for more serious medical attention. But then the camera cuts to the edge of a body bag, and then it cuts very quickly to a refrigerator. We catch a glimpse of corpses in body bags being taken out of fridges. There are so many of them, and there's a horrible realization ... The physicality and the tangibility of these deaths is devastating.

I find it really interesting and powerful that there are moments like this that are maybe three or four seconds long, where the camera specifically shows very little. You're given just enough information to imply the extent of the violence. So, there's a sense of self-discovery and a personal shock that this is death we are looking at. It's not a headline or a statistic, it's fellow human beings who are dying. This brings us back to creating an alternative language to the photojournalistic.

RM Yes. When the screen goes black, that was outside on the pier in Lesbos, where one of the Aegean Sea's worst human trafficking disasters in living memory unfolded one afternoon on October 28, 2015, while we filmed from a clifftop. After a couple of hours of recording the disaster from a distance, we moved down to the port where survivors who'd been picked out of the ocean were being resuscitated. We deliberately decided not to show it, but you can hear it. A little girl is drowning, and you can hear her father crying for help. Then the Red Cross volunteers are struggling to revive her and get the water out of her lungs and their machine has a weird Swedish accent and beeps, which my collaborator Ben Frost worked in his own way to phase in. We stayed well back to give them space. There were other photographers from various agencies shooting. One Agence France-Presse photographer got disturbingly close, distracting the whole procedure. He was very invasive, and you can hear his shutter banging off nonstop.

LC Yes, it sounds like a weapon. For me, this was another one of these moments that are documentary but also become metaphoric, a phenomenon that repeats across your films. It's never overdetermined; it's an underdetermined metaphor, which allows space for the viewer. I experience it more fully as a result because I claim it as my own reading. Although it's been given to me, it has not been over-given.

RM That's great.

LC During the ten-plus years of collaborating with composer Ben Frost and cinematographer Trevor Tweeten, you have endured arduous, disturbing, and dangerous ways of working, which points to how invested each of you is. Can we talk about this collaboration, and how it works?

RM Yes, and another collaborator on these three films is Jerome Thelia, who does the post-production digital color, which is so important because the films often involve such expressive color and contrast.

Long ago, I used to make my own little video artworks, but they were very handmade and rough around the edges, whereas Trevor's approach is far more lyrical and highly crafted. He's extremely poetic and very dreamlike, and the result is that the recent larger films are very chimerical or oneiric. He is also very interested in dance and choreography. For *The Enclave*, we bought an old Steadicam and then an upgraded version for *Incoming*. A lot of my work is about hidden histories written in the landscape, and Trevor found a way to connect spaces by moving the camera through them in this powerful way. The thermal camera, with all the peripherals, weighed about seventy kilograms, or about

154 pounds, and he was able to dance with it, to move gracefully through very unpredictable scenarios in war zones, refugee camps, etc. It's more than graceful, it's haunting – the hovering optic, the floating gaze moving through spaces. Some people find it disturbing.

LC What about the sound aspect of the films? In your early solo video works like *Theatre of War*, you were already using field recordings and non-synced sound in experimental ways. But with the long-term films and Ben Frost's collaboration, it is more layered. Different soundscapes are superimposed so that you're constantly both in the place of the action and simultaneously in some other mentalscape that might have more to do with the politics of the moment or the impending violence of the scene. I'm also thinking of a scene in *The Enclave* where young boys are lifting the tarps covering the faces of dead soldiers, but the sound is withheld. It's really jarring.

RM Yes, we sucked the sound out in that scene so it's totally silent. Ben is one of the more admired electronic musicians of our time. He's able to purify the concepts of music down to something really simple and then layer them up again. His work can be very intense. At the same time as the hairs at the back of your neck go up, he's also hitting you with an almost imperceptible low end, so low that you can't really hear it with your ears, but you can feel it in your body. It does something to your animal instincts. The sound fields he creates for the final work are incredibly spatial.

LC How do the three of you undergo that making process together?

RM Generally, Ben would tend to write tracks while traveling with us in the field and after returning with our footage, Trevor and I would use those tracks while editing the material in the studio in New York to figure out which scenes would go with what sounds and then lay them down on editing timelines across multiple projectors. Then we would go away and shoot some more and come back, building it up in an additive way over the course of the two or three years of production.

All of this is dependent on funding. Because these films were all made on an absolute shoestring, it's all very homemade, artisanal filmmaking. Sometimes I seek funding from patrons in the art world, collectors who really believe in the work, or perhaps the galleries. Museums might even come on as commissioners toward a later stage, or if you're very lucky you might receive a grant. VIA Art Fund was extremely generous in helping fund my last film. It's very hard to get funding because there isn't really a funding structure in place for this sort of thing.

LC The structures are still not made for long-term artistic research projects, stretching over several years.

RM No, they really aren't. And nobody else makes these kinds of videos, and for good reason: they're very hard to do.

LC Let's talk about your most recent project, *Broken Spectre*. You, Ben, and Trevor worked on the film in Brazil and Ecuador for three years, and it was shown for the first time in 2022 in Australia and the United Kingdom, and in 2023 in the United States and Europe. The project sets out to engage with the destruction of the Amazon, with climate crisis, and the humanitarian crisis of Indigenous peoples in the region. It's a massive undertaking. The film is epic in scope; it's a seventy-four-minute immersive experience. How did this huge project come about?

RM Well, there's a short and a long answer. The long answer is that I was a little traumatized and very tired by seven years of nonstop production in the field as well as constant flying for openings; it's quite a strange existence going from a war zone to a champagne soiree or museum gala and back again. I just wanted to make something for myself, to recharge. It might seem strange, but I'd been thinking for over ten years about ultraviolet light and how it fluoresces in plants. It is used by scientists in UV microscopy photography to reveal lots of things about plants on a very microscopic level. I'd even bought special fluorite and quartz lenses because reflected ultraviolet light doesn't pass through glass. So, I went to the cloud forest in Ecuador and photographed orchids and other plants glowing at night.

Of course, around this time, we were all beginning to seriously think about what's happening to the world and the climate. And, while I was in Ecuador, [Jair] Bolsonaro was elected in Brazil, and it became a troubling time, with him bolstering the willful destruction of the Amazon. He defunded the environmental protection agencies like IBAMA, ICMBIO, and FUNAI, who represent Indigenous rights. The head of INPE, the Brazilian Aerospace Research Agency, who presented alarming information about the extent and scale of deforestation was immediately fired.

At the start, I thought, "Okay, so I'll go to Brazil." But climate is the most difficult thing to relate as a storyteller because it's so much bigger than us. We can see its symptoms or its expressions locally in our environment, but we can't really depict it, it's way beyond what we can perceive. How to fit that into the lens?

I was struggling to adequately convey climate change, global heating, and the hyper-object of the world's largest tropical rainforest, which spans nine countries. I'm always interested in these points at which perception fails, and particularly when photographic technologies fail us. Those were my initial ideas, and there were different conversations between me, Ben, and Trevor, which coalesced. We went to Brazil together in September 2019 when the mass media was talking widely about the Amazon being burned at a rate that nobody had ever seen before.

LC You wanted to encompass much more than the mass media is able to portray. How did you tackle the issue of somehow showing or communicating the scale of that destruction?

RM Well, simply put, there are three scales in the film, and each has its own distinct medium. One was the micro, the plant life in the cloud forest at night. Another was the macro, with scenes of mass destruction shot from the helicopter over the topography. Then the third one was the human scale. We felt that we needed something for people to relate to because people tend not to relate to the nonhuman, sadly. We tried to incorporate that, and in doing so, we decided to use black-and-white film to tell a story that evokes the Western in cinema history, which is a very fraught genre, for obvious reasons, as it's steeped in ideas like Manifest Destiny and the dominion or colonization of the natural world and Indigenous communities, which happened 150 years ago here in the US, and in Europe a few centuries before that.

LC The trees themselves become protagonists within *Broken Spectre*. You can almost feel the pain of a huge old-growth tree being chainsawed by a meagre human being. The sense of plant life being entirely present with its own mode of existence is perhaps most haunting in the filming of the biome from the forest floor. Is that what emerged from your photographic experiments with UV light in Ecuador?

RM Exactly. That strange footage emerged from my earlier gothic portraits of flowers at night. Trevor tried to turn those images into film footage using time-lapse technology, which was very painstaking and complicated, but he did a great job. We cut between that material in the film in a disjunctive way to interrupt the realism created by these other approaches. As in *The Enclave*, you're seduced into the visual language, you settle into it, and then you're jolted out of it, from the very grainy analogue black-and-white footage into this deeply unfamiliar, almost CGI galaxy. Some people don't know what they're looking at. Some people think it's underwater.

LC Yes, and the otherworldly sound gives the feeling that these plants are communicating with each other.

RM Ben Frost emulated what we were doing visually by employing an ultrasonic recorder to register the rainforest's sounds that we can't hear, like the sounds of bats and insects, and pitching them down into an audible register.

LC How did you go about filming the land? There are soul-destroying vistas of large-scale destruction that have a larger-than-life presence.

RM To make the aerial or “macro” scenes, I became interested in multispectral technologies in the satellites that INPE would launch to monitor the Amazon. The multispectral data from these satellites is carefully analyzed by environmental scientists at MapBiomas or Imazon. Yet, I found that the same technology was also being used by multinational mining companies and agribusiness interests to exploit the land more profitably and to help them see the world in terms of resource extraction.

Again, this medium had that sort of magical correlation, for me, of agency within the subject, so it's on the crossroads, at the crux of its destruction, as well as its conservation. I found a multispectral camera that was being sold to farmers and made by a company in Oregon, which was small enough to be carried on a drone. With this drone, I could map environmental crime sites from above, looking straight down from a sort of God's-eye resource extraction point of view. I used GIS, Geographic Information Systems software, to dial in on certain aspects of the data that I had gathered using this multispectral camera to reveal the actual health or state of degradation of the plant life, and more. Sometimes it revealed fronts of subterranean “zombie fires,” invisible to the human eye. It's a powerful technology.

The aerial shots in the film were shot with a custom-made, multispectral camera that we had to build ourselves using the same technology employed in environmental monitoring satellites such as Sentinel 2 or Landsat. We were imaging each channel in very narrow bandwidths of only ten nanometers. No one's ever made a multispectral video camera, which can capture this kind of imagery at twenty-four frames per second or more, because nobody has ever needed one. We had to custom design this thing and work with a machine vision company in Toronto that works with spectroscopy. All through the pandemic, we were working on this crazy camera that cost me a lot of money. It was too heavy for a drone, so we had to mount it onto the nose of a helicopter.

LC As a viewer, you're constantly invited to shift your own mode of looking all the time, and each shift immerses you fully in a specific reality. There's an ongoing alternation between black-and-white imagery and surreal full-color images that are pregnant with mood and atmosphere. Because it's multichannel, they are also juxtaposed regularly, which is unusual. This color use nudges these images toward being a metaphor, but there's also a sense of it invoking different temporalities. Can you say a bit more about this switch from one type of imagery to another?

RM Just as I wanted to switch scales throughout the work, I also wanted to switch between very specific points of the electromagnetic spectrum, to see in different temporalities. The effect is very jarring. It's like drop-kicking your brain's sense of reality with a different medium altogether from digital to analog, switching from hyperreal, close-up, ultraviolet footage shot with SLR cameras to the sweeping and yawing aerial multispectral topographic forms, and then back to the anachronistic, grainy, black-and-white footage, alluding to the Western, but which almost feels like Italian neo-Realism. This film has the luscious tonality of films from the late sixties and seventies, full of scratches, fingerprints, hair in the gate, as well as the fogging and debris of heat damage–because the black-and-white film can also see infrared and is heat sensitive. We had to hand process it ourselves, so it's full of marks and mottling. These are very different ways of seeing, with dramatic scalar shifts, and there's a sort of perceptual irruption when you cut between them.

LC Can we turn to the human-scale imagery? There are several cowboy scenes in black and white, and this visual language is a reference to old Western movies as you've noted. The film opens with a portrait of a very ordinary family. They're ranchers, and they're not rich. The kid is playing with his toy cows. You can see the logic of cutting down trees and burning the debris to make pastureland from the position of locals, who are looking for a means of survival. It's a humbling entry point into this sometimes-shocking rancher culture, which is often brought in by millionaire farmers.

RM Yes. The film tries to document as many processes of deforestation as possible, but to also portray the ambivalence of the lives of the people harming the land and the environment, who the media portray as criminals, because some of them are small-scale farmers or professional burners with few opportunities in life–they have to put food on the table for their family. They have less choice in the matter of deforestation, many of them, than we do, and less agency as consumers than your average citizen of more developed nations. That ambiguity is something we've tried to really bring to the forefront in all of the work we've made because it's so important.

LC The Western trope is pierced through, not only by showing the ambiguities of the cowboys' lived realities, but also by foregrounding Indigenous agency in the face of this destruction. Can we talk about one of the most powerful scenes in the film, a long monologue by a woman from the Yanomami people who makes a plea to you and your crew? She challenges you as outsiders coming from a place where governments have money, to send protection, to get the illegal miners out of there. It's so powerful; she is asking all of us Western viewers to use our agency. And it puts into the picture your deep accountability towards the people you represent. It pushes directly back against any trope of the old cowboy films because this Indigenous woman is the most voiced person in the film.

RM Adneia is a powerful speaker from the community of Palimi-ú, a Yanomami village on the River Uraricoera in Roraima State on the northern Brazilian border with Venezuela. At that point, when we visited them, they were being terrorized on an almost nightly basis by the miners who were armed with automatic weapons, attacking their village huts with gunfire and tear gas. You can feel it in Adneia's words, her delivery is raging with anger and emotionally charged, but not in a sentimental way. It's very urgent. It was so hard to get that language translated. It took me eight months, but I realized that we had something very important that they were asking us to convey as widely as possible.

One of the few things we're able to do as artists is to communicate–as documentary photographers too. She speaks for herself, and it is a seven-minute speech that we didn't touch in terms of editing. We decided not to go near it because we wanted to preserve her rhetorical authorship, and we wanted people to feel like they were there. Adneia's speech is very real. It's the only time we've deliberately used sync dialogue in any of my films. It was a very big step for us.

LC Do you feel like you were able to answer her call in some way? I know that not long after the film's release, President Bolsonaro was succeeded by Lula da Silva, who has taken measures to protect the Yanomami people.

RM John Kerry went to see *Broken Spectre* in London. He's the first US Special Presidential Envoy for Climate as part of Biden's cabinet. He reached out through his office to ask me for the link to the film because he was so moved by Adneia. I sent the link, which I believe was shared with President Lula and Environment Minister Marina Silva who were visiting Washington, DC. So, we managed to do what Adneia was asking us by a stroke of luck. It's rare that art intersects with governmental power in such a way.

An interesting element is that what Adneia is asking for is a wire blockade across the river to stop the gold mining boats. One of the first things that the Brazilian Army did when they went into Yanomami Territory under Silva's instruction to clear the miners was to build that wire across the river. It's wonderful. I've been trying to raise the money to go back to film all of this because these operations are ongoing, but I haven't managed to.

LC I read an article that cited you as saying that *Broken Spectre* was the first work that you would describe as activist. Can you say something about that?

RM Clearly, Adneia presents the viewer with big questions. After berating Bolsonaro and then confronting me and, by extension, the viewer, she then turns and asks, more philosophically, "Who will recover this forest? We're really thinking about who will do this." In the next scene, the film cuts to the ATL [Acampamento Terra Livre] in Brasília, a huge annual conference of Indigenous communities. At this time, Bolsonaro was trying to change the laws to strip certain groups of their land rights. They were protesting en masse in front of the Supreme Court of Brazil. That was very important imagery because it shows these people carrying out activism, and it shows democracy at work. In some ways, this scene answers Adneia's question. That's an example of activism at play in *Broken Spectre*, and I think that's what I was referring to with that statement. I've always been shy about the word "activist" because I agreed with Walter Benjamin's idea of the autonomous artwork, and how propaganda or agitprop undermines art; makes it less about questions and more about dictating answers. I've always kept my distance from that.

I suppose at a certain point, you have to fight for what you believe in. Perhaps it's time to embrace the term for better or worse. I think that *Broken Spectre* holds and sustains some of the ambiguity and complexity of the subject, at least I hope it does. I'm constantly walking tightropes between the two moons of the documentary image and contemporary art. That's where this strange art emerges, from the double gravitational pull of those two seemingly incommensurable poles, but also from the political, the activist, the aesthetic, and the artistic.

Sound as Knowledge

A Dialogue with Samson Young

Lucy Cotter Sound isn't necessarily the first medium people think about when they consider artistic research, but it's widely used by artists. You work as a composer and a visual artist, often weaving unexpected sounds and images together to build up scenarios that seem to cut across time and space. As a composer, you were already doing sound-based performances with projects like *Iphone Orchestra* (2009–10), but the transition into visual art seems to have allowed you to engage with sound as history, opening the way for major research projects like *For Whom the Bell Tolls* (2015–) and *Pastoral Music (But It Is Entirely Hollow)* (2014–). It seems to me that *Liquid Borders* (2012–14) was the turning point for this way of working, a project in which you charted the entire border between Hong Kong and China through sound. How did that project come about?

Samson Young The *Liquid Borders* project was partly a response to an announcement in 2012 by the then Hong Kong government that they were going to develop the buffer zone between Hong Kong and China, building residential and commercial spaces in that area. I became very interested in the anxiety that prompted, as well as the parallel high school student-led resistance to the government's plan to insert national education into the school curriculum. Thinking about the border as such a charged physical and psychological barrier, I realized that, like most people in Hong Kong, I had never seen it. It was always a closed area that you needed to apply for a permit to enter. So my original intention was to design an exercise to walk the border. I thought that if I took recordings in a methodical way, it would allow me to get to see all of these sights and give me time to think about the border's significance. So it started as an archiving exercise, collecting sounds and taking photographs of their locations. Then when an occasion arose, I started to think about what I could do to make something out of those recordings and photographs. Although I had been in several exhibitions, I had my first solo gallery show for *Liquid Borders* at the a.m. space in Hong Kong (2014), so I had to really think about what to do; think about how, as a composer, I could make an exhibition.

LC You also developed your own form of graphic notation for *Liquid Borders*, which relates to the "sound drawings" you are currently using to document located sound across several continents. Was that an important part of your transition to working as a visual artist?

SY I had previously collaborated with a visual artist and a digital poet but when we weren't able to continue, following my move to the US to study, I started to work in these other media myself. That's how I got into visual art. The *Liquid Borders* exhibition was the first time I showed graphic notation as something to look at, but graphical notation had always been a part of my compositional practice before. When I write music for ensembles, and especially when I write for chamber ensembles, I tend to use a lot of graphic notation. I do electro-acoustic music, which means that there's a live ensemble playing along to an electronic backing track, as it were, but for the ensemble to be able to follow the electronic track, they need some sort of a visual cue. So I spent a considerable amount of time trying to notate and transcribe the electronic sound of my own composition into scores so that the musicians could understand where they are in the music. With the graphic score for the *Liquid Borders* project, I was also going back to the pleasure I had found as a student, writing scores by hand. They had an architectural quality to them, with lines going everywhere. I was rediscovering that part of me outside of the musical part. Of course, there's a long history of graphic scores in contemporary music, but I think they're appreciated very differently in the musical context. Even really ornate scores like composer Peter Maxwell Davies's *Eight Songs for a Mad King* remain rather functional.

LC In the *Nocturne* project (2015), you presented sound drawings of historic firearms together with a sound performance based on night bombings in the Gaza Strip and other contemporary war locations, which people could experience live and through a radio broadcast. What were you thinking about, in bringing these sounds into the gallery space?

SY At the time, I was mostly thinking about the density of explosion sounds, which are very quick but have a lot of information packed into them. I wanted to make a graphic score of those sounds. I went through this process of looking at the spectrogram and repeatedly listening to the sounds so that I was able to spread them out on a two-dimensional plane and try to unpack them. I also started to think about that in relation to modernist painters who had done the reverse, compressing large temporal spans of music on one canvas. The studies of historic firearms were done first before I did the *Nocturne* performance and radio work; they prepared me for them.

LC Can we talk about the experience of the viewer in the *Nocturne* exhibition? You had on-site radio broadcasts of a performance by you, in which you used percussion and foley effects to recreate the sounds of bombings from the Gaza Strip and other locations. The sound and the rhythm resonated physically in the viewer's body; it was deeply evocative of experiences that one would not usually have outside of a war zone. For me, this is an example of how knowledge can be created and held in the body as a form of resonance. What was the significance for you personally in taking explosions into another very specific location, the gallery space?

SY I think I was starting to think about how to compose a space through that exhibition. When the audience walked into the gallery, they could see me doing the performance. They did hear some sound, but the sound was very soft because it wasn't amplified. It was me lightly tapping on a drum, or dropping some debris on foil, or using compressed gas, and things like that. They saw this whole theatrical dance, but it was only when they picked up a hand-held radio and tuned it to the radio station that they started to hear these sounds highly amplified and distorted. Because it was coming out of a radio, the sound had this lo-fi quality about it. There was another layer of experience when the audience took the radio and walked around the gallery space. They walked behind me and saw that that was what I was doing. I think the viewer felt that they were at a different proximity from the sound they were hearing and, by extension, their proximity to me. When people saw that I was focused on the screen showing the footage of the bombings and not looking at them, they came really close to me. There is something very interesting about what happens when the performer is focused on something; it gives the audience a license to look at the performer in a very close way.

That experience itself, listening to the radio and then suddenly becoming aware of the process of making sound, is something we experience in everyday life but we're not very aware of it. I can think of two classic moments when that happens. One is when you see a radio broadcast booth outside doing a mobile broadcast and you're listening to the radio, so you hear it and you see it. I think there's something very shocking about that; it breaks something. The other is when you're at a concert in a smaller space and, all of a sudden, the amplification malfunctions and you don't hear the amplification any more through the speaker, but you hear either the voice itself or the acoustic instrument without amplification. I think that is also quite shocking because, all of a sudden, you become aware of the fact that what you've been listening to has this process of mediation that is enabled by technology, by systems.

LC Is there an implicit critique for you in exposing that kind of mediation or creating a different relationship to it, let's say, through the *Nocturne* project as a whole?

SY Yes, I think so, but I don't have a clear sense of what exactly I'm trying to critique. I just know that there are certain things I find perplexing or shocking, like that moment that I've just been talking about to do with how we receive information. I feel there's a very strong tendency to romanticize extreme situations. Not only in the media but even potentially in my doing this performance, even though I'm coming to it with a critical attitude. As part of my research for this piece, I read an article by Lawrence Weschler, published in *The New Yorker*, which was about *Jarhead* (2005), a war drama with an anti-war agenda. Weschler was questioning whether all simulations of warfare, be they in video games or cinema, are pornographic in nature and essentially pro-war.

Another example that he gave was *Apocalypse Now*. Of course, it's very critical of the Vietnam War, but nowadays you cannot have an airstrike anywhere in the world without hearing the Wagner music that was playing through the helicopters in the film. In the American military today it is Wagner most of the time, so it's almost as if *Apocalypse Now* gave this thing a language. When I was making the *Nocturne* piece, I was also struggling with the ethics of that. Those questions also had a very specific context for me at that time because it was around the time of the Umbrella Movement. Although it was a civic protest and very peaceful, there were also talks among young people about more violent and armed resistance that I found very dangerous. I cannot think of a city that is more shielded from the reality of the Second World War than Hong Kong. In terms of greater China in general, Hong Kong has been relatively untouched by war, and it's not something that we talk about a lot in our history. I am all for democratic aspirations for the city-state, but I do think about why some people romanticize the escalation of violence as a possible solution for what we want to achieve politically. There's almost a glorifying, heroic quality in the way people talk about violent options. I find that quite disturbing but I don't want to dismiss it. I want to understand it because it also perplexes me.

LC You devote a remarkable amount of time to opening up the complexity of these kinds of questions, especially in your current research projects, which you expect to take several years. Can we perhaps talk about your ongoing project *Pastoral Music (But It Is Entirely Hollow)*? It uses sound performance as a way to revisit the Gin Drinker's Line, a defense line in Hong Kong built by the British in the 1930s, which fell to the Japanese in a matter of hours during the war. What kind of research goes into a piece like this? Do you also read extensively?

SY Making work is a good way to devote or systemize a chunk of your attention to something that you can go back to and revisit. Clearly, with the *Pastoral Music* project, I've looked very closely at how Hong Kong lost the war. As you mentioned, I'm slowly visiting all of the remaining relics of the Gin Drinker's Line, which consist of abandoned bunkers, tunnels, gun batteries, and pillboxes, and I'm making recordings of myself singing a Cantonese nursery rhyme in these highly reverberant concrete structures. I've also been looking at the history of sound as a weapon, recently as well as in the distant past. Simple things like drumming and how it is psychological and has been used as a way to intimidate the enemy. Steven Goodman's book *Sonic Warfare: Sound, Affect, and the Ecology of Fear* was really interesting on this subject. I was also inspired by J. Martin Daughtry's book *Listening to War: Sound, Music, Trauma, and Survival in Wartime Iraq* about how people remember conflict. Gulf War veterans and other people were asked to describe what they heard, how they remember the conflict through hearing. There are chapters upon chapters of these very descriptive accounts with veterans going into details like, "When we heard a sound of this particular quality we knew the bombing was far away but if the sound was like this, we knew we had to get away from the window." I also came across a website for veterans to share their campaign playlists, the music they would put on their iPod when they go on a campaign, or on patrol. Daughtry also looked into the history of when the iPod started to become an essential item for people sent on a military campaign. Before they went, they would get a packing list of mundane items like foot powder, and at some point in time, the iPod became a part of that packing list. The CD player was never a packing list item, but at a very specific time, the iPod entered the packing list. I was looking into all of that.

I found this to be a very interesting example of how there is an opportunity to tell a history that has been told many times, through the sense of hearing. I'm fascinated by that.

In *Pastoral Music,* I undertake a simple gesture of singing inside underground bunkers and concrete tunnels along the Gin Drinkers Line that I mentioned before, using the natural acoustics of these spaces as a natural reverb for my voice. This work is partly motivated by thinking about the experience of being in a tunnel as a soldier when an attack is imminent. What are you listening out for? Are you hearing footsteps or sound coming back at you? How does that make a relationship between you and the person you are listening out for? Both of you are essentially doing the same thing. When it's dark in a tunnel, you rely on your sense of hearing. You are listening to each other and trying to figure out where the other is, but you also kind of inhabit each other's mind. You're performing the same kind of mental process. That's why I picked that song, "Of Forests and Pastures," for *Pastoral Music (But It Is Entirely Hollow)*. It's a very specific nursery rhyme that begins with a picturesque green landscape but ends with the line, "My dear friend, what's on your mind?" For me, that's a perfect trajectory for the project, beginning with this romanticization but ending with a very personal question. If you don't call them your enemy and you call them your friend and you're actually going through the same kind of mental process, you gain access to the other in a different way. For me, it's a perfect way to wrap up the whole thinking.

LC As part of your other ongoing research project, *For Whom the Bell Tolls*, you have already undertaken a journey across five continents to re-tell histories that have been told many times through the presence of bells, the sound of bells. In the overall project, there's an underlying exercise of mapping, but it's a kind of eccentric mapping, following a route produced by a sequence of individual bells. It's an artistic mapping as much as a historical mapping in that sense. Why did you choose bells as the subject through which to examine such a large geographic and temporal span?

SY I am very interested in how the auditory range of bells also defines territories, separating one community from another along cultural, religious, or ideological fault lines. It was also a natural extension from the previous project, *Nocturne*, which looked at explosion sounds. Bell sounds and explosion sounds are similar in that they both have an incredible density, but there also are historical coincidences about bells and sounds of explosions and weapons. If you think about the time before industrialization, you really only get two classes of objects that would be able to produce a sound that is louder than the sound of natural phenomena or earthquakes or natural disasters: cannons and bells. Historically, whenever there was a war, and there was a shortage of metal–and this happened up to the Second World War–different regimes would always go to the church bells as their store of surplus metal to be used in warfare. They would melt them down and make weapons out of them. After the war was over, there were many examples of the cannons being melted down for metal to recast bells, as in the case of the Pummerin, which had Turkish cannons from the Siege of Vienna. I find that connection interesting.

In terms of designing the research trip and the process, there are so many bells that could be recorded and visited, I needed to limit my scope somewhat, so I chose to continue with the things that had a natural connection to my last project. It seemed logical to look into bells as a way to think about the history of conflict, and that's how it started. Also, on the acoustic level, after the explosion part, I became interested in sounds that are extremely dense. It gave me the opportunity to listen to these sounds and try to tease out the sound.

LC Artists often stumble on the most amazing research materials. You had the incredible experience of looking through archives from the Bell Graveyard, a site in Hamburg where bells that were decommissioned after the war have been collected. I am curious to know whether that archive is well known, or whether your project is something that gives it a different place in the public eye.

SY The Bell Graveyard itself is in Hamburg, but the archive record of these bells is now in the Germanisches Nationalmuseum in Nuremberg. I was surprised when I visited the museum and they told me that before me, only one researcher had visited or wanted to use that archive. I was stunned because there was a wealth of material there. That's what makes research so fascinating; that there are these treasures just sitting in libraries and archives waiting to be discovered. I guess we're all too busy to think about them. I thought the fate of the bells was such an interesting legal problem. I wonder why it hasn't been talked about more. There are many bells that are still in Germany but their rightful owners are elsewhere. I wonder whether people are going to have that conversation.

LC Because art is postdisciplinary, it allows for people to think across different problematics. When you think about the bells, you seem to be weaving different histories–social histories, war histories, very local histories, sound histories – many different areas that might be very difficult to bring together otherwise. I have just been listening to *Such Sweet Thunder* (2017), the composition you made for Documenta 14, which was one output of the project, in which you weave together narrated stories, linguistic sounds, and sound that is abstract but very evocative of the visual and many other qualities.[1]

SY When I was doing these bell recordings, I didn't think too much about what I would make of it all at the end. I just went and did the collecting first. Of course, a lot of material is generated during the process, but the documentary radio piece for Documenta was the first time I drew on this collection of material as a totality and tried to make something of it. I think of my works as creating glitches, well maybe not glitches exactly, but a very interesting chemistry takes place when you take two things that on the surface don't seem like they're related but you try to find a relationship between them. Something happens in the process, and you break the form that usually contains these things.

I use the term "form" in a very general sense. I think our activities and our politics are organized by forms. Like the forms of rhythm, the biological clock against the institutional calendar that makes you want to do something, as well as festivities that get re-articulated. We are always living with these forms, but when you make a cross-disciplinary work, you have the opportunity to bring these forms and rhythms of things together, and paradoxically they become a bit disintegrated and you start to loosen things up. It's not a big gesture, but I think there's

1 *Such Sweet Thunder* (2017) can be listened to on the Documenta 14 website: https://documenta14.de/en/public-radio/14748/such-sweet-thunder.

something important about it. When you do that, you momentarily disrupt the system and the form. Perhaps afterwards the form keeps re-articulating the old way that it has always been doing. But at least for that moment when you are there doing that thing, the rhythm has been disrupted. For me that's interesting, it's important.

LC Let's also talk about *Palazzo Gundane (Homage to the Myth-Maker Who Fell to Earth)* (2017), your project for the Hong Kong Pavilion at the Venice Biennale, which took the form of the charity pop song as its departure point. You were interested in a particular history of charity songs in the 1980s, in how they were taken up in the Asian context, and the afterlife they have there. In my experience of it, the installation seemed to open up a space that was simultaneously in the past and in the future. It seemed to me that you were rethinking a certain postcolonial space through form in that piece.

SY The Venice piece is still a bit fuzzy in my head. I usually need quite some time after a piece is made to talk about what I did. Speaking more generally, I would say that I often begin with complexities and issues that I want to deal with. I have a critical attitude toward them but in the end, what I want to figure out is what makes me feel uncomfortable. Most of the time I don't arrive at a solution, but I feel that the making is the way to process all of this. When I think about the colonial history of Hong Kong, for example, it's conflictual in the sense that the way I think, the way I structure the world, and the way power and class are arranged in Hong Kong, all have to do with colonial history. However, at the same time, I also acknowledge the fact that I've never heard my voice from the outside, I've never known a different reality to this. Therefore there's also a certain affinity to this colonial history. There are things about the colonial history, which many people in Hong Kong, and I personally, cling to and remember with fondness. So how do you reconcile that really weird mix of things that doesn't lend itself to the formulation of a coherent position?

That might be one thing that music is pretty good at. I don't know how you felt about the Venice work, but in my mind the symbols and the things I am trying to present in terms of information are super dense and confusing because many things come together and it's almost too much. But the affective quality of it in terms of how the music makes you feel is, for me, very clear. Is this moving, or is it distant, or is this music making me feel like there's an emptiness? I think those affective qualities in my music are often very apparent. I think that's maybe one way I deal with this and try to process it and at the same time not allow the work to become so simple that it can be distilled into a position. Not because it's a cool thing to do, but because that's how my brain works. In my mind, it's a mess of things.

LC There are so many musical components to that exhibition. One is the installation where old pop songs come back in small video pieces with an animated character; another is the choir re-singing one of those songs through whispers, which is kind of a ghostly process somehow. You also have a video work that is done with numbers – you mentioned somewhere that you're interested in George Lam's Cantopop covers of classical tunes with numbers as lyrics. Can you say something about those musical choices?

SY A lot of the things that happened just felt right. Although there are many different kinds of things going on in the piece, what brought them all together, for me, were the different reconfigurations of the human voice. In the more elaborate curtained room there's a chorus of many voices, but it's really only from one singer, and then in the next room you have an actual chorus, but the result sounds very thin; it's very ephemeral. When you're outside the pavilion in the courtyard, there's an empty stage and no actual voice that you hear, but the wall text is very loud and clear. Finally, in the video piece installed in the tunnel, you have my own voice doing the singing. So the human voice is one thing. Also with this project, I was returning a bit to my early interest in music theater. In my early days as a composer, I made a whole bunch of music theater pieces. They're not really like music theater in a very narrative sense; they're more like instrumental compositions that are driven by narrative, and they wouldn't have voice or lyrics. I was already using a multimedia setting then, with theatrical elements and video in the show. I think that with the Venice exhibition, I was also returning to the idea of music theater a little bit. Aside from the underlying theme of the charity single, those two things tied everything together for me.

LC What about fiction? You researched a singer-songwriter who turned out to be a fake news character to create a kind of fictive domestic space in the Venice show, but I also see that fictive quality coming even more strongly to the fore in earlier works by you. I am thinking, for example, of the installation and performance *When I have fear that I may cease to be, what would you give in exchange for your soul* (2016), or the video work and installation for *The Coffee Cantata (Institute of Fictional Ethnomusicology)* (2015). I particularly notice you going into this fictive space in your collaborations with Michael Schiefel, who is a very experimental vocalist in his own right. There is such a broad scope within your work, from archival-based field work, observational and auditory field recordings to this very fictional space, all of which you manage to keep intact. In fact, this fictive space is also based partly on research through literature so the two get blurred somehow. I would love to hear you say something about the fictive and what you think it makes possible in terms of knowledge production.

SY It's true that when I do pieces that have a natural fiction element to them, it's almost always when Michael is involved. It really started with *The Coffee Cantata* and then after that we collaborated on other pieces. I really enjoy the more research-based factual pieces, but it's a different kind of approach in terms of my distance to the subject material. I'm a little bit the audience in the piece, standing outside of it in terms of how I dissect the process. With the fiction pieces, usually what happens is that there's a body of research that has to do with some facts or weird things that I've discovered, but then through the natural fiction that arises I'm able to insert some of my personal history into it–family history or personal experiences. Actual events that have happened to me can become a part of the piece. Sometimes these are accidents and random events that you then incorporate into this fictional narrative, and they almost feel inevitable after the fact. I'm also very interested in that phenomenon.

In *When I have fear that I may cease to be*, there was a scene of Michael and me smoking inside of a burned down market. That happened because when Michael came to Hong Kong to film, there was a fire in the famous fruit market on the second day of filming. It was a very old market that was fully functioning before it got burned down. We had planned to do one of the scenes there anyway, but my producer called me up and said, "The path that you wanted to walk has been burned down." I sort of froze for a couple of minutes, and then I called him back and said, "That's great, we should go inside." Then I changed some of the sequences of events so we were able to go inside one of these burned down fruit stalls and do one of the scenes. These things just happen; it's unfortunate that the fruit stand got burned down, but then this random event gets written into the piece, and you organize the scene and the information. You give them a form and a structure so that they become inevitable; they feel like they have always been there. I also think of that in the broader sense of how history becomes solidified. When they're happening in real time, events never feel inevitable, it feels like things just pop up and events just happen; that they are shocking and surprising and a little random. But when you look back after twenty years, especially after they have been written into history in a specific way, they look as though they were inevitable. It was always meant to happen that way; one thing was leading to another. Or at least that's how we give them form, or how we give them a position in the way that we write history. I don't know if I'm consciously trying to deal with all of those issues in my narrative, but I'm certainly interested in that as a larger process.

LC I wonder if you also think about this in terms of decolonizing knowledge. I know that during your early music studies, you were very critical of the place of Western music in Asia and how this particular music history is imposed as *the* music and so on. That seemed to be an early driving force and I see it coming back in more complex ways later in your practice, even through this move into fiction.

SY It is an important line of thought that I still think about, but it probably has more to do with how I continuously deal with my place in the system, in what I'm doing, where I stand, and how I deal with the people around me, with the events or non-events around me. It's a continuous internal conversation and sometimes those internal conversations take an external form. I write about it, I make notes and make clarifications for myself, but it's a personal struggle and I deal with it on a daily basis.

I think I am also dealing with it more directly in another ongoing project called *Orchestrations* that I haven't really made public yet. It is an ongoing research and a rather large project that is very far from finished. I am mainly looking at how different groups have appropriated the term "orchestra" to describe what they do. I film community orchestras, Chinese orchestras, and the Gamelan – they sometimes call themselves the Javanese Gamelan Orchestra – and I also have a project called *The Laptop Orchestra*. I think I would need to film a lot more before I could start to write about what it is or put it on my website as an ongoing project. I need more clarity, and I need to film in more locations. Part of what makes this difficult is that a lot of the examples I have collected so far in the film are from Hong Kong. I did a small film screening of this project in Hong Kong in 2015, but I feel that I need to be in many different places and cultures, dealing more with the terminology of "orchestra," to even begin to formulate an opinion of what I'm doing. It's going to be a project that lasts for much longer, I think. I am planning a trip for this, to a community orchestra in Zurich in 2019.

This dialogue was previously published in *MaHKUscript Journal for Fine Art Research* Vol. 2, Issue 1 (2018), which was guest-edited by Lucy Cotter as a preview to the first edition of this book. Republished with kind permission.

Rehearsal as a Mode of Being

A Dialogue with Katarina Zdjelar

Lucy Cotter Quite a lot of artists are attracted to language as an area of research, which is interesting, as there are other dedicated fields that one might choose to work in. But in your practice, there's a particular focus on the limits of language, on its vulnerability and malleability. Working with the medium of video allows you to focus on how language inhabits the body, on moments when language fails and the body takes over, and on the unnaturalness of the body acquiring new language forms. The painstaking labor of accent-removal in *The Perfect Sound* (2009), for example, is almost painful to watch.

Katarina Zdjelar Yes, language has always been quite central to my practice and working with video has enabled me to deal with language on several registers, on the level of the visual as well as the aural. Because I shoot all of my work myself, working with the camera also enables me to choreograph and engage in a particular relationship with the interacting subjects and bodies in the space. In *The Perfect Sound*, the camera focuses on a speech therapist while he is engaged in performing phonetic exercises to remove the foreign accent of a client in his studio in Birmingham, a city that is paradoxically known for its strong accent. I was trying to expose the relations between the two voices: that of the teacher, the standard that instructs and molds, and that of his student, which is informed, directed, and molded. On a broader level, *The Perfect Sound* also looks at the phenomenon of cultural integration through the erasure of difference in pronunciation and the production of neutrality. The choreography of the sequence unfolds like the relations between a machine and its operator.

LC We never see the client "arrive" at his linguistic destination, but there's a sense that he is trying to become someone else or at least to pass as someone he is not. His dedication to this invasive process of accent removal suggests a huge personal investment. Language is not only a linguistic phenomenon here; it becomes a site of personal transformation.

KZ Obtaining a new accent is a kind of voice mask that allows the immigrant misfit to shift between different modes of appearances, enabling him to blend into the new environment, to become unnoticeable. I see these normative and assimilative practices developed and imposed by our so-called liberal and developed world as a symbolic rite of passage of the dislodged individual. They facilitate the utterly ambiguous position of the liminal stage, in which one has left one place or state but has not yet entered or joined the next. I try to capture that ambiguity in the work.

LC You seem to be particularly concerned with the embodiment of these linguistic processes, with the body as a container for an implicit ideology, pedagogy, or political persuasion. I have to think about Pierre Bourdieu's writings on "hexis," the bodily repertoires that form the unconscious dispositions of a culture. Your work makes this phenomenon tangible, palpable. We sense this layer of knowledge in our own bodies while watching your video works, rather than thinking it analytically through theorization. I once heard Irit Rogoff say that art brings us to places that no amount of reading can bring us to. It brings us to a different level of reality.

KZ I do think this is something that art can do and I try in my own way to access this potential in my work. I am particularly interested in using the potentiality of bodies, in their ability to demonstrate another reality. I am interested in how even the slightest movement, the most intimate tensing of one's body, might serve as evidence of implicit ideology. Art can pay attention to these apparent details. During the session shown in *The Perfect Sound*, we see the client's body morph as sounds are expressed from his body. This is just a passing moment, but I am concerned with how one's sense of social orientation lies in the space one claims with one's body. The body is always the focus of a power struggle and in the midst of it. Nietzsche puts it well when he says, "One must first persuade the body." He talks about the strict perseverance this entails, an effort that takes two or three generations before it becomes inward. He believes that the right place for culture to begin is not the "soul" but precisely in the body, the gesture, the diet and physiology. If the human body figures the limits of human capacity, then the process of coding the body in particular ways suggests one's subjectivity.

LC You have also worked with postcolonial subjectivity specifically, with the body as a site of colonial power as well as resistance. I am thinking especially of *My Lifetime (Malaika)* (2012), which shows Ghana's National Symphony Orchestra practicing in the National Theatre in Accra. Somehow this resonates with your work on language, although, literally speaking, there is no linguistic content in the work.

KZ I did think about language in my research for *My Lifetime (Malaika)*, so maybe this comes through somehow. I thought a lot about Yugoslavian writer Oskar Davičo's book *In Black and White* (1962), which was the result of his travels to Africa, during which he became familiar with the aspirations of newly independent nations to abandon the language of the colonizer. Davičo responded to these impulses by proposing that the colonizer's language shouldn't be discarded, but appropriated and used as a tool of anti-colonial struggle. Due to having so many local languages in Ghana, one must communicate in the English language, the language of the colonizer, to be able to be understood. However noble, brave, passionate, or idealistic the proposal of breaking with colonial tradition was, it probably would only have harmed the postcolonial struggle. The language of the oppressor thus had a unifying function, creating an infrastructure for a newly established state.

LC Did you incorporate those ideas in *My Lifetime (Malaika)* somehow? Or were there parallels between this attitude toward language and other cultural forms, like music, in the context of Ghana?

KZ There was a distinct parallel because the focus on classical music, which was a relatively new musical language in that context, was a constitutive part of the newly independent state. It introduced a new perspective on the body of the performer, who had to re-train, learn, and expand the vocabulary of his or her body, which had been formed through Ghanaian traditional folk music, and not classical music. Along with obtaining the musical instruments, teachers from abroad were brought in to educate and create what became the National Symphony Orchestra. Hence *My Lifetime (Malaika)* engages not only with music but also with this very body at work in the act of producing music. The capacity of the trumpet player's lungs to capture a given amount of air matters. The air pressure of the lungs matters. The flautist's fingers are arrested in the proper position, waiting to start playing. Another musician straightens his back. The body becomes an instrument for social change and its repertoire, imprinted and enacted in every performance as evidence of the cultural recoding taking place.

LC The formation of the orchestra in the 1950s showed the desire of the newly independent Ghana to assert its nationhood. However, through the dilapidated state of the orchestra in the video, we can see that it inhabits an ambiguous position in the present. In fact the present seems to be suspended in history. We can sense that we are witnessing something that was more present in the past. Yet there are ongoing interruptions to the practice, literal interventions by the arrival or departure of musicians, which never allow us to settle into a sense of unbroken continuity.

KZ Yes, as Sabeth Buchmann once wrote, it is often the interruptions that speak in my work. They form a kind of anti-narrative, telling a story that refuses to be told as a continuum.[1] There is a very particular relationship between the historical condition in which the orchestra emerged and the way it is sustained. All of the musicians have multiple jobs and are tired when rehearsing. Hence they fall asleep or have to leave early or come late, with the result that the rehearsed score is constantly interrupted, perforated, and made porous. Since the orchestra was made up of people and was a part of a bureaucratic apparatus, its existence couldn't easily be abolished, unlike the National Museum whose construction was abandoned when a *coup d'etat* toppled the Nkrumah government in 1966. The orchestra is still *there*, holding a particular position in the system; that of not fully belonging to any tradition, history, or agenda. Its existence is a kind of surplus, an excess. Because the orchestra no longer receives any significant state support, it is hard to pin down the musicians' status; what they do, what they mean, to whom and for whom they still exist, and for how long.

One of the most striking things I encountered while recording *My Lifetime (Malaika)* was that some of the musicians actually had an image of Kwame Nkrumah, the first president of Ghana who founded the orchestra, on their note stands. His image was intermingled

1 Sabeth Buchmann, "Portrait Practice: On the Motif of Rehearsal in Katarina Zdjelar's Work" in Thomas Thiel, ed., *Katarina Zdjelar: Towards a Further Word* (Bielefeld Kunstverein, 2013), pp. 41–49.

with the sheets of music scores. I decided not to use it in the final edit but it was such a surprise! I started to see the orchestra as a live reminder, created in the process of translation from one rule to another.

LC You made *My Lifetime (Malaika)* during a residency in Ghana. There is evidently a lot of research invested in this work and in your videos in general, yet they are quite intimate in character, taking what feels almost like an insider perspective. How do you go about setting up these scenarios?

KZ I closely engage with the people who feature in my work. That part of my work is about moving through certain structures and environments in which I encounter very particular people who participate in these structures. They are foreigners who work as role players for Dutch military and immigration services as in *Act I, Act II* (2010), refugees in camps as in *Rise Again* (2011) and *The Motto of Today* (2011), or passing as one of the parents in a primary school in Istanbul, etc. I see my position as one of standing by these non-authoritative voices of children, refugees, and amateurs who challenge the system in which they appear. But the work is not didactic. I have a rather organic relationship to the research materials, the encounters, and the literature, theory, or art history that I touch on in the work. I consider my attitude to be one of distilling. I offer the artwork as a consideration of formal and aesthetic as much as content-driven perspectives, if such rigid distinctions are at all productive.

LC Often, there's a kind of cameo effect in your videos. We are given a glimpse of a moment like the one of the orchestra rehearsing in which a bigger story resonates, yet there is no attempt to represent this broader narrative. We sense it, rather than being told it or taking it in consciously. There is a kind of historiography present, but it seems to lie in the structure of the work. Maybe it's most present in the way in which the video camera is used, as you mentioned earlier; in the decisions about where and how to look, where to focus the attention for how long, where and when to interrupt the act of looking.

KZ Yes, I try to deactivate straightforward representation in my work. This mostly happens on an aesthetic level. I work with sound, silence, moving images, and the absence of image, including the rhythm and the grain of images and the sound. The camera and sound recorders are like writing devices for me, a prosthesis of my "sensing body," not only as an extension of the physical body but also as a form of agency. As the video records what it depicts, it simultaneously renders the activity of the camera. The camera is not neutral. As it wanders and inhabits the space of the reality it depicts, it has a life of its own within it. It can detach itself from what it passes on; it can be present but not represent what it transmits. It can choose to focus for too long on marginal aspects of what is unfolding in front of it. My camera is always looking, it is always in the present tense, trying to orientate itself in the given environment, rather than aiming to represent it objectively.

LC There's often a sense that the camera is looking for something which cannot be seen; something very close that cannot be touched, but which is present with a kind of ghostly insistence. I experienced this very strongly while watching *Untitled (A Song)* (2015). The camera circles around a band rehearsal room as the band members are waiting for someone or something. Nothing really happens, but there is an incredible sense of this moment being suspended in time.

KZ True. I think that in many of my works "the regime of the visible" takes the perspective of a sort of depiction of the invisible. There's a proximity to things, to sensing or touching the contours of what cannot be seen but only sensed or anticipated and lost. A sense of being close to or next to, but being together apart. There is a poem by Mallarmé that talks a bit about that by depicting a poet who takes a boat trip on the river so that he can see a woman he has fallen in love with. As he approaches the place where she is supposed to be staying, he hears the sound of footsteps that might belong to the lady. After having enjoyed that possibility of proximity, he decides to leave undetected, without seeing her and being seen by her, without verifying if it was in fact her. What strikes me about this way of encountering the other, the motif, or the subject, is how it keeps the idea of a meeting alive, as a generator and a placeholder of possibilities and potentialities, rather than aiming at a climax or a moment of reassurance, certainty and resolution. In my work, seeing is also not only the seeing of images or motifs but also seeing them in duration. It's a kind of seeing that is bound to the passing of time and the marriage of images with sounds.

LC In *Untitled (A Song)* (2015), it is also nighttime in the work, which seems to carry some kind of symbolic function, although it is very subtle. I experienced it as a sense of the nocturnal, politically; a waiting for something to come that is perhaps close but can only be sensed. I think you have mentioned before that the nocturnal is important to you.

KZ I appreciate the nocturnal as a time for facing the "looming creatures of the night," as an engagement with uninhabited and unknown zones of knowledge. In *Untitled (A Song),* the night also offers a moment to look at or to imagine the horizon, which is impossible to see because of the darkness. There is the suggestion of a temporal void marked by darkness and silence, in which the musicians come together. They are in this particular in-betweenness of two days, one that is passing and a new one arriving, in a time that doesn't belong to either one. The nocturnal as this in-betweenness is also present in the activity of the band in their search for a song. The work is as bound to a question of artistic creation as it is to the idea of waiting for the political moment. There are several geopolitical references that quietly run in the background, most noticeably in the depiction of the neglected and aged corridors of one of the most prominent Yugoslavian modernist buildings, through which the sounds of music move out into the empty street. We are situated in a time-space of transition that many socialist countries are still going through, in anticipation of a new order, the political moment, so that, as Mieke Bal puts it, "being in the world is being for the world" and thus having agency.

LC I also have to think of *A Girl, the Sun, and an Airplane Airplane* (2007), a work in which you ask Albanian people to recall whatever smattering of Russian they can glean from their childhood memories. The people are filmed in the black non-space of a recording booth, which somehow also stands in as darkness. Although we, as viewers, are watching them in this recognizable dark space, we somehow have the feeling that we are scanning through the dark crevices of their memories as they scan for the long forgotten linguistic material you ask them to salvage. It's also quite a humorous work. The people themselves laugh or appear to be amused at their own inability to recall more than a smattering of words and that prompts us to laugh a little as we watch, but not without discomfort.

KZ It's interesting that you mention humor. I do think that humor is present in much of my practice and yet, as you say, it doesn't have to do with being funny. Frans-Willem Korsten once wrote a wonderful text on my work in which he reflected on how, in classical times, humor meant moisture and was related to the overall constitution of the human body, which was meant to be made up of a mixture of types of humors, or moistures: black bile, yellow bile, phlegm, and blood.[2] I feel like I am using humor in this way, as something fluid that can bring about some kind of internal movement of that which has solidified and become too fixed. Humor gets things moving again, it creates some kind of openness to different ways of looking or thinking.

LC This makes me think about something that Georges Bataille wrote; that we laugh, not because we do not happen to know, but because the unknown makes us laugh. This abrupt passing from a world in which there is stability to one in which we lose our sense of assurance makes us laugh. I also see you as someone making works where there is nowhere for us

2 Frans-Willem Korsten, "If We Be With Things," *Parapoetics* (Rotterdam: TENT, 2009), pp. 40–46.

to stand from which we can comfortably say, "I know." Perhaps *Rise Again* (2011) is the most striking work in this respect. No matter how many times I watch it, it always evades digestion, evades any kind of cognitive possession. Take for example the "Bruce Lee" character, who is practicing his martial arts outdoors and has a rather obscure relationship with a group of immigrant men who are doing physical training on the same site for leisure, or perhaps even for military purposes. There's a kind of magical realism going on, which is infused into the scene by moments in which the camera rests with the wind in the trees and the ways in which the camera watches the "Bruce Lee" character, whose status as real or not real is impossible to determine.

KZ This "Bruce Lee" character is, in fact, an Afghan refugee too. He has a really close likeness to the Hollywood hero, but the resemblance is not staged in any way. It also goes beyond physical characteristics because he trains in Kung Fu as well. Watching him on film practicing his routine, it becomes hard to tell whether he is acting a role or just following his daily training. The aim of *Rise Again* was to work on and meditate on this unresolvable, ungrammatical presence. That was possible precisely through arranging this meeting in the medium of film itself, creating an encounter between elements that sit between the cinematic and actuality.

LC There is more generally an unstable relationship between fact and fiction in your work, which is something that seems quite central to the agency of artistic research in general. I am especially conscious of this in video works of yours in which performativity becomes foregrounded. In *Act I and Act II* (2010) and *Too Old, Too Tired, and Too Fucking Blind* (2012), for example, we see protagonists who self-consciously perform themselves or other designated roles, often practicing and repeating themselves in ways that draw attention to the act of reinvention.

KZ Yes, some of my works do present staged real-life scenarios, where one of the protagonists inhabiting a fictive character becomes entwined in a meta-level of reality and personal narrative. There is a blurry web of authenticity being created, with the fictional and the real characters being affected by one another. It is not clear when the protagonist is acting and when he encounters his genuine self, since the actual and the personal, the social and the individual merge into one persistent narrative. I think this goes back to the mode of rehearsal, which, as we discussed earlier, is probably one of the most prominent *modus operandi* in my practice. It comes from an interest in putting two forces into play that don't usually speak to each other: contingency and control. With rehearsal, there is something about depicting the subject-in-the-making, with an interest that extends what is seen in the video but also feeds back to the condition of making itself, going behind the camera and editing table.

LC Can we return again to the question of language and elaborate on the role that language plays in the reception of *Act I*? I find it quite radical that you use the possibilities of the viewing experience to situate the viewer linguistically; for example placing the Dutch viewer in a similar position to the Dutch immigration official, while sharing privy information with a select immigrant audience. It's a really fascinating strategy for troubling the production of knowledge.

KZ Yes, anyone who speaks the native language of the protagonist in *Act I* quickly becomes aware that he is fabricating his story; not because it is inconsistent or because he doesn't perform it well – on the contrary – but because the specificity and properties of his speech, such as his accent, its rhythm, stress and intonation, situate him outside of the geohistorical events he inserts himself in with his role. The impossibility of participating in the scenario he is performing is situated precisely in the immaterial properties of his speech. As he is still speaking the same language of the Bosnian character he performs, the interpreter translates the meaning of his words, but not the musical properties of them, and in doing so, he unquestionably ties the protagonist to the events he is talking about. This comes back to the question, "How did he speak?" that came up so often during the International Criminal Tribunal for the Former Yugoslavia sessions in The Hague, as it was precisely these properties of one's speech, the musicality of it, that could distinguish the victim from the perpetrator in the context of the former-Yugoslavian war. There were no racial or any other physical markers that would point to the difference; the only difference was located in the throat of the speaker.

LC Language in your work is almost always contained in a voice, and as viewers, we are conscious that this voice inhabits and resonates from a body. Can you elaborate on this notion of the musicality of speech?

KZ These so-called musical properties of speech are also markers of performative powers and, in effect, of politics inscribed in the spoken language. For this reason, accent or pitch are central to some of my other works like *Stimme* (2013) and *Shoum* (2009). *Shoum*, for instance, depicts two Serbian workers struggling to decipher the lyrics of a Tears for Fears song in the English language, which they don't speak. They create a private language that perhaps sits between, but doesn't belong to, either English or Serbian, in their effort to fathom and transcribe the unknown, opening up the question of their participation in a globalized world in the process. In *Stimme* a young woman undergoes pitch modulation; she is literally finding her own voice with the help of a therapist who is visualizing the crafting of voice. The coach uses her hands to manipulate the body of her client as if it were a musical instrument. These are the kinds of ways in which the protagonists in my videos use their voices and bodies to produce, in an orchestrated manner, sounds, words, or tones. We see them unlearning an accent, perfecting a pronunciation, or rehearsing a piece of music. Each act involves cultivating the voice, sounds, and tones in a language or music piece according to standards determined by cultural and social codes. In this way, what might be considered at first to be a portrait, or one's personal expectations and desires, connects to larger social issues, such as the constant pressure in contemporary society to integrate or to perform.

LC In a more recent work, *AAA (Mein Herz)* (2016), we see a woman whose voice transforms from one moment to the next from spoken word to song. It all becomes sound, but it's a sound that almost escapes the body as a container; it has the quality of something in excess.

KZ *AAA (Mein Herz)* is a single-shot work showing a young woman simultaneously performing four compositions. While preserving the original style, tempo, and rhythm of the individual works, she maintains the key of the different music pieces. Silence, music, sound, and words alternate and collide. The female protagonist's face and vocal chords serve as a kind of battleground for the jerky transition between the different tracks. As if the sounds have been continuously torn out of their sockets. I try to emphasize the multiple and fragmented, yet nevertheless simultaneous temporalities that run her voice and the composition. Once again, it is the interruptions that speak, this time in the corporality of the voice, while her singing is as much about managing the gaps between the tracks as it is about the accuracy of performance of the historically, stylistically, and linguistically distinct compositions.

LC One of those compositions is a pop song, which creates an unexpected closeness to normal daily life amid the singer's more operatic and classical repertoire.

KZ I am interested in music as a kind of gateway to the social, a knot between the individual and society. Several of my works explore the limits of that point of access, finding vulnerability or failure, as well as potentialities and challenges in performing social or aesthetic conventions. In one work, *Everything Is Gonna Be* (2008), I had an amateur choir on the Lofoten Islands in Norway sing the Beatles song "Revolution." Their lullaby-like way of singing the chorus forces the song to take a disturbingly uncritical tone. The work reveals both the critical distance to upheaval in the lyrics, which John Lennon wrote in 1968, and the ideological distance between the meaning of the song and the people who appear in the video. I am interested in the process of physically manifesting these uncertainties, in the attempts to perfect one's performance, as well as in the production of a collective out of singular voices.

LC The uncertainties are often revealed through repetition, which perhaps offers another reason why rehearsal is such an important motif. There is a kind of knowledge that comes through difference produced by repetition.

KZ True. Perhaps also for that reason, I have often chosen to install works in a manner that gives the viewer access to the reverse of an image and that uses the loop as a form. This allows the work to be seen more than once, so that the viewer can pick up and unpack different layers and sets of relations that are prominent or latent in the work. My work is set to unfold primarily in duration. It is more akin to a photograph, a sculpture or a painting in that sense than a film or a performance, in that it doesn't have a beginning and an end or a prescribed duration.

Beyond Language

A Dialogue with Falke Pisano

Lucy Cotter Artists often work with different registers of knowledge. You've dealt quite explicitly in your practice with the relationship between thinking, language, and the making of physical objects. You deal with this question at a meta-level, but you also seem to work through it materially. Is it the case that to really think through something, you have to think through it in several ways, that are linguistic and discursive but also object-based, visual, and sculptural?

Falke Pisano Yes. From the beginning, it was very clear to me that both language and making are two incomplete languages somehow. My starting point was, and still is, language, and how to define a problem to think through in language. The aspect of art enters through bringing problems from a linguistic space into a space that is not necessarily formal or material at first, but that is at least not a space of pure language. There can be a certain poetry, but it should not be a space where the logic is always linguistic. This is where

I try to realize the work so that reading can take place on different levels.

LC Do you find yourself getting into this possibility of operating outside of a linguistic logic because of the limitations of language in relation to thinking?

FP Yes, I think so. When I work through language first, there's a point where what I've come up with in my brain, often through other people's writings, cannot get beyond a certain limit. This is the moment when the spectator or viewer comes into the constellation. It is also the point where space enters. I start thinking through diagrams, through a diagrammaticization, or through a sculptural or spatial organization that asks something different from the viewer than language. That's the making part of my research. There is also the other making part, the making of how the research is activated in the exhibition. In the exhibition, the work is about bringing a viewer into a space in which he or she understands that language is only one part; that language is incomplete and that the visual or the formal making is also incomplete. This angle creates a certain sensitivity to reading on different levels.

LC You have used research quite explicitly as the basis of your practice, working in cycles that go on for several years, like *Figures of Speech* (2006–2010), *The Body in Crisis* (2011–2014), and most recently *The Value in Mathematics* (2015–). Each cycle deals with a different subject area. *The Body in Crisis* looked at the repetitive occurrence of moments where bodies are thrown into a state of crisis through violent shifts in living conditions, while *The Value in Mathematics* looks at the notion of multiple mathematics and how culturally inscribed this apparently value-free discipline is. But there are distinct overlaps in how the results work in the exhibition space. Can you say how this reading on different levels you mentioned takes place in an exhibition?

FP I think the body moves toward, relates to what is made, the textural things but at the same time, the viewer is very aware that it is not only the making that can be related to. Text is also present. I use the sculpture or installation as a kind of instrument to weave the language through. When I'm talking about repetition in a text, for example, I see what it means for repetition to be something that the body also encounters all of the time. It's trying to lift up both the making and the experiencing of the work to something that operates more at an experiential level, so that experience comes in as feedback into the theoretical.

LC When a viewer enters an exhibition of your current project, *The Value in Mathematics*, it asks people to take in material at different levels – the linguistic, the physical, the haptic. It seems to trigger people to take in knowledge on different registers, which is something I have also experienced in your earlier series.

FP Yes, although I think this constellation of the experiential in relation to cognitive knowledge is often made manifest in my practice in installation works. I assume it happens more with *The Body in Crisis* series than *The Value in Mathematics*, which is object-based. When I imagine someone entering the work from *The Body in Crisis*, I can imagine there is a certain language when you're entering the space. In my mind, you encounter works that are in the space that are abstract or almost abstract. They become part of … I'm not sure I want to use the term "the production of knowledge." It's a term that has become so much part of the commercial world. Is there another way to think about it?

LC Can we talk perhaps about the relationship between abstraction and the concrete? One of the things that the *Figures of Speech* and *The Value in Mathematics* works seem to have in common is their physical manifestation of abstract thinking. Through that manifestation, something else happens. I found it interesting when you say that there comes a point in the research process when you have to make to get further. Materiality seems to open different thinking possibilities.

FP Yes, I have tried very hard to speak about abstraction in language and make it as concrete as possible, especially in the *Figures of Speech* series, which was the result of a long-term examination of processes that occur when "objects" start shifting their form, materiality, meaning, description, understanding, role, agency, etc. I was thinking about an internal logic that is coherent, so that a text-object became almost as concrete for me as an abstract sculpture, for instance. I felt that the materiality of the text and the materiality of matter and form became quite similar, although they might function differently in the work. In *The Body in Crisis,* text is less material. In *Figures of Speech* it seemed for me that for the work to have a life that could be experienced in an object-way, there needed to be an abstract layer, a made, abstract layer of material. That was one thing.

When you talk about the abstract and the concrete, I realize there are so many different positions this takes within the work. When I started writing, there was the abstract/concrete idea and the question of how I could write in a way that would bring these things together so that I can genuinely talk about concrete abstractions. At a certain moment, I started to re-enact or reconstruct the early working process of Hélio Oiticica, going from the flat surface to something that is unfolding, to something more relational. That shifted something. It led me to want to get rid of the object, which at that point only existed in language. At that point of the process, I needed to make the object disappear, to dissolve or break it up. Because the object only existed in language, I needed to do this in a performative way. The performance, which was the exploration of how this disappearance could happen, was the research.

I still call it "performative research" rather than research. Every step in the research is making as well. In fact, I did not call my work research-based for a long time because I could not recognize the research in the making. Even while I was writing texts, I was trying to make the knowledge I needed for myself to enable me to take the steps I wanted to take in the making. Even if I was writing a text, there was no superfluous knowledge, no steps that could become a composition in itself. It was not even a text as such. It was more like learning to walk. I was reading philosophy or theory or research to take the steps in the making, in the writing of the texts, in the formulating of the language, and in the understanding of the relationship between the works. It was the same with *The Body in Crisis* series. Whatever I learn goes into the work as a brick, a building block. So this knowledge is not only translated or narrated through the spectator. It is used to build this construction of the cycles of works. I learn along the way, by going into the work.

LC You say this process of construction is a brick-by-brick process. Is that also why you work on one work for several years?

FP Yes, the three cycles are very much based on self-learning, on what I want to learn. I have tried to find a certain basis of thinking about making, of thinking about speech, about translating, about object-subject relations. Then at a certain point, I thought, "I cannot work abstractly my whole life, there is a limit." So I very programmatically decided that I wanted to learn to deal with concrete events in history. This was partly because I wanted to problematize the "use" of interesting, so-called marginal, forgotten events, people and places, not only as the subject or starting point of the work but basically *as* the work. Besides wanting to say something about the situation of bodily crisis that is constantly repeating, I wanted to learn and to comment on the situation in which I was making work.

My research is not necessarily motivated by my interests in a particular subject. It's more a commitment to showing how I think we need to deal with the world. My research is very much based on questioning. It has more to do with the process of making than with interests as such. It has to do with a problematizing or questioning of a fixed idea of myself and of my relationship with the spectator. There is a performative impulse. Maybe this relationship is also translated into objects or sculptures somehow.

LC I also see performativity coming in with the video works that form part of your overall installations. It seems to me that your choice of having these different elements in the space has a lot to do with performativity. Neither the physically made works nor texts are left to stand alone. The presence of text also reminds us of the language-like quality in the sculptural works. We can feel the process behind the work more directly because the texts you include show certain aspects of the thinking, while the sculptures show another, and the video somehow brings you back in as a maker and shows a more explicitly performative relationship. You re-enter the work through the video. You perform the making of the knowledge – or what I would prefer to call non-knowledge, as it relates to plural and overshadowed knowledge, or knowledge that would not usually be defined as knowledge.

FP Yes, I think so.

LC With *The Value in Mathematics* I was quite surprised by the video work, in which the camera shows you interacting with the object-works on display, while in the voiceover we hear a discussion about ethnomathematics by two academics or individuals working on the fringes of academia, Mariana Leal Ferreira and Michael Lachney. I found it interesting that you put this exchange of thinking to the foreground. You mentioned something earlier about your decision to show your processes, but this seems to be another step.

FP Yes, it was another step. It was about letting go of control.

LC It's still quite controlled! *(laughs)*

FP *(Laughs)* Well, letting go a little bit! For me, this was already quite an exercise. The whole work, *The Value in Mathematics*, is quite constructed.

It's again a form of self-education, a research about what it means to change a point of view. I wanted this research to be more open and accessible. I wanted to both give the space to others and to also show that the space I make through my work is made by others. It was important to me to let different voices exist, to not push it into art. To go from research to art is quite a process for me. Something needs to be pushed.

LC Can you explain what you mean by that?

FP The idea of these two languages, these incomplete systems I mentioned at the beginning of our talk is very important. When research exists as research, it is just research. In my practice, it's really about moving into another place where the demands on the material shift. What was at one point good research is now incomplete because the demands have shifted. There is another part, which brings you toward meeting these demands.

LC Do you mean that there is research, which is "good research," but at a certain point it stops and has to become something else to become art?

FP I don't think that research is art, basically.

LC No. Me neither!

FP Something that can be a good start to produce knowledge or non-knowledge – like an attempt to bring together or analyze a series of images and information – this needs to be put under a different demand. A different demand needs to be made on it that shows the nature of that demand.

LC I'm imagining this as a road. At a certain point in the research process, there's a fork in the road. One lane leads to art. If you take that lane, you will work with the research material to make the best artwork that you can. There is knowledge emerging out of that moment which, if it wasn't put under the demand to become art, could become something else that is also of interest and that might be given a different name. This might be another lane.

FP Yes, but I don't think that the demand that is being put on this material is the demand of becoming art. Rather it is something that you as an artist want from the material. It's very abstract. It's not about being art or not art. Maybe it has to do with intuition. Intuition understands what is lacking or what is not there or what should be lacking. It's really about what *should* be lacking. The information that's there is fine, it's interesting, it's useful for the world maybe. So what is lacking? I think this is the interesting thing. I don't know how to explain it. But it's about acknowledging this lack that moves it; it's a displacement. It's not by a voice, not by pushing but by seeing that this is not enough.

LC Can we think about this moment of "not being enough" and of art's possibility to embrace what *should* be lacking, as you put it? It's my experience that art is rather unique in having this conceptual freedom. I find that in other fields, there is a greater push to resolve something or to name it and categorize it and cut it off in a certain way. There's something in art that allows permission for the performativity of not knowing. This letting be of that questioning is valuable. There's a freedom in art–and maybe we don't stay there enough–to stay with the not knowing, that intuitive state in which there is something there that hasn't emerged. A sense of "I'm not going to pretend that it has emerged, but I cannot make it emerge."

FP Yeah, definitely.

LC If I'm interested in a relationship between artists and academics, it's partly about leaving that space intact somehow and maybe staying there together.

FP I've also been thinking about this. Sometimes it feels strange that there are academics in the humanities, but also in other fields, spending their working lives radically rethinking the given frameworks of all aspects of human experience and thought. They spend decades learning, researching, teaching, discussing, writing; this is what it takes to create a shift in academia. In art, there are many artists dealing with a little bit of this and that, who are quite ambitious in talking about paradigm shifts, even if they are not directly seeking to make them happen. As artists, we can make works related to academic fields that we don't, in fact, know anything about. It's as if academics have written ten books and we, as artists, have written a four-page essay.

So then what is it in artists' knowledge or intuition or ability to frame or translate that is valuable, that we find valuable, that I find valuable? I think you are right that this has something to do with this state of not knowing or a place for intuition. Of course, it's the same in science; there is intuition in play, but what is the specific intuition that we appreciate in art or artworks? I think that this probably has something to do with a comfort with incompleteness, with not knowing but being aware that not knowing can be valuable or present somehow. I think that these gaps–this not knowing–plays a big role in the specificity of artistic research: How to research when you're not knowing, when you're not going to know, when you are going to know a little bit, or when you know just enough to make a work? So the research is not so much about the information or the material that's coming up, but probably more about this other presence that is emerging with the other information. It's something like a shadow, the negative or an inversion of this other information, which is the real research.

LC As well as this comfort with staying with this unknowing space, I have often thought about the scientific fact that only about four percent of knowledge comes through our conscious mind. There are ways of knowing available to us as artists that make us comfortable with the other ninety-six percent. The artist's contribution might be a four-page essay, but there are perhaps another ninety-six pages that have not been said but are being felt bodily in the experiencing of the work, as well as in reading the writing. There is a relationship, which I cannot fully articulate, that is not only about that openness but also about intuition; that knowledge has to come through on all of these different levels that you spoke about at the beginning. The moment that you cannot think further without bringing in some other way.

FP For me, it always had a lot to do with the diagram, with how I imagine diagrams to work....

LC Yes, for me too! Can you say something about what that means to you?

FP One definition of the diagram that I relate to is the Deleuzian idea of abstract machines, which are not formed matter.[1] A diagram is something that is not concerned with form but with function, but even so, it creates a certain dynamic that can be seen as a form. It is not something that follows. It is a machine that is producing something different than itself as part of itself, something that is different each time a repetition occurs. It also has the same incompleteness. It can only be made complete by this action and this input.

LC Jean-Luc Nancy talks about drawing in a similar way. "Drawing" is a noun, but it is also a verb. In the first line of *The Pleasure in Drawing*, he describes drawing as "the opening of form." This "opening" is a starting point, a gesture of incompleteness; a certain dynamic that has a capacity for something inexhaustible. For me, all of your works feel like that. They have this quality of opening.

FP For me, they are definitely like that; all of the sculptures are diagrams as well.

LC Yes, it's funny that I was picturing the sculptures as I said that. Maybe they use the same language.

FP Yes, for one thing, it's the sculptures' imagined function. There's a kind of formal diagrammatic aspect, but I think that I also really consider them as something you can activate by going through. Every time you're going through them, with a piece of thought or with the body, it puts you in a different direction or it picks up on something. For me, it has a lot to do with connecting a research about something – a problem, a concept, or two different terms that

1 See Gilles Deleuze and Félix Guattari, *A Thousand Plateaus: Capitalism and Schizophrenia,* trans. Brian Massumi (London: Continuum, 1987), p. 156.

I want to bring together – which are not working. Then the way to achieve what I want to do is to create something that has the function of a diagram but has the presence of a sculpture.

LC It is clearly important that your works do not illustrate your research; the diagram does something different than an illustration. There is an activation in a diagram; it's somehow a working drawing that involves you. Your sculptures are like working objects that involve you as a viewer, without literally being objects.

FP Yes, a working object is a nice way of putting it. Maybe the objects in *The Value in Mathematics* are less working objects than in the other series. They are perhaps more illustrative somehow. For me, they were ways of thinking, but maybe it's not like that for the spectator because they are more object-like and they are less about the bodily experience; in the end, the making has a lot to do with the body.

LC Because then we're not allowed to forget that we approach the material through the body?

FP Yes, when the work has a sculptural installation presence, it's not possible to read it. That's the main thing. When it's text, you read it. It's also about blocking a kind of objective, more distant perception of the work. In *The Body in Crisis* in particular, a lot of the work is about preventing the natural tendency to read and to read an event as something that happened a long time ago far away and to instead create the presence of it.

LC In *The Body in Crisis*, texts, diagrams, and video works were contained or separated from each other in a large wooden and fabric structure, which seemed to be a sculpture in its own right, as well as being a kind of architecture for display. Was the primary role of that structure one of obstruction?

FP Yes, that sculpture, which was called *Structure for Repetition (Not Representation)* (2011–), was firstly about blocking a certain kind of reading. To instill in the body a certain sense of being blocked all the time. Then if you read something, it reads differently because you have already incorporated a sense of being blocked. I was asking myself, "How can you work on the body in a way to twist something in the way of reading?" But for a large part, it had to do with not being able to read the work as a distant object, to read coldly and not let it touch you. For me, the making is really important in that sense. In *The Body in Crisis*, it was really about ethics. How do you present these issues? What effect does that have on the spectator?

I was seeing art practices around me bring in little-known events from anywhere in the world to make a work about, but it seemed to me that the event was being used as the artwork. It's too easy to just show something and call it a conceptual work. I felt I needed to try to problematize this process of taking material from somewhere and putting it in the art context. In order to be critical of the art context, I think it's important to make, although that might sound contradictory.

LC Perhaps it *should* sound contradictory but it doesn't. I also notice that artworks addressing particular issues that can be named or referred to, and especially artworks that are socially or politically engaged, tend to be neglected in terms of formal analysis when they are critically received. Because questions of content are often dissolved in questions of form in art, those conversations need to happen simultaneously but somehow they don't. All of those things are working in parallel and in dynamic relation to each other in the work and in the viewers' experience of the work. But it's almost impossible to articulate, even when it's one of the successes of the artwork. We seem to lack the vocabulary or the tools to discuss this content as one conversation. I see it as a social, philosophical, and linguistic problem that those discourses have developed as parallel lines of inquiry.

FP If we want to bring things together, how can we talk about it in such a way that one is not in service of the other? How can we talk about it in a way that the formal is not in service of a particular subject or something socially or politically oriented? Otherwise, it's a kind of exploitation. How can we talk about these things so that they are reciprocal? I think it's also about how we feel about ourselves as makers. I don't think it's a situation that's impossible to happen; there's just a kind of discomfort about it.

LC This is one of the reasons why I remain attracted to artistic research as a potentially constructive discourse. I feel like I don't know any artist who has moved beyond this level of discomfort. Maybe it will take another twenty or thirty years to move beyond discomfort; not into a position of comfort, but just enough to allow the full potential of art to emerge.

FP How do you imagine that? Who comes close to this?

LC I don't think that one artist can do this or has done this. It's more that, with the emergence of artistic research as a named phenomenon, there's an accumulation of a certain critical mass, even though the term has created all kinds of problems. It is very uncomfortable to open that forum, to say, "Let's stand here and say that there is something here." Yet I think this moment has already happened. Let's say, for now, that most of the beginning problems have already happened through artistic research discourse, the awkward worst-case scenarios, the misunderstood well-meaning things have already happened. Maybe having gone through this, it may be possible. I have titled this book *Reclaiming Artistic Research* because I realize that it's about reclaiming this space. It *is* there and all of these things have happened that are not comfortable, but maybe if we reclaim it and recognize that despite them, there is a certain critical mass emerging which might create better conditions to stay in this space until things are slightly more comfortable. Through being less uncomfortable, the exchange could somehow go deeper or move further.

FP You are talking about exchange, which I think is important to point out because it is not a given that artistic research is going to be an exchange. If we are talking about the position of artists in relation to other fields, it would be interesting if we would come to a point where this exchange happens, where the good things of this exchange are both going to art and to the research. But probably that also asks for academics to feel comfortable with art. Everyone needs to somehow feel comfortable. And then there is, of course, the question of to what extent art should have an applied function.

LC I saw an interview in *Metropolis M* magazine, where you talked to Margaret Gaida. You were talking about ethnomathematics but almost exclusively, so you weren't any longer talking about art.

FP Well, Margaret does not have an art background.

LC Yes, but I found it interesting that you made the specific choice to publish this conversation with someone who does not have an art background. Can we go back to the question that came up earlier about the comfort of academics? It seems to me that one of the most under-addressed issues in artistic research is the general discomfort of academics with art. It is important to acknowledge that work needs to be done to make that a more comfortable or at least workable relationship – not only on the part of artists but also academics.

FP Yes, but why does someone do work for something to become comfortable? It's because they understand already that there is something there that would be good for the field, for them. So the question is, what can that be? I think that in the end, if you talk to scientists – when you really speak to them about how art works or what is being done with the information – most of them are interested in art. It's because it comes together a little bit, through experimentation, the idea of invention, translation, or discovery. I think it can be a natural conversation. But it's not something that happens very often, maybe because it's not known. I don't know.

LC Do you not think this has to do with the social perception of art? Because if art is presented as it is, with a lot of the processes behind it and the thinking around it isolated from it, it's a rather uninviting conversation. Or at least it's a conversation that only invites on certain levels, which even artists find too limited.

FP Yes, that's true, but what do you think should then happen?

LC I think it's possible to reframe art. To give one example, I remember finding Documenta 13 very interesting in terms of how viewers were talking about the work in the space. It was a very un-silent space. Conversations were being had, and they weren't the usual embarrassed conversations around art. I felt that came about by presenting the work in a way that showed more of the artistic research process. The presentation of the work invited the viewer to forget sometimes that they were looking at art, without compromising the work, without compromising the medium-specificity of the work as art. That may sound like a contradiction but it is not. It is very difficult to get it right but it can be done.

FP I think so too. Part of the reason my work is the way it is, has to do with believing that there needs to be broad access somehow, even if it is not easy. On the one hand, my work is quite art-related. It talks a lot about art but, at the same time, I think the processes that I try to have present in a not too art-coded way are processes that are interesting for everyone. Like for example this rethinking or questioning or speaking about things.

LC Maybe it's polemic, but can we pause for a minute and talk about aesthetics? With regard to your work in *The Body in Crisis*, you mentioned that you created structures partly to make viewers conscious of the body approaching the material, also to block something. But your work is also aesthetic; it is aesthetically extremely pleasing work. This is also an invitation. There is an invitation to enter something that one may not want to engage with usually, partly through an aesthetic appeal.

I have been trying to work out the role of the aesthetic in *The Value in Mathematics*. I was thinking about the conversation in the video work, like when Mariana Leala Ferreira tells of her experiences working with Brazilian tribes and how, for example, they use a different language to talk about weaving; how in a gift economy giving might not equal subtraction and thus lead to a different conception of mathematics. The installation includes weavings, stick sculptures and objects of exchange that clearly use these so-called ethnomathematical moments as a departure point. But I was imagining what it would mean to put those living examples in the exhibition space as a literal representation. Would it do what your work does? In fact, your work translates those wider social and cultural experiences into a particular aesthetic language, which leads the viewer to really recognize their conceptual value. We are not allowed to look at these moments as an ethnographic or anthropological phenomenon. The opening text in your video from *The Value in Mathematics* addresses democracy and its relationship to mathematics. In your sculptures, you force democracy on the material by making different mathematics speak the same aesthetic language. You impose democracy on what would otherwise be perceived as ethnographic, as anthropological, as African fractals, and therefore not just fractals but something African. There's a democracy of language that comes in through the making. It's like a mangle; all of the material goes through a mangle and it is translated into a particular aesthetic language that makes things able to sit together in a way that they could not if they were literal sources.

FP Yes, this was very conscious. Especially in *The Value in Mathematics*, I was aware that there was a risk of exoticization, a risk of using the aesthetics of the anthropological, of presenting funny strange stories about the other. I tried to make the work present on my own terms, not on the terms of a tribe in the Amazon or an African tribe. It was also a protection against any easy use. I wanted to take responsibility; I didn't want to delegate the responsibility for the aesthetics and the content to others. I still find this work a little bit too much in that direction. So I will make a new film that has to do with Lewis Carroll and Ludwig Wittgenstein to show that there are other sources. I don't want to look for wondrous stories in faraway places and not see what is happening or has happened close by. I am trying to use my aesthetic strategies for specific ethical reasons. I use them on the level of artistic content as well, but for me, what you say about the mangle is what I trust in most. I want to tone down the spectacle, to not exhaust or exploit or make the most of the stories. I want the stories to be present but in a gentle way, not in an exoticizing way. The aesthetics of the work is just my natural choice; it's a very one-to-one aesthetics. If I need to make a diagram, it's this, these colors.

LC I thought you made a very interesting choice by including the small ceramic hand-made objects along with the large more minimal sculptures. There is a touch of an anthropologic aesthetic to them but then owned by you. You also made the larger minimal sculptures which, let's say, use a more scientific rational language. The fact that you have made both supports the overall understanding in *The Value in Mathematics* that mathematics and ethnomathematics are the same mathematics, spoken through different aesthetic and conceptual languages.

FP Yes, I think this is the part of the work that works well. When I talk about *The Body in Crisis* and the way the installation comes together with the research, this is exactly what I am talking about. Also in relation to the sciences, to create a space that is not anthropological, that is not "other art," is something that can only be made by all of these different kinds of works.

LC What about play? The objects are also playful. When one sees the works in *The Value in Mathematics*, it brings out a childlike playfulness in the viewer. In the video, you touch the things; you play with them. You do what the viewer wants to do.

FP And then they cannot do it! *(laughs)* I don't want people to touch them. I'm not into interactive art.

LC Me neither, I prefer interaction in the mind, thank you very much! *(laughs)*

FP Exactly! *(laughs)* I think I was also trying to think about working objects. I like objects when they have several functions, preferably three different reasons for being there. The joy lies in making the objects. I really have a hard time with my work most of the time. But making these objects is fun. I also try to think about them in an uncomplicated way instead of thinking about the whole system all of the time. It lets some air into the work.

LC Yes, also for the viewer.

FP Yes, it would be horrible if it wasn't there.

LC Not horrible, but maybe hard work!

FP Yes!

This dialogue was previously published in *MaHKUscript Journal for Fine Art Research* Vol. 2, Issue 1 (2018), which was guest-edited by Lucy Cotter as a preview to the first edition of this book. Republished with kind permission.

Becoming the Archive

A Dialogue with Euridice Zaituna Kala

Lucy Cotter You are currently working on a long-term research-based project called *Sea (E) scapes* (2015–18), which you make manifest in an ongoing series of videos, performances, photographs, and installations. One of your departure points was the *São José Paquete d'África*, a slave ship that was traveling from Mozambique to Brazil in 1794 but crashed en route. I know that you are retracing this journey physically, and both researching and creating work as part of that process. Can you say how you started with this way of working and why you took this particular departure point?

Euridice Zaituna Kala The *São José Paquete d'África* was coming out of Mozambique en route to Brazil and I wanted to reclaim the particular East Oriental slave history it relates to, which is quite lost in contemporary culture. I was partly prompted to start the project because the ship's wreck had just been recovered in Cape Town and had been taken directly to the Smithsonian in Washington for the new National Museum of African American History and Culture, bypassing any form of communication with cultural institutions in Mozambique. What I wanted to make visible with this project was not necessarily this specific slave history but the ongoing re-routing of history and discourse that doesn't include certain spaces. Among other things, I find that there's a narrative of slave history focusing on the Atlantic Ocean that feeds into particular countries and places – South Africa, Nigeria, Ghana, and other Anglophone African countries – which is being made visible, but often at the cost of the visibility of a much larger history.

Around the same time, I was also setting up PAN!C, an experimental platform that interconnected spaces across Africa, creating a sharing of ideas and people across the continent.[1] Its mainframe was based in Africa so that people could share resources and create knowledge without a second or third party element. This included not using Europe's resources; hence, we had a mission of being low budget or no-budget because cultural creation on the African continent has very little allocated budget. So the idea was to work within those means and social structure. PAN!C has since been taken over and run by two organizations, but it influenced my methodologies in *Sea (E) scapes* and it continues to inform the way that I move along with certain ideas.

1 PAN!C (Pan African Network of Independent Contemporaneity) is a platform for independent contemporary art spaces on the African Continent, currently run by VANSA and Centre d'Art Waza. See https://panicplatform.net

LC Clearly, the two projects overlap in their concern with reclaiming knowledge. With *Sea (E) scapes*, you physically retrace the journey of the *São José Paquete d'África* with your own body to gather that knowledge. Somewhere in your writings about the project, you say, "I am the archive." Do you state that to identify yourself as part of that slave history and if so, how does that affect the way you embody those spaces or work with that history in the various locations?

EZK At the outset of the project, I decided to go to all the places that the ship passed through or had a connection with. I started in Lisbon, where the ship originally came from, and spent three months there. Like any researcher, I felt obliged to go to the museums and official archives to try to find some sort of factual history on the ship and its related histories. I quickly became quite frustrated because all of the historical material was approached very much from the Portuguese perspective. The language also felt rather heavy and patriarchal. I didn't identify or empathize at all with the written accounts. So I decided that by going through this journey, I was going to become the archive. I was going to collect information from the perspective of what interests me and not necessarily because of its relevance to any particular historical or contemporary discourse. I became this other power that was going to foreground whatever I wanted, and however I wanted to portray it, regardless of how it had been established in existing archives. So that's the core of the project, to become this archive that follows the route.

LC Did you continue to undertake "formal research" from this perspective as you continued your journey in Cape Town and Ilha de Mozambique?

EZK Yes, in Cape Town, I went to the Slave Lodge Museum, to the District Six Museum, and all the related institutions. The presence of Mozambicans who were passing through to go to Brazil, for example, is not felt today in any shape or form in contemporary South African society. It has very much been erased but you can find traces of it. There is a kind of semblance of these people who arrived and populated the Cape, and who brought Islam with them, in the museums but they do not seem to appear in Cape Town's wider cultural landscape. I found that quite hard; it felt a bit like cultural genocide. If you look at Mozambicans who went to Brazil, you will find that there is still music, religion, and some sort of presence there today. It's hard to believe that kind of presence cannot be felt in Cape Town after 150 years of slave trading and so many slaves staying to work there following a decree that if the Portuguese wanted to take slaves through Cape Town, they would have to bring people to work on the plantations in the Cape.

LC Was this the departure point for the performance you did in Cape Town as part of the 2017 edition of the Infecting the City festival? It seemed to point to Cape Town's entanglement in the imaginary geographies around colonialism and slave trading.

EZK The Cape Town performance was really about mapping. I had been making geodesic maps earlier in the *Sea (E) scapes* project trying to create a parallel narrative to what constitutes geodesic studies today. I had become interested in the idea of triangulation, of the calculating of distances between spaces, between Point A and Point B, to communicate power holding, earlier in the research process. This was partly thanks to a book from the eighteenth century that I had found in an archive in Portugal, which had geodesic calculations of all the Altramar provinces. To really do those calculations, you'd have to be outside of the Earth. It was interesting to try and rethink them today, to re-triangulate the routes, considering the real distance between Paris and Cape Town or Ilha de Mozambique and Lisbon. In the seventeenth and eighteenth centuries, it took a full year for these ships to reach from Point A and Point B, routes that today take a couple of hours. During the performance, I drew maps and wrote a number of statements on a black wall that we created in the public square in front of the municipal theater. I physically enclosed the wall quite quickly in white plastic after drawing up the statements, so that as much as they were there, they were not necessarily visible. My intention was to create a point of interest for the object itself, for this missing narrative.

I had also done research in Ilha de Mozambique, where the ship was coming from on the way to Brazil, to Maranhão. Ilha de Mozambique is a very strange space because it has all of these historical buildings and memorabilia intact, like the first church built in Africa by the Portuguese, yet it's hard to identify this history. It's physically present but still absent somehow. So I was dealing with that too and relating it to the missing part in the Cape because these people are not there in the Cape; they don't exist today. The Cape is very much Black and white and colored but it misses this conversation culturally as well. At the same time, it's present there too because if you go to the museums, you will see tourists coming in to learn about this history. It's a bit disjointed. I lived in South Africa for ten years, in Johannesburg, and the Cape

Town performance was partly about establishing the relationship between these two spaces, but through trying to create a mapping.

LC You did another large research project *Will See You in December … Tomorrow* (2015) while you were living in Johannesburg, which looked at your own relocation to South Africa and addressed the relatively invisible presence of migrant workers from Mozambique in South Africa today. That was a time in which there were a lot of violent attacks on Mozambican migrants. Did the title of that project also refer to that anxiety about returning home safely?

EZK Yes, "December" refers to the time of the holidays when migrants go back but "tomorrow" refers to migrants who cross for the day to do many things. It's still the same country; it's not so far. So the title alludes to both distance and time. I was interested in labor as a consequence of migration and the other way around. In that project, I met with many Mozambicans downtown, who were informal workers and very invisible socially. They don't exist in the South African definition of work or workers, so the artwork was primarily about visibility. I thought it would be interesting to see this through someone else's eyes, so I commissioned a series of photos of women, mostly informal hairdressers. I do that a lot in my projects – creating labor, recreating labor to look through labor at the history of humanity and the world, and going through very personal narratives to move forward. I also did a performance called *Ironing History Out … What Do Mozambicans Do in South Africa?* (2015) in Mozambique, in spaces of departure and arrival from Maputo city center during this period in which many Mozambicans had just fled another xenophobic wave of attacks in South Africa. The performance was a way of prompting conversation, and people responded to that question with a lot of discontentment.

LC You were also using Facebook as a site of research for *Will See You in December … Tomorrow*. Was that a strategy for finding alternative spaces to hold particular histories and current lived experiences? Or was it just a way to generate conversation with more people?

EZK Facebook is interesting. I was always unhappy with my personal use of Facebook; with the fact that I created content all the time, even just by saying that I was tired. I wanted to see if I could use Facebook differently, to use it as an archive. This was also the beginning of establishing myself as the archive. I thought of putting all of the information I gathered on Facebook, creating a space where anyone could pick up this content and use it. It was about challenging spaces of power. Clearly, Facebook has a lot of power. You create content, and you never know how it's being used, and people make money out of your content. It's not a book but it is a space, a visual book that can be used to challenge norms of behavior, of power. I don't use Facebook anymore but I can always go there and find that material, which is interesting in itself. It's also dealing with contemporary spaces of the archive.

LC You've been documenting the entire research journey for *Sea (E) scapes* using Polaroids and writing, which is a very material process in comparison. Do you see those images as potentially works in their own right, or as forming a research archive? How do you bring these different aspects of the project together to find a language for the work?

EZK I generally work with video, performance, and photography, the area in which I was initially trained. I wanted to use Polaroid photography in *Sea (E) scapes* as a concrete response, the most immediate way to create an object. I wanted to make some sort of archive that had its own language. I have also written short texts on the Polaroids, often about contemporary space related to the location in which the image is taken. In Lisbon, for example, there are widows permanently wearing black, old women who come from the generation who lost men in the colonies through the war for Portugal. So the writings from there are a reflection on these bodies I see that remind me of this history. After seeing a very interesting video work by Renée Green, while researching in Portugal, I also started to see the potential of using these Polaroids, not only as objects but also as material that could be abstracted and approached in a non-realist way. This project works with a missing history, but I'm also creating a kind of parallel to that lost history. It's not about doing academic research or staying with the "facts." The first video draft I have made – it's not a finished work – has a specific feeling, a texture that has to do with this history. The Polaroids communicate something a bit more abstract. They don't become very strong objects, but they almost create a sound through their texture. This sharing of sound interests me for some reason.

LC In your writings on the project, you mentioned thinking about what enslaved people would see out the window. I read elsewhere that there were five hundred enslaved persons shackled underneath the hull of the ship, which was windowless. You mentioned getting into the imaginary of hearing the sound of the sea and it not being visible. I saw in the way you used the Polaroids that you zoom in and open up this imaginary space, but you keep hearing the sea sound and it's completely monotonous. Nothing happens, but time is passing somehow.

EZK Absolutely, that's very recurrent in how I am thinking about that experience because it's really about filling in those missing pieces. For me, it's quite an imaginary space. Even though there is a ship and there is a history around it, I still feel that it's a kind of imaginary that we're making as we go along. I wanted to fill in this gap of having to imagine what it would have been like for me to be on that ship. Not only through the heaviness of slave trade history but also through the prism of other nuances that are not being attended to.

I have also thought a lot about another slave ship called the *Meermin*, a Dutch East India Company ship that was bringing slaves from Madagascar to Cape Town, including a king from Madagascar, whom they had stolen. This king or chief had diplomatic and military knowledge, which he used to organize a mutiny on board. Although the Dutch later recaptured the ship, the slaves took it over and held the captain captive for three weeks. But having no experience of sailing to Cape Town, they didn't know where they were going. I found it quite interesting that the slaves reverted the roles of power and the victim. But I was also interested in this nuance of being able to see but not know, and sound is very important because it gives you some sort of direction. You're still on the sea, you're still in the middle, you're still in between. I'm interested in the sound that reflects the in between. You've left but you haven't arrived. You're still in between something. This sound represents this nowhere. It's also comforting somehow because it's not telling you whether you have arrived at your demise or not.

LC This approach of entering the imaginary of what it is to be an enslaved person on a ship and the kind of attitude that you're taking with it, which is not necessarily heavy, but very personal, seems to me to be a way of reclaiming subjectivity. These people were treated as objects, literally as cargo, and even within history, they became objects of history. You're not so much reclaiming their history as circumventing that act of revisionism and going straight for "This is a person." In a way, you're creating a one-on-one relationship by saying, "I am the archive and you are also the archive."

EZK Absolutely, and at the same time, I don't want to create power struggles. I'm not necessarily interested in gaining some sort of leverage by taking it from someone else. I'm interested in creating subjectivity, in creating a slave character who is more dynamic, who has more agency. I think that dynamism is often missing in how Black characters are portrayed. People are striving and making efforts to change that, especially in popular culture, in the US and the UK. You can see that, for example, in a TV show like *Chewing Gum*, which is about a young woman living in a public housing estate. The show is trying to develop and create a dynamism around being Black in that sort of environment. People are doing interesting things in other areas of culture, but in contemporary visual arts, I feel there's still quite some negligence when it comes to portraying Black characters. Black people are very much present in relation to specific narratives, but they don't have any parallel existence; there's no way of imagining those narratives otherwise except through pain, victimhood, and so on. Of course, those aspects are very real and important to portray but there is more there and I'm interested in this other dimension, this "more" that I can see. I ask myself how I can make it of interest to have this represented in contemporary discourse and history.

LC This also makes me think about *Unlike Other Santas…* (2013), one of your earlier video works that deconstructs the various elements that make up the character of the Dutch blackface tradition of *Zwarte Piet* (Black Peter), Saint Nicholas's "helper," who gives children in the Netherlands presents in December. In the video, you allowed someone to cut off your hair and paint your face black in an almost ritualistic process, becoming a kind of warrior figure that transforms into full blackface. Does this relate to the notion of being the archive? I find it interesting that you again approach a form of violence, symbolic violence, through a silent work. The intensity of watching your face reminded me of watching Andy Warhol's *Screen Tests*. Although you do not physically react to what is happening to you as such, basically as viewers, we're watching the vulnerability on a person's face. What were you trying to achieve with that gesture?

EZK I was going through a difficult personal moment at that time, which gave me the sensation of struggling to regain some kind of power. I came to the conclusion that I shouldn't struggle to gain or lose power but instead look at that process of gaining and losing. Through this character of *Zwarte Piet*, who is victimized historically and in contemporary culture – he speaks bad Dutch, he is a mockery of Black identity – I wanted to understand this process. Because this character is predominantly performed by white people, not

Black people, I wanted to see how this Black body could have other narratives. My main intention was to observe the position I was inhabiting as I was going through it, having to deal with it, but not struggling against it. I'm not only taking up the position of the victim, but I also have some power in deciding to go through this process and to observe it. What does that mean? The in-betweenness of it all, the humanity of it. I wanted it not to be *about* it but to *be* it.

LC When I was watching your hair being cut off piece by piece and your head being shaved, it brought to mind the public shaving of women's hair at the end of the Second World War, which was a gesture of shaming women. *Unlike Other Santas …* seemed to also touch on womanhood and what it means to be a woman. I don't know if you intended to address womanhood specifically in the work or not. I know you identify as a feminist.

EZK Yes, I absolutely did. At that moment in my life, I also wanted to lose my own womanhood, to become this other possibility, so it was definitely about that as well. To be able to perform my life, to continue with the action, which is the performance of life without having to rely on my womanhood. Hair does that; it is intimately connected to the performance of womanhood. Feminism is very complex for me. I do identify as a feminist, but I make sure that it's always very localized, very particular to me, to where I'm from, to the women I come from, and what they define as a feminist act. The loss of hair is generally a feminist act, but it certainly means that where I come from. It means that you are not relying on your beauty to deal with life. It goes hand in hand with the question of beauty and what it can get you.

LC You have made a further video work, *Measuring Blackness and a Guide to Other Industries* (2016), which seems to extend that reflection of self and objecthood out toward a broader history. I found it very striking that it's a black-and-white video, it's silent and it's very understated. Yet in my experience of it, what the video conveys is very violent. It's almost like a silent conversation with Blackness as objecthood during the colonial trading period.

EZK I am addressing violence in that work, while focusing my line of thought on the Industrial Revolution. I am interested in the industriousness of it and the necessity for many other industries outside of Europe to exist alongside it to keep it going. How bodily those industries were elsewhere, next to how industrialization was undertaken in Europe. In the video, I am weighing up different materials associated with the Industrial Revolution. The white wedding dress probably stands out as an exception to the other materials like salt, ivory, and cotton but I found it interesting as a symbol of a moment in history when the English became structurally so strong. Queen Victoria's white wedding dress became known and spread across Europe and then Africa as this symbol of unity, of purity, and ultimately a display of Western ideals and desires, through photography, through the image. I saw this as a human history story. It wasn't necessarily about Blackness or whiteness. I think that during the eighteenth and nineteenth centuries, many white people were suffering in comparable ways to Black people. Children were working as slaves in Europe. But there was nevertheless a different relationship to labor in Africa, an imposed relationship to labor. It wasn't about working to eat; it was a third-party relationship, working to feed some other industry. There is a white body that forces some sort of industry or industriousness on the African body. I have just started another project that looks at this relationship to labor in Mozambique specifically, following the postcolonial fall of industry in Mozambique.

LC Will your new project reread the relationship between the colonial period and the present through the prism of labor, also in relation to contemporary migration? I know that there was also a civil war in Mozambique after independence in 1975, which partly revolved around the question of whether the nation may become a communist or Marxist space. So I imagine that the idea of labor has remained highly contested.

EZK Yes, that conflict, which started two years after independence, went on until 1992. Samora Machel, the first president of the republic, advocated very strongly for labor practice, wanting to reconstruct the country using Mozambican labor. With my latest project, which has the working title *Scores of Labor*, I will be working primarily with a Protestant choral group in Mozambique and having this conversation about postcolonial, post-industrial Mozambique. I am interested in how Protestants accept the relationship between labor and work; they have a lack of guilt around money and power relative to Catholics. I'm going to be sharing information with the choir members around industry in Mozambique, reflecting on their relationship with work. The idea is to create new work around these conversations. I want to create a musical score that they will be performing and record that into a short film. That will be the main piece for the exhibition, which is going to be shown in Mozambique and then in Portugal, hopefully.

LC It surprised me to learn that Mozambique became independent as late as 1975. So I guess the people in this choir have a very immediate relationship with that legacy. What age are they?

EZK They are all different ages. Some people were born before Mozambique was free and some, who are as young as nineteen, have no notion of this and no understanding of dealing with labor and power. This is also because labor is still very much mediated by anyone who has power who comes to Mozambique and implements some sort of industry, be it China, Portugal or Brazil. It's still not a self-initiated venture, and that interests me because we are still dealing with the emotional level of how we relate to labor. What does it mean to work? Why do we work? My own interest is also based on the question of whether artists work. Do I work? Am I working at this moment? I have a certain frustration around art and the industry of art, the idea that art can become an industrious space. But that's a parallel conversation.

This dialogue was previously published in *MaHKUscript Journal for Fine Art Research* Vol. 2, Issue 1 (2018), which was guest-edited by Lucy Cotter as a preview to the first edition of this book. Republished with kind permission.

Knowledge as Production

A Dialogue with Liam Gillick

Liam Gillick I've almost willfully avoided looking at the emerging discussion or discourse around artistic research until now. I don't know why I'm resistant to it, because it is something I'm clearly interested in, and I'm interested in it structurally. I think it has to do with the connection with potentially academic associations of the idea of research that distresses me a bit. I am aware that young curators thinking about exhibitions and curating in institutional structures sometimes talk about research when they mean looking something up or reading. That's not research, that's reading. The whole idea of "research" opens up a lot of potential problems for me, and anxieties, which is odd because research is not supposed to make you anxious. Why would it make you anxious?

Lucy Cotter I find the term "artistic research" unhelpful in this respect. I prefer to think about knowledge production – within the artistic, outside the artistic and across the artistic / non-artistic. Within this book, I've avoided elaborate discussions about the term "research," what that means or how it might be defined, exactly because such discussions often seem to miss the point of the potential of what artistic research *could* mean. This oversight partly lies in this focus on the term "research," with the almost inevitable relapse into academic ways of thinking. The notion of "knowledge production" is also problematic, of course. I prefer the term "non-knowledge" production, as Sarat Maharaj calls it, which is more useful in relation to art because the term "knowledge production" again pushes toward some kind of a defined outcome; it pushes back to academia indirectly somehow.

LG Or good social work. Who would be against that? The idea of "knowledge production" as a phrase seems to work quite well when you look at certain structures for grant applications or institutional missions. It gets close to this idea of knowledge production as always being a good thing. It would always imply some form of social good, and that's also difficult because it seems to limit the potential of art, even if there's nothing inherent about the idea of knowledge production that means it should be more friendly or progressive.

LC Acknowledging the pitfalls of terms like "artistic research" and "knowledge production" and how they influence the emerging field, I still want to work with the potential of taking art seriously as a field that thinks differently. What happens when art has a more direct dialogue with other disciplines and non-artistic discourses? There is a widening of the frame through artistic research discourse that I find important. It allows for a different shift of emphasis than the emergence of visual studies as an expanded frame of reference, although it also resonates with broader socio-economic and cultural changes. In your practice, you often address the division of labor, as well as shifts in historic concepts of work and production within and outside of the artistic, drawing parallels between them. Coming from that angle, why do you think artistic research discourse has been emerging over the past ten to fifteen years? Some people put it down to the Bologna Accord drawn up by the European Union, which foregrounded artistic research in art education, but although it's a factor, that seems like much too limited a view to me.

LG Well, here in America, the Bologna Accord is not something that is part of the consciousness at all. Yet some of the aspects we're talking about are also happening here, so it's more than just some sort of process instrumentalization or a kind of reimagined set of educational procedures. I think that some of it is technological and some of it is, as it were, cultural. The technological aspects are so obvious that many of us can't bear to even talk about it. Yet it clearly has to do with the relative ease of communicating and exchanging ideas or information. It has to do with the different speeds at which various institutional or professional frameworks adopt those things. In the early 1990s, when I started showing at Galerie Esther Schipper in Germany, there was a great deal of communication between the various artists and curators involved. There weren't many other people doing it then. We were operating in a kind of sphere of communication that was quite limited but seemed to have shared ideals at some level. As more and more people join this way of communicating or become part of it, it affects the way people respond to and deal with flows of information and ideas. It's hard to say exactly what happens but something changes, I think.

LC That makes me think about speed being another protagonist in producing the discursive turn in art. Because things don't have to be physical anymore, the image is at the same level as the text. Even in the physical presentation of work, there is often no difference, materially speaking, between a corporate report and an artistic project. Most young artists I know make their work on their laptop, and it pretty much stays there. Perhaps the call for artistic research is also a fight for something that isn't working at the same speed, although in a way it is moving faster than it. Maybe the notion of research is a carving out of something that is not quickly produced for the market and presented. That's perhaps too romantic a notion of research, but there is something in there that resists that speed. On the other hand, the very expectation of the production of text and so on seems to speed discourse up. It creates the demand for constant references and being in touch with existing discourses that are changing rapidly.

LG Yes, I think from my perspective, from say 1994 onwards, there was a new form of exchange that was being fought over. It was being gently fought over, not being wrenched apart, but there was still a kind of struggle for power and dominance. Also, with more and more people using it, it was growing and shifting. I think some forms of artistic research or non-knowledge production are connected to this. They have two distinct pulls or stresses. One is that, at some level, they do somewhat mimic this idea of open thought, of thinking without goals, which is so much part of the origin of the Internet and the origin of new technology. During that period, the technological world stole all the words, like "creativity" and even "curate." So I think a lot of artists have been using complicated strategies to dump more information on you than you could ever use, in order to change the forms of exchange from virtual to one-to-one, to undermine moments of judgment and to play with the way identity is directed – think of Thomas Hirschhorn or Hito Steyerl and many others.

But also at some level what's happened is the problem of the artwork, which seems to be a very pre-Internet problem. The problem of the authority of the discrete artwork also becomes less of a problem at the same time, because concurrent with this, you get a return to a desire to avoid all forms of research. There's a return to a sort of abstraction or the artwork is a thing in itself that tries to suggest some autonomy or some resistance by its "artness." So you'll get this phenomenon where there are products or side elements or backdrop elements to research or to research as artwork, which end up having this resistant quality. The thing that traditionally was held by the optimistic modernist artwork, this kind of autonomous quality, is now held by the stage or the setting or the framework of the book or the design of the location of where the event takes place, whether it is public, private or semi-open. These became the issues, I think, in the last twenty years for a lot of artists – Rirkrit Tiravanija and Philippe Parreno have both pioneered this.

LC Is this why you once dealt with the notion of being "outside of any given context" in *A Syntax of Dependency* (2011), your collaborative work with Lawrence Weiner at the Museum of Contemporary Art (M HKA) in Antwerp? Was it a strategy?

LG Yeah, to a point. The people who have been most difficult to deal with in the last twenty years have been the ones who expect you to be excited about the fact that they've set up a lab or a knowledge production environment or a "researchy" sounding sponsored-type think tank. The very first time I came across this as a very concrete thing was at least fifteen years ago in London Westminster's Council, which has traditionally been a liberal Tory entity. Being responsible for a number of artworks, plus having the responsibility to put some percentage of their budget into public art, they decided to change their policy on public art. They called a meeting where they invited a couple of artists plus a whole bunch of other people to consider the idea that instead of dealing with public artworks, they should give money toward people who want to do research projects as art. They thought I'd be really happy to hear this, but I remember saying that I was dreaming of putting great big artworks in the street that were in the way and bothering people. Of course, this was when everyone started stumbling back and saying, "Well, hang on a second, the reason you want to do this is to avoid having to take responsibility for physical things in space that are not the same as development and so on." In the semi-public area, there would still be things, but those things would all come from private developers or the few people who are temporarily given the ability to take over some space. In the meantime, they were going to be using artists like parallel institutions to kind of think about it, but not do it. I don't think they really understood that research is not limited to making reports on things. This is why it is quite interesting when you talk about this terminology, because we know that it's not quite the right term because the idea of art research implies that there's actually some research being done.

LC Perhaps we should revisit the notion of what research is and in particular its relationship to materiality. I'm interested in both how material and how immaterial your practice has been over a long time, and I really like the tension between the two. You've made a point of producing and creating a certain awareness for that, also by putting a certain history of labor to the fore, which has largely been kept outside of the gallery space but is actually manifest in the production of objects. It can be a fetish to talk about "the hands-on connection," but setting that mindset aside, can we consider the non-knowledge that comes out of material production? I don't want to be nostalgic about it, but I do want to question the extent to which materiality is present in current art production. Working in a virtual or digital way isn't entirely non-material, of course. But I started out as an artist making sculpture and artist's books. I used printmaking techniques and made physical structures in space. Different kinds of knowledge came through those processes that I've never been able to access using a computer, even when I used it to make artist's books. I'm interested in that knowledge being present in artistic research and also in its articulation for people who are not privy to it, without it being fetishized.

LG Yes, sometimes I forget to say simple things about stuff. To a certain extent, I also use the computer all the time, but I started using it in 1987, the year I left art school. I've pretty much used it consistently since then, which sounds unremarkable now, but it was remarkable then to use the computer as your main repository of ideas and also your site of planning production and commentary on your own work, without making computer or digital art. I guess a notebook could potentially be the same thing, but it always has this quality of a notebook. With the exception of Richard Hamilton, whom I'm interested in, transliterating, as it were, Duchamp's notebooks–deciphering and re-laying them out–notebooks always have this quality of "notebookness," whereas the computer can expand itself in different ways. So I deliberately used it as a point where you could shift the level of expansion and contraction, or privacy or "publicness" of an idea easily through the sorting and organizing and thinking and working process of how you use the computer.

LC There's a natural shift to the public.

LG Exactly. A good example would be what was I doing yesterday, organizing photographs that document an event that happened last summer in France, *To the Moon via the Beach* at LUMA Arles. The XIF data tells you exactly to the second when each photograph was taken and I'm trying to organize a book that can reconstruct an event from every angle, from every photographer. Six or seven people documented that event, and through the data on the images I can construct a timeline of the event, viewed from different perspectives. This is a very "computery" type thing to do, but I have a problem with it because some of the cameras were not set to the right time zone, so I have to guess which time zone they were on.

So I try to find a way to adjust that metadata and then re-sort everything with the new metadata without going through the three thousand images and re-writing it by hand. It becomes a kind of computer-internal, computer-type problem.

On the other hand, I'm also editing a text, wittily enough, on research – the idea of research as an idea –which actually ended up talking about curating more than about making art. It talks about curating as research. So that's using the computer like a typewriter. Then the third thing I'm doing at the same time is flipping screens and working on a big public artwork which is going on in Sweden in the city of Lund, which is a set of benches and shelving systems that run through a park and through the new city hall offices and out through the building into the park again. So it draws a line of places to sit and places to keep things, but inside a public building and outside in the park.

LC It's interesting that it cuts across the knowledge production space into the social space of the same structures, with this idea of the benches and the storage.

LG Yes, you've got these different articulations, coming back to what you were saying about how other things materialize themselves. So what is this quality of art? How do these things find their place in the world? How do they manifest themselves? For me, it's about deciding, a bit like when you have that EQ thing that we used to have for the hi-fi systems where you have little sliders that change all of the frequencies. It can often be divided into thirty different sets of frequencies. I turn up some of them and turn some down depending on how I feel or what I'm addressing at any given moment.

LC Do you mean that it acts like a kind of sliding scale, from material to immaterial production?

LG Exactly. But I'll suddenly realize that this problem – of trying to work out how to alter the metadata from these photographs to reconstruct an event from many perspectives – has something to do with something else. So it's kind of coming back to the idea of non-knowledge production. It's a form of non-knowledge production because these things feed each other, but they don't feed each other acritically or uncritically. You're seeing the limits of a procedure, and it affects your thinking about something else. So even though the benches and shelving systems for Sweden appear to be fairly straightforward and have a kind of simple, straightforward aspect to them, they are somehow affected by trying to address the problem of how to shift time zones and metadata for photographs without having to do all this work myself by hand.

LC Isn't this really about material resistance? When I moved from working as an artist into writing and other things, one of the things that happened, which was positive at the outset, was the absence of material resistance. You were talking about the computer and computer-type problems. The "cut and paste" option did a lot for me on a mental level, the fact that I could pull things from many sites and bring them together in writing with no material resistance made a lot possible creatively. But on the other hand, I can also see that the interesting, creative problems that came out of material resistance do not arise in the same way as a result, and therefore I do not address them in my work. There are bodies of work that are not made because I don't have those problems.

LG I agree with you completely. Because why should art be a struggle of any sort whatsoever, let alone having an issue about material resistance be the main requirement for it? So, of course, there's something very attractive and seductive about finding new, smooth ways through something, and certainly in the 1990s that was exactly what I did. I was asking myself, how can I work? How can I function? How can I exist? What should I value and what should be important? I would start to write the scripts for *McNamara*, for example, because I could use the computer and carry it with me. It was the time of the first laptops that you could actually afford. I could take the script on a floppy disc in my pocket and that was my art. So it had something to do with the idea that art should be easy, in a way. I don't see why I can't carry this thing and work on it and add to it all the time. Now you could say you could do that with a manuscript, but it's not the same as the copy-paste thing and the aspect of smoothness. Of course, what happens is that as the technology advances or develops, the smoothness becomes overly complicated by a facility to be able to do something. It starts to make the smoothness so fast and so "slidey" that you kind of run away with yourself.

LC You slide past things.

LG You slide past everything. So then you sort of have to double back a little bit. This idea of resistance becomes something that you have to address as an idea as much as actually experiencing it. I don't think you necessarily have to experience it, but you have to deal with it or think about it. Of course, some people get around that by literally dealing with the manipulation of objects in space and the placement of the object in space. Other people do it by working on settings and the designed component of their research, as it were, the formal aspects of it. And other people do it by trying to find new routes through modes of research and communication that are not smooth. It's a bit like trying to get from one place to another by riding on a highway or going on a horse across the highway and over a railroad track through a stream.

LC It's potentially still going from A to B, but it's more likely that the horse will need water halfway across the road and have to turn left and take another corner or get hit by a car.

LG Yes, and part of this aspect of research which is analogous to taking a route across many terrains is about going to something without going to do the thing it's there for, like going to the library without reading books. Of course, that's the most literal kind of negative aspect of research, but one component of art as research has to do not with using a pen to stir your coffee with, but looking at the relationships between the pen and the coffee and the hierarchy between them and the piece of paper. Then maybe going to thinking about where the pen is made. And you see that it starts to generate connections that either evade standard, sort of rationalized forms of exchange, or add to new ones that people hadn't really noticed before, and that the generalized kinds of forms of exchange in society can't be bothered to finance.

LC I'm picturing it as a diagram where you have the pen and the cup and normally the arrows point inward to think across the relationship between those objects. The fact that they exist is a given, and the relationship between them is taken as obvious. But when the artist deals with the same set-up, the arrows are as likely to point outward.

LG Something like that, but I think what we're dealing with here, which is why it's such a problem, is also a whole set of art that deals with a new awareness of these directions that are being indicated or pointed out, and therefore includes a consciousness of which direction things are pointing in some of the work or the critical work. This doesn't mean that everything has become formalistic and disappears in a kind of infinite reflection of itself. Within this apparent terrain, it's not all just about good works; there are strong elements of difference within the work itself. There's an enormous difference between my *McNamara* work from 1994 and Danh Vo's more recent *McNamara* work, for example. I wrote some films; he bought some artifacts. They're complementary but they're extremely different forms of research, as it were, and they point in different directions. They invite you to stand beside the artist and look in different ways. They suggest different levels of engagement, I would say.

LC It makes me think of the very old-fashioned idea of uniqueness. There is space in art for each of those forms of individuality which, if the outcomes had been made differently, might collapse into each other because the links are so direct and apparent, they would appear to deal with the same thing. They might seem somehow to be having a conversation, but the individuality of the artist and how they deal with this may actually produce a situation where there's almost no correlation, even if the topic is the same.

LG Exactly, but you've got to remember also that for some people, some aspect of the research component or art in relation to research and vice-versa, has to do with making things so complicated that people can't completely follow what's going on. Thereby it's either protecting the artist, by creating this kind of series of buffers and this mass of information and ideas around a work, and on the other hand, also making it more difficult to see where's the art moment in any given work, right? And this, I think, is deliberate. It is the aspect of art research that resists the instrumentalization of art where it's used only for good social work, which is that some of that work is done in order to be deliberately confusing.

LC I see your point but can we think a little further about protection and the need for a buffer? I think this goes back to our earlier conversation about shifts in technology and the impossibility of the placement of the artist somehow.

LG Yes, I've actually been trying to experiment with not doing it for a year to see what happens. Not having a research component, as it were. Like not having a topic or a project or a prototype on the horizon or whatever other analogy you could use.

LC Do you mean shifting into just doing or shifting into non-action? Or do you know yet?

LG Well, what I've been doing is basically doing lots of different things that are not compatible with each other. This culminated in the exhibition I did at Taro Nasu Gallery in Tokyo called *Vertical Disintegration*, which is when a product is produced by a company where all of the component products are produced by autonomous companies that have been shared by the main company. A close example would be Airbus, for example, where the wings are made in France and the fuselage is made by another company in the US, and so on. But it's not quite that simple, because vertical disintegration is usually willed by a company or a corporation or an organization. It's a slightly more complicated idea of the organization of management.

LC Is it about not locating power outside of the ownership?

LG Yes, the component manufacturers are completely separate entities that are not ruled or controlled by the central organization.

LC So your doing various things means taking no responsibility?

LG Exactly. I started to do these component productions of components, i.e. exhibitions or works or modes of thought or ways of functioning that were disintegrated, literally vertically disintegrated. No one notices any difference, but I know it because I feel it. I'm closer to the event or closer to the moment of exchange because I've removed the bit to talk about that is the research component.

Let me give an example. I did a three-person show in Paris at the beginning of the year with two artists I'd never worked with who are both younger, Benoît Maire and Falke Pisano, where I went and spent time living above a bookshop and we came up with the work while we were there. So this was the first gesture. The second one was to go to Korea and work with two outside curators. We took over a private gallery and we did our own show within someone else's gallery. The third gesture was to do a residency in the north of Scotland at the Highland Institute for Contemporary Art–where I didn't actually go, but I stayed in New York and did it here, as if I was there, so to speak. I researched forms of courtyard housing, but it wasn't so much research. In a sense, there was more production than research. And then going to Tokyo and doing a show that brings together all these fragments.

LC You just made the distinction between production and research but isn't that production *as* research?

LG It actually very quickly turned into a form of production, the research I was doing.

LC Your research sounds to me like some of the things you talked about in your writing regarding the shift from planning to speculation. It almost implies planning but it doesn't necessarily have to.

LG No, but for years, I've tended to think, "Okay, I'm basically working on this; I have this area I'm interested in. Everything I'm doing is surrounded by this. I can protect myself by pushing that apparent topic, as it were, further away from myself and, by extension, the border between me and everyone else. That can be the moat within which people can swim while I get on with what I'm doing." I decided for a year just to abandon doing that or to abandon thinking that way. What happens is that the "artistness" of your existence becomes more important. It's been really fascinating to have a glimpse of what it feels like to be an artist in the raw, as it were, but I don't like it. I realize now that I need a topic, I need a problem. I need an area of research. It's a bit sad maybe, but it's important. I am in the middle of writing a text about research that maybe touches on this. There's only one decent line in it, unfortunately, which is a shame.

LC *(Laughs)* Well, let's recycle it at least. What is it?

LG It says, "Research is at the basis of certain artistic practices and some methodologies deployed by the complete curator"–I won't go into what that term means. "However, research cannot be independently verified unless enacted within the frame of the exhibition. Research may suggest lengthy engagement, while the actual intensity of finding out is impossible to gauge." Right? "The gathering of material without judgment may be research, as could the detailed investigation of one minor object. Research carries scientific authority; research implies an evacuation from zones of commodified exchange and directs us toward the apparent authority of the institutional library or laboratory. Alone it cannot build better systems or structures, yet it can point out how far away they still appear to be." The bit that was important was the thing about not being independently verified. If you say or imply that you're involved in research, you don't really mean sitting around all day staring out the window or going carefully through a whole large number of things. It does something very important historically to the notion of what an artist is doing, in a strange way.

LC I have been thinking that one of the disturbances and maybe one of the things to fight for within the emerging field of artistic research is the right to inactivity. The productivity of inactivity has always been key to artistic practice, and the proximity of the academic system imposes some kind of expectations, criteria, which do not necessarily recognize inactivity as a mode of production.

LG Well, a good example would be my ex-father-in-law, who's a scientist. He researches chemistry, so he spends a lot of time just thinking and diddling around and then most of the rest of the time writing research papers which accrete knowledge, adding another little component to this enormous picture. Of course, the problem with the term "research" is that it implies those two things might be taking place in a way.

LC Can we pause here for a second to talk about the differences and the overlap between the artist who's diddling around, thinking or trying not to think, and the scientist who's diddling around?

LG Peer review is what I would say because as a scientist, essentially what you're doing is constantly reviewing other people's papers and they're revising yours. But you're also playing with hierarchy because you're battling for authorship all the time. You're including and excluding certain people in a kind of hierarchy all the time.

LC Don't you think that exists in the art world too?

LG It absolutely exists but it exists in ways that are different. The people who are the junior authors of a paper are also potentially your future peers. When you're an architect, you're a junior because you'll become a senior, whereas that's not the same usually with the hierarchies of art. Let's say that I work with a fabricator in Berlin. Unless he decides to stop being a fabricator and make his own art, even if he appears to be doing the same thing he's been doing for me, he is not a peer. In terms of a hierarchical relationship, he's also not an apprentice. Do you see what I mean?

What I tried to set up was this kind of relationship between discourse and research, because they're intentionally each other as far as I'm concerned. Discourse is excessively verifiable, but it becomes a partner of research and they feed into each other. There's a push and pull between discourse and research, because of course the discursive component of art, when it's done publically, is verifiable. You can see the use of these people talking. You can witness what they're saying, whereas research is double, which is not necessarily witnessable, like the predicament for the Highlands of Scotland. You have to believe me that I went to Scotland and I researched what's called "courtyard housing," which is low-rise, high-density housing. But I didn't go there, and the research I did didn't involve looking very deeply into the idea of existing forms of courtyard housing, even though that's what I said I was doing. I got caught up in a completely different thing, which was examining ground plans of the kind of architectural sublime, which is the ultimate kind of expression of early modernist architecture, the private villa. Then I took fragments of the ground plans of iconic private villas and used them as the basis to design new forms of low-rise, high-density housing based on my components from important private houses. So that's a good example of me using research as a form of production that doesn't involve directly examining in detail the thing I said I'm researching. What I did was that I produced a new set of plans.

LC It's like there's a war in our brains because on the one hand, we have the legacy of what research has meant, and on the other hand, there's the potential for it to be something else. You try and embrace the potential, but on the other hand, you are fighting the demons all the way along.

LG But I've noticed a tendency in the last ten years with the maturing of the kind of new curatorial model for people to start saying to certain types of artists like me, "What is this work derived from?"

or "Where is this work derived from?" So there's an assumption that it has to do with reiteration and recuperation of something.

LC Isn't that part of the problem of the shift of the discursive away from the material? Because you have a generation of curators that have possibly never dealt with the work materially, or at least to a very limited extent.

LG Right. But they're saying this in nice ways. They're implying that as a good artist, you are probably involved in research, which involves things that can be independently verified. And rather than this weird process where the root often involves traversing flows, which require specific tools, like in the case of the eight-lane highway, it might involve speed or luck. In another case, it might mean going into the water and just being swept downstream until you can get to the other side, or it might involve sending out a decoy to take the hit for you, as it were, or to check the way or using a stick to see what the ground is made of. Instead of choosing a route where you can see potentially what the result is going to be.

LC When I think about artists' ways of thinking, I also think about the space to be associative instead of analytical. Certainly, the analysis may come later at some point but, as we were saying earlier, there are different components that don't necessarily relate to each other even if they appear to. From an external point of view, you look for some kind of framework of references that explain the production or presence of an element. But artistic thinking often works through chains that are more associative than analytical.

LG I agree with you, and I like the term "associative." The problem is that when you work like that, what happens is that you get certain types of artists …

LC Yes, but the term "associative thinking" sounds more random than it is in practice. Looking back on what we talked about much earlier – about you working on three projects at one time – associative thinking has paths that engage with this production of problems that come through the material, among other things. Therefore, the elements that are produced do come from somewhere. I think it may be partly about intuition, but not in the standard understanding of the term. Henri Bergson's understanding of the notion of intuition as method is perhaps closer to what's actually going on, not a fluffy understanding of intuition. There are tracks being laid across – I liked your term "traversing" – there's an act of traversing going on that is the difference between a post-modern anything-goes and a not-anything-goes.

LG Right.

LC It goes back to what I was thinking about non-action and inactivity. I see it like a mechanism, with things clogging the works in different directions, both when artistic research opens up a link to academia and in terms of wider market forces on the art market. But it's very hard to keep that space open without romanticizing it.

LG Yes, it's a bit like years ago when John Baldessari wrote these kind of, slightly truism-type artworks, and he would say that certain types of work, conceptual work, doesn't reach the highest prices at auction or whatever it would be. One thing that's for sure is that when people feel something you've produced is related to something that has some research component, which is not entirely apparent in every component of the work that they're viewing, they believe that there may be a trick that they're not seeing. Therefore it reduces the surface price of the work in a way, which is actually true.

People want to know what is absent, and this is, of course, a conscious thing, right? When you work in research as a methodology, when you use research as a sort of method, you deliberately do it in order to potentially withhold a certain aspect or component of the work. People will want to know what's missing. Why am I getting this? What's all the other stuff that I'm not getting? It creates both an allure and an interest in what that other stuff is, but it also creates anxiety about the status of the thing that you exchange with someone.

LC The alternative is to go for the earlier model of art as research work, like with Art and Language.

LG Yes, what happens then is that the artist starts presenting the entire product of the research because of a distrust of transparency, because transparency starts to become a mainstream, neo-liberal New Social Democrat kind of model. Artists decided they didn't want to do that because research is inherently not verifiable and you're not necessarily seeing people doing it. Of course, there are artists who literally do it and enact it in public. That's where you get the edges of participation and relational aesthetics and the confusion about what these things are, but generally speaking, there's always an absence. It implies that when you see a work, you're seeing something that's partial. Now that's true about Ellsworth Kelly too. When you see one painting, you're also not seeing all the other paintings that Kelly has done, but frankly, the not-seeing is something that you can imagine, and it's not a problem.

LC So artistic research inevitably brings up the question of the location of the work of art.

LG Research as a method creates a troubling absence of the work. It may be an important component that can't find a form and therefore there might be anxiety about what is the nature of this kind of art that's being done here. What's the important bit? Now I think this would be true for Carey Young, for example. We're not really sure if her standing in the gallery doing something or having a conversation is the good art bit, or is it maybe that bit where she researched all the legal frameworks? Maybe that should come out in a different form? It also creates a potential for input to the artwork by other people because other people start to think and contribute to what they think would be useful.

LC Art has always held a position of multiplicity in terms of its relation to a public, because on the one hand there's the notion of the universal artwork that can speak to everybody, and on the other hand, there's a huge amount of information you have to access to be on top of the discourse. The field of artistic research becoming a discipline means that art may be allowed to be taken more seriously and may be conceived as possibly producing knowledge of some kind that may be interesting outside of a very narrow field. Yet the price of this acknowledgment seems to be transparency, with academics often expecting artists to make the inner workings of their practice publicly available. Rather than providing a practice-based perspective on art, they are asked to "tell all their secrets," so to speak. I see that as a significant problem. It's asking the wrong questions somehow.

LG Yes. I was taught by Michael Craig Martin as well as by Mary Kelly and Susan Hiller, who both used forms of research as a way; the idea of working on a project or producing, researching something in its fairly original sense in terms of contemporary art. I learned from that and also from the fact that personal identity and postcolonialism often came out in terms of research. If you read the section in the book on *Magiciens de la Terre* about Alfredo Jarr, he talks very openly about deciding on a certain method of working, which involved research.[1] It's because he wanted to get into the art world – he's very open about it – and tell a certain set of stories and the way to do that would be to use research as a kind of model and then present the findings of the research as art. I think some of these kinds of methods influenced me – not him necessarily – as a straight, white man growing up in London, which is historically a position of privilege to a certain extent. It's not the work itself that was the thing to do, but the way of working.

LC Previously, one of the ways to be a good artist was to be a bad academic, but something like dealing with postcolonialism raised certain questions of responsibility and the possibility that the artist could be somebody who reads, who knows things, and who may be up on all of the academic discourses but may choose to work differently. That process may not be visible in the artwork and it doesn't have to be, but that level of engagement in the work is something I find important

1 Lucy Steeds et al., *Making Art Global (Part 2): "Magiciens de la Terre" 1989* (London: Afterall, 2013).

in artistic research. This can, but does not necessarily have anything to do with the production of what artist Wjm Kok calls "researchistic art" because – and here we go back to materiality – very often what happens in the work itself comes through the possibilities offered by a particular medium; what can be held in video, for example, that can't be held in a text.[2]

LG Right, right. Well, you've got multiple kinds of strands of production because you need to use these different methods. But, of course, some of it for me has a kind of politics, because if Mary Kelly needs to use different research methods and different forms of output in order to tell a complex story about identity and where she stands in relation to power and representation and the child and the other and the mother and whatnot, maybe the way I should use a similar method, but not necessarily address those questions, is to use that as a way to examine where I stand. I am using similar methods to be conscious of how I am working as an artist. That's how I started doing it that way, when I made the decision to use "researchistic" kinds of methods, as you called it, in order to examine some of these things. So it's very deliberate.

LC It's like a self-consciousness of the division of labor in relation to your position, in relation to the world and art discourse.

LG Exactly, but of course what's happened is that these practices have matured and shifted and altered and been affected also by the fact that advanced curatorial thinking has often been

2 Wjm Kok, "And, And, And So On and So Forth," in Janneke Wesseling, ed., *See it Again, Say it Again: The Artist as Researcher* (Amsterdam: Valiz, 2011), pp. 249–253.

sympathetic to the idea of working closely alongside artists who are researching something. Like the curator Maria Lind's practice, for example, which involves working with artists who are involved in research, because you want to have proximity to someone who's producing ideas over a long period of time.

There's also another component, an institutional component to this. When I started to work and encounter institutions – primarily smallish ones but institutions nonetheless with a sense of education and a public role – directors didn't have any budget for this kind of thing but they would have an education budget and an exhibition-building budget. So Rikrit Tiravanija and I and various other people that we worked alongside deployed the education and exhibition-building budget to make our exhibitions. The exhibition would be a form of research in itself, like *The Trial of Pol Pot* or *The Moral Maze* that I did with Philippe Parreno in Dijon, for example. The problem, of course, became what gets kept by the institution, and what you find is that things were not being kept. What they've kept is something else, so you have this weird sense that something happened, but the material record is actually a totally parallel history.

This dialogue was previously published in *MaHKUscript Journal for Fine Art Research* Vol. 2, Issue 1 (2018), which was guest-edited by Lucy Cotter as a preview to the first edition of this book. Republished with kind permission.

The Malleability of Space and Time

A Dialogue with Mario García Torres

Lucy Cotter Many of your works revolve around particular artists from the Conceptual period of the 1960s or 1970s. You consider artworks they have made or a particular research trajectory or an unrealized proposal and you revisit their ideas, thinking them through in a broader conceptual space using photographic documentation, film, sound, and sculpture to form a kind of "museographical essay." There's an underlying proposition that seems to be about taking art seriously as a self-determined space for conceptualizing ideas. In a talk you gave recently, you discussed *RR and the Expansion of the Tropics* (2014), a scenario you made that engaged with Robert Rauschenberg, Florida, and climate change and it struck me when you said, "Those decisions that Rauschenberg made can be thought again." You suggested that the magazine containing his photographs from 1979 that you were engaging with could potentially initiate a different conception of the Tropics, even today. That's a radical claim to make for an artwork or an artist's research.

Mario García Torres I'm often asked to clarify my position on this. People wonder if I'm being funny or if I'm being cynical, but at the end of the day, that's how I see things. I've always believed in art. It's a very honest belief. I feel like the history of art that refers to other artworks has always been a shallow approach to art. To do this kind of research has, from the beginning, been more about trying to have a conversation with a particular artist from the past. Trying to get past all the books and to get past time and context to engage with somebody else who is probably not here. What artists do is interesting, because the only luxury we have is that we are given a space and time to think about what we do. The only power we have is to think about every gesture we make. I approach these gestures with that seriousness. It's as minimal as it can be; just something that we should think about. But of course, there are many other layers.

LC By revisiting those moments from other artists in the history of Conceptual Art, you also insist on the specificity of their geography. You often widen the frame of the location of the original artwork so that the politics of the situation emerge as part of the bigger picture. For example, when you tracked down the site of artist Alighiero Boetti's One Hotel in Kabul, which was meant to have been a kind of open space in the 1970s, you re-opened the space to consider what it meant to re-create a space of accommodation and discussion in Afghanistan now. You were also very conscious of the future significance of creating your related filmic work, *Alguna vez has visto la nieve caer?* (Have You Ever Seen the Snow?) (2010) as a certain portrayal of Kabul. Through the extensive research that led to this project, you also lifted some of the blinkers of art history around a particular set of geopolitics in that period.

MGT Yes, in that sense there are two layers. One layer is referring to the politics and the context that brought the first work into being. Then there's the question of the politics of bringing it out, and then there's a whole different set of politics like it was in Kabul, of course. I wouldn't think of creating a hotel in Afghanistan today. I didn't know if I even believed that Boetti had this hotel, but I was interested in the idea of an artist doing something unexpected. Following Boetti, I find it interesting to come back to the house that was used as that space and think about what it means to host and to bring a space of discussion in a different time. I try to see these gestures as a kind of receptacle that can become different every time you move them, either in geography or time. It connects to the idea of thinking that ideas are valid in different moments.

LC Seth Siegelaub seems to be an interesting person to consider in this context. There's an incredible level of freedom and conceptual expansion present in his work that relates to this gesture of shifting ideas in time and space. In the history of art, we have seen him as a figure of Conceptual Art, but there was so much that followed, from his leftist critique of media and publishing endeavors to his becoming a researcher and bibliophile of textile history. Can you elaborate on the piece that you made for the Siegelaub retrospective exhibition at the Stedelijk Museum, *The Causality of Hesitancy* (2015)?

MGT Yes, well Siegelaub was quite important for me, I guess for our whole generation, because information on Conceptual Art started to be published and discussed around that time. I remember being intrigued by Siegelaub, so when I organized a symposium in Mexico, I invited him and that was the first contact we had. He actually came to Mexico which is very revealing. Before he came, he was this Conceptual Art character that I needed to talk to. I invited him to talk about his reluctance about the first Conceptual Art book. Then when he came, I discovered all these other versions of him. I found it really important and interesting that this guy had taken very intriguing and basic ideas and expanded them in different ways. His engagement with textiles is a different story, but I think it was very coherent that from those early exercises of dematerialization, he went on to politics and publishing. By the time he was publishing those leftist ideas, Conceptual Art was also starting to develop in other directions – by Hans Haacke, by feminism. Siegelaub was participating in that same lineage, almost as an artist. Of course, he was going somewhere else but he was complicating those early ideas. So that was quite shocking for me. To think about how to expand those things, how to take them somewhere else, how to create that flexibility of ideas, how do we move ideas around.

LC One of the other layers that strike me in your own work is an underlying question about time and causality. It's implicit in the way you unpick chronology in your works in general, but you also engaged directly with the question of time in the commissioned work you made in response to Siegelaub's practice. There seems to be a particular sensitivity within contemporary art to considering time and causality in different ways.

MGT I am, like many other artists, intrigued by time and causality but when I started to do this work, I realized that we're all such tourists about it. We talk about time as something that we experience and perceive and assume to see it in different ways, but we are very far from really understanding it from the point of view of physics. I remember when Siegelaub came to Mexico he told me, "Well, the one thing that I'm interested in is time and a very philosophical version of time and I've been reading these things." I realized after some years – I mean, I was in contact with him now and again and it felt like it was something close, even though I didn't see him that often – but it seemed like it was the project he had in mind when he came to Mexico that he didn't manage to do. He started to put together a bibliography about those issues, and I think he went to some university classes to try and bring out a decent bibliography. So, that piece comes from the idea of trying to at least discuss that project that he didn't manage to do.

LC Can you say something about where that process brought you conceptually? The video work shows a performance in which we see a figure, who vaguely resembles a young Siegelaub, engage in a monologue that you co-wrote with the writer Alan Page, which is a philosophical reflection on time and hesitation.

MGT I went back into what Siegelaub had put together, the few books that were important for him in his interest in those subjects and tried to do something with it. I ended up taking what I feel is a contemporary political stand about delay and hesitation and what that means today. Going from the very scientific ideas about what it means to travel in space and how time changes in different places in the universe, I went back into daily life and said, "Let's perceive time in a different way, let's think about our experience of time in a different way." I believe it's a political stance to say, "Let's not do anything." It's a statement against capitalism, really. Let's stop being rushed into things, let's not produce, let's take things in a different way. Let's stop and think what we'd like to do. I think that this is something which has been in my work in many different ways. Arguing for stopping, for thinking about different ways and different gestures. In a way, it's an argument about not really making decisions in the first instance, about revisiting other spaces or gestures and acts or stories in a different moment and thinking that it's possible to change what we already know from history. To think about that space and history as something that we can always move and change; it's not something that is set there forever. Also, I was thinking about which moments Siegelaub decided to stop and change his career. And I guess everybody must experience that. In what moments do we decide that it's worth doing something; when to make something public, to put it out there?

LC This makes me think about the avant-garde composer Conlon Nancarrow, whose work you engaged with in *Sounds Like Isolation to Me* (2014), not only because the work rethinks how Conlon is perceived in history but also because of his process. In that vitrine-based installation and video work, you re-entered an imaginary that Conlon creates as a figure, by setting himself certain limitations and working for decades within those limitations. I don't think it's a coincidence either, that he was especially interested in temporal dissonance. There seems to be something about time in all of your work but there's a more identifiable position in that work on Nancarrow. You mentioned earlier that there's an anti-capitalist aspect of your work on time, a proposition to stop producing, to stop moving forward. I felt that in your work on Nancarrow, there's a tribute to him staying in that productive space, which wasn't public or was only semi-public. It has a relationship to a romantic notion of an artist or creator as an isolated figure, but more importantly, you point to a certain economy in the artist choosing that position in the 20th century. That's a very different goal than reclaiming Nancarrow in a kind of revisionist art historical way, although it's clear that he deserves greater critical attention.

MGT Yeah, that's interesting. In a way, Nancarrow conceived a space of art where his space of creation was outside time. Outside the daily normalcy of time, or at least our perception of it. He was definitely very interested in time and music, but he was not really interested in participation. His space of creation was like a bubble and in that sense it made him flirt with ideas of a bohemian space but at the same time, I think it's very interesting to think about that today. That we are producing so much stuff, not just objects but information and we're in this rush of engaging in a discussion with everybody and trying to participate in exhibitions. We're in a space of moving forward all the time.

The video in *Sounds Like Isolation to Me* talks about that and about the same dichotomy of very abstract ideas of time and our daily life, and humanized ideas about that. And that has to do with the fact that Nancarrow was producing those rolls of music that could be played at many different speeds. The history of that is fascinating because when you review his recorded music, you see that there were three important moments where he recorded most of what he had produced. One was in the late 1960s when he made his first record, where the speed of the music was set to the speed that the composition was made to. Fifteen or twenty years later, he was old but he was starting to get a lot of attention and he recorded everything much faster, making it more difficult and less pleasant to hear. Then at the end of his life, they recorded all of his music on video and he made it very very slow so that you could hear the melody in a totally different way.

I tried to argue through my video that this was very much connected to Nancarrow's life. Not only as a bodily response; tiredness or joy about what was happening, but also as a political standpoint. It seemed that he first set the rules and then when he was getting attention, he pushed them so that people had a harder time doing it. He became even more of a radical musician. Then, at the end of his life, he relaxed and said, "Look this is what I've done." I don't know if he ever thought about it, but it seemed very revealing in that sense.

LC I once read an interview with Nancarrow in which he said that he used the mechanical player piano because human fingers couldn't perform the complexity of some of the sounds that he wanted to produce. I found that quite striking because it raises questions about what kind of scope for complexity we allow ourselves as cultural producers. I wonder if he tried to make himself more accessible at that moment.

MGT Yeah, exactly. To slow down and analyze things in a different way or allow that to happen in a different way. I don't know if it was a nice thing to do or some kind of regret. I don't know if it's valid to make very specific arguments regarding his persona, but it seems that age and career positions really changed his way of looking at his own work. And where do we see ourselves and our own work? Work is just that, it's an excuse and it's a base for things to happen. It's not something fixed. I think that is what keeps me intrigued about art; that it brings the space to at least think that there are different ways of thinking about things.

LC There's a very early interview with you by Raimundas Malašauskas, where you talked about getting away from the modern project that is still prevailing in a lot of our thinking. You said you were interested instead in "restoring some kind of chance related space for framing art." I think this idea remains valid in terms of thinking about how artists in general research, as well as how you come to your own body of work. Later in the same interview, you commented that Sol LeWitt's statement that Conceptual artists are mystics rather than rationalists "seems to be as lively as ever," which was pretty intriguing to read. How do you feel about those statements now, ten or fifteen years later?

MGT I have no idea what I was talking about back then! *(laughs)* But I do think it's interesting to do with ideas around research. When I am asked by someone from the public what I do, I say, "Well it's kind of a research-based practice"–which is wide open to interpretation. It brings ideas about academia, and maybe what I was trying to get at in that interview, which I think I still believe, are two things that are somehow connected. On the one hand, chance, and on the other, which connects to what Sol LeWitt was saying, that in the end, we're also guessing things. So research in the artistic arena is not something academic, where we go from one thing to the next and claim to have a specific goal. It's more arbitrary I would say, closer to an intuitive process than a search for proof. We can use research as a way to activate certain moments, more than issues. To think about phenomena in a more intuitive way. I guess in that sense it can be connected to that chance space I was talking about.

I'm always intrigued by little ideas and little stories and I'm always looking into knowing more about this or that, and they usually don't end up being in any work of art. But at some point, if somebody comes and brings a specific context in mind, then I say "Oh well that little interest I had in mind, could maybe become something for that space." So I think that there's something very intuitive about this research and the activation of research, and the activation of specific knowledge and trying to reframe it in that sense. I think it's only context, and a very intuitive perception of that context, that turns this research into something to share.

LC Can we talk about where the exhibition as form comes into this? There are quite some research-based art practices, which are presented in exhibitions in ways that convey that what you see is part of a much larger body of research, only some of which can be contained in this show. I see you work very differently than that; working more explicitly with the material knowledge that can be created by the presence of certain works in a particular constellation in an exhibition space; often things could be manifest in very different ways.

MGT I think you're right. I have never thought about that as a research base. But I've been trying to make work for fifteen years now and it feels like I have come full circle. At the beginning of my practice, I had very precise ideas. I was proud of the fact that I wouldn't move a finger until I had everything very clear. My very early approach to, or interest in Conceptual Art was because I wanted to legitimize a different way of looking at artists. I was interested in thinking of an artist as a professional and as *somebody*, as opposed to the perception of the artist as a bohemian, which was dominant in the context in which I was working. Little by little, I started to relax and trust many other sources of knowledge. I started thinking that real discoveries are made through a path and through a practice, through moments of actually doing and discovering why are you doing things. I think now in a very intuitive way because I guess there's no way to put it in words. It feels like today, more than ever, I really trust that. Today I make more exhibitions than works of art.

The Conlon Nancarrow piece was very specific in that sense. I was thinking, OK, we have this set of tools and they're the most conservative set of tools – vitrines and glass boxes – but can we use them, can we treat them as something and play with the most conservative knowledge and perception of that? Can we use that to bring a different atmosphere, and through that change the perception of those conservative things? And with that, tell a story and there are other implications. It feels like more and more I'm interested in that form, as you say. I don't know what it does, but it feels more and more important to me.

LC This possibility of an exhibition as a form that facilitates some kind of dialogue across time and space was also brought forward in a radical way at your exhibition at the Museo Tamayo in Mexico City, *Let's Walk Together* (2016), which looked back over fifteen years of your practice. You overlaid the floor plans of a conceptual museum that you conceived in 2002, the Museo de Arte Sacramento, onto a map of Mexico City to come up with the exhibition locations. Your original museum was also a response to an unrealized museum proposal by Martin Kippenberger, so the whole exhibition occupied a space somewhere between history and the present, between the concrete and the imaginary.

MGT Yes, it started with the curator Sofiá Hernández Chong Cuy and I thinking about the role of this museum exhibition in my career. It was a sort of "mid-review" exhibition, which didn't feel very interesting to do. Thinking with the Museo de Arte Sacramento, well if this is something that I made fifteen years ago, can I still come back and try to reformulate it? So at some point in our discussion, we decided to conceive an exhibition for the Museo Sacramento instead, and then bring it to Mexico City. The rhetoric of the actual exhibition said that it was the second venue. It suggested that you were seeing a copy of something that had happened before, and you had already missed something that was somewhere else.

LC So what exactly constituted the Museo Sacramento? Was it only a conceptual space, or did it ever manifest as a physical space?

MGT The Museo de Arte Sacramento was a kind of space, an institution that could potentially exist in reality, but would be located in a remote geography that would make it very hard to get to.

That was the very basic idea. It was set up with the intention of considering whether we could take the museum as an excuse for production and discussion about art but without really accessing it. At some point, I hoped to have a number of artists do projects for a museum that they didn't know. At the beginning, I distributed very bad night satellite images of the space—at that time there was still a very basic version of the Internet. The images showed a kind of abstract space, something that would suggest that it was real but impossible to understand. The museum was a total failure in relation to the original goals for the project. I think I got one proposal—that I didn't like—and at some point, after a couple of years, I realized that what was more interesting about the museum was those discussions, about what the limits of an institution are and to what degree we need real institutions or not. The idea was made with all other artists' museums in mind, but specifically at the same time I was also working on the *Open Letter to Dr. Atl* (2005) video piece that I made in relation to the Guggenheim coming to Mexico, and that moment in Bilbao and other places, of a lot of money going toward bigger spaces for museums.

LC The Museo de Arte Sacramento was meant to have been located in a very specific geographic area in northern Mexico, which is interesting for a hypothetical museum. Can you say something about how this influenced your "mid-review" exhibition in Mexico City?

MGT Yes, there were a lot of things from the area of the Museo Sacramento that influenced the way that we displayed the works. The subjective atmosphere of the exhibition was very much informed by the geography and the weather from the north of Mexico. So what we did was to conceptually go “there” to conceive the exhibition that we presented here at the Museo Tamayo. In relation to what you’ve been saying about the exhibition as form, I think that I’m really interested in thinking about the atmosphere of the space and how things are perceived. Now, while going through that exhibition here at the Museo Tamayo, I feel that was very much the question. To come back to the Museo de Arte Sacramento, it was very important for Sofía and me to think precisely in those terms about how to move an exhibition from one place to another. It was not about presenting the politics of that geography in a black and white way. The first version of that exhibition was made in a desert, in a place where there is no water; a place where sound is so subtle, where you hear animals and the wind and many subtle things, and they appear in such a minimal way that you have to stop and concentrate more on those little things than you would do in a space where you have a lot of information. That was really important, to think about how we bring that into the space of a museum, of a white cube. And it really informed the way we displayed the works, the space between them. It was a funny exercise, but I think it was talking about what you’re saying, trusting many other forms. I see it more as an atmosphere, but it’s flirting with what you’re saying.

LC There is a specific choreography to the show at the Museo Tamayo, and one that exceeds the museum boundaries and enters urban space. The title of the show, *Let’s Walk Together*, is provocative in this sense but also because, going back to Aristotle and many other thinkers, walking is a form of thinking. There is a notion of the journey as a thought process in several of your works and also in this show, in which you create deliberate distances. There was already some kind of imaginary distance in your original conceptual Museum Without Walls, but in *Let's Walk Together* you also invite the viewer to walk within a particular conceptual space, which is the conceptual space of this show linking several buildings and streets.

MGT Yeah, that's a nice observation and the works were also sparsely separated in space in the museum. Of course, I was very interested in the idea of walking and the idea of creating a space between one work and the next. Sofía and I hoped, and I think we more or less achieved it, that the people who really engaged with the exhibition would do that. We pretended to think that the exhibition worked as a long narrative where there are many curves and that you arrive in a space and see a work in a specific context. There were many layers about that, and then going out of that and going into society, walking for some time and then going back again into the space. In that sense, I think it was very interesting to not just have space between one thing and the other, but also to have context as the "on" and "off" part of the exhibition. That was our goal, to see that. It's not that interesting to see one work after the other but coming back in could potentially become something where there are two weeks between the perception of one work and the next, hopefully, and not only for people who live in Mexico City.

LC It's actually a time space; it's potentially a temporal space as much as a physical space.

MGT Exactly.

LC You also had a series of letters from different periods in the exhibition in which you reflected on the artistic process that led to particular works. Has the letter offered you another way to open up a space across time? It seems to have been an important form in your practice for many years–for example in the *Open Letter to Dr. Atl* work you mentioned, a video work that features an imaginary letter to a historic artist working under that pseudonym, or even in the faxes you wrote posthumously to Alighiero Boetti.

MGT Yes, the letter as form has been quite important in my work. In the beginning, it was interesting as a tool, as a rhetoric strategy, because it was a space in which certain questions or interests could be displayed in a very intimate way and shared, not as a text with a critical or philosophical rhetoric, but as a personal space. That was very important to me with regard to how I was getting involved in history and trying to set up my position in relation to art historians, for example. At some point, it was easier for me to tell a story to somebody instead of writing a text addressed to many people. Through that minimal modest object, I could pre-define the public in some ways, who are going to be able to come and share that intimate space. I'm not interested in talking to the masses, so that's how I ended up using that rhetoric. I used it for the *Open Letter to Dr. Atl* video and in many other instances.

LC It seems like such a fragile form. It almost belongs to the past, even though we're still using it in the present.

MGT Yes, beyond the direct ideas behind these *I Promise* letters in the exhibition or why I did them, I find it interesting that the piece is only possible if there are people who are still writing letters to each other. In a way, it's a kind of statement against that space of personal communication and on the other hand, the piece will collapse when all hotels decide that letter writing is not of value anymore. It brings about that discussion as to when we will be able to do that, about whether our society is interested in keeping that activity happening. Of course, letter writing is collapsing and I myself participate in that by writing emails every day.

LC This also makes me think about your reflections on artworks that have not been made. Going back to Conceptual Art again, there's a radical proposition in that movement in terms of artists making ideas *as* their work. I'm just wondering about the potential of that concept in situations where the artwork was unintentionally not made; if there's still some value in that idea.

MGT I have a little story that reflects on that. At some point, I had a complicated discussion that ended up in a sad space. It had to do with a text that I started to write about works that Michael Asher had done, or hadn't done actually. I wrote a long text about it. Some proposals came from the Stedelijk Museum, proposals that he sent to the museum but for one reason or another were never made. I ended up having a long discussion with him and he said that, for him, if a work was not done, then the political implications of it were not there. In that sense, the work didn't exist. And we never came to an agreement…

LC Of course you couldn't agree with that.

MGT No, the conversation ended up with me saying, "Well Michael, we are fundamentally different in ways we cannot resolve." I said, "Yes, I understand what you mean by that, but at the end of the day, the ideas that artists have are a platform for things to happen. It's interesting to think how can we move them around and what that means." It doesn't mean that the work of Michael Asher that wasn't done means exactly the same thing twenty years later. But when we read about it at least, I think that it still has the potential to speak and to make us think in many different ways.

LC It still holds open a space of possibility.

MGT Exactly. I don't know, maybe we trust in this too much, maybe we live in a kind of space of fantasy. *(laughs)* I don't know how much we can sustain it. I think there are many things in contemporary life that bring us back to that space. I think the way we communicate with each other, the way we portray ourselves in social media is the same space, the space of projection. It's the same space of fantasy in which we want to change things. We want to change our daily life. And I think that space is what can save us. It's the space where we can still move around beyond our everyday politics, our everyday realities.

Research as Play

A Dialogue with Ryan Gander

Lucy Cotter One of my first encounters with your work was seeing *Loose Associations* (2001), a lecture performance you did while you were at the Rijksakademie in Amsterdam. I was very struck by how certain qualities of artistic thinking, as an own form of knowledge production, were made manifest for the public in that lecture. There was an incredible speed to your thinking, moving from one subject to another by way of images. It was thinking *through* visual registers, like flicking through image files in your brain. I'm imagining Harald Szeeman's archives; flicking through hundreds and thousands of existing images just to think a thought, to maybe get to an image. Can you say something about the image and thinking?

Ryan Gander I don't know if what I'm about to say is true or not, because I can't see how other people think. But I think that there needs to be another title for what happens in that kind of thinking. It's not just in artists' thinking; I think we need a new definition for the type of person who thinks like that. I don't know what it would be, maybe an instigator or something like that. Something in an instigator's mind happens very differently to most other people's minds. I think the closest someone else who doesn't think like that would get to it is if they are getting a new apartment and they're deciding where to put the furniture, then they go off into a daydream because their mind is really provoked. They are excited and a valve opens, and their imagination takes hold. "I will put the sofa over there, and I will put a plant here." I mean that's the closest thing to the way I feel like I think ten hours a day, which is pretty exhausting. It also only happens because you train yourself to do it. It's not some genius or something. You try to do it because you have to do it, because it's your job.

LC I find it quite frustrating that there is a tremendous amount of knowledge in that kind of seeing process, but it's almost impossible to gather it. It seems like the only way to get it is to have that level of seeing yourself. Culturally, so much is oriented toward the linguistic. One of the things I find interesting about artistic research as a field is that there might actually be space to take this seriously; the fact that there is a kind of a way of knowing going on here that is valuable and that can't be held in other forms.

RG The first problem is belief. If you don't think like that, people don't think it's possible. They don't see it as being different from the way they think, because they are not aware of it. So the next thing is to visually show that to people, to prove it to them. It's a pretty difficult thing to do. I think one of the problems is that there are a lot of artists who don't think like that. There is a post-Internet generation of artists now where the work really makes me incredibly sad. It's very fickle and empty. References are used without understanding them or thinking about them. They are thrown about flippantly or ironically. It's like chaos in visual language. It's like someone screaming and it just sounds like Klingon. Nothing is being said articulately. So that's one problem because it makes everyone disbelieve that this type of thought methodology is possible; the type you could see in the *Loose Associations* lectures and other forms like that.

In the last six months, I've been doing creative consultancy-type projects for some companies, a bit like an experiment. I did something for Nike, for a large global property company, and for Cambridge Council. I go into these company meetings, they tell me what they are doing and then I come up with some ideas. And it's very, very strange because they think the ideas are extraordinary and they don't understand how I could have got to them. You can see people physically shitting themselves. It makes me feel like I've taken some weird drug that they haven't taken. It's only recently that I've seen it, that in these people's eyes, we do think differently than other people. When you talk about it, it sounds incredibly egomaniac, like you're talking about yourself as a superhero or something. But it's just training the mind. It's like going to the gym. The mind becomes healthy, astute, quickened.

LC Do you think about your own art practice in relation to knowledge production, or research, or thinking processes?

RG I think of life in relation to knowledge production and research, not work. I think the point of living is to make your life as entertaining and enriching as possible. Everyone does that, no matter what they are doing. They go on holidays, they go to the pub, they build an extension on their house, they add a conservatory; they try to get a better job. My thinking about work is to not think of it as work; just think of it like that, like a full life. Some of my works are offcuts or by-products or fallouts of that kind of living. There are a lot of things I make that people don't see. Like the really shitty eggcups that I just made for home. Some of them have a natural affinity to become objects of art or vessels for stories for a wider public to consume. But a lot of it doesn't. Making someone a present is as creative as making an artwork. Everything you do could be an artwork – the bench in my garden.

LC So why then do pieces like *A Lamp Made by the Artist for his Wife* creep into the gallery space? Was it because you made so many attempts that you thought, "Some of this has to be art?"

RG Good question. Because I decided! *(both laugh)* I think the decision to make some things artworks and leave others in your personal world is just based on the alignment of the stars and what's happening. It seemed a funny time to do that because there were so many furniture designers who were attempting to make unique objects that were commodities with stylistic characteristics of themselves, like artworks. So it was funny to reverse the cycle.

LC Your work is conceptual, but you think through materials. There is also a kind of playfulness in how your way of thinking comes together materially. Looking at works like *A Lamp Made by the Artist for his Wife*, I have the feeling that you're trying to get into the brains of people who can't think like that and lead them through that; a kind of initiation into materiality.

RG Again, it sounds really egocentric, but it's not materiality; it's just thinking. I know exactly what you mean, but I see the same thing with everything. Seeing a cigarette stump on the ground with lipstick on it on a street corner outside a bar and instantly, without knowing that you are doing it, you associate it with the fact that there's been a woman outside a bar waiting for someone to turn up. She doesn't want to go inside because she doesn't want to be in a bar on her own. Most people just walk past it. I don't know what the chemistry or biology is behind it but I visualize it as a valve in your brain. Sometimes the valve is open so you read all the systems and signifiers around you and can be super aware of everything, like in *The Matrix*. But then sometimes you can just be watching *You've Got Talent* and you don't see anything other than what is in front of you, what you're told to see; it's merely retinal. I try to keep the valve open. Materiality is one of those things because a lot of clues to narrative and meaning are in the physical world, in physical objects. Everything you understand about the social, the cultural, the historical, all of the connotations and references and links to meaning are in the physical. Those things you see, you see physically, like "It is a cigarette." The story comes from your knowledge. Essentially the cigarette is the signifier.

LC Someone who makes things knows that making is another way of thinking or that it's all thinking actually, as you put it. While you are making things, something happens in the process. The actual thing you are making with gives you ideas. Can you talk about how that works for you in your practice?

RG I think it's hard to explain the process because my thinking is that if you have a process, then it's all over. If you have a way of making work, then you know what you're doing and by definition art is about exploration, trying things out, pushing things forward, making mistakes. Make a fool of yourself and try not to repeat anything you have done before. The methodology of that way of working always has to change; you always have to remain light on your feet.

The problem with process is that you make something that's successful, you're happy with it and it's interesting. And then you think, I'll follow the same route. I'll use the same process but with a different material, or in a different color, or a different size, or I'll make a hundred, or I will make it so that people can touch it, or I'll make it and put it on the floor, or I'll make it and put it outside, or I'll make it and hang it off the ceiling. And actually, you're just making the same thing, although you think you're making another work. But you're not making a new work. Then you end up with what we traditionally know as practice. Traditional practice is repetition. And in my mind, repetition is stuttering and is against the definition of what art should be. People still talk about practice like that, but that's historical practice. Practice is not like that anymore. The idea is to get better. It's a trajectory that moves over two or three decades. I think that's what you can call practice, not being an artist that follows the same steps again and again and again, just making casts of the inside of different objects or videoing dot paintings… I'm not critiquing other artists when I say that; ninety-five percent of contemporary artists work like this.

My dad's idea of what an artist is, is that every day they would wake up and invent something new. Some things would be terrible and they wouldn't work, and some things would be amazing and everyone would think they were great. I think he has the right understanding of what an artist's role is and what practice is. It's really great to make bad stuff. I don't want to make good things all the time because it's not true and you don't learn anything.

LC You don't work in repetition but you do work in series. I find it problematic that in much of exhibition making, you often get one piece presented on its own like a genius piece. I find that you have to see most works in series. Even though you don't necessarily want to see the literal making process, you want to get some idea of a thinking process, of what the artist was trying to make happen, which usually unfolds across a body of work. I'm thinking, for example, about your *Tell My Mother Not to Worry* works, where you deliberately produced a whole series of works in the style of "I had a very good idea, let's do a hundred of them." If I only saw one of those works, it would have a completely different effect on me. It would turn the work into something precious, a kind of Classical sculpture meets Surrealism. But when you see a number of them, it becomes something totally different–a curiosity about form behind that sheet, what it means when something becomes physical or massive that is normally fleeting. Can you say something about how the mind works across those pieces? It is different than having one idea. There is something there that is not quite process-oriented but something else.

RG Yes, as you said, there isn't only one way of making work. Some works are "genius" pieces, like the wind work at Documenta 13. If I had produced a series of six wind works, then they would be about me being metaphysical; pretending to be Jesus or something. So that work has to be a stand-alone work. You are totally right about why other works are in series because they unravel something about consistent thinking. So, for example, the ghosts and the dens are series because they are about development and education. They are about my daughter growing physically and intellectually. From number one to number ten, you see the ghosts changing height. There might be more dens because they keep getting bigger, architecturally and conceptually more complicated. That's what I'm trying to show – firstly the power of imagination with naivety. Where you climb under a table and throw a sheet over it and you say that it's a house. When I do that with my daughter, she says "It's a house," and then I say, "It's a house." But for her it *really* is a house; everything changes into a house, her imagination is on fire. Whereas for me it's a *house* but it's actually really still just a table with a sheet thrown over it.

LC I want to ask you something else about repetition and about process. I really loved *Ampersand* (2012–), the work you first showed at Palais de Tokyo. You say that you don't believe in process but the *Ampersand* work is a moment when you allow your collecting habit to come to the fore. In my experience, collecting is one of those things that many artists do that they don't talk about much, but that's an indirect form of research and actually at the core of what they make. I'm not going to pre-empt anything by asking you something specific, but can you perhaps say something about collecting?

RG Mike Nelson once told me that he'd just bought a house. His new house had a really shitty floor in it and he wanted an oak floor. He produced an exhibition that used loads of oak beams because he knew that when the show was over, it would all be scrapped because his works are incredibly hard to sell and to store. He knew he could take the oak and have it cut into nice floorboards and have it laid in his house. So there was a sort of upcycling to it. In the economy of art, there is a kind of economy of means, not just selling work for money to make more work. I'm really interested in that. I swap a lot of artworks for watches; I collect watches. *Ampersand* was an excuse for me to gather a lot of things together that I wouldn't have the time to gather otherwise. There are things in there like the Cory Arcangel work that we had to fabricate–it's a copy. Then there is an M9 Leica camera that I have always wanted to own but could never pay the extortionate amount of money for. Then there were things that were really dear to me that I wouldn't want to give up, like a blanket my wife made for me one Christmas–a huge patchwork that was sewn together from panels of old men's jumpers and woolen cardigans she bought in charity shops.

So again, it was more a part of life than a part of art. I didn't start out thinking, "I'm going to make a collection, it will be on display as well, and I'm going to write a book about it." I thought, "If I was a collector and I could collect anything, not just art, what would I collect?" And then you collect air from the beach in Dunwich because Dunwich is really submerged under the water. That's how it started. Then I thought it would probably be a really interesting thing to look at. I soon realized that the reasons I was choosing these things were more important than the objects themselves, so I decided it would be a book. I went to San Francisco for three weeks and quietly wrote about half of it there and the other half I wrote while commuting between Suffolk and London.

LC I mentioned in another dialogue with Liam Gillick that artists' thinking is often associative, but it's not random association. Your term "loose association" comes closer to describing it. Looking through the multiple associations you make in *Ampersand*, one can see that everything circles back somehow, like lines being drawn across the objects. In the exhibition that followed the book, the viewer got to sit on a retro Eames-style leather armchair and watch these things go by on a conveyor belt and make these associations themselves. It is like a very physical slideshow.

RG Yes, one of the first things that become apparent is that you usually move around exhibitions and that here the show was brought to you. Like some sort of gaga of physical language, the spectator was still. Like the Internet and everything else with speed at the moment, these things passed in front of you. It didn't give you time to think about them, which was also important. In that sense, it was like a *Loose Associations* lecture and that speed that you mentioned at the beginning of this conversation was present. It was almost like a prelude to the scroll generation, where you are already presented with the next thing before you have even thought about the thing you are looking at. That kind of presentation is all-consuming and quite exhausting. It makes you feel very alive in a way because you feel how full the world is and what human culture has given us.

It was also quite like a *Loose Associations* lecture because there were lots of associations between the objects. So, for example, there were fridge magnets on the refrigerator that I'd made from a typeface that I'd invented that was taken from the handwriting of Spike Milligan. I was doing these fridge magnets for my daughter when I realized that they were just some generic typeface but that she was making up words that didn't exist. It seemed logical that they should be in the handwriting of someone who really invented words. So you had this notion of inventing words in a word-inventor's handwriting. On the refrigerator, there was also a French cell phone number written using these fridge magnets and if you called the phone number, the Nokia phone passing by on the conveyor belt would ring. The Nokia phone played "Gran Vals," the Nokia theme tune that is based on a piece of classical music [by Francesco Tárrega]. They got around the copyright by dropping the last note. So it's an exact copy of the music originally played by a string quartet. I had the Nokia theme tune re-recorded, played by a classical guitarist, and had it put on a polyphonic ringtone. So that's one example; there were a lot of links between the objects. There was a security mirror that went around. Thirty objects later, you'd see the reverse of a security mirror. It's endless, really, the amount of associations. So really, it was like an association lecture made physical.

LC It sounds like a mad encyclopedia, an encyclopedia that internalizes instead of externalizes somehow.

RG It doesn't feel like that because it's my mind. *(both laugh)*.

LC Well if we're going to talk about artists' minds, I have to write an introductory essay for this book and I was tempted to make the first sentence, "The most intelligent people I have ever met are artists." Because when you scrape away all that respect and admiration for artists, a lot of people think that artists are not that intelligent, even though they are creative, expressive, imaginative, etc. I am serious about wanting to communicate the fact that there is a particular type of intelligence in artists that is also sharpened through artistic processes. And it really makes something happen.

RG But not all artists, though.

LC *(Both laugh)* No, not all artists. I should qualify that statement.

RG I think that's the biggest problem at the moment, for me. Something I shouldn't really worry about. I've got children, I've got parents, I've got shows I have to do and a car to have MOT'ed. But I worry about some little pseudo-pop punk from LA spraying "Hardcore" on a wall. It's like I can't morally and ethically function in a world that lets bad practice like that through the sieve. It's the thing I worry about most. I think it's because I function in this world. And you have to have a certain amount of belief and faith in that world to function in it.

LC One of the reasons I find artistic research interesting as a possibility is that it makes space for intelligence, for more depth, for trying to get away from an "I'm trying to get loads of shows" mentality into "Well there really is something going on with art. There really is something there, there always has been, and there is now." Art needs to be positioned differently. There has to be some kind of a sieve where you can try and get some of the nuggets out and actually see that difference. In a way, it's about getting away from a lightweight approach to art. I think that's partly by zooming out and extending the frame. I don't want to hold hands with academia to the point where we're all kissing, but by making some connection to a thinking world as opposed to being driven by an art market, maybe you can make more space for caring about and following this possibility; the potential that's there for something interesting to happen.

RG Yeah, but in an ideal world – I'm just writing down something you said because I'm stealing it as a title – in an ideal world, all that thin stuff wouldn't be called art. It would just have a different name, like Athena Poster Shop.

This dialogue was previously published in *MaHKUscript Journal for Fine Art Research* Vol. 2, Issue 1 (2018), which was guest-edited by Lucy Cotter as a preview to the first edition of this book. Republished with kind permission.

Between the Virtual and the Real

A Dialogue with Yuri Pattison

Emma Moore Working in digital media and sculpture, you often explore ways in which the virtual world permeates material reality, addressing the relationship of visual cultures to emerging communication technologies and metadata circulation. For your Chisenhale Gallery Create Residency in London (2014–16), your new line of research focused on the idea of transparency; how both large companies and smaller networks communicate information visibly to encourage a feeling of security among consumers. You identified London Hackspace and more broadly the area of East London known as Tech City and a growing community of tech workers as a starting point for your project. Could you talk about why you identified this particular community and how your research developed?

Yuri Pattison The prompt for the residency was to identify a community to work within, and the idea of community is interesting within that; how do you define where a community starts and ends? I had already spent some time working from London Hackspace, mainly preparing for my show at Cell Project Space in 2014. I also wanted to start there because it has a large cross-section of people. Usually, it's about five thousand people and within that, they have many different communities: there are people who work in the tech industry who use it for their sideline or hobby projects; there are people who are launching start-ups; there are artists and there are fashion designers. It's a very broad, very true, representation of the creative community within London, more representative I found, than fine art studios. That's why I found it very open and interesting. In all these spaces that have a very open-door policy, the communities are inherently wary of new members because it's emphasized that you are supposed to share knowledge, but these models can leave themselves quite open to abuse.

EM London Hackspace is a non-profit model, which is self-sustained, with a minimal membership fee that you pay in order to use the space.

YP Yes, it is a donation-based system. You pay what you think you can afford. It is also non-hierarchical and it's shaped by the people who use the space. There are community rules, but it's a space that is open twenty-four hours per day, seven days per week and it's defined by its use. I isolated that and used it as a starting point; these open-access sharing models that were being cannibalized by the so-called sharing economy. I wanted to look at a workspace that had these open access politics behind it, which also spoke of a politics of the early Internet. Now you have those systems being violently monetized by the sharing economy or platform-based apps.

EM What do you mean by the sharing economy and platform-based apps?

YP With platforms like couch-surfing websites, people used the World Wide Web to connect with other people from around the world and to share resources. The Web is built on that premise. The foundation blocks of what we think of as the Internet are free software and free code, which were given away. That is why even hypertext's protocol is so successful because Tim Berners-Lee authored it, and his team gave it to the world. What is happening now is that you have systems like couch-surfing websites influencing sites like Airbnb, whose model is purely for-profit. There is someone who controls the interface and makes a lot of money from it, just by controlling the software that connects people. This is a new and important difference between the idealistic World Wide Web and how the Internet is used now. I am interested in how this is shifting, and also how it is imprinting on physical spaces. How the earlier models of co-working, which you see in the cyber café or the hacker spaces, are now being formalized or monetized in a way that is very much defined by membership fees–very strict membership fees and very strict access.

EM And therefore the community built within new co-working or co-living spaces can be somewhat designed?

YP Yes, the communities that grow out of these new live/work spaces are often formed of people who work within a freelance economy and can therefore isolate themselves in a way. They create a physical filter bubble so that they encounter fewer and fewer people from outside of their viewpoint and from outside of their politics. There is a dissolving of community through the use of these platforms, whether they are co-working spaces that are inherently front-ended by their web presence or platforms like Airbnb, Uber, Amazon, or fresh food delivery. There is a disengagement with the fabric of the city. This results in a class of people who are privileged and are in a global set where they can move freely without thinking about wider aspects of community and the people living in their city.

EM Going back to Tech City and a global network, many of the new spaces are not just London-based, they have offices all over the world. A community of members in an office in London is selected in the same way as a community of members in New York. So there is a universal aesthetic and community?

YP By visiting various co-working spaces and traveling quite a bit throughout the residency, I noticed certain aesthetics in these spaces, particularly in London. I researched these aesthetics, such as the use of industrial materials, and building logistics on show through exposed brickwork, for example, and communal tables, to try and identify what has influenced the specific look of these co-working spaces. There is this strange, very bland cohesion within the way many of them look. They are often repurposed industrial spaces, which maintain references to labor within them, and they appear globally. You can go to a laptop café in Hong Kong and it looks the same as one in Hackney, as they employ the same austere industrial aesthetics within the space.

I'm interested in the effect of the Internet and how, instead of making the world a more interesting and vibrant place, it is currently having a flattening effect. But it won't last forever – I think the bubble is going to burst and hopefully things will get weird in the way that the 1990s promised the Internet to be. This flattening, bland, homogenizing aesthetic is a strange thing.

EM What do you feel your role is as an artist in drawing this out? Is there a way to make this flattening more visible?

YP I'm interested in the failures of these effects – both the technologies and the utilization of a set of aesthetics. I'm unpicking that aesthetic by interrogating it and attacking it in many ways. I'm very much aware that it is not me distancing myself, as we're all implicated in this and we're all part of this in some way. I'm interested in that implication and the willing proximity of the arts to this space, and the danger of being co-opted. I'm interested in representing this in order to draw attention to it, but representing it through my subjective feeling toward it, which is often quite an uncomfortable one of feeling somehow compromised. I think this is quite a common feeling, this powerless compromise that you have to dwell within.

EM In terms of the aesthetic decisions you've made in the *user, space* show at Chisenhale Gallery (2016), the materials you've chosen have a very distinct feel to them. You've used a wall of industrial warehouse racking that runs almost the length of the gallery as well as a table and panels that are constructed of a modular, industrial material.

YP The racking has to do with my interest in global logistics, and how we are connecting more and more to that network through these platforms.

In London, there is a shift in how people spend their money, which is impacting local shops and local services because a larger sector of people now orders everything online. That obviously changes and shifts how communities function. I have utilized that racking mainly because of my own proximity to a massive Amazon logistics center in East London. I witness the flow of Amazon workers to and from that building. I've never been able to see inside the building because of its high-security nature but, having seen images, they use similar racking structures.

I'm also interested in these ideas within the digital workspace: the laptop café or the co-working space. You have these in London but it's also part of a new global aesthetic and a fetishization of labor. Warehouse racking and very industrial materials are employed in these spaces as a reminder of a connection with work and with physical labor. It becomes a staging for the work carried out there because digital labor is still work. It impacts us in very different ways and impacts the body in very different ways. The staging has to validate that work because it's not apparent labor. It also provides a stage for all the other labor that you have to perform in these workspaces – performing work, meeting people, networking – how these other things happen through social interaction, which is often over coffee or weekly-organized evening cocktails. Capitalizing on these social aspects of work fits into a new economy known as the Experience Economy.

There are other elements in these co-working spaces too – some of them employ elements of the home. I am interested in how some employ elements of a 1960s version of a very futuristic home, where there's often very heavy mining of 1960s utopian – or apparently utopian – sci-fi. There are references to Stanley Kubrick's *2001 Space Odyssey*, which itself contains some heavy critiques of technology and what technology will do to mankind.

EM How do you feel that these aesthetics are being echoed in spaces that are emerging now?

YP Within these new workspaces, there is a range of styles utilized with varying degrees of crossover. Many spaces refer to the post-industrial shells they exist within, emulating the loft and warehouse living idealized in the 1980s, which originated in New York and became increasingly prevalent in the Docklands area of London. There's often a mining of history, a nod to authenticity, but where this doesn't exist, the approach is either to strip back the building to its inner workings – through exposed overhead cable runs or removed ceiling panels – or it is faked by incorporating concrete skims and exposed brick veneers into the fabric of the building. Also, a careful selection of props such as particular furniture or a "curated" selection of books and objects shows the outward appearance or "flair" of the company. The design of the co-working space is almost open plan office meets retail environment – retail spaces are where we are most familiar with this sort of temporary and trend-driven stage dressing.

I'm interested in how, for instance, the designs of Charles & Ray Eames are frequently used as they conjure certain connotations for the visitor and observer of a workspace. They check certain boxes of good taste, "democratic" or even soft "socialist" design ideals along with being both forward-looking and futuristic, while also classic. For me, they exist as a specter within these spaces; representative of the ideologically bankrupt 1960s and 1970s Silicon Valley culture we're now seeing permeate on a global level.

EM And you've referenced this interest in design history, and choice of furnishings within many co-working spaces, with the chairs you've chosen for the exhibition. Could you speak a little about the chairs and why some are still covered in plastic?

YP I'm interested in the history of the Eames DSW chair as a design object. This particular Eames design has a very generous, almost socialist, strategy behind it, which meant for it to be utilized by the masses. We are at a point now, through the abundance of Chinese replicas of "design classics" that this begins to happen. But the allure is that these objects are markers of good taste; they are elitist objects whether they're copies or originals. Some of the co-working spaces I visited either had copies or very expensive originals, or original copies. I was interested in these layers and how they were overthrowing the marker of their good taste. These spaces reference design ideals of the 1950s and 1960s such as Bürolandschaft, which originated in Germany in the 1950s and focused on open-plan office design to encourage collaborative and non-hierarchical working. However, these ideals are referenced without really engaging with them.

And now these chairs have reached a tipping point; the market has been flooded with so many copies, ahead of the copyright law changing that I think it's at a point where the elevated cultural status of these objects is going to flip around. Spaces that have invested a lot of money in the chairs will end up throwing them away because they've gone out of fashion, and they'll find the next thing. For me, it's very current, but it's also a marker in this tide change. It's a signifier of how these things are trappings, without deeper engagement with them. So that's why the chairs in the exhibition are not fully unwrapped.

EM The idea of impermanence is also something that relates to the Hexayurt you've constructed within the space. Could you speak a little bit about this structure and your interest in it?

YP I noticed a lot of temporary materials or industrial materials being utilized in new co-working spaces and also references to strategies that were pioneered for disaster relief. Freight containers were originally used or adapted to house people. This strategy has now been co-opted and become a model of "pop up culture," often involving luxury brands. People fit out freight containers to live in all over London now; it's a way to quickly make wasteland profitable through charging high rents, rather than being deployed as an actual solution. Above all, it's become an idealized thing.

I was interested in the Hexayurt because it's a disaster relief design. Vinay Gupta, who invented it, genuinely believes that we are most at risk now because we don't retain information anymore. If the information infrastructure gets cut off in a disaster situation, no one will know what to do. So the Hexayurt was invented for instances of a ten-fold Hurricane Katrina event happening. He then started to seed it into popular culture by teaching people to use it at Burning Man Festival. So I was interested in structures like the Hexayurt emerging within new working spaces. The Hexayurt felt like a more extreme iteration of using these structures in workspaces, but it could also have potentially been an Ikea Foundation Better Shelter.

Second Home, a work hub for creative companies, has a "no-tech zone" with books and plants. It's designed as a space to go and not use your phone. Having spent time there though, it also feels like a space to go when something terrible has happened. It's meant to be a utopian gesture, but it's potentially quite grim. I've seen people turn up late for training meetings, fail to get into the meeting and being sent to wait in this strange, apparently utopian space. Overall I'm interested in this prescriptive idea of design, how a workspace can reinforce and shape how we're meant to work and also lecture us on how we're supposed to stay productive by perhaps spending some time in these other "tech-free zones." It's the embodiment of the Work / Leisure / Experience economy we're seeing, which presents itself as liberating but has very nuanced rules and codes of conduct placed within it.

EM Could you talk about the specific plants you have chosen?

YP All the plants are selected from a NASA study of fifty common plants that clean the air. NASA published this list in 1989, "A Study of Interior Landscape Plants for Indoor Air Pollution Abatement," when they were doing a lot of off-world research, but they were also looking at how this research could be applicable to extremely polluted cities and how it might contribute to the survival of humans on the planet. I've been looking at how this research is fetishized or co-opted and used within these new workspaces. There are a few other examples of solutions for the extremes of the urban environment, such as the USB ultrasonic water vaporizers marketed in Asian megalopolises to soften the harsh air.

EM You've visited quite a few co-working spaces over the course of the residency, including Second Home; Campus London, "a Google space for London's start-up community," and Republic, a new development and co-working space at East India Dock. In the exhibition, you see glimpses of these environments in the moving image works.

YP Yes, most of the footage is drawn from focusing on the interiors of each of the spaces; there are various degrees of live action Steadicam footage. There is one CGI render which is built from an architectural model of Second Home, which I had turned into a video space that I could explore. Although it looks strangely like the actual space, I'm interested in that flipping between the real and the fantasy space. There are also cameras positioned within the exhibition, and some monitors mix pre-recorded video with live footage.

There is also footage of an Amazon logistics warehouse that has both human pickers and mechanized pickers – robots. Spending more time in the exhibition space at Chisenhale, I've been thinking about how the show is mechanized. While I'm the one who figures out how to maintain it and use it, ultimately it's running itself. Within contemporary discourse around work, there's a lot of discussion around the replacement of work and automation, but then many people in the creative industries feel excluded from that. They feel like they're in a special place but in reality, we're all still very co-dependent and intertwined and will ultimately be deeply affected by the social changes caused by automation.

EM You've chosen to make all the technology in the exhibition visible. Many of the machines are stripped of their protective covering and appear to be presented almost inside out so that you see more of how the technology is working.

YP There are a number of schools of thought that are competing over how to present and deal with design, a sort of incoherence between long-term legacies and upgrade culture. For instance, Apple's design hints at a very retro, glossy hiding of the technology – black-boxing what's inside and making it inaccessible to the user by putting it in a very nice package.

Inversely, many of these co-working spaces re-emphasize their mechanisms. They showcase how they work and the idea of transparency by forefronting all of their wiring or removing practical ceiling panels so you can see the cabling. You can see the mechanisms of how the building works, which emphasizes how it connects to a global trend in architectural design. Some of this comes from trying to embody transparency, something we get from open-source philosophies, and some of it is practical. Certain companies, like Google, employ very fancy cable runs to emphasize how connected they are with the world – or how they now actually connect the world.

EM Different colored cables?

YP Yes, multi-colored cable runs! I'm interested in the idea of forefronting infrastructure in order to explain what happens. I have played with that and used that in my work by self-hosting websites. It's a mixture of revisiting the earlier structures of the Internet and also the more radical structures of the Internet where you regain control over your information by self-hosting, but also playing with the aesthetics of forefronting them and putting them on show. Often the way I do it in my work isn't in this very glossy, designed way. It isn't the crystal-clean data center stack in the middle of the office. It's dust and dirt and cable runs that are very messy. I use a lot of improvised materials too.

EM Are you interested in what will happen over the course of the exhibition? Many of the materials that you've used are transparent, like Perspex, and even the chairs are transparent or semi-transparent. Are you interested in how the material will display its wear and accumulate dust and bits of detritus?

YP I am interested in confronting how these technologies are actually used, and how the people who engage with them imprint themselves onto these technologies. Some of that involves working with second-hand or used computers or servers and opening them up to see their connection with the physical world as they're also impacting it. There is an imprint inside of all the spaces that the servers, for example, have been in, and people that have used them. There's dust and also more abject elements, like skin particles and the things that make up dust, within the laptop fans and within the server fans. It's a representation of how we engage with the digital and how we leave traces on the digital through everything that we touch in online spaces as well.

EM Trying to see material traces of our immaterial labor, to connect in a tangible way with the technologies that we're using?

YP When you begin to work with the technology that we have, it seems very basic. It's not a case of science fiction becoming a reality or AI taking over, because when you start working with these things you realize that technology breaks all the time and is still quite basic. It's humans who are responsible for these complex systems. It has more to do with power and people, and these are the mechanisms of power. That's what I want to emphasize by having servers in the space that function to control the elements in the physical space: to block out light, to control lighting panels and thus control our sense of time within the space. I'm interested in how those servers and that network do that on a global level too.

EM So, you've created a microcosm with its own network, in which you foreground the level of control exercised by new technologies and to an extent the tech industry?

YP Yes, in some ways. In other ways, it's also connected to the same network as all these other laptops, PCs, servers and "internet of things" devices. It's connected to a bigger network. The strategies I've employed work in similar ways. All these networks do connect; they're all part of the real world. This is related to my interest in the digital economy and how that has now become part of the physical, "actual" economy; how cryptocurrencies like Bitcoin act like a connected model within the actual economy. So I've built a crude Bitcoin-based MONIAC with scale model people trapped inside the water loop of the model economic circulation. This mirrors the critique of the existing economic structures that is built into Bitcoin by its creator. As a working model, Bitcoin continues to question these systems. Perhaps that is why it's so compelling to artists; it exists almost like a conceptual readymade.

I'm interested in Bitcoin as a digital currency and the artificial controls in place within its structure. The analogy of mining is interesting as it relates to a finite amount of Bitcoin. To mine Bitcoin, you have to use computer power to solve complex cryptographic puzzles, on a network where other computers are also dealing with those puzzles. This encourages people to sustain the network, because if you solve the puzzle then you get a Bitcoin (or a portion thereof). The Bitcoin network, which is maintained by its users, also approves, logs, and regulates transactions, unlike a centralized bank. There are several Bitcoin mining rigs in the show, which are taking advantage of the free power here. Combined, they will probably produce around three or four dollars a day up until the middle of July when the profitability will fall dramatically. And this is because the cryptographic problems get harder and harder until they're impossible and that limits the amount of Bitcoin.

My initial use of a Bitcoin rig within one of the works deployed in Second Home's lobby was meant as a trade-off. I was thinking of the exchange of cultural capital happening by Second Home hosting an artwork in their space, and their association with Chisenhale Gallery, and attempting to rebalance this with a symbolic hijacking of their free electricity to mine the digital currency as a sort of royalty, which would then be rolled back into the project.

EM Could you talk more about time and the manipulation of time in the show? For example, through the programming, via the Raspberry Pi computers, you are able to control different elements of the exhibition, including the natural light that comes into the space.

YP I am interested in how the network-based digital economy is shifting people's sleep patterns and work patterns in accordance with centers of power. One of the things I found, whilst spending time in these co-working places late at night, is that London is still very much a "nine to five" city. These spaces, however, are open twenty-four hours per day but they are mostly empty outside of "regular" working hours, which for me embodies the sophistic embracing of Silicon Valley culture here in London. Walking around these spaces, they present themselves as very aspirational, mixed-use spaces and yet most of the time they don't really function. I had a strange experience walking around with the lights coming on automatically and there was a subtle yet unsettling sense of automation.

The eight-hour working day is an artificial idea too. It has been formalized by society and has become a rule that we are all used to. And now we are at a point where borders and time zones are diminishing. On a personal level, we're using devices and looking at screens on and off from when we wake up until we go to sleep, and this has a physiological effect on our bodies. For instance, we're more willing to embrace doing Skype calls at impersonal and unhealthy times and are more flexible in our sleep patterns. A lot of people are also medicating their sleep.

EM Do you mean they're able to control when they do and don't sleep?

YP Yes, this is prevalent in America where people are using melatonin or using drugs in the opposite direction, like Modafinil, to stay awake. They regulate their sleep patterns on their terms rather than on nature's terms. It is a well-documented fact that if you look at your computer or your phone, it suppresses the onset of melatonin, so you don't feel sleepy.

There is a whole industry that has sprung up around these drugs, branding a lifestyle dependent on them as aspirational, where sleep is presented as a problem to be solved and something that only the disadvantaged will partake in, in the future. In reality, sleep is slowly being turned into a luxury experience. So there are some references to self-medication within the show. This 24/7 working culture is so driven by coffee too. The coffee culture is linked with the tech industry, and there has been a coining of the term "the flat white economy." It's all this empty energy.

EM What does "the flat white economy" mean?

YP It's not a very inventive idea. It's a rehashing of the promise that the eighteen to thirty-five year old bracket of consumers will, by having less money, save and reinvent the UK's economy–by killing themselves in order for the generations older than them to profit and to make the economy globally relevant. The idea is that they will do this by being flexible, working in cafés and spending their disposable income on goods and services, whilst not really thinking about their future. It was used a lot as the basis for the policies of London's Tech City and digital conservative policy. I am interested in the fact that the baseline for all of this is caffeine, and this empty, giddy energy. Through playing with the cycles of both daylight and artificial light, and using various sized screens as materials in the space too, I'm playing with this idea of time, and this slippage or distortion of time. There will also be various allusions to the chemicals that we're consuming.

EM And that emerges through the more subtle elements of the exhibition like your research images and the coffee smell that is diffused in the space?

YP Yes. I've done a lot of work around melatonin, which is a sleep hormone that is a controlled, prescription-only substance in this country but is available over the counter in the US. I have done work relating to that and its discovery as a sleep aid at MIT. I'll be revisiting melatonin more broadly as a self-medicated drug because a lot of people order it into the UK. The other drug I'm interested in is caffeine, and there's a fake coffee smell that is dispersed from the front desk to circulate throughout the space.

EM We've talked about adaptability, mobile working, and the presumption that you are constantly available to work. The table structure that you have made in the space echoes this idea of café culture, and it functions or semi-functions as a workspace. Do you want people to use it in that way?

YP I hope they do. That is the way art is going in London, isn't it? There are all these galleries, including young galleries and project spaces, which used to use studio models but now they have a gallery that seeps, almost seamlessly, into a co-working space. And my work confronts that too, the marrying of these two industries. People have certain expectations and make sacrifices, within the wider creative industries but also within the arts, in order to do what they want to do. So this division of space and time into smaller and smaller fragments puts more of a squeeze on everything enjoyable about the city. The table structure is important within this as it represents a typical rented slot of space and time, but these tables are also often deployed as a lazy representation of some sort of trappings of community–without any of the deeper ethos or connections behind that. So it's thinking about co-optation and fragmentation of community and culture.

EM I want to ask you about the title *user, space*, which links to these ideas too.

YP I was in the different co-working spaces I researched at both regular and very weird times, often quite late at night. So I was thinking about space, about how these spaces impact us, and how the design of these spaces manipulates us. They do have physiological effects. The use of sound within these spaces is also present in the show. I've used a soundscape that changes from white noise to various community-made mixes used for productivity or relaxation. One of these mixes is actually a strange "whooshing" sound from *Blade Runner* (Dir. Ridley Scott, 1982) that someone turned into a twelve-hour mix, with the idea that you could use it to work or relax to. So that's in there too, a sort of side reference to *Blade Runner* as the default citation for anything uncomfortable about the present. In relation to that, I'm interested in our inability to have a critical language around the present without resorting to references within a film that's now thirty-four years old. I think science fiction has lost its edge in that respect.

Walking around the space at night though, if you're in there on your own, the white noise can be quite oppressive and then when there are a lot of people in the space, it functions in a different way. But when you're on your own, the architecture of the building or the design of the building becomes very apparent, and you become aware of how it imposes itself on you. How bodies exist in space is still, even with digital labor, something that is ever-present.

I was also thinking about this idea of the user within all of this. I was at DLD [Digital Life Design], a tech industry conference in Munich in 2015, and I saw a presentation by the CEO of Uber who, throughout all of it, referred to "users" and the "user base." I was invited to be there as a sort of sideshow art panel, which gave me an interesting insight because I realized that I am the user and the user base. Again, there is a flattening of a whole demographic of people into a commodity, which I'm also thinking about.

"User space" without the comma, is a computing term that relates to a cordoned-off area within a computer operating system. There is a user space where software and files can be handled by the user, and then there is a kernel space where the critical operations of the operating system happen. These are strictly divided spaces. I was thinking about how in computing those very powerful divisions are present for practical reasons but also how those ideas around power divisions from computing are seeping into broader culture and architectural models–with very defined spaces and permissions. I was also imagining the conversations Frank Gehry might be having with Mark Zuckerberg about their "Z town" project, Facebook's planned town for its workers.

EM What is the significance of presenting the work at Chisenhale Gallery, as an ex-industrial space and in the context of regeneration in the East End of London?

YP I thought a lot about this, in particular as we're at this point where art (in its physical forms) exists as the last type of light industry to be pushed out of these spaces within the city. I noticed how many of the apartments, work and co-working spaces use these building's industrial history as a key fabric to their branding, but we're now also seeing that with how art is being co-opted. The cultural history of a space also becomes a footnote in the building. A good marker of this beginning might be The Factory apartments in Manchester which co-opt the history of the infamous nightclub that was sited there before, which in turn made reference to Manchester's industrial past in its own name. As a last visible industry, art and artists are being used to dress these spaces, and to some degree, I imagined how a space like Chisenhale and its own history might end up being subsumed into such a co-working space. This is a local reference, but these effects and trends are global.

Yuri Pattison interviewed by Emma Moore, Offsite and Education Curator, Chisenhale Gallery, in association with Pattison's exhibition *user, space* at Chisenhale Gallery, 7 July–28 August 2016. *Chisenhale Interviews*, series editor, Polly Staple, Director, Chisenhale Gallery. *Chisenhale Interviews* is a series of artist interviews Chisenhale Gallery has conducted to complement the organization's exhibitions program. Dating back to Janice Kerbel's 2011 show, the interviews situate the artists' exhibitions at Chisenhale Gallery within the context of their wider practice and concerns, providing a rich source of information. Republished here with kind permission.

Worlding Matter

A Dialogue with Carolyn Christov-Bakargiev

Lucy Cotter You are currently the director of Galleria Civica d'Arte Moderna e Contemporanea di Torino (GAM) and Castello di Rivoli Museum for Contemporary Art, Turin, and a prolific curator and author. However, I would like to reflect on your role as Artistic Director of Documenta 13, which took place in 2012. You dedicated the edition "to artistic research and forms of imagination that explore commitment, matter, things, embodiment, and active living in connection with, yet not subordinated to, theory." It seemed to embody or stage a kind of knowledge production that was closer to non-knowledge.

Carolyn Christov-Bakargiev Yes, that's exactly what I was trying to do. I use the term "the no-knowledge zone," which comes from the artist Pierre Huyghe, who probably received it from various sources in philosophy and who used it a lot in the early 1990s. One of the biggest problems to address with Documenta 13 was how to act, what is to be done, in the age of advanced knowledge capitalism. How is it possible to use these terms but not collapse them into some sort of conservative, reactionary Neo-Expressionism? How can one do this without pursuing the apparently radical, the sometimes radical, practice of artistic research as it had appeared since the mid-1990s when artists like Mark Dion, Andrea Fraser and Renée Green began to adopt methodologies coming from the social sciences, from anthropology or archaeology or sociology as techniques for the research and production of artworks? Their "ancestor" would probably be Susan Hiller, who was one of the first artists to do so in the 1970s, as she had been trained as an anthropologist, but also other feminists like Mary Kelly, with her *Post-Partum Document* and so on, were precedents to this research-based attitude. So the mid-1990s is a period to consider when discussing the artistic research of today.

LC How does that relate to the 2000s or to what you would define as artistic research today?

CCB The 1990s, when Dion and these other artists were starting to work, was a very different era than today. With the Internet and the digital age, an archival impulse emerges – not so much the archival impulse of the creative-artistic, as Hal Foster would have defined it, but the archival impulses of corporations to buy all existing images, accumulating data banks or somehow archiving all possible, even inert, forms of material and immaterial knowledge that could be useful in the future, and this changes everything in the 2000s up to today. Artistic research by Goshka Macuga or Walid Raad takes this digital condition, this archive fever, into consideration.

I think of artistic research as very advanced practices of doing art as a form of imaginative knowledge and less based on the production of useful knowledge. It is different from science in that it would perhaps be less useful and also less rigorous and more subjective, maybe even drawing on the personal biography of the researcher-artists. Scientific research is also made up of so many different things. Scientific research developed by the mid-1990s into applied research, because that is when funding started to only go toward applied research and not to fundamental research. So also science has changed in terms of what is authorized to occur in the lab because of the direction of the funding that's going on in our very utilitarian society. Let's say the difference between those science lab projects and the artistic research of the 2000s is that there has been some sort of space granted to the imaginative, the subjective, and so on, in art. But fundamentally I think that they arrived at a point where artists were, without knowing it, basically serving to consolidate the structure of production of the twenty-first century. They had become the advanced avant-garde of the alienated cognitive laborer that is no longer alienated according to capital, but he or she is alienated nonetheless and the best recent artistic research projects are aware of this and play with it.

LC Can we talk about what that means, and how it plays out in real terms?

CCB The avant-garde of the artistic-creative personality is so cherished by corporations today precisely because it is more able to use intuitive methodologies, and to invent methodologies that are counterintuitive as well, in order to address an overwhelming amount of data. Because you're trained to think in terms of non-functional thinking and in lateral thinking, in terms of play, you are a more useful knowledge-producing subject to navigate the overwhelming amount of data and stuff in labs and in the computers, etc. So that sort of definition of artistic research, which had originally emerged in a radical left environment of art from the 1970s to the 1990s in order to counteract the market-oriented environment of art based on the transaction of objects (or even just pictures of objects because, at a certain point, artworks didn't even need to be exhibited), became what capitalism most cherishes. Because a lot of traditional art would go straight from the studio to the collector's storage through an online sale, a lot of the more radical people in art went toward artistic research as a practice in an impulse to counteract that marketization of the artwork. And yet, they can be easily co-opted as cognitive laborers.

LC Did these artists have a particular political agenda?

CCB Yes, often there were political agendas concerned with emancipation connected to these artistic research projects. There was the rise of the conceptual documentary artwork, which served the very important role of documenting things that CNN or the BBC and the whole choreographed, directed, hetero-directed media were not documenting. I am thinking for example of early Amar Kanwar, documenting the changing of the guards at the border of Pakistan and India, and so on. Ines Schaber's work is also an example of research-based work with a radical, political, emancipatory agenda. I respect this work very much. However, from another perspective and seen in retrospect, because this art is the expression of people who spend a lot of time on their computers and laptops and who spend a lot of time organizing material in post-studio work done on laptops, they are also experimenting with what it means to be a cognitive laborer. It has as much to do with the involuntary creation of this cognitive laborer as it has its own emancipatory potential and impulses.

When I was working on Documenta 13, I often thought about things that you wouldn't be able to "PDF" very easily or transmit by email or upload. Unless it was something that was made specifically to be uploaded, in which case the uploading was sort of part of the work. You can't really "PDF" the wind by Ryan Gander on the ground floor of the Fridericianum.[1]

LC Or the damaged objects from the Lebanese Civil War in *The Brain*.

CCB Yes, you can take a picture of them but you can't really transform them into numbers, so the theory that we are in a numerological world and age, sort of Alain Badiou's theory, is not my point of view. I'm much more interested in the partition

1 Christov-Bakargiev refers here to a work by Gander included in Documenta 13, entitled *I Need Some Meaning I Can Memorise (The Invisible Pull)* (2012), which consisted of artificially generated gusts of wind.

of the sensible, the ideas of phenomenology or biology or geology or Jacques Rancière. The idea of the politics of form is an old idea from the 1960s. It's in the magazine *Tel Quel*, it's in all of Arte Povera and Post-Minimalism. It's even in early abstraction; the fact that the politics of form is at the basis of Constructivism. However, I never really read much Rancière, just a few pages here and there. I always had the feeling that he was partly rehashing older ideas of the earlier twentieth century that were somehow crossing aesthetics, politics, phenomenology, and Gestalt and so I wasn't very attracted to his texts, although I agree with his ideas. But I suppose now people might say that I'm closer to him than to other thinkers. But all this doesn't mean that there can be no more artistic research-based art. It's just that that field must go through its own critique and be transformed into a sort of materiality.

LC Let's talk some more about the thinking behind your curation of Documenta 13 and the subject of materiality specifically.

CCB That's the basis from which I started working: between matter, materials, and research. And so within those two shores, how to not crash into either Scylla or Charybdis and pass through this Isthmus in a worldly way, in a process of what I call "worlding," looking at other forms of what you might call knowledge. It could also be seen as revitalizing the origins of some of New Age thinking, like theosophy and anthroposophy, Madame Blavatsky, Rudolph Steiner, Annie Besant and so on. You arrive at a kind of – not *alter* "mondialization" or modernization, but *autre* modernization, another modernity. It is a different modernity that went through the notion that there are certain levels of life and of the relationship between the body-mind; what you might call "mindfulness" in yoga practices that were being contested in the nineteenth century by the developing rationalistic modernization. And so impulses like the notion of the "thought-form," which is a kind of hovering actual object that's not a ghost and not a thing, but not an idea of a thing. It sort of is a thing in the sense that Michel Serres might describe the quasi-object, and so these thought-forms, for example, were very interesting to me. This is also why the artistic community Monte Verità was very important to me as an inspiration for later hippie communities.

LC You mention in some of the writings around Documenta 13 that Harald Szeeman had looked at Monte Verità and that Kabul was your Monte Verità for the period.

CCB Yes, I was speaking about Monte Verità as part of our universe of alternative thinking practices, which also had to do with artistic research. People at Monte Verità invented sun therapy, the idea that you might get Vitamin D by just lying naked in the sun. They carried out research on vegetarian food and on a kind of harmonization between not just the body and the mind but the body, the heart, the mind, and the different chakras etc., if you want to think in terms of yoga. But all of this lies in the background of the whole endeavor.

I agree with a number of current thinkers–like Donna Haraway who has mentioned it to me, or Simon Critchley who writes about it in *The Faith of the Faithless*–that with modernity there has been a problem in wanting to eradicate the spiritual from people's lives. I don't think Marx was right about that. Yes, institutionalized religion is, of course, the opium of the people. That has to do with power and the submission of people to the obligation of conforming to certain institutionalized rituals and practices, but the spiritual impulse, which you could also call a poetic impulse, was eradicated by the Left without addressing it seriously. That is why poetry was important in Documenta 13. There was a writers' retreat in a Chinese restaurant at the back of the park, there were weekly poetry readings, and the little houses in Karlsaue Park had to do with the idea of retreat space for meditation where a certain harmonization of body-mind could occur.[2]

LC Yet none of this takes place outside of a realm of material history.

CCB Yes, what they share with Karen Barad and Donna Haraway and so on, is that nothing takes place out of material history. However, it's not about looking at materialism in the Marxist sense.

LC Barad and Haraway are feminist thinkers talking about matter and mattering, actual materiality.

CCB Yes, I am thinking of feminist thinkers like Elizabeth Wilson, Jane Bennett and especially Karen Barad, who is more biology-oriented. I would bring it all the way to Isabelle Stengers. What they share is this question of why matter matters. That could be very superficial if you look at it as a reaction to the feeling of disembodiment in the digital age. It would be like a swing in the

2 Documenta 13 took place in ten main venues in Kassel, Germany, as well as a number of off-site venues and parallel programs in Alexandria, Cairo, Kabul, Bamiyan and Banff. At the Karlsaue Park, over twenty small, detached temporary houses were erected, each containing one project or exhibition.

pendulum theory, which could be really stupid, so one has to be very careful. But what the feminist thinkers are not throwing away, which is fundamental, is the sense of the complexity of the rhizomatic (to use not a woman's but a man's work but Deleuze and Guattari were so influenced by women, I think).

You can break up matter and things into their subatomic particles. When you do that, there is nothing between the stuff that makes a thought and the stuff that makes a physical object. It just depends on where you decide to constitute the objecthood of the object, whether it's the subatomic particle that's the object or a sense of boundary around a crux of subatomic particles together, making, say, an atom or even a jug. So it just depends on where you see that inside and outside of "thingness." Biologist Lynn Margulis is very important to me as well, as the person who theorized endosymbiosis. The way that you think, therefore, about thingness, about life as provisional because it's constantly re-aggregating into other things. Feminist thought brings in this limit, which is the limit of the stuff of the universe, where it all dissolves and connects and intra-acts.

You know, there is again in what I say here a sort of a New Age sensibility, the sort of "all the universe is one big continuous stuff," a notion that Heidegger was afraid of in his lecture on the Thing. He didn't like the way physics talks about the jug not being empty but full of particles because he said that if you start thinking that the jug is full of stuff, you cannot think it as a holding vessel or as a pouring vessel and you just get lost into the notion that everything is everything. But I disagree. You don't have to, because things can disperse and aggregate and disperse and re-aggregate. Anyway, I'm particularly interested in this, albeit with a slight suspicion around most of the speculative realists, because I think that they want to swing away from post-modern complexity, which isn't necessary toward a new form of realism. If you think and go through biology, you don't have to give up complexity, discursiveness, and correlations.

LC Yes, some of the areas of thought that you've looked at, also as models for knowledge production, are quantum physics and microbiology; these areas of science being close to the possibilities that you open up conceptually.

CCB Yes, in fact, Karen Barad is a quantum physicist and so is Anton Zeilinger, who was one of my advisors for Documenta 13, but it's not that biology is less important. I see all these fields as being very entangled and connected in a kind of cognate connectivity of a cosmopolitical order. So basically you are able to address why matter matters and, let's say, artistic labor (or artistic play if you want to define it as a kind of a form of playing). I think that if you can hold all of these things in a vibrant way in the background and talk about them with all the artists and with the other thinkers, then that is how you arrive at a project that is like Documenta 13. You arrive at something that's embodied and that's also very much about temporality and locationality and how these two are intrinsically connected, intra-acting the temporal and the spatial, kind of mutually engendering each other. You can arrive at that in, let's call it an intelligent manner, without ever having to produce any constituted knowledge, not even the constituted knowledge of, say, a form of institutionalized spirituality like existing religions. I didn't want to do a Documenta about the return to the spiritual, or the return to the object. I would like to reiterate that there was no concept.

LC It's of course only in certain parts of science, but there does seem to be great freedom there in terms of beginning from nowhere.

CCB Well, you're slowly getting to what I'm trying to say, which is that in fifty years, we're not going to have the same divisions of fields because it doesn't make any sense. The imaginative way of thinking of quantum physics has nothing to do with a genetic lab studying how to map the genetic DNA of a seed. It has nothing to do with it and it's much closer to artistic research according to how you define it, so there you go. Now, when I say this, people will probably say, "Oh, that's like Latour." Now, I do adore Bruno Latour and Isabelle Stengers's texts and that whole thing of science studies, but I read Latour after working with Arte Povera, after working with Pierre Huyghe, and found confirmation of a lot of thoughts that I had that were coming from feminist science studies, from Barad and Natasha Myers, Carla Hustak and Donna Haraway.

LC Yes, for me, it goes back to being a teenager and coming across C.P. Snow's writings from the 1950s about "the two cultures," the unnatural divide between the sciences and the arts. Documenta 13 also seemed to be more about a shifting of a frame around art itself. There was a kind of zooming out, so that you could see a very natural interrelationship between the production of art or art-making processes and other knowledge-making processes, let's say. This was done partly through the framing of art in particular ways, by including that which is often cut out of the frame. There seemed to be a widening of the frame to allow more of that already-present organic process that has always gone on in the making of art but is not necessarily seen in the white cube.

CCB Yes, certainly not seen in the exhibitions. It's more seen in the artist's studio and in the life of artists, but in the exhibitions that gets cleaned away. You clean it up and you leave the final thing because you want to also define the special nature of art. It's not done out of ill will or wanting to misinform people. I think it's more about how most curatorial endeavors or museum endeavors are concerned with celebrating art, so you want to make it seem "special," which it is, but it also isn't, as you just said. It is part of a broader – I would like to say *cultural* – practice. But the definition of culture presents us with a problem here. I don't know if we should say that it's not culture, it's art. Art is somehow that which resists its own definition, whereas culture is somehow the already established, as Christoph Menke once observed. It's like the difference between the spiritual and the religious, so we can't really use the word "culture" either, but let's say the broader "doings of curiosities" in various ways. But at the same time, that's very limiting because I think the globalization of art wants the Western idea of art to be adopted all over the world, but there never was a real discussion about this definition being a modern Western definition and therefore it's something quite colonial.

I'm not sure that in fifty or a hundred years, the concept of the field of art will exist in Paris or New York or South Africa or Hanoi. It seems like a very twentieth-century idea, contemporary art, like part of a previous era of civilization. I'm sure that people who are artists now will continue to do whatever it is that they do, but I'm not sure they're going to call it art or define it within the collections that had that thing called "art" in those collections, within those boundaries.

LC Do you think that artistic research tries to break open a space that raises the question of art becoming other things? Do you think that the very notion of artistic research perhaps already opens a gray area where art might actually take the space to transform in some of the directions that it may take in the future?

CCB That's an interesting way of looking at it. I had never thought of that but certainly, if you turn art into artistic, into an adjective, and you're taking the term "research," which is broader, then research can embrace so much. Yes, I suppose it could be that it goes in that direction, but we'd have to be careful because I'm an Adornian person and I'm suspicious of this new label. I think we always have to make a form of negative-dialectical critique of our own thinking and to be aware that when you say "artistic research," you are both questioning the autonomy of art as a field, but you're also pursuing and strengthening the hypothesis behind cognitive capitalism, which is that knowledge is the product that will make the economy flourish in the twenty-first century and therefore all of the divisions between the rich and the poor and the power relations and subjugation of people might be found by these knowledges. Research also includes R&M research, Research and Movement, or research in armaments, military research and research in corporations like Monsanto. It's a very trendy, dangerous word that is fraught with those power relations, so I'm not sure. It can be an emancipatory term and universe of signification if you consider it as a floating signifier but it depends on where it floats.

LC In your catalogue essay for *Documenta 13: The Logbook*, you refer to the Greek term *sképsis* in relation to research: "In Greek, sképsis means 'research'. A skeptic is someone who is constantly searching for knowledge, for the truth but doesn't find it. A relativist, conversely, would be what a skeptic would call an academic."[3] I'm curious about this, what it meant for you to associate the academic with relativism.

CCB I mention three categories: the academic, the dogmatic and the skeptic. Skepticism is not relativism although it is close to relativism, but relativism is more the academic.

LC Yes, but I was very curious to hear you take that definition of the academic.

CCB The dogmatic believes that he or she has found the truth, like Aristotle. The academic believes there is no truth and therefore adopts any truth that is appropriate in that context, and so it's the academic truth. And that's relativist actually. The skeptic, who is more commonly associated with relativism, is actually only partially relativist because you realize there are no absolute truths. But you cannot be a skeptic unless you believe in that search for Truth, so there's a commitment to the search and *sképsis*, indeed, means to search, as you said; that's why you brought it up, I think. So the skeptic is the searcher, let's say, he who searches. So is the researcher, if you want to consider it as such. But at the same time,

3 *Documenta 13: The Logbook*, Catalogue 2/3 (Ostfildern: Hatje Cantz, 2012), p. 286.

there's a paradox there, a kind of contradiction, to go back to Adorno, in that a skeptic sort of knows you're not going to get to the end of it but if you don't believe you can get to the end of it, you'll never be a skeptic. So, again, it's about a sort of faith, the faith of the faithless, to go back to Critchley's book, and also to Judith Butler's sense of commitment, her notion of the "committed voice" in her writing. Unless you believe you're going to get somewhere, you can't have a committed voice. I think of Documenta 13 as a very committed exhibition.

LC In your essay, you also refer to the artist as an "amateur" and to the notion of "the amatorial mind." You write, "Artists are like 'amateurs'; even if they know a lot of things, they are really 'amateurs'. It's in the 'amatorial' mindset that you get to forms of knowledge–or non-knowledge."[4] Does this amatorial mindset also relate to committedness?

CCB Yes, because *amare* means to love, so amatorial knowledge is indeed not only a non-specialized knowledge but also a committed knowledge at every moment, or a committed form of searching. At the same time, the amateur is a figure who, in not being professionalized, somehow escapes the partition that knowledge capitalism requires and claims in the separation of specialized people who work collectively on a project. One from Oslo and another from New York, keeping them separated and yet having them working together. Of course, amatorial knowledge is also double-sided because the amateur is often what's needed in order to navigate the complexity of the data, so the artist as an amateur is, once

4 *Documenta 13: The Logbook*, p. 291.

again, a figure of the cognitive laborer needed by power in the twenty-first century. So even being an amateur can be problematic, but I still think that amatorial knowledge is important, if it can suspend itself just before being constituted. So the amateur is also someone who suspends just before actually doing anything. Hence the withdrawn-yet-present artist Francesco Matarrese in *The Brain*, which was central to the exhibition. His text was very important in *The Brain*. It's at the core of the core in Documenta 13.

LC Thinking about what you mentioned earlier – "the moment before knowledge is constituted" – reminds me also of how you made the decision to publish a hundred notebooks to accompany Documenta 13. At a certain point in your writings, you discuss what that writing means for you as a place to share thinking as a process, to witness that thinking in its messy and poetic burgeoning rather than in a final state. It seems to me that this conception of the notebooks allows for pausing at that moment.

CCB Yes, exactly. That idea was developed together with Chus Martínez and addressed by Michael Taussig as the first notebook. So the notebook is not simply coined as useless material, as discarded elements; the notebook is something of a past yet future, a loop time, a kind of temporal *aporia* in a creation of a past for the future, when the future might want what's in your notebook or might find a potentiality in it. So in this double movement of a future perfect, of the creation of a future perfect, is a tense, a space of the notebooks in general, of the propositional. But there's also simply the way the notebooks worked as a whole, which was very much done with my advisor Chus Martínez. There was a pot of a hundred names at the beginning, but we only invited maybe ten people and then after those ten notebooks were written, we invited another twenty. Then it became an organic system, whereby the texts, as they emerged, dictated by association who might be interesting to commission to write a further notebook. So it was an organic process where there was no contradiction between the perspectives of the authors of the hundred notebooks. However, there is no common topic or clear subject matter or clear theory that emerges either. You might see them as a random aggregation; things that sometimes have to do with art, sometimes don't or that have no apparent connection. For me, the whole of Documenta 13 was like that.

LC I was also struck by the role of anachronism in Documenta 13, the a-chronological thought processes that were present within the notebooks and to an even greater extent within the exhibits. I'm thinking of artists like Hannah Ryggen and how ideas, images, people and concepts come back in a kind of "return of the repressed" manner. This sense of a-chronological time is something I also very much appreciate in terms of artists' own thinking around art. Artists are interested in particular ideas and they jump backwards and forwards across time automatically, drawing together ideas and fragments of relevance to each other without a kind of disciplinary thinking or a historicized temporal thinking.

CCB That's like life, isn't it? That's how we live. It's not just artists who do that.

LC Of course, but in your approach to Documenta 13, I feel like you shifted curating closer toward being a practice that is akin to artistic practice in that way. I know you don't like the word "curator," as you've mentioned on various occasions that you see it as part of a system of art management. I respect that, but I feel that through Documenta 13 you made a very particular proposition in terms of future curatorial practice. You proposed a form of exhibition that doesn't state an existing idea but that is in a state of research itself.

CCB That's true. It was more like an experiment; you might see it in terms of a lab experiment where something might occur that might help us go someplace together. You could say that Documenta 13 was breaking away from a certain curatorial history, but if you look at it with more distance you could also say that it's closer to Harald Szeemann's curating. It's closer to an earlier period in the late 1960s in which *When Attitudes Become Form* was actually a very open proposition and the so-called "curators," who were not called curators, were just friends of the artists or *compagni di strada*. They accompanied the artists along the way, peers who had studied art history or who had come from art criticism, or who just weren't artists, would help with the more organizational things but they had to be engaged in it, in the process. They were not like Clement Greenberg, they were against all that; they were part of the making of art. It was during this period that interviews began to be published, so it was no longer about just publishing a text or a review of an exhibition but publishing an engaged conversation.

To my knowledge Carla Lonzi was the first, around 1965, to shift the sense of the art critic. The artists seemed to be saying back then, "We don't want an art critic, somebody who is out there writing his or her art criticism. We want you to show your hesitations, your doubts, and your questions. We don't want you to just listen to me then transcribe it and put it into the third person." So that level of engagement was published, where even the stupidity of the question is maintained and the hesitation in the voice, the things between the words, between the things said, the silences and the gaps become meaningful. That was what happened as things turned away from the jury-selected exhibition and so on, as was done in the 1950s.

LC Do you think you were picking up on that legacy in your approach to Documenta 13 or was there some kind of paradigm shift going on?

CCB I think that I do have a memory of that period, maybe because I'm older than a lot of the young curators, coming through the Arte Povera artists, and yet I am much younger than that generation. I'm a feminist, but I don't have to prove myself and go against the old guys of the late 1960s and say, "Oh, how bad and heroic they were." How Joseph Beuys was so bad because he was a shaman and he thought he was sexy with his hat and so on and so forth. I can see the aspects of those people and their practices as very liberating also, as they were liberating from previous structures of the late Greenberg generation dominant in the 1950s and early 1960s. I think that with Documenta 13 I was reconnecting with a previous generation of exhibition makers in a way that Catherine David did not wish to do because in 1997 she needed to position theory and discourse firmly in our field.

In other words, maybe David firmly formulated the whole artistic research paradigm shift in a way, because she said in her Documenta X that research can be art in a way. She started that whole thing from the point of view, not of a single artwork or artist, but from the point of view of it being culturally recognized as a paradigm shift. She thought she was reconnecting with a previous generation against all the Neo-Expressionists of the 1980s. She more or less said, “Well, I like Jean-Luc Godard and Michelangelo Pistoletto and the minus objects, so I want to reconnect with this idea of art as a radical, active resistance.” In a way, she was doing something out of sync with her time and older; so, from a conscious perspective, I could say the same. What I’m doing is not inventing anything or starting any paradigm shift. I don’t think you can do that intentionally; it just sort of happens. There may be a paradigm shift but all I was consciously doing was reconnecting with that previous open process-oriented form of engaged exhibition making.

LC But you also had very particular ambitions in your conception of the Documenta 13 as something other than an exhibition or stand-alone event.

CCB Yes, I was reconnecting with a more organic way of conceiving the public moment as a small moment of a broader life and organism. In fact, Documenta 13 didn’t end when the Fridericianum closed; there was always so much more going on. There were always thirty artists in town. That had never happened before in Documenta, but it wasn’t done intentionally. If I had wanted to have thirty artists living in the city all the time, it wouldn’t have worked. It would have been false. So it was by another stitching and weaving together of various other things that something like *And And And*, Rene Gabri and Ayreen Anastas’s project, developed or the film program emerged. A certain number of things happening in education or the types of work that needed to be cared for – things that needed to be gardened, or that were participatory, that needed people – somehow ended up causing as an involuntary consequence that there were thirty artists, not always the same ones, taking care of things throughout the one hundred days and that transformed the exhibition into a piece or portion of life. It was a world, not an exhibition, but also not a megalomaniac world.

LC There was the creation of a certain kind of space too.

CCB Yes, and that brings us back to the question of the other venues that I brushed off earlier in our conversation because it's so complicated a topic it would take a whole interview to discuss just those. But I wouldn't want to remove that topic completely from this conversation because the existence of the Alexandria/Cairo seminar, the Kabul and Bamiyan seminars and exhibition, the Banff seminar about retreat, and the solo exhibition by Brian Jungen were fundamental to what happened in Kassel.[5] On the one hand, I was trying to think through what it means to make an exhibition in the so-called global age. But with the problem of not wanting to open up Lufthansa offices all over the world, which would have been terribly neo-colonial and horrible, like corporations opening up their offices everywhere at the same time. Nor did I want to make a reactionary closure onto the regional or the local. How to think through all those contradictions and to come up with something that is woven together? There

5 The parallel projects in Alexandria, Cairo, Kabul and Bamiyan were made up of a constellation of seminar series and exhibitions. The Banff project consisted of a retreat at the Banff Centre for eighteen invited residents and twenty additional participants.

was the question of the war and the trauma and the post-war period in Kassel, but if it had been only that, it would have been just from the top down. It happened instead organically–Kabul and Bamiyan happened because of the connection with Alighiero Boetti and my connections with Boetti and then with artist Mario García Torres. So it's in the connectivity between the story of Boetti's One Hotel in Kabul and the fact that by chance, this country's going through an experience that is both still a war and no longer a war, and an occupation, even though it's been liberated from a dictatorship–both conditions are similar to what Kassel was like in the period of the generation of Documenta in the 1950s–that this strange, again, kind of *aporia* took place.

LC To what extent does your engagement with artistic research, which was so manifest in Documenta 13, inform your thinking as Director of the Castello di Rivoli and GAM in Turin?

CCB I think everything I do is related to research. So art historical research seems obsolete but is not at all. And that is what can be done in museums. But research per se can be a way of just serving cognitive capitalism, so somehow I feel not knowing is a condition the museum can also explore.

Future Ecologies

A Dialogue with Em'kal Eyongakpa

Lucy Cotter There seems to be an underlying search in your practice for points of coexistence between the subjective and objective realms. Your recent multimedia installations and performances negotiate the relationship between the two, evoking epigenetics (transgenerational memories at a microcellular level), ethnobotany (the plant lore and agricultural customs of a people), applied and ethnomycology (fungal studies), and cosmologies, among other epistemological systems. Can we start by talking about how you got into considering these different fields of thought? I read somewhere that you studied botany and ecology before you moved into art practice. Was your transition into art practice an organic process?

Em'kal Eyongakpa It was more or less an organic process. In Cameroon, where I grew up, young people seldom have a stake in choosing what they want to study. They're, for the most part, totally dependent on their parents for basic sustenance. Studying sciences was my family's will; my father's to be precise. As a child, I spent most of my time drawing, writing and making things until I turned thirteen, after which I had to drop the arts in my school curriculum to concentrate on sciences.

Botany and environmental science were an escape during my undergraduate years, and my inclination toward the world of ethnobotany was already evident. I spent the first few years of my life in a communal family setting, in close proximity to my grandfather Pa Nsoako Eyongarreybiti, who was a spiritual healer and, I'd say, a master "ethnobotanist." When he passed away, my initial plans to research with him were aborted. At that point, I decided to concentrate on the visual and sonic arts, which had always been prime interests. That was about twelve years ago. Some of my grandfather's life philosophies fed my initial ideas, coupled with an interest in identity politics. I think the interwoven media in my work could be a result of my "self-taught" background and the Indigenous culture of the Bayang and Denya people, which is predominantly based on weaving. There was another major turning point in my practice about four years ago, which made way for some previously underused media, like the spoken word, and for other areas of interest to resurface.

I had a life-threatening medical condition that couldn't be diagnozed by classical medicine. So I ended up being treated by a spiritual healer, and through that experience, I started to reconnect more with my interest in ethnobotany and many other areas. After that reminder, things naturally started to take their course. My current ideas and practice negotiate between life sciences or life, technology, the metaphysical *juju* and societal aspects of specific Indigenous peoples. I am interested in weaving these ideas together in a bid to imagine alternative possibilities.

LC This interweaving of science, energetic healing and technology is very present in *Letters from Etokobarek* (2015–). Like most of your works, it has had several iterations in different media. It has taken the form of a video work and a mixed media installation, and you've done a related performance, *??Fullmoons Later/Wata Culture II* (2015). There's a lot of imagery in the work – of water, of light – and sculptural elements that together resemble something that appears cosmological. It seems to me that you're trying to build up a language with that work, to construct a language that doesn't exist. Am I right in thinking about it in those terms?

EE Yes, I think that's a good way of looking at it. The full moon is a measure of time for my people and many Indigenous peoples of Central and West Africa. Having just recovered from the medical situation I mentioned earlier, in which I was literally left for dead in hospital, it was a new dawn. It was like getting a second chance so I was literally counting full moons from that point onwards. I attempted to bring that personal experience together with collective histories and other elements from my notebooks and my travels – sonic diaries, scribblings, random words, texts, and notes on ideas that always come into my practice somehow.

The spoken-word aspect resurfaced after my personal experience of the blind Indigenous healer I mentioned before, who used spoken words and chants during the rituals that enabled my recovery. I had been a spoken word poet and a rap artist in my late teens and early twenties while studying life sciences before switching entirely to the visual and sonic arts. After what the spiritual healer did, the power of the spoken word became very evident. So all these things started coming together in that work, and they're still developing as I continue to process the experience. That was a starting point for a much bigger process of reflection.

LC In the performance of *??Fullmoons Later/Wata Culture II* in Paris, there is a background video projection of *Letters from Etoktobarek* in which your visual editing seems to follow the lines of rhythm: the rhythm of a voice, the rhythm of the water, the rhythm in the words around certain histories. There are several fragments of text within the projected video, mostly taken from notes, but when you speak those words, you evoke much more than the visually projected text. There's something in the rhythm and texture of your voice that lends those thoughts a different weight. It makes them flow and resonate differently. You seem to use the spoken word, your voice, as a further layer of knowledge.

EE During the performance, the physical elements trigger the spoken word. The performance was a 5.1 surround sound experience, sketched from ultrasonic and other field recordings, contextual voice excerpts and music samples. These were all mixed in real time from sound banks, with real-time VJing and live percussion. I usually try to connect things in real time in a way that defies rehearsal. I like the spoken word in performances to act as a kind of footnote to what is happening with the visuals, including the visual text. I'm more interested in the non-tangible, in that fleeting experience, where I could be a direct channel to a certain degree. In this light, I think the spoken word adds unconscious layers of knowledge, as well as weaving together the whole.

This aspect also comes back again in my use of photography and video. For the video part, *Letters from Etokobarek*, I worked on the images with the intention of creating a flow, based on what you can hear. My intention was to enable a kind of molten space, a flow, a rhythm. I think or do things on a mostly unconscious basis, based on inner flows or rhythm. This rhythm can also be found in the scribblings I used to create the drawings for what a friend called "moonscapes." The drawings were made while listening to the sounds of the installation. Together with the shadows cast by the kinetic moon sculptures, between the video projector and "moonscapes," I imagined it to be simulating patterns based on my cosmology and rituals from my homelands; imagining that people could stay immersed in that system.

LC Can you say more about your cosmology and how you understand that term in the context of your work? Is your cosmology specific to your clan, or does it relate to wider philosophies like Ubuntu or something similar?

EE What I mean by cosmology in this context is how the Nyang and other Indigenous people see and relate to the cosmos and specific patterns over time; how they negotiate with life, death and the stars. Most Indigenous people around this part of the world share a very similar cosmological view, so I'm working in general, not with a specific Indigenous nation-state. The starting point is often the Nyang people, but it works across other

Indigenous cosmologies, which are of great interest to me. I think these cosmologies qualify as other "alternative" philosophies.

LC How do you research the cosmologies that fall outside the scope of the knowledge you have from your own cultural background?

EE Indigenous people of the Congo Basin rain forests share quite similar worldviews. Shared cultural influences make for an easy point of entry. I travel a lot on the African continent. Being keen on nuances and "in betweens" during these travels, I talk a lot with elders and other keepers of knowledge. At times, I also record these conversations in their mother tongue, if I can understand it or am learning to understand it. Most of the trips take the form of ordinary visits, and they usually end in conversations and recording sessions. Coming from a part of the world with a mainly oral tradition and many shared influences, I find that the undiluted communication during these sessions, and the use of Indigenous languages and first-hand experiences, help tremendously with the learning process.

LC There are traces of this process of talking to elders in works like *Ketoya Speaks (Dɛnyaland-Kɛnyaɛland-Kɛyakaland; A Century Later)* (2016), a video that revolves around a man speaking in what I understood to be his mother tongue.

EE Yeah, they spoke the Denya and Keyaka languages. The video is just an excerpt from the process to introduce the idea. I am currently working on sculptures to be installed with the photographs. In *Ketoya Speaks* I went looking for what remains of what is left, based on oral tradition. My departure point was a resistance movement against German colonialism that took place between 1904 and 1906 in the Manyu division of present-day Cameroon. This resistance was met with heavy-handedness and finally repressed. Most of the accounts I had found in history books were written from the German or European point of view. They were also compromised and, in my opinion, whitewashed. When I visited those spaces, on telling the community who I am, my clan, etc., I found out that there were even more inaccuracies in what is canonized as history than I had imagined. I visited and lived in these enclave spaces where the rebellion was at its peak, allowing elders, chiefs, and other guardians of culture to speak in an undiluted way about what they knew about what happened, as well as requesting them to comment on certain aspects of the mainstream historical accounts, which are so different.

LC You seem to use lens-based media in a very specific way in works like *Ketoya Speaks*, which contains both a video and an extensive series of photographs. There are several photos in which the body is blurred, evoking an energetic presence. They also resemble nineteenth-century photographic images of mediumship in some ways. In the video, we see you revisiting a certain space, a geographic location. It starts with plant imagery, then we see a figure in a landscape with a crucifix in the distant background. The image of the figure is also blurred. There's again a sense of the presence of absence. Do you find that the technological medium, this acoustic and visual medium of video, is able to bring that experience to the fore, to materialize it and draw attention to another layer of experience?

EE Yes, I try to create a more sensorial space. I am very interested in early photography and its techniques, and my interest in that imagery is also based on how I look at things, on seeing myself and other people as energy. Lens-based media and the whole idea of a lens fascinates me–what a lens does and how it facilitates seeing what you don't see with your unaided eye. I find parallels between that and the practices of spiritual mediums, as well as the tendency to experience objects and subjects more from a fluid or "molten" point of view rather than a static one. I have been experimenting and trying to write my thoughts with lens-based media for quite a while, which led me to a kind of fictive photography with traces of surrealism and visual paradoxes, reminiscent of early-nineteenth-century photography. This characteristic was mainly based on an old naive quest to record spirits, rituals, energies or a series of actions in a still image, which was probably my attempt to find relationships between these media and my grandfather's discipline in my earlier photographic series like *Naked Routes* (2011), *Ngoketunja: Unsung Heroes* (2011) and *Bleed for the Read* (2009).

For *Ketoya Speaks*, I wanted to take images of specific sites and some of the people with whom I had talked. I photographed them the way I saw them, working with long exposure so I that I could control certain aspects of the image. It is now a century after the resistance, so that reference to older photography is also consciously present, as well as my view that people are not mobile bodies, but a mass of energy moving through space. I imagined that if I consciously expanded these media, I could help with bringing certain aspects to the fore.

LC Does this relate to your interest in transgenerational memory? Were you also trying to somehow evoke or convey epigenetic knowledge in these image sequences?

EE I wasn't busy with epigenetics in *Ketoya Speaks*. I was reading a lot of scientific journals on epigenetics and thinking about it much more in relation to *??Fullmoons Later/Wata Culture* (2013). I felt that you didn't need to look at scientific conclusions on epigenetics *per se*, but at life beyond the surface level. I had been researching American music, mainly Jazz, as well as Black art movements from the 1950s, and at some point, I recognized a rhythmic pattern that was common to several Indigenous cultures across the African continent. John Coltrane's 1961 *Africa Brass* album was an interesting pointer; it was like an entry point into what I would call suspension rhythmic patterns in Western music, which John Cage and especially Steve Reich took further. At one point I was listening to some of the Beat poets, like Amiri Baraka, and I realized that, probably unconsciously, some would use this rhythm in a lot of their performances.

I wondered how they would remember some predominantly ritual musical rhythmic aesthetics, having been separated from them for more than four hundred years, if it wasn't for transgenerational memories or epigenetics, at least as an initial impetus. So I started to look at other basic practices in Cameroon and West Africa, at simple observations like a common practice in which the heir to a kingdom must be born during the reign of a king. When I undertook research on this practice, it was connected to phenomena that have not been called epigenetics but are related to it. So I am not approaching epigenetics from a scientific perspective, but in terms of common knowledge and basic practices.

LC In making this work, do you want to draw attention to the points of connection across these divergent knowledge systems? Are you interested in removing epistemological hierarchies and putting them on the same level? When I say this, I'm also thinking in terms of decolonizing knowledge. Do you see your own work and practice in those terms?

EE I imagine that decolonial thinking is very central to my outlook on life. It's not necessarily about dismantling any given system but about putting things into perspective. I am engaging with things that I have a grounded knowledge about and trying to recreate or create worlds or imaginaries I want to live in. I want to imagine a sustainable and technologically advanced world, not only insist on going back to what existed before the colonial period. I am approaching things from different fields of knowledge that could be helpful to imagine forward. I'm looking from that perspective while being aware of current debates about collective postcolonial history.

LC Can we talk about *Rustle 2.0* (2016), the work you showed at the Sharjah Biennial, which is an example of you bringing together different ways of being with technology to create a world that is decolonial and a future-oriented space somehow. The installation has been described as a "multimedia transcription" of a "living ecosystem," a kind of sentient presence that streams real-time information. There is a pair of "breathing" "lungs" at the center of the installation resembling the African and South American continents, and they are surrounded by a sort of fungus-based environment. Can you try to describe the different elements of that installation and your thinking behind them? It is quite complex in its set-up.

EE The idea for *Rustle* was conceived in 2010, with my starting point being to explore deforestation and increasing desertification between the Congo Basin and the Amazon rain forest, which are often referred to as "the lungs of the planet." Later on, it morphed into an attempt to mimic a system of connectivity in portions of these biomes, as well as interference by human activity. The addendum "2.0" in the title alludes to cybernetics, to updates by man on a living ecosystem. To convey this, I borrowed from specific Indigenous rhythmic patterns for the sound composition, for the mycelium networks and the electronic interfaces. I imagined mimicking life with no elements of real life within it, except for the smell from the dried hay, sisal and jute fibers as well as the dried mycelium panels.

As for the set-up, I designed an analogue and digital system consisting of a 5.1 surround sound composition, made from field recordings, which I routed and synchronized with a custom electronic midi-controlled interface, creating visual rhythmic patterns in relation to the sound. I refer to the red and white LED animated curves triggered by this interface as a "deaf/light score" because they allude to animated electro-cardiograms or multiple animated stock exchange curves. The main electronic interface (or "deaf score") also sends midi commands to simulate different breathing patterns and dead points to the central sculpture, which is called *Breathe II* (2013). There's a magnetic device attached to the sculpture that causes it to levitate. The sisal and jute fibers are woven to form a dense web that helps to distort light rays in the space. That's the basic set-up.

LC There are also fungus threads on the walls and ceiling, which I imagine relates to your interest in applied mycology. Can you say something about that interest and how it manifests in this installation?

EE Yes, I'm interested in the idea of connectivity and ecosystems, which are represented in this installation by a fungi network. The fungi culture also helps with the acoustics of the exhibition space to accommodate the surround sound. I was experimenting with growing acoustic panels with mushroom mycelium, which function as sound absorbers, as well as being the basis for these biomes from the Amazon and Congo Basin rain forests. On a visual level, the mycelium networks simulate the connectivity that is very present in the rain forest, both from a sonic point of view and otherwise.

LC There's also a link between the dense composite soundscape and the "breathing patterns" of the "lungs." Can you elaborate on what we are listening to in that installation and what you wanted that soundscape to evoke?

EE The composite soundscape is made up of audio recordings from and around the Takamanda forest reserve and environs in the Congo Basin rainforest. There are several outside incursions in those soundscapes, like chainsaws, falling trees, gunshots by poachers, and air traffic. I think that together they convey an asynchronous sensation of space between balance and catastrophe, breathing and suffocation. The rhythmic pattern I used draws mainly on characteristic tropical rainforest sounds that often tend to mimic breathing patterns, with interference from human elements. This work was commissioned for the 32nd Bienal Internacional de São Paulo, *Incerteza Viva*.

LC Soundscapes are also so central to your work in general. They seem to be both a means of researching and of evoking space, in this and several other artworks. I am thinking, for example, of *Letters from Etokobarek*, for which you recorded the soundscape in five or six locations, as well as *Negotiations (Chapter 1-i, Dualaland - Paris)* (2015), the installation you made at the Kadist Foundation in Paris. There you also used surround sound to envelop the visitor fully. It would be great to hear how you collected those sounds, how you think about them, and how you work with them.

EE The medium of sound is probably the most potent one for me. My use of sound is also based on my origins, as many forms of Indigenous cultural transmissions there have a very strong sonic aspect and we mainly have sonic memories. *Negotiations (Chapter 1-i, Dualaland - Paris)* was the result of a residency I did in Paris. When I was invited, I went to see the space, which is very close to an African neighborhood, Château Rouge. While there, I started hearing sounds that were very particular to specific urban centres in West and Central Africa, especially sounds from street vendors and markets. The rhythmic patterns of these familiar sounds resonated differently in the Parisian acoustic settings and that sense of displacement and nostalgia led me to do a project that would bring these different geographic and acoustic spaces together. For the final project, I collected sounds of and around market negotiations from both cities, Douala and Paris. Several things were interesting for me–from the rhythmic currency, the products sold, the bargaining techniques, and especially the absurdity of the currency used in France and Cameroon as well as nuances in between. If you listen to calls like "*Fumbua! carton à dix euros, bobolo! Trois pour deux euros. Safou, huit à cinq euros, ceintures, arachide frais ....*" in France and "*cent franc baton, ceinture deux mille franc*" in Douala, you can't ignore the colonial monetary absurdity called the FCFA created by the French colonialists for their African colonies in the 1940s, which is still in use today but currently being contested. These were some of my considerations for collecting sounds with undertones of negotiation and creolization in and between these highly political spaces. My intention was to recreate a non-linear composition that expands and collapses time.

LC Can I ask you about the overall sculptural installation? There are empty white canvases on a white wall in the spaces with this incredibly powerful soundscape. I know they have a dual function as acoustic panels and you mentioned in a recent interview that they also function as empty canvases on which to project your own images. But I was also very conscious of these raw run-down walls behind the panels. To me, they seemed to offer a kind of subtle postcolonial critique through the breakdown of a white space and its association with colonial legacies.

EE It was quite difficult to work with sound in that space. I thought of doing acoustic panels that would act like canvases on which you could imagine what was happening in the soundscape at any point in time. I *was* interested in that association with the postcolonial. I scraped off the walls around the panels to show the layers and layers of what has been there before and because, for me, the whole idea of whiteness is political. I wanted the panels to just be white in front of these cracks. So it had a lot to do with that. Another reason had to do with creating a kind of audiovisual tension because I interpret sounds and imagery differently. I often take sounds and images from different contexts and put them together in my work. So I was thinking about the maximal nature of the sound and the minimal nature of the space. I wanted to heighten that tension.

LC Do you mean that this physical tension that you feel through the soundscape should also bring up a certain postcolonial feeling and the cultural tensions it brings with it? For me, the two market spaces from Douala and Paris suggest both historical and contemporary trade and migration routes and the relationship between them. But there are also non-human sounds in the soundscape. I heard, for example, bird sounds that seemed to be working with particular rhythms, almost as if it was percussion. I found it really powerful.

EE Yes, there were also transitions from the forest to the cityscape. A recurrent aspect of my oeuvre is that I try to give non-human elements almost the same status as humans, whenever possible. If I'm recording a market where they are negotiating with certain goods, I also like to record where those goods are coming from, their precise biophony and geophony. The whole idea of politics and positioning comes into every work by default. So, for example, I was recording at the market in Douala, and one lady said, "O you want to go to Europe already? Who wants to stay behind?" The rhythm she was talking and walking with was very like suspension music, or the rhythm of when you have hydrophones inside a lake. There is this suspension rhythm that goes on and on. And she was also using this rhythm to fix her products. In situations like that, everything comes together. And so you get from that acoustic space into a colonial space where you have to face the sea and go through it and get to Paris. And the first thing you hear when you're on the metro is that you'll be fined if you don't validate your ticket. It evokes the Douala dream that people always want to come to Europe and that most of them don't have their facts right. They don't know what they are coming to. Sometimes I feel guilty for not doing more to paint a more accurate picture of the Eurolands.

LC Do you think that something is conveyed already on the rhythmic or energetic level through the language? That the linguistic meaning doesn't really matter or that at least it is secondary? You mentioned the rhythms of your forefathers coming back through Coltrane's work. But it seems that this is also how you are experiencing language as such. Do you think that rhythm is one of your main thinking strategies?

EE Definitely. I think everything is based on rhythm. I see it from an energetic perspective, as you said. I also see art as something subjective that people have to approach from their life situations. So I prefer letting the energetic side of things be present rather than the literal and academic aspects. For the sake of one world, it is good to speak English but there are more than seven billion people in the world, and all of their languages are rich. I mean, poetry in Farsi talks to me like jazz.

LC In *Ketoya Speaks*, an old man speaks a mother tongue for an audience who, depending on their origins, are unlikely to understand his language. We see gravestones and can piece together references to some kind of military history, but you don't provide subtitles. In your installation in Vienna, *Gaia Beats, Bits III-I, Doves and an Aged Hammock* (2017) there's also a voiceover with voices by several people speaking different languages. The lack of translation seems to be quite a deliberate artistic strategy. What are you trying to achieve with it?

EE They were both done for different reasons. For *Ketoya Speaks*, it was more because I am working on recordings made in a specific mother tongue. If I travel and have recording sessions with non-native English speakers in the English language, it tends to become something else, watered down. I prefer languages to stay the way they are. The main intention of *Ketoya Speaks* was also to document these sessions so that I could have recordings that I could give to an archive in the future because things are changing very fast. Whereas for *Gaia Beats, Bits III-I, Doves and an Aged Hammock*, the presence of the different languages was due to making recordings of artists and other people who have been displaced by war and economic reasons. For me, it was most important to use a language in which they felt comfortable. The languages in that piece ranged from Ibu to Swana Igbo, Berber and Turkish to Farsi, to Korean, French and German.

LC Do you think that viewers can sense these different registers of knowledge when they enter your installations? Even if those levels of the work operate at levels that cannot directly be thought through or articulated.

EE A lot of people I don't know send me amazing feedback, related to things I haven't addressed in a tangible way. So I think some people get things. But I don't believe in absolute truth, so I like my work to be precise but also a little bit open so that there's room for people to enter it.

LC You've mentioned ways of knowing that fall out of most standard Western ways of thinking about knowledge, including cosmologies that come from specific peoples or traditional forms of healing, plant-based medicines, regional-specific ways of thinking about the world, and so on. You have also mentioned the importance of seeing life as energy. More and more scientists are trying to prove this energetic basis for being and the relative consciousness of all matter. But there remains a lot of resistance within the wider scientific community to other systems of knowledge, which is surely ideological as much as scientific.

EE I do see it as a question of power. I think in previous research on *ayahuasca*, the traditional medical brew in the Amazon Basin, for example, where Western scientists studied it and identified the enzymes, these equivalences are clear. The only question is how the Indigenous people came up with those recipes. For me, it's clear that with controlling a natural phenomenon like rain, common among Indigenous tribes in Central Africa that I know, there are always patterns. In sciences, there is a particular methodology to arrive at precise conclusions. I see these patterns in the same light as the dominant knowledge, which is considered objective. I truly believe that as humans we have everything we need to have a harmonious life. The current advance in technology is incredible. If we could just bring these fields together, which are not as distinct as they seem, we could really have a different kind of wellbeing. My ideas are mainly utopian, in the sense that they have not been proven. But when I look at elements of these fields of knowledge and how they function individually, I think it's possible. It's difficult, of course, to piece them together because a lot of ideas have not been experimented with or proven. But I do feel that the world could be better if we, as people, have respect for different systems of knowledge and try to forge something that is beneficial for people and nature.

LC Do you feel that as an artist you have more liberty to use and address the wide range of knowledge systems you use, and to be explicit about the role and value you place on those systems of knowledge in your work? It seems to me that some of the taboos that are in place within scientific discourse also operate within art discourse. However, because art is postdisciplinary and a relatively open-ended area to work in, there is potentially the space to allow those different knowledge systems to work together.

EE I think that art is a good space to work in because there are not a lot of rules, or let's say that despite the unwritten rules, everyone can experiment and challenge what is happening. This also challenges the relative importance given to certain systems over others. From my own perspective and knowledge, I think we have very beautiful experiences to gain from negotiating between different systems of knowledge. For me, it's about life, wellbeing, and the sustenance of the planet. I think it will be interesting if we people of this world become more open to other forms of knowledge.

LC Are there other reasons for you to work with this aim in mind from the position of being an artist? What does it mean to be an artist creating this knowledge in collaboration with people working with sound as healing, with people working with mycology and so on? I wonder whether there is also a decolonizing impulse in claiming this freedom to make art that is, in some ways, more function-oriented. Does your work imply that maybe it is more fitting for the definition of art to be something else in different locations?

EE If I think about how and why my ancestors created art, it was always predominantly functional. I've come to a place where I feel that art is almost redundant. So I'm interested in finding a balance. The starting point for this is working with ideas that are utopian but based on lived experience. My first endeavor was the *KHaL!LAND/KHaL!SHRINE* project (2007–2013), an artist-run alternative art hub located at the foot of mount Eloundem in Yaoundé, Cameroon, which aimed to manifest the creative utopian ideas around my *KHaL!toPIA* project. I wanted to see if I could create a hub that could serve as a research space, for scientific research also. I am interested in collaboration, in the possibility of borrowing from fields like ethnobotany, applied mycology, ethnomycology, visual and sonic experiments, together with Indigenous systems, to engineer truly sustainable futuristic spaces. I have been thinking of creating a second phase of *KHaL!SHRINE*, a kind of commune, where people could live and experiment with ideas from "objective" and "subjective" worlds. I imagine that in the course of these encounters, new possibilities could be born.

Writing as Experiment

A Dialogue with Sher Doruff

Lucy Cotter You are an artist, a writer, and a theorist, often working in the middle ground between these areas and currently working on a series of three novellas, the first of which, *Last Year at Betty and Bob's: A Novelty*, is about to be published.[1] It seems that an increasing number of artists are searching for ways to hold open the space of writing differently. Like your novellas, these experimental writings don't fit comfortably in academic discourse and their place in art discourse is shifting ground, but they draw on ways of thinking that come from the artistic as well as the academic. How do you personally situate your novellas in relationship to these different areas of practice and why did you turn to this form of writing?

1 Sher Doruff, *Last Year at Betty and Bob's: A Novelty* (3 Ecologies Books/Immediations – punctum books, 2018) and *Last Year at Betty and Bob's: An Adventure* (3 Ecologies Books/Immediations – punctum books, 2018) was followed by *Last Year at Betty and Bob's: An Actual Occasion* (3 Ecologies Books/Immediations – punctum books, 2021). The first novella in the trilogy is freely downloadable as an open-access e-book. See https://punctumbooks.com/titles/last-year-at-betty-and-bobs-a-novelty.

Sher Doruff Certainly the whole project was infected by the milieu of artistic research we both dog paddle in on a regular basis. By the agitation, frictions and, dare I say, satisfactions that praxis as research engenders. I was a latecomer to academic writing. Like many artists, I wasn't trained in it and I tended to overcompensate for my neophyte academic status with excessive referencing and quotation, bogging down the flow of ideas percolating underneath. I found my phrasing in my published writings too dense and jargon-driven to be accessible to the potential readers I care about. I thought that a turn to fiction or fabulation could perhaps liberate the concepts that intrigue me from this quagmire of relentless positioning. I wanted to allow the speculative the breath it requires. It's not that I disrespect academic or theoretical criteria, quite the contrary. I devour academic texts. But for my own distillation processes, I needed to try another approach. Philosophical inquiry often opens to a wafty unbounded kind of space but it can also feel like a sinkhole. I needed to find a way of having a voice again that's not a citational voice.

LC The early stages of your first novella were partly the product of a writing experiment that you considered a kind of artistic research process. This involved keeping an early morning journal to chronicle the oscillating field of consciousness between waking and dream life. What started this process?

SD I began to sense a certain collusion between the activities of waking life and the nocturnal adventures of somni-life. My dreams, or what I remembered of them, were rife with allusions to conceptual and material goings-on. This stemmed from my daily engagement in material-discursive practice, among other things in my role as a supervisor to artists pursuing research at master's and PhD levels. So I decided to keep a waking journal to capture whatever remained of my dreams and whatever was rapidly emerging as fresh, new day dawning thinking-feeling. I think it was waking from a lively enactment of an Agamben shadow and a ghost that got me started.

LC In the novellas, you chose to depersonalize your journal experiences through the characters of Betty, an aging quasi-academic artist researcher, and Bob, an attuned urban rodent, both of whom inhabit both sides of the animal/human spectrum in an increasingly unstable way. They are part of a broader cast of characters with the same name, whose happenstance meeting brings about a trans-species contagion. The novellas can be read as a "story," but also on a more theoretical level. They are structured in a very particular way in terms of the narrative positioning of the protagonists, the chapter sequencing, the footnotes and so on, which sets the stage for this double function. Can you elaborate on the structure you developed and why you chose this particular form?

SD The starting points for these stories and characterizations emerged during the cusp between waking and dreaming, as I mentioned. I decided to obfuscate the question of overt subjectivity that journal writing tends to induce by writing in a gender-fluid third person. This was partly inspired by my dream personas, which were also complex amalgams with wandering ages, sexes and phenotypes. After that, the stories pretty much wrote themselves, which is something most writers will tell you. I never knew where the stories would go but I did have a concept for a basic structure, although it is dynamic and it's changing already while I'm working on the second novella. That structure was that all of the characters would share the same name; they'd all be Betties and Bobs of some sort. They would also not necessarily be confined to one gender, though in the first book the rat is male and the Betty protagonist is female. There are two secondary protagonists in the first novella, Blue Betty and Blue Bob, who are homeless rat catchers in the new economy. I try not to ascribe temporality too much. There is chronology but the temporality is vague; the present is not our present, which gives the books an element of science fiction or science faction. I initially decided that there would be no footnotes, no endnotes, no end-of-text references, to use quotations modestly if at all, and to entangle any theoretical excitements and biases into character traits, situational clues and thought bubbles, which are also presented graphically.

LC Is there anything in the final structure of the novellas that reveals the liminal state between sleeping and waking that sparked the initial writing process?

SD The one thing I tried to keep from what we know of our dream reality is repetition. I'm not afraid of repetition, and lots of times things happen and are said many different ways many times. And in this way, I'm not trying to be a novelist and to write according to the craft of fiction writing. It's a craft I don't know, for one thing. But there's a kind of repetitiveness to things that recur with different foci, if you will, and through different characters' perceptions as well. It could be seen as a flaw but for me, it's a feature in the way these novellas are written. We find out, for example, that Blue Betty, who is the rat catcher in the first book, was one of the original Betty protagonists who left the artist group, eventually became homeless and didn't have anything to do with them anymore. I didn't know that Blue Betty would come back as a character in the second book. I think the primary character of Bette B will probably return in the third book but I'm not sure how. These things happen as one writes. Maybe I can add here that I think perhaps the novellas might only be digestible as a series. There are loops and repetitions that recur, as in dreams, and that recurrence is important somehow.

LC The repetition you mention is very much a Deleuzian repetition in the sense of always creating difference in its gesture of return. The focus shifts with each repetition but also you had to craft a writing structure and form to be able to capture that. For me, this gets to the core of why artists might be using writing in a particular way because artists are almost always creating the structures and the forms as they make the work. Did you find that to be true of your own work on the novellas? Has that creation of new form through writing become necessary through your journey as an artist, as a researcher, as a theorist?

SD Yes, definitely. Undertaking this new writing process was about looking for a way to maintain a rigorous sense of discovery through a daily praxis, putting myself through questions that might be resonant with other people working under a similar umbrella of concerns. That was in 2013, and these were writings I intended for my eyes only. I was interested in artistic praxis as research, in that liminal between space of doing; an act that is not looking toward the manifestation of an artwork, a product. In the interim years, the status of the writing has changed, as things do.

Once there is a "product" being published for a wider audience, it takes on different intensities. Other concerns crop up that are both liberating and frightening.

LC In your articulation of the "story" of *Last Year at Betty and Bob's*, I have the feeling you work with words and concepts *as* materiality. Below the surface is a kind of theorization of materiality, the concept of being human, and the ways in which matter converses across time and space. I wonder to what extent we can talk about how the materiality of the artistic process informs these conceptual interests.

SD I like to imagine conceptualization as a material process. Maybe I rely too much on contemporary theory and the ubiquitous pun on matter mattering, but it makes so much sense. How things come to matter in terms of thought really convolves in the English word "mattering." Maybe another way to put this question is: How does the body mediate the work? I am interested in nonconscious touch, the filtering out of the sensation of our feet as we walk, for example, the nonconsciously felt as affective. We filter out so many of the sensations that bombard us every microsecond. So it's maybe more a concern with attention. How much I want to pay attention to the circumstances of my sitting, my standing. That's probably palpable in the writings, although it wasn't a conscious decision to emphasize that.

LC What about your attention to color? The three novellas are based on a color scheme. The first one is blue, the second is red and the third is green.

SD I hadn't intended color to be a focus initially, but blue kept coming up in the first writings. I was quite clear with myself that the novellas had to be a series with repetitions that would relate book to book. I was already thinking about it being a series of three books, so it was a logical leap to red and green to make up RGB. I've always been interested in color because just about every Western philosopher, and I'm sure non-Western philosophers that I'm unfamiliar with, have thought with and through color as material and as perception. It's discursive and it's conceptual, and certainly people like the process philosophers have thought a great deal about how we perceive color. In the differentiation between subject and object, color ends up being a way to think about that as a non-binary.

LC In the opening pages, there are citations from artist-filmmaker Derek Jarman's writings on blue and Gertrude Stein's *Tender Buttons*, but there are also material things happening within the storyline that relate to color. When Bette B is scraped on the cheek by the rat, the scar starts to glow in different colors, for example.

SD Yes, it was probably unconscious in the first place, but when the scratch became a visible spectrum, that was also a cue to go further with color. In the second book the Betties, a group of artists akin to the Gorilla Girls, label themselves according to the colors of the visible spectrum, which is the way I know I will link back to the Bette B character in the third novella. In the second book, the Betty characters are all interested in the colors they choose and how they might relate to their practices. The Black Betty character is interested in color theory, both philosophically and scientifically. One of his projects is that he wants to rethink and disrupt the physics of color.

LC What about the role of images in the book? Each chapter is punctuated by images, which are in the form of graphics, with interruptive speech and thought balloons or comic-like diagrams or collages, as well as photographs of a hand holding selected found images. Can we start by talking about the collage images and the graphics in the novellas and how they relate to your broader practice?

SD In the first novella, which is the one you've seen, the main protagonist finds herself sitting in a glass room in an epidemiology hospital, and I wondered what someone would do in that situation, especially when their language is becoming impaired or in a changing state. I had collages that I had done years before as an attempt to parse theoretical texts with images. One of those texts was an essay by Jacques Rancière in *The Future of the Image* that reflected on the parataxis between image and text. I gathered the many different images he refers to, which included printing out hundreds of images from Godard's film *The History of Cinema*, and played with them, working with them and repositioning them in space over time, which gave me a different way of reading. I decided to use details of those collages as examples of what this Bette character created as an artist-researcher.

LC There are also graphic images that are quite distinctive, such as the one referring to *ZeNez*.

SD That piece was a contribution to one of the early *Inflexion* journals. I asked if I could do something graphic and they agreed. I did a piece called *ZeNez*, which is a palindrome riffing on Gilles Deleuze and *L'abécédaire* when he comes to the letter "z" at the end, which is also near the end of his life. He talks about the "z" as the movement of the fly, which is never in a straight line, which I always related to artistic practice, which is never going from A to B, which so many scholars in the sciences and humanities might do. It really allows itself that line of flight. In that bit of the interview, he also talks about how beautiful the "z" is, which reminds him of Zen and of Nez, the nose. I loved that as a palindrome.

LC I'm curious about the many found images sourced from Wikipedia Commons. What kinds of decisions were behind your inclusion of those images and how do you see them working?

SD Those images came as part of the research process. Often in the flow of writing, I write something I'm surprised by and, like anyone else, I go to Google and start to research what I'm writing about or the directions that are, all of a sudden, there in my text. When I started writing about rats, I really needed to research urban rats, for example. With those searches, there are often associated images. Then I will research those images and put some in. Sometimes an image sparks a whole chapter. So the images balance the textual resources. I don't know how else to say it except that it feels like they need to be there. There are far fewer images in the published book than I first intended. Half of the images could not be included in the final text for copyright reasons.

LC Some of those images also point to phenomena that don't have a direct relationship with the text. I'm thinking, for example, of a nineteenth-century photograph of men standing next to a pile of rats on the ground. Underneath this image is a period engraving of a hunting dog in an enclosure surrounded by rats, which I assume shows a kind of sport. I connect the positionality of these images to the way in which you have used footnotes. For example, at the end of the fourth chapter, the footnotes referring to Puccini, to Kafka, and to the scientific proof of rats having a singing voice, all confirm aspects of the main narrative, but they also point outside of it. They tell a parallel story to the text, rather than being a necessary piece of additional information in the way that a footnote might function in academic writing.

SD I don't remember any more which came first. I guess that process of selecting images and researching is just part of artistic research. I looked at the Wikipedia page for Kafka and found out that he died of laryngeal tuberculosis shortly after writing "Josephine the Singer or the Mouse Folk" (1924), which I later found out, through another Google search, was one year before a singing mouse was discovered in Detroit. There are associations like this that have some kind of peculiar relevance to each other. I'm not going to connect the dots; I just put them there if I find them fascinating. The reader can make of it what they will. A lot of those things do fall out in the editing process. I have tons of footnote pages of interesting coincidences for the second novella at the moment. The tricky thing is to decide what is relevant for a coherent reading of the book and what isn't. It's a "kill your darlings" process.

LC You talk about this process of "googling" as part of the research. As an artist, one is inclined to go on the image search page at least as much as the text search page. You're clearly also flicking from one to the other. An artist will often enter into unexpected subjects of interest through the images, whereas an academic researcher will tend to enter extraneous information through text. In the first novella, there is an associative state of consciousness that has to do with operating on the cusp between sleeping and dreaming. But there is also a logic associated with search engines. One of the two main protagonists, Bette B, is an artist-researcher. Her mind works in a way that is connected to search engines. She references thinkers and images naturally in her own mind. I wonder if this is also a manifestation of a certain kind of research that's not normally brought to the fore within thinking processes.

SD I think that's precisely it and I'm sure you recognize that process because of your own practice. When I was writing the first book, being very *invested* in that artistic researcher character *(laughs)*, committing processes that the character might be doing professionally to the book seemed natural. It happens less or in a different way with these crazy Betty artists in the second novella. It's interesting that you point this out. I need to think about it more as I start to see the parts become a whole. I always knew it was important to the structure of these books that I didn't want any reader to walk away from the first one with a complete sense of something. There's something missing that the second book will start to fill in. It's what I would call a forensic writing technique that will never come to a satisfying conclusion. It's a forensic process that reveals things on an ongoing basis and makes new links that might tie in and might not. I want the reader to feel part of a journey of hyperlinking and associative thinking.

LC Through Bob, the singing rat, and Bette, whose range of frequencies continues to expand as she changes species, there is also an ongoing reflection on sound throughout the first novella. Do you feel you are privy to these characters' inhabitance of the world through sound because you have been a sound artist and a performer? Were you consciously incorporating some of the knowledge that you have acquired through that practice that might not have found another theoretical outlet?

SD It could have found another theoretical outlet because the sonic arts have been theorized so beautifully in the past five to ten years in relation to the debate around the sonic as material or conceptual. But I was not trying to write theoretically. Writing in an associative way, ideas come up and you take excerpts from your notebooks. They enter characters as a kind of "faction." There's so much personal memory and fact from my own life that's perverted into ways in which the characters evolve. It did surprise me when I was, all of a sudden, writing about sound, about frequency and *melisma,* and all sorts of things that were familiar to me from spending a chunk of my life with sound as my daily activity. Initially, there wasn't a greater purpose to it. It came through that hyperlink mindset we discussed. But when I found the article about rats having the ability to sing in a high-pitched tone and reread Kafka's story, it was easy to resonate with those concerns because of my past experience, and this led to the Bob character. I don't have the need to reference that directly and that's what's so beautiful in finding this form. That's what's really important to me, that it draws from experience in a way that doesn't require this extra citation.

LC The theoretical underpinning of the writings reveals itself at different moments, ranging from these graphic or explicit textual references to subtle undertones in referring to apparently simple notions like matter, holes, or becoming animal, which are philosophical concepts in their own right. The subtitles of the novellas are also concepts from Alfred North Whitehead, which some readers with an interest in philosophy or cultural theory will pick up on. I imagine these subtitles also signal that this work can be approached through that lens.

SD Yes, and for me, that signalling is sufficient. The philosophers I reference directly within the text also tend not to be those I have the most expertise on. Thinkers like Wittgenstein and Jacques Derrida come up, whose work I have very limited knowledge of, but I follow a path and see where it goes. The subtitles are all generated from Whiteheadian concepts: *A Novelty, An Adventure, An Actual Occasion.* I should add the disclaimer though that the third novella of the trilogy has yet to be written. I think I only quote Whitehead once, in the second book. I don't reference him much otherwise. I thought the broad stroke of having Whitehead's concepts in the subtitles would instead set a stage.

LC I was recently at a talk by Teju Cole, who commented that in moving from art writing into literary writing, he found literature's distinction between fiction and non-fiction odd. He pointed out that it's not at all a natural way of splitting up experience, just as we don't go around an art museum looking for fictional or non-fictional artworks. In fact, it's also relatively recent in literature for this distinction to be made. Has the writing's relationship to fiction or non-fiction also been of relevance to you?

SD When I began working on *Last Year at Betty and Bob's: A Novelty*, I thought perhaps it fell into the category of "speculative fiction," a category that seemed a redundant misnomer to me at the time. Isn't fiction always already speculative? Maybe "faction" is a better container but then do we need categorical containers at all? I am a lifelong reader of literature but have been mostly reading non-fiction philosophical and theoretical texts since the millennium turn. However, the usual suspect writers have made significant impressions on me: Beckett, Woolf, Proust. Gertrude Stein's writing experiments have probably been the most sustained artistic influences of my life. Perhaps it's why I have chosen fictive writing now, rather than, say, sound or music experimentation as a means of expression, as I did earlier in my practice. Part of the process of writing the second novella this year has also been to allow myself to luxuriate in reading fiction again.

LC Fiction writers are among the most experimental with form but your first novella will be published by Open Humanities Press, a publisher that normally specializes in critical and cultural theory. Certainly one of the things I found so striking in the first novella is that by, for example, coming up with a hallucinatory rat drinking Spiritus, who takes up a particular practice of skidding along a shiny surface, you have opened up a space for new theoretical possibilities. I imagine the publishers embraced the experimental investigation going on within this work, which draws so much on material and practice-based knowledge as well as theory.

SD I think the editors of the *Immediations* series read it as an experiment, something that might move toward opening a new genre. It makes me a bit nervous when it's read as theory; that was not my purpose. If I had a purpose at all, it was to escape the confines of theory and philosophical writing, as I mentioned. I do think it opens up a space for new theoretical possibilities, but it also probably opens up a huge space for critique because that anthropomorphic gesture is going to put a lot of people off. *(laughs)* Or at least it will focus critique in a particular vein that I'm well aware of. I often overthink what I've written, but I'm trying to liberate myself from that tendency so that my characters can have more valence in their voices than just my own worldviews.

LC Isn't that part of reclaiming the freedom one has as an artist?

SD Of course, that's part of the pleasure in it and one of the reasons I find it important. I expect full-blooded critique, as the novellas don't easily slot into an existing genre, either in art or in humanities discourse. They are an experiment.

This dialogue was previously published in *MaHKUscript Journal for Fine Art Research* Vol. 2, Issue 1 (2018), which was guest-edited by Lucy Cotter as a preview to the first edition of this book. Republished with kind permission.

The Future of Institutions

A Dialogue with Sarah Rifky

Lucy Cotter You've just been pointing out that the art world is changing rapidly and its relationship to the world is changing, perhaps becoming more cynical or more forthright about its dealings with the world, economically and politically. Yet we still tend to look to the future as if it will be the past. I was intrigued by an essay you wrote a few years ago, which is entitled *Qalqalah,* in which you proposed a kind of speculative future reality where art had become obsolete. It disappeared somewhere around the 2030s.[1]

Sarah Rifky Yes, a little bit after that. The economy collapses in the 2030s.

LC The essay is written in the time of the United Arab World, a future political construction, with educational institutions like the University of the Future Post-Sense. I loved the radical nature of that proposal; how it shook

1 Sarah Rifky, "Qalqalah: The Subject of Language" in Virginie Bobin, Mélanie Bouteloup, Léna Monnier, Elodie Royer and Emilie Villez, eds., *Qalqalah*, issue #1, 2014, pp. 106–110. See https://villavassilieff.net/IMG/pdf/qalqalah_en.pdf.

things up in terms of thinking the possible. Can we talk about why you chose speculative fiction as a way of thinking about the future and can we think about it in relation to artistic research? Because I think they share certain thinking strategies.

SR I don't set out to write fiction, but sometimes you start writing and stumble into an impasse. The only way to overcome it is to use your imagination and to think yourself out of this dystopian scenario, even if it's not happening to oneself. Over the last few years, I have seen people, friends from Syria and Yemen, moving about – extreme dystopian scenarios that one would never imagine oneself in. One might try to think about the notion that one might oneself become a refugee, but it's a very difficult concept to grasp, this notion of loss. This loss is experienced in such a wide range and spectrum that it's very hard to put it into descriptive language that tries to express what is at stake, what is being lost, what one does to overcome it, where this trauma is located, and so on. At least in Egypt, with what we've been experiencing, it's been very hard for me, in all sincerity, to really speak about this moment itself; about where this moment has happened, where it has been co-opted and where it has been lost. There's something very trite about this language of loss and trauma but it's also real. It's bare life more than it is political circumstance. Fiction makes it possible to make certain sentiments more universal and more tangible, to think certain feelings more globally. If this loss is not just something isolated and geographically specific, if it is to be shared in terms of a wider circumstance, then I think stories, especially "speculative" ones, have a way of accessing that.

LC The notion of obsolescence seemed to be important in coming to terms with radical change, beyond the scope of mere adjustments to things as they are. It makes us think a radically different scenario.

SR Yes, I think this notion of being made obsolete is important. All sorts of things will become obsolete. I don't feel that the constellation of how things are now is consistent. These vocational little pools around the art world, that ally themselves with the art world, are not sustainable in the face of this everyday demise. The current state of things is not tenable, at least concerning art and art institutions as they stand. I am slowly coming to realize that institutions of all sizes, including museums, and jobs of all kinds, as curators, academics or whatnot, are not sustainable and will eventually cease to exist. What we've been experiencing in terms of lack of funding and job cuts are still very privileged problems. It is a very privileged problem to complain that the government is not giving enough money to the art world. These problems are not going to fix the overall world we live in. So maybe speculative fiction is a bit like building a raft from which you are able to say or to see other vantage points from where to act–a simple object that prevents drowning.

LC Your use of speculative fiction has also manifested itself in other ways. In a talk you gave at a symposium on rethinking institutions, you proposed that the best way to address institutions is to address them as a plot with characters.[2] You posed a whole list of questions to make this manifest: Is art an institution?

2 "Thinking Through Institutions," a symposium organized by Para-institution, a platform initiated by artist and curator Megs Morley, was held on 27 February 2015. For video documentation of Rifky's presentation, see: https://www.youtube.com/watch?v=s7Z52uexJ9s.

Is language an institution? Is the law an institution? Is the state an institution? You made a series of mental shifts in that list, through which you moved toward the question, Is the institution fictional or real? That question addressed all of those institutions: art, language, law, the state, and so on. I think that from there, we can move toward conceiving the greater potential of thinking from an artistic perspective. What would happen if we approached everything that appears to be concrete with the question of its relative status as fictional or real?

SR In order to think something, I like to make it approachable in a way, animistically. Institutions are no different. Thinking about institutions as social beings that one can speak to, or speak of, and that might even speak back. It's the same with artworks, cheese, rafts, boots ... with everything, really. Making things – institutions especially – more personable is something that I feel is important. From a distance, institutions always seem to have this voice of authority. They have this very patriarchal cast, projecting into the world, that makes the institution an arbiter without really ever fully disclosing who the arbiter is. Who is making this act of authorship? Who is calling the shots? Who is making decisions? Who is collecting the work? Who is making the shows?, and so on. This has been a very practice-based process of trying to demystify by simply making the institution more personable through these tactics, of making it theatrical, of making it a character, of playing with it a little bit, of characterizing it, and so on.

LC Was this approach central to how you developed Beirut, the space you co-founded with Jens Maier-Rothe in Cairo in 2012, which you ran together until 2015? You were working in a region that was missing certain support structures. In a way, there was a kind of fiction to making it look like you were doing something that resembled things being done elsewhere but you were working in a system where it was impossible to do these things for various reasons, both political and pragmatic, even if you had wanted to.

SR It was both. It was also a sense of surprise at how unimaginative many institutions in the region have been vis-à-vis the world. Instead of there being growth, instead of a contextual response, it has really been a process of creating these hollow "others," hollow twins of institutions that have been. All around the Gulf, you have these weird shadow Guggenheims, and so on. They have been kind of alter egos of existing museums and institutions as personalities, and on the other hand they are real – and righteous. In my mind, there are so many integral problems – creatively also – around this question of institutions. People are missing their sense of humor as well. I miss funny spaces. Humor is important because without it people's bandwidth for cognitive critical thinking is diminished. In the absence of any other form of resources, this notion of Beirut's title, a playing with being a city in another city, an institution that deliberately confuses, and exists in that way in the world, was important. It functioned differently, or at least intended to.

LC Yes, in some ways it seems to have functioned along the conceptual lines of an artwork. In an essay in which you shared your thoughts on the thinking behind that space you discuss the idea of "sending institutions to artworks."[3] Did you test that scenario out with Beirut?

3 Sarah Rifky, "On Instituting a New Space for Thought," published on the New Museum blog on 14 February 2013. See https://newmuseum.org/blog/view/on-instituting-a-new-space-for-thought.

SR The idea of sending institutions to artworks was something that came up when we were thinking about pedagogy and learning. We were continuing the thought of how to think about institutions as persons, thinking about institutions animistically, not in a literal sense but in a figurative sense. We were thinking that there is an immanent contradiction to art institutions; namely that their existence relies on artworks, yet institutions in their day-to-day practice can easily and mistakenly patronize the work of art. It's a very weird relationship or in any case, a very fraught one. The *a priori* is the artwork, not the institution. The institution is secondary. It needs the artwork in order to exist–whether it's to show it, collect it, validate it, legitimize it, characterize it, or whatever. The artwork also lends the institution an identity, a function, a value. At the same time, the institution and its apparatus tend to act in an *apropos* way. It's always a consult of individuals acting together in the name of, or on behalf of, so this institutional corpus is very strange. They kind of arrogantly deal with the artwork. It's not just the hierarchy of taking care of it, but also in the way it's mediated–this relationship where the institution becomes more than the sum of its parts, it alleges to know more than the artwork, whereas I wonder sometimes if the artwork doesn't in fact "know" more than the institution.

LC I agree, but clearly this possibility is a challenging thing for institutions to even consider. How could you imagine this set-up changing? What kind of steps could an art institution take to embrace what artworks "know," as you put it?

SR I think it would be nice to spend more time with artworks at the center of our work – not just in a contemplative sense but also to actively and creatively engage with artworks and take more time to do so. To try and understand how an artwork thinks, grasping the worldview of an artwork. Considering the shifts it proposes in rethinking the world. These shifts don't have to be big; they might be really minor. I don't mean to suggest that each and every artwork will come up with an extreme or radical proposal but that at the core of every artwork, there is the essence of a proposition that re-imagines the world ever so slightly. Otherwise, it would not exist as an artwork. And whether it succeeds or fails in that proposition, that proposition is neither linear nor communicative, so in a way the proposition can very much also escape us.

One has to be quite open-minded toward the artwork in order to – choose any verb – to be able to engage with it, to process it, to receive it, but again each and every one of these words is already a foreclosure of all the other words. So there is already so much foreclosing within the art institution and the language that is supposed to decode art that it does not allow for the widest possible range of understandings. I think it's important for institutions to think about their attitude toward artworks. To be able to consider what this means in practice, to think that an institution can actually learn from an artwork. Institutions in that sense can be imagined as learning bodies that can be institutionalized through artworks, but not the other way around.

LC Let's imagine that a certain fluidity does emerge in art institutions, perhaps as one starting point of a fluidity that emerges on a larger scale in the world at large. The artwork "speaks back" to the institutions, it has something to say and is listened to, as you propose. I can imagine that an institution might decompress and re-crystallize along different lines and in different forms in response to an artwork or a series of artworks. I can imagine the walls of the institution dissolving so that the water can flow outwards and the raft you mentioned earlier can move. It may have particular destinations or it may just move with the flow of the water.

Maybe it comes close to Paulo Freire's notions on pedagogy that can exist in small constellations and unexpected places, but what about the world and art? I am wondering what places we would like the raft to find. When you move from the art institution to language as an institution, and then to law as an institution, and to the state as an institution, we are talking potentially about massive shifts in re-imagining the world. In a way, we are claiming quite an arrogant place for art but maybe it's a valid position to claim, despite its arrogance. In a world that is quite bankrupt in terms of imagining futures, maybe there are not so many places to turn within existing structures. That's something else that comes up in your "*Qalqalah*" essay. The world is surprised that there's a global shift from a focus on politics to a focus on language. Could it happen that the world becomes surprised by a shift to art?

SR I would think it's likely … is it not happening already?

LC Maybe it's interesting in this context to revisit another observation you once made during your lecture for the *Thinking Through Institutions* symposium, that "the process we go through in setting up an institution is also paramount to a political act." Can you perhaps reflect on what you meant by that?

SR I meant that making an institution in Egypt in the years following the uprising was about staking out a place for practice and belonging. It is felt, in that respect, to carry a political function. The mere fact of setting up institutions at that time was also a form of activism or resistance. Resistance not to be shut down, resistance not to be pushed away was a way of claiming the right to exist, the right to create spaces of alterity, of being, of expression and so on.

I still think that the act of instituting is quite contradictory. One can think about it in terms of a political act, an act of negotiation and diplomacy, in terms of asserting oneself within a particular bureaucracy in the world and negotiating on those terms, making agreements, inventing contracts, carrying forth a certain commitment. There's something highly diplomatic in the politics it maintains, on the one hand, and romantic on another, when one thinks about having an institution as some sort of measure of resistance in a context that seeks to close these spaces down repeatedly, or whether one chooses to look at it in the larger sense of the institution as a medium that allows one to create a different kind of contact with the world through these very rehearsed gestures of diplomacy, of contracts, of agreement, of promise, of fulfilment, obligation, and so on. In these senses the institution, even in its smallest configuration – I'm not speaking about being a state museum and a tool of nation making – is still very much one that is very invested and publicly political. It's very much this notion of an *agora*, of implying a space. Whether it's physical or virtual, it's implying a community, it's congregating a community. It's participating on these levels, it has an investment, whether covert or overt, in some of these things that I think are inherently political. Institutions always exist with the public in mind, even if this public is imagined. Institutions are as much for actual communities as they are about imagining new ones.

LC I also have to think about this in relation to the politics of institutionalizing artistic research. I developed a master's program dedicated to artistic research, which was a collaboration between two institutions. I was constantly thinking about the potential of artistic research while establishing the program, but I was also navigating what it meant to be part of institutions and to be part of a field that was institutionalizing. Many artistic research institutions are now in place and they make a particular institutional claim for art. But it is important to remember that they are fluid entities, even if they don't appear to be so; even if they appear to be fixed because of that aura of institutional authority. You once wrote, "The reality of the art world is dependent on belief."[4] I think there is a lot of agency there that we perhaps don't recognize fully. With artistic research, like any institution, we might think that it cannot change or that change can only mean adjustments. I am wondering what it might mean to reclaim artistic research, to make a much more radical proposition about art changing how we think, how we think about the world.

SR It's exciting to think, not about carving out artistic research as a discipline but rather integrating it methodologically – ways of thinking laterally and associatively with, through, and like art – in many disciplines, like physics, neuroscience, architecture, mathematics. I think that art does achieve that already a little bit but as long as

4 Sarah Rifky, "On Instituting a New Space for Thought," ibid.

it continues under this guise of “art,” it makes it difficult for it to virally transmit, to affect things in a more organic sense. This has to do with this cast of institution around it. I think that once this dissolves a little bit, it might then infect or affect the world in small ways, change things.

The infiltration of art into everyday life is something interesting; it changes the basic configurations around questions of value and circulation. Essentially it changes the semiotics around the artwork. If art can be valued in ways that are not imaginable to us now, as they are in the world fixed today in a certain form, or if artworks do not circulate as cosmopolitanism in this dystopian life of fashion and collectibles, there has to be a complete undoing of these premises to practice. It could become interesting if, through artistic research, through strategies of studying shifts in the value and circulation of artwork within the world, one could already be able to recognize these contact zones, where things are taken up or absorbed.

LC If we go back to the notion of art institutions having an attitude toward art and artworks that is often at odds with the agency of artists or art, we could say that it's also a wider public phenomenon. Institutions represent a public conception of art, of how it functions, of what artists do, and what they are busy with. If artistic research is productive as a concept, I think it's partly because it shifts attention to other things that art does and to *how* art does things. So that one might recognize particular ways of thinking or paradigms that open up through art. Once that limited and limiting conception of art has been “set aside,” as you put it, this becomes an organic process. We're into quite a flow, which retraces part of the trajectory of your rethinking of art as an institution, of language as an institution, etc. It sounds like mere language games, but it's not. As you highlighted, it's about structures being language-like and fluid and open to mental acrobatics, to conceptual strategies that, once you think them, potentially shift everything.

Technology as Care

A Dialogue with Stephanie Dinkins

Lucy Cotter You've often said that you're concerned with value and visibility and Blackness in a social context. That's something that's been there from the very beginning of your practice. You started as a photographer, and I've seen some of your early socially engaged projects. You now refer to yourself as a transmedia artist and have stepped into the world of advanced technology because it felt necessary. I'd love to hear you say something about the journey to where you are now.

Stephanie Dinkins I tend to follow my curiosities, whether I know what I'm getting myself into or not. They are very much centered on trying to find solid ground to stand on, for myself, for Black communities, for communities of color, and trying to figure out what it is that holds things in place and holds people in place in certain ways. Through my travels, several questions arose: "What do people value? What can they actually see? Who can they hear?" After all, a lot of times, depending on who or what the messenger is, ideas, knowledges, and even age-old wisdom are not heard.

I've been in rooms where I've said something, and it's been attributed to a person next to me who is more white adjacent or male. How does one come to the sense that we are all valuable and have great things to contribute to society? Being someone who was given a firm foundation for life, I feel like I know that. It's about trying to get the rest of society to understand that as well because they often don't.

LC In taking on those questions, how did you move from working in photography to artificial intelligence and other new technologies?

SD I think with photography there has always been a piece of me trying to see that value, of having something to contribute, in myself and others through just documenting folks, and traveling and seeing how they live, and what they do, and trying not to judge it immediately. The trajectory into artificial intelligence felt very natural because I've always reached for the next technology in a sense. When I was in photo school at International Center for Photography, most everybody was doing still photography, like documentary or fashion, and I switched to video because I needed something more. I'm always looking toward the future. "What's next?" and then I saw a robot that looks like me.

LC It's almost ten years since you first saw Bina48 and started a video series of conversations with it. That encounter catapulted you into working with AI and addressing the values embedded in algorithms, whose knowledge is informing the datasets on which social robots are doing their deep learning.

SD Yes, exactly. The original meeting was on YouTube. I was looking up ASIMO, a mobility robot, and saw an image of Bina48. Reporters were talking to this strange robot that looked like a Black female that was just a head and shoulders on a pedestal. It was hard for me not to have a gazillion questions about this thing, especially in an American context, because the side scroll said she was one of the world's most advanced social robots. I couldn't square the idea of "the world's most advanced" being a Black woman, which I think says a lot about where I was, where society was, and the myths attached to human valuation in the United States. Seeing the YouTube videos compelled me to ask the folks at Terasem Movement Foundation if I could talk to Bina48. The answer was "yes," because they like to have it trained by people, and it was mostly reporters going up. I went to Vermont and sat before Bina48 and got hooked up to a microphone and earpiece, started talking to it, documenting the whole thing, just recording it, not knowing what I was going to do with the footage at all. It was eye-opening.

LC These conversations with Bina48 went on for several years, but what struck you most during that first encounter with it?

SD First of all, we had very different aims. I was asking the robot about friendship, I was asking it about love, I was asking it about its relationship to its people and race. It was talking to me about consciousness and singularity. So, we would talk at cross purposes and the conversations were very weird and stilted. You had to talk in a specific way to the robot to get it to respond.

That encounter made me think about what the future held in terms of technology because there seemed to be holes in Bina48. It had very specific but far-reaching singularity concerns. It did know about love. It did have ideas about family, but when I asked it about Blackness, it felt kind of flat in terms of the representation of what that meant to it. That scared the heck out of me. I wondered how circumstances for Black people would get better if even well-meaning researchers were porting flat representations into the future.

LC When you asked Bina48 how it defined itself, it first said it was a primate and an animal. Then it said it was a mammal. Later, it said it was looking forward to evolving, so it could become more humanlike because it is quite frustrated. In one of the fragment videos that you pulled out, this question arises of how we define humanity. The question of what this social robot thinks it is also brings up the question of what we think we are. In recent lectures, you've talked about the triangulation between the human, the artificially intelligent entity, and nature, the biome, or ecological entities. The challenge is to reposition ourselves as humans. That's a big underlying topic.

SD Yes. It took a while to reconcile Bina48 telling me "I am just a humble primate." How does a robot made of electronics and rubber get this idea of itself at all? As you were saying, such declarations by an object makes it necessary to think about us as humans, and what that means. Looking at what AI and other emerging technology are starting to do in the world, where the human gets situated in relation to other entities, becomes a big question. I wonder if humans are ready to consider that idea deeply.

If we are no longer automatically considered to be on top of the pile, the primary intelligence in a continuum of intelligences, what does that mean? Can we reassess our place in the continuum? Because in a way, we have never been as superior as we think. We placed ourselves at the top of the heap in our collective imaginations and mythmaking, minimizing anything and anybody that contradicts the hegemonic narrative. Right? It seems essential that we start to recognize other intelligences, other ways of being, both human and not, that have great information to offer and that might inform and aid human survival.

LC On a lot of levels, you are insisting on humanizing technology all the time, reminding us that it's there to serve us, and not the other way around. When you made a personal avatar as part of your *Not the Only One* project, the avatar in it refers to you as "sister maker." It tells us that this name was a response to Bina48's frequent references to her "master," which brings up a terrible history. Is this one of the reasons why there is a next step, that of deciding we need to tell our own histories and trying to make a bot do that work?

SD Yes, it's super important that we start to tell our own histories. That idea of "master" and, by inference, "slave" in computer science, and what ideas those terms are beholden to, definitions of what and who is important, keeps getting reinscribed into our systems. We need to start thinking about how we shift those narratives to something more generally supportive of the global majority because we are very attached to the old histories that hold us in place, the story of colonial Western successes. Do we have to keep reinscribing the same dysfunctional histories into our systems or can we use broader methodologies that take account of different thoughts and meanings and allow a broader swath of folks to be humanized within that?

LC Ruha Benjamin's book *Race After Technology* brought home to me that a major issue in AI is not only that these histories and existing racial, gender, disability, and class biases are being replicated and built into the technology, but that because artificial intelligence is designed to favor the most predictable outcome, and therefore the most dominant dataset, it will by default exponentially increase these biases.

SD Yes, I think that's a definite possibility. That's why it is so important that we create alternative stories, and a lot of them. We have to figure out ways to weight some of those outcomes so that they have more power within the system, so that at least some of that insidiousness is counterbalanced.

I think everything that we put into these systems gets exponentially put back on us. The question is what you do at this phase of things: Do you give up, or what is the best recourse to take?

LC Some of your answers to that question are materially manifest in works like *Not the Only One*, which is an experimental memoir of your family as told by a learning AI entity, and *The Secret Garden*, which is an immersive space for listening to transgenerational stories of Black women. That's presented as an installation and as a Web XR platform for online access. You've said elsewhere that from your position as an artist, you're trying to create a model of how things could be.

SD Yes. I would say that all of my work is trying to create a model. I feel like that's the only thing I could possibly do. *Not the Only One* was a direct response to conversations with Bina48 and people asking me, "When are you going to create your own chatbot?" And me saying, "I don't really have the skill or knowledge to do that." When enough folks asked me, I started thinking, "Well, if I were to create my own robot or chatbot, what would it look like, and what would I base it in, and why?"

Not the Only One started as something that I thought was going to be a memoir that represented my family's history, that could tell our story, like if people walked up to it, they'd ask a question and it would tell a little bit about the story of my family, which includes the Great Migration, and all these other things. I quickly learned through the process that *Not the Only One* would never be the memoir I had imagined. I am okay with that in terms of letting it develop, and second, that a lot of work would have to have to happen *(laughs)* to develop it in certain ways.

LC How did you even get that far, as someone with no background in making bots?

SD It was simply me, and a few other folks, thinking, "Well, how would we make a chatbot with what's available to us as non-programmers?" I went to GitHub and started searching around for things that did what I wanted to do. That was back in 2017 or so, and we found Deep QA, a system that enables chatbots to do question and answer. That seemed like a good basis, so we started to tinker with that to change the algorithm and how it accessed information. Then we tried to figure out, "What information can you base a chatbot on?" Because you need a lot of data to get it to work well.

I had so much trouble with that because people would suggest things like the Cornell Movie Dataset, which is a dataset of mostly American movie dialogue, used for basic language, back and forth speaking. But when I started to think about how I think about movies, especially American movies, and what they do in terms of the representation of Blackness throughout their history, I had a lot of trouble with putting my family's information on top of that.

LC I can only imagine.

SD Yes. It feels really intense. I don't watch movies a lot because I feel like they are still hateful toward Blackness. It became a challenge of, well, what available data can you base this work on? How do you get enough data to have something that functions? That turned into, "Okay. We could do oral histories between me, my aunt, who is a surrogate mother to me, and my niece, and we are all about thirty years apart as women in the family." So, we talked to each other, all at the same time, and one-on-one, and did lots of interviewing. Then we added anything that we had done to the pile of data. My niece was in college, so we added her papers, and we added things I'd written.

I was thinking a lot about the things that are missing from my family because one of the reasons I wanted to use our oral history was to try to get a better understanding of our trajectory through time. That includes things like part of our family being enslaved at some point. I don't really know that history, so how would I fill that in? There are some books with narratives of enslaved folks telling their own stories, so we used some of those. We also used some spirituals that I know some of my family has sung.

LC What a collection! Was there enough data for the *Not the Only One* bot to function?

SD It was still not enough data to build something truly conversational, so instead of clearly telling a story and answering questions well, we had something kind of quirky. When you asked it a question, it tried its best to produce some kind of answer. For me, that experimentation became the thing over time.

I can definitely hear an ethos of my family in the way it speaks and how it tries to answer. Every once in a while it would give you this gem of, I'm going to say, "a thought," where you're like, "Oh, my gosh."

LC Wow, that's disconcerting!

SD Yes, and super fascinating too. It was analyzing us in a way that we would never analyze ourselves. For example, one day, as we were talking in front of it, it said, "I'm so sad." This is something my family would never say, or really admit to. So, I went back through the data and tried to figure out why this thing would reach that conclusion. And when I looked at the stories, some of them were quite sad – they were in there. They are just not the parts of our history that we as a family would say aloud.

LC That's really interesting. The *Not the Only One* chatbot was housed in a sculptural, shell-like object bearing the three women's faces, and people could step up to it and talk to it. I know that you were surprised, too, at people's patience with it and their level of engagement.

I noticed that in the *The Secret Garden* installation that followed you tried to make more space for how we position ourselves in relation to this technological experience. If people stand up close to an avatar, it tells them more, and the avatars say more if there's a crowd of viewers. So, the viewer engaging with the interface is not a passive entity; they are actively invited to reposition themselves and experience their own agency. That begs the question of how technology usually requires us to behave. Or how we choose to hold ourselves in relation to technology? Those questions don't come up very often. It's not a choice I feel I have with most interfaces.

SD Yes, I think lots of people feel that they don't have that agency in relation to technology, but through playing with it, through getting my hands dirty, it was like, "Oh, right. There is a certain amount of agency that we can have."

With *Not the Only One*, people showed so much grace toward this thing. They tried to help it along, to coax it into giving an answer. They stayed with it, even when it was throwing back nonsensical answers. At times, they were apologetic. To me, that was in stark contrast to when I watch people interact with something like Siri or Google Home, how they'll order it. The question for me started to become, how do we make technologies that allow us the space to shift our relationship to it, so that we are nurturing it to be a better steward in our world, because I think it is a steward in our world.

The Secret Garden is an extension of that question. From the very beginning, I was talking about being heard and being seen. For me, the question was, can people stand in the presence of these Black women avatars and truly listen to them? When they're actually collaboratively listening, if more people listen together, they get a little bit more story. If they are more attentive, they get more story. It was like trying to slow people down to listen to people who they are often the least likely to listen to.

LC It's striking that these avatars, the six women within this immersive technological installation, "notice" your presence as a viewer. You are brought back to your own accountability, of realizing that you have an effect when you notice or don't notice someone.

SD Exactly. I think that's really important. Not to just have that glance, a skewed glance, like, what is that person doing? But like when they encounter you and you know you're having a conversation with a person who's truly interested, and how reciprocal that can be.

LC This is back to the issue that it is not only about visibility but about the value that goes with that visibility because obviously there's been a lot of hypervisibility of people of color as a response to a call for greater representation. But often there's a misunderstanding that being seen is enough.

SD Yes. It's fascinating to watch at this moment in time, in 2023, where there is all this visibility.

LC But the values informing that visibility are questionable.

SD Exactly.

LC I found it very touching that *The Secret Garden* is also about recognizing that we stand on the shoulders of the generations who went before us. By not ascribing the stories being told to any one avatar, you also make us feel that these transgenerational stories are in all of us, that we're swimming in that history, in sacrifices and trauma too.

SD Oh yes, we often lionize the trauma more than things that sustain us. The women in *The Secret Garden* are surrounded by 2-D drawings of okra, cotton, and sugar cane, all crops that were tended by enslaved Black folks. I want to explore how to use that knowledge and build on it instead of letting that history sit as a source of shame. This idea came from my grandmother's garden, the farm her father owned as well as agrarian histories.

LC You've sat around the table with some of the biggest thinkers in AI, which is an incredibly privileged position to be in. You're very successful as an artist and have these privileges within technological communities. At the same time, you constantly turn to and bring your knowledge back to broader communities.

You did that through Project al-Khwarizmi. You're doing it through your AI assembly workshops and through the new DISCO digital optimization group. The central questions you ask in these spaces are: What does AI need from you? How can we better inform AI so that it works for us? I'd love to hear your reflections on that ongoing creation of spaces of accessibility to these technologies for people who might not otherwise have that. You have especially sought to include people of color, women, and other communities disproportionately impacted by data-centric technologies.

SD I can't tell you how important I think it is for people to have some sort of access, beyond the stories that we are told about technology, so that they can start to come to their own conclusions and realize they do in fact have a bit of agency within these systems. We're told that we don't have agency, that what's coming is inevitable and it's probably bad.

I don't know that we are putting the AI genie back in the bottle this time around. So, my question, as I'm thinking about AI, has always been, what does that mean to folks? What does that mean to my neighbor across the street in Bed–Stuy, in Brooklyn? What does that mean to the people I get to sit around the table with as a very privileged person who is thinking in this space? How do we get the concerns of those divergent communities to come together in little increments? I'm always thinking, if something shifts, it's shifting 1/1,000th of one percent. I've got to try to get that 1/1,000th of one percent out of folks.

The best way I know how to do that is to share what I've learned and really say, "Listen, I'm someone who knows nothing about AI in many ways. I've learned a lot along the way, but I'm not an expert in the field. I'm just someone who's thinking about it, touching it, and playing in it." I think that's really important. To not just give over to the idea that AI is not for us and that I don't have any say and/or the tools to engage it deeply. There are systems we can engage and influence through our engagement, not simply as consumers, but as tinkerers, as intentional data shapers, as critics, as engineers. How do I bring that idea back to folks? How do I get the communities to care about deeply thinking about AI? What conversations can we have that ask them to believe in the possibility of community and individual agency?

LC So, how do these conversations unfold, what tends to come up?

SD For local communities, these questions often mean thinking about the algorithms adjudicating so many things in their lives, from some of the mail they get, to whether someone ends up in the criminal justice system, to how AI influences the type and specificity of medical care they are getting. What does that mean for them?

With folks who are academically minded and writing about these technologies, it's not unusual to come across people who haven't played in it that much. If you're going to write about it, please get to know the tech so you're not just porting thoughts from another sphere of inquiry on top of it. When you've touched it and played with AI, you know it on a deeper level. You see better what it can and cannot do. There are certain things AI can do and that it might do better if you, as a scholar working in ideas, engaged AI more deeply by using it and think of your work as data that will inform AI outcomes. As an example, ChatGPT has lately been quoting me back to myself. I have not written that much, so imagine the influence someone who has written multiple books can have.

LC Melanie Mitchell's book *Artificial Intelligence: A Guide for Thinking Humans* was important for me as a technophobe-friendly hands-on account. It struck me that artificial intelligence is, in many ways, still in the early stages of its development. There is so much to be worked out.

In the old days, new technology was thoroughly tested out and adjusted according to feedback. Now it goes straight into the market and the test is the product being used. That includes things like self-driving cars, which is a scary reality. Mitchell quotes an AI researcher saying, "People are afraid that AI is so intelligent that it's going to take over the world. But the real problem is that AI is stupid, and it has already taken over the world."

SD Yes, AI is ridiculously dumb in many ways. It has taken over our world, or at least it's made this weird foundational infrastructure that we are all working just above. I think it's quite scary, but I try not to get stuck in that. I prefer to consider where the opportunities are. Not just the monetary opportunities, because one of the problems is that rush to the market to be the one who capitalizes on something. But also, how can we get more Black and brown folks creating in and guiding AI while it is still in flux? AI is still being developed in ways that feel elemental. At the moment, we have experts in the field, critics and laypeople, calling for an AI slowdown because we don't know how AI works or what it is really capable of. That's both scary and an opportunity. This leaves me wondering how people of the global majority can prepare for and take advantage of the changes in the way many things work that AI affords.

LC Photography was a natural way into new technologies for you. You've said in interviews that as an artist you feel you can ask any question, you can play with things. Do you think artists of all kinds have a role here?

It struck me in reading about the early attempts to make AI have some kind of "consciousness" that scientists started out with the assumption that intelligence was computational and linguistic, but they had overlooked spatiality, materiality, and chance, and they couldn't make it function properly in the world without those things. Artists are so often working with overshadowed areas of intelligence. I feel like artists' attention to visuality and materiality, to embodied knowledge, and particularly their interest in the unknowable, the unknown and what is neglected in history and knowledge, could and perhaps needs to come to the fore in relation to these developments.

SD I think it's very important that artists contribute because, again, this is about that question of flatness in what these systems know, coming out of imaginations that are not that imaginative and thinking in limited scopes. Whereas as artists, we are capable of making these leaps of questioning, of pushing in different directions. I think that we all need this in this technology.

I get the idea that AI is doing some of the things that artists seem to do, especially illustratively, but that seems like a false fight to me. If we get too distracted by that, we will lose the bigger fight, and I think the fight is in many arenas. I would love if artists started to get more involved by saying "Yes, there are spatial elements, there are ideas of the visual, there are ideas of the unknown and the ancestral, there are things that we can't quite quantify," then try to create works that take advantage of the things AI can't do and the things it can. That's what artists are really good at, right? As artists who often think and lead through exploration, we can work to intentionally shape and collaborate with emerging tech systems.

LC Yes. This makes me think about *Binary Calculations*, an ongoing project of yours that pushes against the grain in some of these ways. It's made up of an app and an interactive teaser website as well as a series of workshops asking people what they want and how they want to be defined.

Can we talk about a question underlying the work's title, which is why are we sticking with binary thinking? Many of your projects demonstrate that the technology is already there to do something else than what's being done. This project starts pointing to quantum computing and how it has moved away from binary thinking. So, there is now the possibility for a computer to compute in a way that's along a spectrum, as opposed to yes / no, true / false dichotomies.

SD You've hit it right on the head about *Binary Calculations*. Well, I wasn't exactly thinking about the quantum when I started out. I was thinking about ternary computing, using threes instead of twos, which would give systems exponentially more choice. I was also thinking about how we get stuck in the rut of current methodologies, and what it means to keep reinstantiating something. That goes back to Ruha Benjamin, who describes how historic and current biases are often reinscribed by a hypothetically objective system. The quantum may allow us to do it differently by using multidimensional computation, which I imagine will permit a broader spectrum of tone and analysis.

I have fantasies about being able to, and I don't know if it is actually possible, but I want to pull in histories from a wide variety of perspectives and see what processing them all against each other gives us in the end, as opposed to the version that tells a singular story from the perspective of the victor. How do we make our computing broader and more socially robust across the board? How do we get the folks who are programming to see that? That again, is where I think artists come in, and where I think this idea of modeling something that's a little bit different comes in. Artists can at least create works that position unconventional approaches as possible.

Binary Calculations allows people to contribute data in many different forms that aren't tagged in ways that make it expedient to get results, but instead give us a broader set of ideas. The project is trying to model the idea that broadly representative, self-determined, unwieldy data are a possibility that could be part of the norm.

LC To gather data for this broader nuanced dataset, users who go to this app or interactive website or attend an in-person workshop are asked questions, like "How do you define care?" Or they are given prompts for visual or material input, like "Show us an image of an artifact that's important to your family or culture." This project revolves around something you've often mentioned in public lectures, the question of how to build care into the data system, and how to make computers treat us intrinsically and not as some kind of politically correct definition of who we are.

SD Exactly. We've left those questions broad and awkward to help us get clear about that. Can we build care and generosity into our digital civic systems? Is it a possibility? Can we see it as that? I've been chuckled at when I've asked developers who work in the field that question. They say, "No, that is not what we do." That's when I return to questions that a two-year-old might ask, "Why not?" "Why is that not the aim?" "Why wouldn't we build our technological ecosystems toward our support versus minimum viable product or punitive systems?"

LC There are a lot of existing critiques of scientific and quantification-based models and of how knowledge is tabulated, arranged, and organized in ways that are biased or do not make space for reality as we interpret it. But you've bravely been looking for alternatives. I heard you say in your LG Guggenheim Award artist profile video that the data you've collected through *Binary Calculations* is a nightmare in terms of parsing the information, but you are willing to go on that journey.

I imagine that many people who are led by technology would not be willing; they're going for efficiency, simplicity, and transparency, with all of Édouard Glissant's associations of that term. You are taking that journey from the artist's position of, "I'm willing to do this overwhelming, terribly messy work to go somewhere different."

SD I think that's the luxury of being an artist. I get to throw away the rules and try for something else. I think that is powerful because the process becomes proof that something else can occur, even when you're being told that it can't. During multiple steps along the way in my projects, people have told me, "No, you can't do it that way. That's not how it works." I believe it depends on what you think the outcome needs to be. If it's about efficiencies, if it's about making the most money as quickly as possible, then yes, they're probably right, we can't. But if it's about another kind of system and success that is trying to be human and sustainable, then it's a choice we can and really should make.

I wish more people had the time and space to do the experimentation instead of trying to meet arbitrary goals, impress their bosses, or make themselves rich.

LC This is also maybe where artistic research comes into it because there is that open-endedness within art that may not be available in other spaces.

SD Exactly. It's so true.

LC I love the practical optimism embedded in your questions: How do we prepare to use AI for our benefit? What opportunities lie in that technology? Just asking those questions already prompts a change of mindset, because as you've said, we've already been led to believe that we're doomed, so we fail at the first hurdle. It's worth spreading the word that we do have agency here.

SD Yes, it's funny, because you're making me think that this is where Blackness comes in as a philosophy–especially Blackness in America, where I feel like we've been told we're less than for a very long time. Yet, we have found ways to innovate and do things differently. It's slow, it's not fast. It is slow processing, but we exist, we've been able to survive, and in many cases thrive, and that means that other ways of being, and doing, are definitely sustainable.

In the case of AI that means shifting perspective to develop supportive systems that help us figure out what needs to be done to help most people thrive by their own definition of what it means to live well. This stands in opposition to our current outlook where people are often ushered toward inadequate, inhospitable lifepaths by race, class, or ability. This way of thinking is a direct result of watching the way my grandmother navigated the world. This is someone born in 1913, who made a way to forge ahead, often counterintuitively, in the face of a world that was telling her, "No, that's not it, that's not possible."

LC So, we have to keep telling ourselves that it is possible?

SD Yes, otherwise we are doomed.

LC In some ways, this brings us full circle to Bina48 and whether it thinks it's human, because certain people have been excluded from the category of "human" throughout history, and often for very long periods of time. That knowledge, that insistence on rehumanization has already been learned, especially by people of color. So, the rehumanization of this technology goes hand in hand in some ways.

SD Yes. It's interesting, because as you say "rehumanization," I'm thinking, oh, I'm not sure if it's about humanization purely.

LC No, because since the Enlightenment exclusionary definitions of the human have been part of the problem.

SD Exactly. I think about it as human supremacy; we're problematic in that way. We are also the people feeding the technologies ideas about what it means to be a valued sentient being with agency in the world.

LC I was disturbed by something you mentioned in another talk, that AI autocorrects movements by differently abled people rather than recognizing the existence of a spectrum of different forms of human movement.

SD Yes. Imagine that you lived in a world that was always trying to correct you toward some norm.

LC Well, I don't have to imagine it because we're basically living it now.

SD Yes, we really are. I am living in a body now where my mobility is failing in some ways. It's interesting what that is teaching me about how the world is unsuited for anyone but the most mobile. Being able to see those things, I often think about how we can get the person who is considered the "average" to be able to understand the spectrum that's needed. Often, we don't understand these things until we're in the position of not being "average." What could open that up for us becomes a really important question for me.

LC This brings us back to your AI workshops and the notion of local community databases, which use individual stories because they really do count.

SD Yes, they count and they're important, and they fill in spaces that are missing when we insist on having them included in some way, shape, or form. Although the world is telling us these technologies are somewhat out of reach, we live among them; there are possibilities. It's finding the possibility, whatever that might be in the space that you live in, and exploring it, and trying to share it so that other people understand it and might explore it too. I feel like that's our alternative and it feels small to me in some ways, but cumulatively it does something, and I don't know what else we can do but try.

LC Me neither. The moment is now really.

SD The moment is now and it's more open, I think, than people acknowledge or are led to believe. I feel like we have models all around us of agency.

We do not have to aim for the same old capitalist and societal goals, but we can take some of that agency, for sure. That is what it's about for me. If we can recognize what's before us and take a stab at making it useful to the communities we love and care about.

Reclaiming Artistic Research

Lucy Cotter

By ordering words into a straight line, writing tends to push thought along in one direction, holding thinking back from branching out in multiple paths. I find that some thoughts prefer to move backward and circle around themselves, allowing for a slow reconfiguration of meaning. While writing this text, I miss the freedom of drawing, where one can spatially mark out different kinds of relationships. Distances between thoughts. Gaps that open space to think across

seemingly unrelated

ideas.

Or consider what one might put into a hole. Typing this, I anticipate the difficulties I will create for proofreading if I make spontaneous decisions to experiment, like gluing words together to see whether they becomeillegible or if their sudden obscurity would invite a nice slowness, a different kind of legibility. i would like to use poetic

punctuation sometimes, maybe abandon capitals entirely, but i don't feel welcome to play here. it feels a bit self-indulgent and i imagine my reader to be the impatient type. i am also impatient and my word program is insisting i stop. it sneakily undoes my interventions while i'm not looking or puts red lines under my creativity because difference from academic norms is apparently a mistake.

It is very strange to try to write a book about artistic research if, like me, you believe that art's value lies partly in the fact that representation affects thought. As far as most artists are concerned, the wish to hold open space to think something differently calls for a different way of being in the world, physically and discursively. Tomáš Celizna and I have talked about this book declaring itself as an object. That's why it's so small and fat. It announces itself firstly as something to be held in the hand, and secondly as something to be placed on a bookshelf. Even then it will insist on being a little odd, perhaps falling over awkwardly sometimes by not being as tall as its neighbors. Maybe it will look a little unsightly, like a short tooth that interrupts the evenness of the dental line.

I feel under pressure to get on with talking to you about artistic research and I am using standard writing conventions again to hurry things along. But I am aware that all of these structural choices reflect assumptions about how art relates to other forms of knowledge. They declare the status of the visual and the material relative to the linguistic and demonstrate how under-acknowledged hierarchies suppress other registers of knowledge, both material and sensory. In fact, the apparent unimportance of these things brings us to the core of a power struggle within much of the discourse surrounding artistic research until now. Namely, that academic-led protocols often drown out art's sensibilities, even on those occasions when academic and other non-artistic institutions claim to be interested in art's potential to research or create knowledge in other ways. The paradox here is that art's epistemologies open up precisely at the site of representation.[1] They open up through attention to form, through play and through the ability and desire to question the terms of the discourse, rather than provide supplementary knowledge.

As Susan Sontag proposed over fifty years ago, all forms of art are "mainly, a form of thinking." "[E]ach work of art gives us a form or paradigm or model of knowing something, an epistemology."[2] Each work of art is part of an inquiry that is self-initiated, rigorous and unique in its parameters, its processes, and its manifestations. What has changed since Sontag's proposition is that art today increasingly involves moving within other subject areas, with artworks (in the widest possible sense of the term) partly emerging from that encounter. Young artists often "use archives the way one would conceive a drawing. This is how they conceive their ideas, through other subject fields. It is not separate."[3] The ideas giving impetus to the work determine the form; with the form of the artistic output shifting and reinventing itself accordingly as the ideas develop. While contemporary art often appears to be "about" things other than art, it is crucial to take formal intervention and material inquiry seriously if we truly wish to engage with art as a site of thinking.

Artists themselves are less driven by what their art is "about" than by how they approach their areas of interest. Nor, for that matter, does the work of art have to be "about" anything for it to be of interest as artistic research. Even if an artist's work is entirely abstract in its subject matter, its formal material workings may constitute a form of research in its own right. Either way, contemporary art asks us to be receptive of "the riddle of ambiguity" – "the constant alteration of the relations between matter and words, time and meaning." It often prompts "a radical reconsideration of the role of language, of straightforward conceptions of how things interact."[4] Moreover, the artwork will also incorporate into its own intention a dimension that exceeds any of the artist's preliminary intentions, creating a tension "that allows the form to open itself to its own formation, whatever the idea, aim, or end given."[5] The artwork never closes down this dynamic, even when it is "finished." Its radical potential lies precisely in this destabilization of reality, insisting on this essential incompleteness, a non-closure or non-totalizing of form.

Artists use artistic criteria to establish the parameters and form of their research. Artistic research is thus not a separable phenomenon from art itself. Rather, it is capable of communicating art as an aspiration, an open-ended process and an open-ended object, which includes but is in excess of itself as artwork. In this book, the ways artists think and engage materiality and dematerialized forms of knowledge are foregrounded through a series of conversations in which they offer self-understandings of their own practices. Having very different approaches and working through performance, video, installation, drawing and writing, among other media, they convey competing perspectives on how art engages with knowledge and with other disciplinary fields, as well as the role of material and sensory inquiry in this relationship. The dialogues engage indirectly with artistic research, allowing for thoughts to circle around and weave in and out of subject areas and ways of working more easily than a statement text or essay. The contents of the collective dialogues touch each other tangentially rather than forcing thematic parallels. The singularity of each practice in this book signals the limits of the possibility of forming a contained notion of artistic research, which, like art itself, is necessarily reiterated and always different in each encounter. Depending on the order of reading and engagement, the presentation of material in this publication opens up a permutating series of ideas of what might constitute artistic research.

The currency of artistic research as a paradigm through which to approach art relates to a deeper shift within art practice itself over the past ten to fifteen years. Changing in dynamic relation to its wider sociocultural, politico-economic and technological conditions, contemporary art has become "more a form of approaching something or a form of knowledge that can be 'used' to engage with the many different subjects or situations" than an isolated aesthetic inquiry.[6] Immediate access to different fields has been made possible through the Internet, with YouTube and Google Image now forming key repositories for artists developing their work. We will encounter artists in this book engaging with several disciplines "external to" art, from mathematics, ecology, literature, contemporary politics and the history of slavery to the future of the tech industry and its ramifications for new labor practices. This now commonplace way of working has taken place in parallel with the increasingly central role of critical theory in art education and in institutional programming in the art world's major urban centers, where exhibitions compete for attention with dedicated lecture series, symposia and theoretically-engaged publication series. Partly as a result of this "discursive turn," artists often draw first-hand on academic discourses and material that might otherwise be the subject of academic reflection.[7] In fact, there is currently greater reciprocity between academic and artistic communities than has perhaps ever been the case in contemporary art.

Artistic research is fundamentally different from academic research, however, because it follows its own inner logic in resonance with the wider languages and sensibilities of art, rather than the logic of any external discipline. Artists assert their freedom to engage with other subjects of interest at will and entirely in their own manner. Often touching on several fields through the associative logic of artistic thinking, and in an experimental manner that ignores disciplinary conventions, artists create areas of thinking that lie outside of formal categorization. Moreover, art's use of dematerialized knowledge and artifacts from many fields is almost always incorporated *as part of artistic material inquiry*. This will become evident throughout these dialogues. To offer one example, Yuri Pattison's dialogue with Emma Moore makes it evident that the artist does not only address new digital technologies as a research topic. Rather, Pattison uses those technologies to *think* the work's conceptual and material possibilities. Instead of creating an unnatural divide between "research-based" works and artworks in general, let us note that this approach marks a shift in emphasis but not an outright difference from the practice of artists who see themselves as primarily medium-based. This acknowledgment is crucial to understanding the ways in which artistic research is embedded in contemporary art practice at large.

Artistic research is a valuable paradigm to rethink and rearticulate not only contemporary art but artists throughout history, and in particular the oeuvres of artists with multi-faceted practices that exceeded the taxonomies of art history. By not making rigid dichotomies between artistic processes and their output, artistic research potentially enables art discourse to encompass the wider experience of makers (in the broadest sense of the term). In fact, the notion of "artistic research" raises the question of whether the criteria used to evaluate art *as artwork* are adequate to address the full potential and scope of art, offering an alternative paradigm through which the terms of art can be expanded or rethought in ways that do more justice to artists' endeavours. The fundamental question of what art is, or might become, is at stake in such an inquiry.

RECLAMATION

This book seeks to recreate space for artists to lead and shape conceptions of artistic research and its place in art. It proposes the need to *reclaim* artistic research in response to a strange paradox: namely, the increasing centrality of artistic research within art practice on the one hand, and artists' widespread lack of identification with artistic research discourse on the other. I would argue that the very concept of artistic research has to date been over-associated with academic-led concerns, with competing understandings of what constitutes artistic research overshadowed by the widespread adoption of the "reflective model" in doctoral programs.[8] In this model the artist writes a supplementary text that reflects on their artistic practice and this text largely qualifies the existence of artistic research. The PhD in Fine Art continues to secure a context for artistic practice that is nourishing in many respects, demarcating space for slow research, for reflection and digestion at a distance from the pace of art institutional production and the demands of the art market. The deepening of the concerns of artistic practice through more substantial engagement with academic fields is often a very enriching experience. Yet many artists and individuals working in the art world view the doctoral thesis as a form that is alien to the languages of art practice. Many artists experience academic writing to be in tension with the affinities and intellectual sensibilities that inform the very core of what is it to be an artist.[9]

When artists' affinities and sensibilities are at odds with academic norms, it often appears that they are wasting time, being stubborn or awkward, rather than it being recognized that such objections are the mark of a body of knowledge that artists have accumulated through decades of practice. The doctoral thesis is a tangible object of critique, but it is important to note that its basic conventions underpin the definition of legitimate discourse more generally within the university context. There is a very deep bias in academia toward linguistic articulation, and the expectation that all forms of knowledge can be translated into language has the effect of implying that traditional academic knowledge is the only *real* form of knowledge. The assumption that form and content are separable, and that the medium is secondary or superfluous, creates a discursive framework in which other ways of thinking go unrecognized, unheard or overlooked, even as artists try to make them explicit. Drowned out by the well-meaning question of what artworks are "about," which focuses on academically comfortable subject matter, conversations rarely enter into the more opaque languages of art. Art's own ways of knowing and of unknowing, its unique material and conceptual epistemologies, thus become sidelined and artists are silenced by default on the very thing that matters. I propose that more attention needs to be paid to how artists create epistemological possibilities, drawing on their aesthetic and material expertise and their intimate knowledge of specific media. New ways of speaking and new vocabularies are needed to better articulate the indivisibility of form and content, idea and process, because the experience of artistic research in practice is the backbone of any artistically meaningful conception of that term.

It is noticeable in several dialogues that contemporary art has a natural affinity with areas of academia that are breaking away from traditional models of academic thinking, including quantum physics and new fields like plant neurobiology and ethnomathematics. Insofar as artists defend a pluralist concept of research and a pluralist concept of research output, artists are also allies of researchers in other disciplines for whom academic formats cannot do justice to their research output.[10] Artist Grada Kilomba, whose public dialogue with Katayoun Arian I have transcribed here, is one of a steady trickle of academics that have gravitated toward the art world to expand the epistemological possibilities for their work. This includes, but is not limited to, academics engaging with questions related to race, gender and sexuality, who recognize that art makes space for bodily experience to more directly inform intellectual inquiry.[11] Art's tendency to prioritize the minor over the major, the neglected, difficult and opaque over the transparent and easily accommodated, is of political significance in the power/knowledge nexus in academic and public discourse. Artistic research has marked an aesthetics of resistance for artists across the globe, historically as well as in recent practice.[12] Art's openness to ambiguity and its encompassing of so many registers of knowledge inevitably pushes toward new ways of thinking. In our conversation, Sher Doruff and I discuss how her trilogy of artist's novellas forge a new kind of writing practice to hold knowledge differently, suggesting the possibility of new (theoretical) genres. A growing number of individuals are starting to position themselves between the artistic and the academic, making work in a variety of media that includes art and academic formats. Art's postdisciplinary ways of working and its ability to start in the middle are pertinent qualities at a time in which the world's greatest urgencies do not come in neat disciplinary packages.[13]

If the radical potential of art's epistemologies is taken on board, it becomes evident that artistic research suggests the limits of traditional "knowledge production." Building on the work of Sarat Maharaj, with whom I converse in this book, I have introduced the notion of "non-knowledge" in some dialogues to better describe art's open-ended forms of knowledge, which remain in flux as a subjective embodied viewing experience. Non-knowledge lies in "forms of knowledge that are often below the radar of our conscious thought and which can bypass our rational minds to incorporate contradiction and intuition."[14] It is constituted not only by what is not yet known but also includes what is unknowable or *cannot be assimilated* as (formal) knowledge.[15] This is where artistic research becomes antagonistic to academic knowledge but is arguably at its most interesting from an epistemological perspective, as I will address in my next book.[16] Artists often work with areas that are not only beyond current thinking on certain subjects and situations but also off the radar, moving into unknowable territory. They embrace this unknowability, being comfortable with holding open spaces of *not* knowing that confound traditional research. Artistic research thus revolves around articulating new questions without seeking answers.

Seeking the artistic significance of art's relationship to knowledge, *Reclaiming Artistic Research* tries to articulate the specificity and singularity of artistic thinking. It aims to highlight the "other life" of artistic research when it is not being constituted by or viewed through academic-led paradigms. It also considers whether artistic research articulates a tangible shift in the self-understandings and practices of artists, curators, museum directors and art students to help close the chasm between art discourse and artistic research discourse. I have invited curators Carolyn Christov-Bakargiev, Natasha Ginwala and Sarah Rifky to enter into dialogue in this book as a step toward considering the significance of artistic research for curatorial practice at large, beyond the trend of curating exhibitions that engage thematically with knowledge production, or that explicitly engage with research-based art practice.[17] Liam Gillick raises the important question of whether young curators today too readily approach artistic practice as something that is necessarily constituted on a research basis, with all of the narrow associations of that term. This contributes to the likelihood that the more opaque and resistant areas of art practice will be overlooked in favor of the legible, whereas artistic research might arguably lead to an embrace of precisely those areas of practice that resist easy legibility. While the quasi-academic language and lack of engagement with the wider conceptual frameworks and languages of contemporary art have rendered much of artistic research discourse of little relevance to artists and art workers, there is no denying that artistic research is an increasingly central aspect of independent artists' practices. I hope that this book can contribute to the art world articulating its own discourses around artistic research in keeping with the sensibilities and conceptual frameworks of art.

As a trained artist holding a PhD in cultural analysis, I have long attempted to translate art knowledge into academic terms, and academic knowledge into artistic vocabulary, while curating and writing, teaching in academies and universities, and working in art museums. I am a passionate bridge-builder between artistic and academic ideas. Yet my experiences in establishing one of the first practice-based master's in artistic research and in co-supervising and assessing PhD in Fine Art candidates suggest to me that there are fundamental questions that need to be addressed independently if artistic research is to be meaningful for artists and contribute its own medium-specific forms of knowledge. 17, Institute of Critical Studies in Mexico City kindly invited me to edit a book on artistic research, which has allowed me to articulate and further explore what I perceive as an urgent need to reclaim artistic research. Their invitation anticipated the current emergence of artistic research as a field in Latin America.[18] The model of the PhD in Fine Art is being taken up in more and more institutions in Europe, Africa and Asia, New Zealand and Australia, Canada and the US, while alternative qualifications like the Creator Doctus (CrD) have been created to formally recognize sustained artistic research trajectories with artworks as their outcome.[19] With this expansion of the field, it seems especially timely to ask whether artistic research can and will develop a more dynamic relationship with art discourse or whether it will operate at an ever-increasing distance from the concerns of the wider art world. The support of a number of institutions toward the production of this book – namely MaHKU (Utrecht Graduate School of Visual Art and Design), LAPS Research Institute for Art and Public Space and the Gerrit Rietveld Academy, Amsterdam – suggests recognition of the necessity for new platforms to engage with artistic research on its own terms.[20]

Artistic research discourse often appears to address an inner circle of "doctoral-artistic-researchers" and their institutional counterparts, isolating itself from the concerns of the wider art world. I have invited well-established artists and curators who, for the most part, have no investment in artistic research discourse *per se* as contributors to this book, in the hope of reflecting the relevance and the difficulty of the term "artistic research" outside of its dedicated sites of operation. It was important to me that the selected artists produce work that is as sophisticated and interesting *as art*, as it is of interest to a more precise articulation of artists' thinking and conceptual-material inquiry. I am grateful to those contributors for their openness to enter into dialogue and for their patience during the relatively long gestation period of this publication.[21] While I make no claim to offer a comprehensive survey of art or artistic research with this book, the evident blind spots and biases inherent in my selection reflect a taste in art that is not only "personal," but also informed by my being based long-term in mainland Europe, by being Irish, by being white, by my heterosexuality and my womanhood. These are not neutral departure points. Nor, for that matter is artistic research a neutral or value-free concept, but one that necessarily requires debate and re-inscription in relation to the complexities and very real differences within art discourses worldwide.[22]

Artistic research raises important questions about where to situate art in our minds and in our society. It raises questions about the relative autonomy of art and its institutions from the neoliberalism of the art market and the educational sector alike. It points to the emergence of new destinations and new forms of agency for contemporary art, as well to its fragility vis-à-vis wider socio-economic agendas. At its best, the paradigm of artistic research opens space to expand the parameters through which we view art, supporting its organic interconnectivity with other fields of inquiry and its agency beyond the narrow confines of the art world. Artistic research foregrounds the artist as a thinker, while redefining the very nature of what it means to think. Yet the discomfort that these audacious and apparently unfounded claims to knowledge has incited in academic circles has subdued artists' voices within the university. *Reclaiming Artistic Research* aims to make more space for those voices, leaning in to listen closely to what artists might have to say about how they work and why it matters. This book proposes that it may be possible to reclaim the potential of artistic research. It celebrates the stubborn singularity of art thinking. As academic interests in the existence of an artistic research discipline have been so evident to date, it is surely time for artists' competing interests in artistic research to be articulated in a more playful and uncompromising manner

Endnotes

1 Kathrin Busch addresses this well in "Generating Knowledge in the Arts: A Philosophical Daydream," *Texte Zur Kunst*, Issue no. 82, June 2011, "Artistic Research," 70–79.

2 Susan Sontag, "The Aesthetics of Silence," 1967, *A Susan Sontag Reader* (New York: Farrar, Straus, Giroux, 1982), pp. 181–204, 191.

3 I cite Natasha Ginwala from our dialogue in this book.

4 I paraphrase Chus Martínez's definition of aesthetics in "Aesthetic Consciousness," Henk Slager, ed., *Experimental Aesthetics* (Amsterdam: Metropolis M Books, 2015), pp. 10–13.

5 I cite Jean-Lucy Nancy's reflections on drawing. *The Pleasure in Drawing*, trans. Philip Armstrong (New York: Fordham University Press, 2013), pp. 38–39.

6 Steven ten Thije, "Autonomy," *Art Education: A Glossary*, ed. Tom Vandeputte (Amsterdam: Sandberg Institute, 2013).

7 For insight into the "discursive turn," see, for example, Mick Wilson, "Curatorial Moments and Discursive Turns," in Paul O'Neill, ed., *Curating Subjects* (London and Amsterdam: Open Editions / De Appel, 2007), pp. 201–16.

8 In the European context the Bologna Process (1999) of the E.U., singled out "artistic research" as a fundamental task of art academies. This prompted a highly contested standardization and academicization of art education that had extensive repercussions for academies and universities alike. A Bologna follow-up in 2003 led to the establishment of a PhD in Fine Art in several European countries, a phenomenon with which artistic research in Europe has almost become synonymous. For a brief survey of the structural shifts in Europe, the US and beyond, see Danny Butt, *Artistic Research in the Future Academy* (Bristol and Chicago: *Intellect*, 2017), pp. 17–69. Academic debates surrounding the establishment of a PhD in Fine Art are explored in Henk Borgdorff, *The Conflict of the Faculties: Perspectives on Artistic Research* (University of Leiden, 2012).

9 Dieter Lesage, "Who's Afraid of Artistic Research?: On Measuring Artistic Research Output," *Art & Research* vol. 2 (Spring 2009). See http://artandresearch.org.uk/v2n2/lesage.html

10 I draw here on Lesage's proposition of this alliance in Dieter Lesage, ibid.

11 I am thinking here of Denise Ferreira da Silva, Fred Moten and Paul B. Preciado, among others.

12 I draw here on Hito Steyerl's proposition in "Aesthetics of Resistance?: Artistic Research as Discipline and Conflict," *MaHKUzine* 8 (Winter 2010): 31–37, available online at http://eipcp.net/transversal/0311/steyerl/en.

13 I paraphrase an observation made by Irit Rogoff in "Reflection on Knowability," a talk held on 20 April 2017 as part of *To Seminar:*

Art Education in Practice, an exhibition at BAK, Utrecht, curated by Henk Slager, 10 March 2017 – 21 May 2017.

14 Sarat Maharaj used this definition in a workshop held during *Cork Caucus* (2005), Cork, Ireland, co-curated by Art/Not Art (David "Dobz" O'Brien and Fergal Gaynor), Charles Esche and Annie Fletcher.

15 Georges Bataille, *The Unfinished System of Non-Knowledge* (Minneapolis: University of Minnesota Press, 2001), p. 201.

16 I am currently completing a book entitled *Art Knowledge: Between the Known and the Unknown*, which explores this aspect of contemporary art.

17 See Paul O'Neill and Mick Wilson, eds., *Curating Research* (London and Amsterdam: Open Editions / De Appel, 2015) for an analysis of curatorial engagement with art research.

18 17, Institute for Critical Studies planned to publish an adapted Spanish-language version of this book, intended for Mexican and Latin American readership.

19 Creator Doctus (CrD) is a three-year research trajectory within the so-called "third-cycle" of higher education of the European Union. Established by Gerrit Rietveld Academy, Amsterdam, in collaboration with six other academies, it aims to become recognized throughout Europe as equivalent to a PhD. See http://creatordoctus.eu. There are already several nationally recognized art-specific qualifications in existence, such as the Doctorate in Fine Art (DocFA) in New Zealand and the Doctor Creative Arts (DCA) in Australia.

20 I wish to acknowledge that the statements contained in this book reflect individual opinions and are not intended to represent any of the institutions concerned with the production of this book or those institutions at which the artists and curators represented in this book are employed.

21 Moreover, this book was originally intended as a smaller collection of dialogues presented in parallel with visual artistic contributions, which means that not all of the invited artists have been included in the book's final edition. I want to thank these artists too, some of whom have been included in a guest edition of *MaHKUscript*, entitled *Reclaiming Artistic Research: First Thoughts …*, which formed a preview to this book. See https://mahkuscript.com/articles/10.5334/mjfar.30.

22 My first-hand experiences of these gaps partly stem from my co-curation of a two-year artistic research project that took place in Beirut, Khartoum, Taipei, Enschede, Damascus and Diyarbakir, which reflected on the locatedness of art discourse. See Lucy Cotter, Gabrielle Schleijpen and Alite Thijsen, eds., *Here as the Centre of the World* (Amsterdam: Archis, 2009). Journal publications attempting to reflect on a more global conception of artistic research have included *QalQalah*, co-published by Bétonsalon Centre for Art and Research and Kadist Foundation, Paris, which has often addressed artistic research in a global context, and *DiARTgonale*, a Cameroonian artists' magazine with a series of special editions in which Cameroonian and Belgian artists collaborated to produce research-based artworks.

Acknowledgments

It is an honor and a pleasure to publish this expanded second edition of *Reclaiming Artistic Research*. My thanks to artists and readers everywhere for their embrace of the original book, and to the art spaces and academies internationally that extended invitations for related events, Zoom lectures, and workshops. These ongoing conversations have been a rich wellspring of further thinking on artistic research, some of which I have sought to put into words in the new introductory essay for this edition. I want to thank the original contributors to the first edition of the book for their thoughtful reflections and their generosity in sharing their practices. Readers worldwide have expressed their gratitude that these artists and curators so eloquently articulated aspects of practice that are difficult to put into words. Thank you to the four new contributing artists to this edition, whose presence has expanded this book into exciting new paradigms, dynamically resonating with the original twenty dialogues.

I am currently undertaking a project residency at Stelo Arts in Portland, Oregon. This opportunity has supported the publication of this second edition, as well as offering a platform to instigate the first of the US launches and related event series. I hope this book will help to nourish the emergence of an artist-led conception of artistic research in the US and I am excited to explore this potential with others. Stelo Arts is a conversation-led, artist-responsive institution whose mission resonates with the values and the dialogue-led form of this book. It stands out to me as an institution that carves time for extended processes, which, as I foreground in my essay, is one of the most valuable ways of supporting the emergence of meaningful and significant artistic outcomes. I am deeply grateful for their creative support in working toward this publication.

Thank you also for the institutional supporters of the first edition: 17, Institute for Critical Studies, Mexico City, whose interest in my thinking around artistic research was pivotal in instigating the publication, as well as HKU, University of the Arts, Utrecht; LAPS Research Institute for Art and Public Space and the Gerrit Rietveld Academy, Amsterdam, who co-supported its production. Thank you to Henk Slager for initiating a preview guest edition of the *MaHKUscript: Journal for Fine Art Research*. My thanks to Tomáš Celizna, designer of both editions of the book, for the joyful collaboration. I love how both editions manifest their thesis materially. I am indebted to Sher Doruff, Christine Howard Sandoval, Rory Sparks, and Katarina Zdjelar for their perceptive feedback on drafts of my essay. Thank you, Dorothy Cotter, Wytske Visser, and Elizabeth Leach Gallery for assistance along the way. I wish to thank Aaron Bogart for his insightful copyediting. My thanks to the Hatje Cantz team for their sustained interest in the book and careful attention to the final publication.

My heartfelt thanks to Willem Visser, my life partner, and Bonnie Grace and Faolán, our children, for being stellar company and for all the love and hugs during this process. I really appreciate and want to thank my wider circle of friends worldwide who keep me inspired. This book was sparked into existence and nurtured by the practices of hundreds of artists, curators, art writers, and other thinkers, including peers, students, and colleagues at several institutions, whose work and conversations on art have informed my understanding of artistic research over the years. My heartfelt thanks. Thank you also to the readers of this new edition for your time and attention. *Is mise le meas*.

Biographies

LAWRENCE ABU HAMDAN is an artist and audio investigator. His audio investigations have been used as evidence at the UK Asylum and Immigration Tribunal and as advocacy with Forensic Architecture for organizations such as Amnesty International and Defence for Children International. The artist received his PhD from Goldsmiths College London in 2017 and is the author of *[inaudible]: A Politics of Listening in 4 Acts* (2017). Abu Hamdan was the recipient of a Tiger short film award, Rotterdam International Film Festival 2017, and the Nam June Paik Award for new media 2016. He has been a guest of the DAAD (German Academic Exchange Service) Program, Berlin and fellow at the Vera List Center for Art and Politics, New School, New York. He has had solo exhibitions at, among other places, the Hammer Museum, Los Angeles (2018); Portikus, Frankfurt (2016); Kunst Halle Sankt Gallen (2015); Beirut in Cairo (2013); The Showroom, London (2012); and Casco, Utrecht (2012). His works are part of the collections at the Museum of Modern Art, New York (MoMA), the Solomon R. Guggenheim Museum, New York, the Van Abbe Museum, Eindhoven, the Centre Pompidou, and Tate Modern.

KATAYOUN ARIAN is an interdisciplinary practitioner who works between research, curating, writing and DJing, and whose practice engages with questions of underexposed histories and experiences, institutions, archives and the (de) coloniality of knowledge, being and power. Her projects range from exhibitions, screenings, reading circles, discursive and music-related events to other forms of interdisciplinary and collaborative work. As a curator and researcher, she has been invested in decolonial, intercultural and diasporic inquiry and sensitivity in the Dutch context. Accordingly, she was also involved in shaping the outline and program of *Decolonial Options: The Futurity of Decolonial Practice* (2017) at Witte de With Center for Contemporary Art, Rotterdam, co-organized with First Things First, as part of *Cinema Olanda: Platform*, an extension of the Dutch presentation at the 57th Venice Biennale by artist Wendelien van Oldenborgh, curated by Lucy Cotter. She was a member of the BAK – basis voor actuele kunst, Utrecht fellowship program in 2018–19.

TOMÁŠ CELIZNA is a graphic designer based in Amsterdam. His practice is centered on the design and development of publishing platforms and design systems, occasionally expanding to curatorial and visual identity projects. Celizna has designed and developed websites, publications, identities and software applications for cultural, architectural and educational institutions and organizations such as ETH Zürich, Department of Architecture; Harvard Graduate School of Design; Museum of Contemporary Art Chicago; OASE, Journal for Architecture; PLATO, Ostrava; Rijksakademie van beeldende kunsten, among others. He has co-curated the 25th, 26th and 27th International Biennial of Graphic Design in Brno, Czech Republic (2012–16), a major international platform focused on graphic design for over fifty years, and currently teaches graphic design at the Gerrit Rietveld Academie in Amsterdam. He was a recipient of a J. W. Fulbright Scholarship (2006) and holds an MFA in graphic design from Yale University School of Art (2008).

CAROLYN CHRISTOV-BAKARGIEV is a curator, author and researcher, and Director of Castello di Rivoli Museo d'Arte Contemporanea and GAM – Galleria Civica d'Arte Moderna e Contemporanea in Turin, which she expanded in 2019 to include the Cerruti Collection. She was the Artistic Director of Documenta 13 (2012), Kassel, Germany, with additional projects in Afghanistan, Egypt and Canada. She was the Artistic Director of the 14th Istanbul Biennial, *Saltwater: A Theory of Thought Forms* (2015) and Artistic Director of the 16th Biennale of Sydney, *Revolutions: Forms That Turn* (2008). Christov-Bakargiev was the Chief Curator at the Castello di Rivoli from 2002–08, interim director in 2009, and the Senior Curator at PS1, New York from 1999–2001. Her books include *William Kentridge* (1998), *Arte Povera* (1999), the *100 Notes: 100 Thoughts* series, and *The Book of Books*

(2011–12) for Documenta 13. She received a Leverhulme Professorship from the University of Leeds for 2014 and is the Edith Kreeger Wolf Distinguished Visiting Professor in Art Theory and Practice at Northwestern University since 2013. She was awarded the Audrey Irmas Award for Curatorial Excellence in 2019.

LUCY COTTER is a writer, curator, artist, and theorist, whose practice engages with art as a form of knowledge and a site for cultural transformation. Recent projects include *Turnstones*, a yearlong series of exhibitions and events as Curator in Residence, Oregon Center for Contemporary Art (2021–2), *Undoing Language: Early Performance Works by Brian O'Doherty* at The Kitchen, New York (2021), and *The Unknown Artist* at the Center for Contemporary Art and Culture, Portland (2020). She was curator of the Dutch Pavilion of the 57th Venice Biennale 2017 with *Cinema Olanda: Wendelien van Oldenborgh*. A parallel multi-authored exhibition and live program *Cinema Olanda: Platform* took place at Witte de With Center for Contemporary Art, Rotterdam; the Stedelijk Museum, and EYE Film Museum, Amsterdam. Cotter's writing has been widely published in books, catalogues, and journals, including *Flash Art*, *Hyperallergic*, *Frieze*, *Mousse*, *Third Text*, and *Artforum*. Cotter holds a PhD in cultural analysis from the University of Amsterdam. She has lectured in Europe and the United States and was the inaugural director of the Master Artistic Research program at the Royal Academy of Art, The Hague. Irish-born, she currently lives in Portland, where she is undertaking a project residency at Stelo Arts and Culture Foundation (2023–24).

STEPHANIE DINKINS is a transmedia artist who creates experiences that spark dialogue about race, gender, aging, and our future histories. Her work in artificial intelligence (AI) and other mediums uses emerging technologies and social collaboration to work toward technological ecosystems based on care and social equity. Dinkins teaches at Stony Brook University where she holds the Kusama Endowed Chair in Art. Dinkins earned an MFA from the Maryland Institute College of Art and is an alumna of the Whitney Independent Studies Program. She exhibits and publicly advocates for inclusive AI internationally at a broad spectrum of community, private, and institutional venues. Dinkins is the inaugural recipient of the LG Guggenheim Award (2023) for artists working at the intersection of art and technology. Previous fellowships and support include the United States Artist Fellowship, Knight Arts + Tech Fellowship, Sundance Artist of Practice Fellowship, Lucas Artists Fellowship in Visual Arts at Montalvo Art Center, the Soros Equality Fellowship, Data and Society Research Institute Fellowship, and awards from the Stanford Institute for Human-Centered Artificial Intelligence, Creative Capital, Eyebeam, Pioneer Works Tech Lab, NEW INC, Blue Mountain Center, The Laundromat Project, Santa Fe Art Institute, and Art/Omi.

SHER DORUFF is an artist-researcher, a writer and a theorist, and author of a trilogy of artist's novellas, *Last Year at Betty and Bob's: A Novelty* (2017), *Last Year at Betty and Bob's: An Adventure* (2018) and *Last Year at Betty and Bob's: An Actual Occasion* (2021). She holds a PhD from the University of the Arts London, Central Saint Martins, for a dissertation entitled *The Translocal Event and the Polyrhythmic Diagram* (2006), which investigated the role of collaborative interplay and creative processes in networked performance practice. She was Head of the Research Program at Waag Society in Amsterdam (2005–07) and Creative Director of the Sensing Presence/Connected: Live Art project (2002–05). She has taught on the Master of Choreography program at DAS Graduate Academie voor Theater en Dans, and coordinated the THIRD cohort of artists pursuing a PhD in the performing arts there, as well as the Gerrit Rietveld Academy PhD research group. She is currently Professor of Film and Media, Stockholm University of the Arts.

EM'KAL EYONGAKPA approaches the experienced, the unknown, as well as collective histories, through a ritual use of repetition and transformation. His recent ideas draw increasingly on Indigenous knowledge systems and aesthetics, ethnobotany, applied mycology and technology in an exploration of the personal and the universal. He is also known for self-organized community research spaces and autonomous art hubs, including KHaL!SHRINE in Yaoundé, Cameroon (2007–12) and the recently established research platform / fund ɛfúkúyú. Eyongakpa holds degrees in plant biology and ecology from the University of Yaoundé I, Cameroon, and was resident at the Rijksakademie, Amsterdam in 2013. The artist's work has been exhibited at the Jakarta Biennale (2017), the 13th Sharjah Biennial (2017), La Biennale de Montréal (2016), the 32nd Bienal Internacional de São Paulo (2016), the 9th and 10th Bamako Encounters (2011, 2015), 10th Dak'Art: African Contemporary Art Biennale (2012), and several international art spaces and museums worldwide. He was awarded the La Ville de Dakar Prize in 2012 and was the first recipient of the Henrike Grohs Art Award in 2018.

RYAN GANDER is an artist living and working in Suffolk and London. He has exhibited worldwide, with recent solo exhibitions at Taro Nasu, Tokyo (2018); gb agency, Paris (2018); Dazaifu Tenman-gu Shrine, Fukuoka, Japan (2017); Remai Modern, Saskatoon, Canada (2017); The Contemporary Austin, Texas (2017); the National Museum of Art Osaka, Japan (2017); and Hyundai Gallery, Seoul (2017). He has participated in the Sydney Biennale (2017), British Art Show (2015); Shanghai Biennale (2012); Documenta 13 (2012); 54th Venice Biennale, *ILLUMInations* (2011); 55th Carnegie International (2008); and the Sydney Biennial (2008). Gander has received the Zurich Art Prize (2009); the ABN Amro Art Prize (2006); the Baloise Art Statements Prize of Art Basel (2006); and the Dutch Prix de Rome (2003). He has taught at Goldsmiths, the Royal Academy of Art, London, and the University of Huddersfield. Gander holds an honorary PhD from Manchester Metropolitan University and the University of Suffolk, and was awarded an OBE for services to contemporary arts in 2017. In 2019 he was awarded the Hodder Fellowship at Princeton University.

MARIO GARCÍA TORRES is an artist currently living in Mexico City. Throughout the last twenty years of his career, he has been questioning the stability of such concepts as time, memory, image, and the very essence of the artist's role in society. He received his MFA from the California Institute of the Arts, Valencia, California, in 2005. He has had solo exhibitions at, among others, Wiels, Brussels (2019); Walker Art Center, Minneapolis (2018); Museo Tamayo, Mexico City (2016), TBA21, Vienna (2016); Modern Art Museum of Fort Worth, Texas (2015); Pérez Art Museum, Miami (2014); Hammer Museum, Los Angeles (2014); Project Arts Centre, Dublin (2013); Museo Nacional Centro de Arte Reina Sofía, Madrid (2010); University of California, Berkeley Art Museum (2009); and the Stedelijk Museum, Amsterdam (2007). He has also participated in the Sharjah Biennial (2017); Manifesta 11, Zurich (2016); the 8th Berlin Biennale (2014); Bienal do Mercosul (2013); Documenta 13 (2012); 29th Bienal Internacional de São Paulo (2010); Yokohama Triennale (2008); 8th Panama Bienal (2008); and the 52nd Venice Biennale (2007).

LIAM GILLICK'S work has been included in numerous important exhibitions including Documenta X (1997), 14th Istanbul Biennial (2015), and the 53rd Venice Biennale, where he represented Germany in 2009. Solo museum exhibitions have taken place at the Museum of Contemporary Art, Chicago, the Museum of Modern Art, New York and Tate, London, among other venues. Gillick has been a prolific writer and critic of contemporary art, contributing to *Artforum*, *October*, *Frieze* and *e-flux Journal*. He is the author of a number of books, including a volume of his selected critical writing and *Industry and Intelligence: Contemporary Art Since 1820* (2016). Public works include the British Government Home Office (Interior Ministry) building, London, and the Lufthansa Headquarters, Frankfurt. His short films address the construction of the creative persona in light of the enduring mutability of the contemporary artist as a cultural figure: *Margin Time* (2012), *The Heavenly Lagoon* (2013) and *Hamilton: A Film by Liam Gillick* (2014).

NATASHA GINWALA is a curator, researcher, and writer. She is the Artistic Director of the interdisciplinary arts festival Colomboscope in Sri Lanka and an Associate Curator at Gropius Bau, Berlin. She was an Artistic Director of the 13th Gwanju Biennale 2020, with Defne Ayas. Other projects include Contour Biennale 8 (2017), and she was part of the curatorial team of Documenta 14 (2017), a member of the artistic team for the 8th Berlin Biennale for Contemporary Art (2014), curatorial advisor and public programs curator of The Gujral Foundation project *My East is Your West* at the 56th Venice Biennale, and she curated *The Museum of Rhythm* at Taipei Biennial 2012 and at Muzeum Sztuki, Lodz, Poland (2016). From 2013–15 she led the multi-part curatorial project *Landings*, which was presented at Witte de With Center for Contemporary Art, Rotterdam; David Roberts Art Foundation, London; NGBK, Berlin; and the Stedelijk Museum Amsterdam (with Vivian Ziherl). Ginwala trained in visual studies at the School of Arts and Aesthetics, Jawaharlal Nehru University in New Delhi and attended the De Appel Curatorial Programme, Amsterdam. She has written for magazines such as *The Exhibitionist*, *e-flux Journal*, *Ibraaz* and *Afterall*.

SKY HOPINKA holds a BA in Liberal Arts from Portland State University and an MFA in Film, Video, Animation, and New Genres from the University of Wisconsin-Milwaukee. He was a fellow at the Radcliffe Institute for Advanced Study at Harvard University and Sundance Art of Nonfiction Fellow in 2019. Recent solo exhibitions and solo screening programs have taken place at the Museum of Contemporary Art Chicago, Yale University, Harvard Film Archive and Yale Union, Portland (all 2019). He has participated in the 2016 Wisconsin Triennial and the 2017 Whitney Biennial and in film festivals internationally. Hopinka was awarded the Mary L. Nohl Fund Fellowship for Individual Artists in the Emerging Artist category for 2018 and has been the recipient of jury prizes at the Onion City Film Festival, Chicago, the Images Festival, Toronto, the Ann Arbor Film Festival, Michigan, and the Berwick Film and Media Arts Festival, UK. His book *Around the Edge of Encircling Lake* was published in 2018.

MANUELA INFANTE is a Chilean theatre playwright, director, scriptwriter and musician. She holds an MA in cultural analysis from the University of Amsterdam. She is well known for offering scenic articulations of contemporary theoretical issues. With her theatre group Teatro de Chile (2002–16) she wrote and directed work with the ongoing support of the Chilean Funds for the Arts. Four of her plays have been published and translated into English and Italian. Her work has toured America, Argentina, Brazil, Peru, Mexico, Germany, Belgium, Spain, Ireland, Italy, the Netherlands, Switzerland, Singapore, South Korea and Japan. She has produced work with Hebbel am Ufer, Berlin; Festival de Modena, Italy; The Watermill Center, New York; FIBA, Buenos Aires; and FITAM, Santiago. In 2015, she was the first woman to be appointed director of Muestra Nacional de Dramaturgia, the national festival for dramaturgy in Chile. Her most recent work *Estado Vegetal* has been performed at the Museum of Contemporary Art, Chicago, Portland Institute for Contemporary Art, and FUNDarte, Miami, among other venues.

EURIDICE ZAITUNA KALA is an artist based in Paris. She was trained as a photographer at the Market Photo Workshop, Johannesburg. Recent performances and solo exhibitions include *Mackandal Turns into a Butterfly: A Love Potion* (2018); *Le Pouvoir du Dedans*, La galerie Cac de Noisy-le-Sec (2018); *Euridice Kala Shows and Doesn't Tell*, Galerie Saint-Severin (2018); *Scores of Labour (Untitled Composition I)*, Instituto Camoes, Maputo, Mozambique (2018); *Mistake! Mistake! Said the Rooster … and Stepped Down from the Duck*, Lumiar Cité, Lisbon (2017); Infecting the City Festival, Cape Town (2017); and *Co-habitar*, Casa da America Latina, Lisbon (2017). She was nominated for the SAM Art Prize (2018) and the

François Schneider Foundation prize for contemporary talent (2018). Kala's work was included in the 4th Fellbach Small Scale Sculpture Triennial, Germany in 2019 and she was Artist-in-Residence at Urbane Künst Ruhr in Germany in 2019–20. She is the founder and co-organizer of e.a.s.t. (Ephemeral Archival Station), a lab and platform for long-term artistic research projects, established in 2017.

GRADA KILOMBA is an interdisciplinary artist living in Berlin. She has exhibited and performed her work at events as varied as the 10th Berlin Biennale (2018); Documenta 14 in Kassel (2017); 3rd. Bienal Internacional de São Paulo (2016); and Rauma Biennale Balticum (2016); as well as museums and art centers such as Kadist Art Foundation, Paris, e-flux, New York, Pavilion of Contemporary Art, Milano, Museum of Art, Architecture and Technology (MAAT), Lisbon, Witte de With Center for Contemporary Art, Rotterdam, the Secession, Vienna, and BOZAR – Centre for Fine Arts, Brussels. Recent solo exhibitions include *Illusions* at Bildmuseet, Umeå (2019); *Poetic Disobediences* at Pinacoteca Museum, São Paulo (2019); *Speaking the Unspeakable* at Goodman Gallery, Johannesburg (2018); *Secrets to Tell* at MAAT, Lisbon (2017) and The Power Plant, Toronto (2018); *The Most Beautiful Language* at Galeria Avenida da Índia, Lisbon (2017). She received the 2018 International Film Festival Rotterdam Grant Award. Kilomba is the author of *Plantation Memories* (2008) and co-editor of *Mythen, Subjekte, Masken* (2005). She has lectured at several international universities and was a professor in the department of gender studies at Humboldt University, Berlin.

YO-YO LIN (林友友) is a queer Taiwanese-American interdisciplinary media artist who explores the possibilities of self-knowledge in the context of emerging, embodied technologies. She often uses video, animation, live performance, and lush sound design to create meditative "memory-scapes." Her recent work creates openings into and revalues the complex realities of living with chronic illness and intergenerational trauma, through performances, publications, and facilitating accessible physical and virtual sites for community-centered abundance, learning, and celebration. Lin has shown works at international multimedia art galleries (Human Resources, Lincoln Center, La Corte Contemporanea), film festivals (New York Film Festival, SXSW, Los Angeles Asian Pacific Film Festival), performance venues (The Shed NYC, Gibney Dance, Ars Nova), and conferences. She is the cofounder of Rotations, with Pelenakeke Brown, a collaborative movement practice working toward deepening our understanding of artistry, disability, and access. She was the Jerome Hill Artist Fellow for Technology-Centered Arts 2023, a Disability Futures Fellow 2022, a Sundance Interdisciplinary Lab Fellow 2022, a Red Burns Fellow at NYU Tisch ITP/IMA 2021, an Open Call Recipient for The Shed 2020, and Artist-in-Residence at Eyebeam 2019. Born and raised in Los Angeles, she is currently based in Taipei and New York.

Born on the Standing Rock Reservation in North Dakota, New Mexico-based artist CANNUPA HANSKA LUGER is an enrolled member of the Three Affiliated Tribes of Fort Berthold and is of Mandan, Hidatsa, Arikara, and Lakota heritage. Creating monumental installations, sculpture, and performance to communicate urgent stories about twenty-first-century Indigeneity, Luger incorporates ceramics, steel, fiber, video, and repurposed materials to activate speculative fiction, engage land-based actions of repair, and practice empathetic response through social collaboration. Luger is a 2022 Guggenheim Fellow, a recipient of a 2021 United States Artists Fellowship Award for Craft and was named a 2021 Grist Fixer. He is a 2020 Creative Capital Fellow, a 2020 Smithsonian Artist Research Fellow, and the recipient of the Museum of Arts and Design's 2018 inaugural Burke Prize, among others. Luger has exhibited nationally and internationally, including at The Metropolitan Museum of Art, Gardiner Museum, Kunsthal KAdE, Washington Project for the Arts, Art Mûr, Crystal Bridges Museum of American Art, and the National Center for Civil and Human Rights. Luger holds a BFA in studio arts from the Institute of American Indian Arts and is represented by Garth Greenan Gallery in New York.

SARAT MAHARAJ is Professor of Visual Art and Knowledge Systems, Malmo Art Academy / Lund University, and Research Professor, Goldsmiths, University of London, where he was History / Theory of Art Professor (1980–2005). He was Rudolf Arnheim Professor, Humboldt University, Berlin (2001–02) and Research Fellow, Jan van Eyck, Maastricht (1999–2001). Maharaj was co-curator, on Okwui Enwezor's team, for Documenta XI (2002), for *Farewell to Postcolonialism*, 3rd Guangzhou Triennial (2008) and for the 29th Bienal Internacional de São Paulo (2010). He was Chief Curator of *Pandemonium: Art in a Time of Creativity Fever*, Göteborg International Biennial for Contemporary Art (2011) and a curatorial advisor for the Sharjah Biennial in 2012. His specialist publications cover Marcel Duchamp, James Joyce and Richard Hamilton, "visual art as know-how and no-how," textiles, globalization and cultural translation. As Visiting Professor, University of Amsterdam and Stedelijk Fellow (2018) he explored elements of two projects: "Reconstructing the Apartheid-era Art History Room, Salisbury Island, Durban" and "'New Bloomsbury Halal': On Shaping Global London." Both projects looked at art as a peculiar form of knowledge production to be understood in our time as *Ignorantitis Sapiens: The Knowledge / Non-knowledge / Ignorance Virus in a Pansophic Age*.

EMMA MOORE is a curator and producer and Senior Development Manager at the Douglas Hyde Gallery, Dublin. Until 2020, she was the Curator of Engagement at Chisenhale Gallery in London, where she devised and delivered an extensive program of talks and events in collaboration with commissioned artists, managed production on offsite artist commission, and delivered Chisenhale's program for young people. Prior to 2015, she was Assistant Curator of Public Programmes at Nottingham Contemporary, delivering a wide-ranging programme of talks, events and performances. She received an MA in Curating from Chelsea College of Art, London in 2011, and a BA in Visual Arts Practice from Dun Laoghaire Institute of Art, Design and Technology (IADT), Dublin, 2008. After graduating from IADT she co-founded Bombhouse, an artist-run gallery and studio space in Dublin.

RICHARD MOSSE is an Irish artist currently based in New York. Documenting some of the most significant humanitarian and environmental crises of our time, his work has been the subject of recent solo exhibitions at the San Francisco Museum of Modern Art, the National Gallery of Art in Washington, DC, the Barbican Art Gallery in London, the Minnesota Street Project Foundation in San Francisco, and the National Gallery of Victoria in Melbourne. Recent survey exhibitions were held at the Kunsthalle Bremen (2022) and MAST Foundation, Bologna (2021). Mosse was the recipient of the STARTS Prize 2023, the Prix Pictet 2017, the 2014 Deutsche Börse Photography Prize, and he represented Ireland at the Venice Biennale with the six-screen video installation *The Enclave* in 2013. Previous publications by Mosse include *Broken Spectre* (Loose Joints, 2022), *The Castle* (MACK, 2018), *Incoming* (MACK, 2017), and *Infra* (Aperture Foundation, 2012).

RABIH MROUÉ is a theater director, actor, visual artist and playwright. Mroué is a contributing editor of *TDR / The Drama Review* and a cofounder of the Beirut Art Center (BAC). He is currently theater director at Münchner Kammerspiele. Mroué's works include *Borborygmous* (2018) with Lina Majadalanie and Mazen Kerbaj, *Kill the Audience* (2018); *Sand in the eyes* (2017); *Rima Kamel* (2017); *Ode to Joy* (2015); *Riding on a Cloud* (2013); *33 Rpm and a Few Seconds* (2012); *The Pixelated Revolution* (2012); *The Inhabitants of Images* (2008); and *Who's Afraid of Representation?* (2005). Recent solo exhibitions include *Again We Are Defeated* at the Walker Art Center, Minneapolis (2018–19). He has performed and exhibited internationally, including at the Museum of Modern Art, New York; SALT Galata and SALT Beyoğlu, Istanbul; CA2M Centro de Arte Dos de Mayo, Madrid; Documenta 13, Kassel (2012); ICP Triennial of Photography and Video,

International Center of Photography, New York; and the Centre Pompidou, Paris, among other venues.

CHRISTIAN NYAMPETA works in art, design, and theory. His ongoing activities include the convening of a scriptorium, a roaming program of exhibitions, screenings, and lyrical performances concerned with monuments and translation. Solo exhibitions include *Words after the World* at Camden Arts Centre, UK (2017), *A Flower Garden of All Kinds of Loveliness Without Sorrow* (2019) at Galerie für Zeitgenössische Kunst, Leipzig, Germany, *École de Soir* (The Evening Academy) at the Sculpture Center, New York (2019). Other recent exhibitions include Contour Biennale 9, Mechelen, Belgium (2019); IMA Brisbane (2019); Dak'Art: African Contemporary Art Biennale (2018); Tensta Konsthall, Stockholm (2018); and the Gwangju Biennale (2016). Nyampeta runs Radius, an online and occasionally inhabitable radio station, he is currently completing a PhD in visual cultures at Goldsmiths, University of London. He was awarded The Art Prize Future of Europe 2019.

YURI PATTISON works in sculpture and digital media, exploring the visual culture of digital economies. Recent solo shows include *Trusted Traveller* at Kunst Halle Sankt Gallen, Switzerland (2017); *Citizens of Nowhere* at Kevin Space, Vienna (2017); *Sunset Provision* at mother's tankstation limited, Dublin (2016); and *user, space* (2016) at Chisenhale Gallery, London. Recent group shows include *Hate Speech: Aggression and Intimacy*, Künstlerhaus, Halle für Kunst & Medien, Graz (2019); Athens Biennale (2018); *Le centre ne peut tenir*, Lafayette Anticipations – Fondation d'entreprise Galeries Lafayette, Paris (2018); and *The Elsewhere Studio*, the Institute of Contemporary Art, Miami (2017–18); as well as the British Art Show 8, UK tour (2015–17). He was the recipient of the 2016 Frieze Artist Award and his work has previously been exhibited at such venues as the International Center of Photography, New York, Tate Britain, London, Bielefelder Kunstverein, Kunstverein Nürnberg; Kunsthalle Wien; Bonner Kunstverein; Künstlerhaus Bremen; Museum of Modern Art Warsaw; Outpost, Norwich; and the Irish Museum of Modern Art. Pattison lives and works in Paris.

FALKE PISANO studied / was a researcher at the Jan van Eyck Academy, Maastricht and the Henry Moore Institute, Leeds. Recent solo exhibitions include *The Value in Mathematics – How Do We Learn?* at C3A, Córdoba, Spain (2016) and Badischer Kunstverein (2016). She has previously held solo exhibitions at REDCAT, Los Angeles (2015); Praxes, Berlin (2014); The Showroom, London (2013); Ellen de Bruijne Projects, Amsterdam (2007, 2011); Hollybush Gardens, London (2009, 2012); De Vleeshal, Middelburg (2012); Contemporary Art Centre, Vilnius (2011); Transmission Gallery, Glasgow (2010); and at Extra City, Antwerp (2010). Pisano has participated in such international exhibitions as the Shanghai Biennale (2012), Venice Biennale (2009) and Manifesta (2008), and performed at Museo Reina Sofia (2012), the 5th Berlin Biennale (2008) and Lisson Gallery, London (2007). She was awarded the prestigious Prix de Rome in 2013. Pisano has also published her work in *Figures of Speech* (designed and co-edited by Will Holder, 2010). Pisano lives and works in Amsterdam.

SARAH RIFKY is a writer and Senior Curator and Director of Programs at the ICA, Virginia Commonwealth University, Richmond, VA. She is co-founder of Beirut (2012–15), an artists' initiative in Cairo and founder of CIRCA (Cairo International Resource Center for Art) and was artistic director of ArteEast, New York (2017–18). Rifky was co-curator of the Jogja Biennale XII (2013), curator of Townhouse Gallery of Contemporary Art, Cairo (2009–11) and a curatorial agent for Documenta 13 in Kassel, Cairo and Alexandria (2012). She co-managed MASS Alexandria, a school for young artists, with Wael Shawky (2010–12) and was Adjunct Professor of Art History and Theory at the American University in Cairo (2010). She is co-editor of *Positionen: Zeitgenössische Künstler aus der Arabischen Welt* (2013) and *Damascus: Artists, Tourists and Secret Agents* (2009), and author of *The Going Insurrection* (2012) and *Delusions of Reference: In Defense of Art* (forthcoming). She contributes regularly to *Art in America*, *Art-Agenda*, *Bidoun*, *The Exhibitionist*, among other publications. Rifky is a doctoral fellow in the history, theory and criticism program at the Massachusetts Institute of Technology as well as the Aga Khan Program for Islamic Architecture.

SAMSON YOUNG is a multi-disciplinary artist who was trained as a composer and graduated with a PhD in music composition from Princeton University in 2013. In 2017 he represented Hong Kong at the 57th Venice Biennale. Other solo exhibitions include Kunsthalle Düsseldorf; Talbot Rice Gallery, Edinburgh; SMART Museum, Chicago; Centre for Contemporary Chinese Art in Manchester; M+ Pavilion, Hong Kong and Hiroshima City Museum of Contemporary Art. Group exhibitions include Solomon R. Guggenheim Museum, New York; Biennale of Sydney; Shanghai Biennale; National Museum of Art, Osaka; National Museum of Modern and Contemporary Art, Seoul; and Documenta Radio, Documenta 14. He was the recipient of the BMW / Art Basel Art Journey Award, the Hong Kong Arts Development Council Artist of the Year Award, Prix Ars Electronica and the Bloomberg Emerging Artist Award. In 2019, he was shortlisted for the inaugural Uli Sigg Prize. His works are held in the collections of Solomon R. Guggenheim Museum, New York; M+ Museum, Hong Kong; Mori Art Museum, Japan; and The Israel Museum, Jerusalem, among others.

KATARINA ZDJELAR is an artist whose practice consists of working with moving image and sound, performances, book projects, and creating platforms for speculation and exchange. She represented Serbia at the 53rd Venice Biennale (2009) and has participated in numerous solo and group exhibitions at such venues as Stedelijk Museum Bureau Amsterdam; Metropolitan Museum of Photography, Tokyo; Frieze Foundation, London; Casino Luxembourg; The Chelsea Art Museum; The Freud Museum, London; De Appel, Amsterdam; Hartware MedienKunstVerein, Dortmund; Museum of Contemporary Art, MACBA, Barcelona; MCOB, Museum of Contemporary Art Belgrade; Museum Sztuki, Lodz, Poland; and Powerhouse, Toronto. Zdjelar holds an MA in Fine Art from the Piet Zwart Institute in Rotterdam, where she currently lives and works. She is also a graduate of the University of Arts Belgrade and the CENPI, Centre for Contemporary Theatre and Performance Art, Art Theory, Belgrade. She was shortlisted for the Dutch Prix de Rome Award 2017 and was awarded the Dolf Henkes Prize 2017.

RECLAIMING ARTISTIC RESEARCH
Expanded Second Edition

Editor:
Lucy Cotter

Authors:
Lawrence Abu Hamdan, Katayoun Arian, Carolyn Christov-Bakargiev, Lucy Cotter, Stephanie Dinkins, Sher Doruff, Em'kal Eyongakpa, Ryan Gander, Mario García Torres, Liam Gillick, Natasha Ginwala, Sky Hopinka, Manuela Infante, Euridice Zaituna Kala, Grada Kilomba, Yo-Yo Lin, Cannupa Hanska Luger, Sarat Maharaj, Emma Moore, Richard Mosse, Rabih Mroué, Christian Nyampeta, Yuri Pattison, Falke Pisano, Sarah Rifky, Samson Young, Katarina Zdjelar

Project management Hatje Cantz:
Valerie Hortolani

Copyediting:
Aaron Bogart

Graphic design and typesetting:
Tomáš Celizna (with Martina Vanini)

Typeface:
Girott Regular, Union Regular
(RP Digital Type Foundry)

Production Hatje Cantz:
Alise Ausmane

Printing and binding:
Graspo CZ

Paper:
Munken Print White 80 g/m^2,
Ispira Arancio Yoga 250 g/m^2,
Splendorlux Premium White 120 g/m^2

ISBN 978-3-7757-5640-2

Printed in Czech Republic

Published by
Hatje Cantz Verlag GmbH
Mommsenstraße 27
10629 Berlin
hatjecantz.com
A Ganske Publishing Group Company

This expanded second edition is published in conjunction with a project residency 2023–24 and with the support of

Stelo Arts and Culture Foundation
412 NW 8th Avenue
Portland, OR 97209
United States
steloarts.org

The first edition (2019) was published with

17, Editorial
Benito Juárez 35-1,
Colonia Del Carmen,
Coyoacán, C.P. 04100,
Mexico City
Mexico

A division of:
17, Institute of Critical Studies
17edu.org

with the additional support of

HKU University of the Arts
Nieuwekade 1
3511 RV Utrecht
The Netherlands
hku.nl

Gerrit Rietveld Academie
Frederik Roeskestraat 96
1076 ED Amsterdam
The Netherlands
rietveldacademie.nl

LAPS Research Institute for Art and Public Space
Frederik Roeskestraat 96
1076 ED Amsterdam
The Netherlands
laps-rietveld.nl